This work constitutes a classic case of microhistory. It reflects the ways in which a seemingly narrow niche study can in fact illuminate all kinds of fields, spreading out into a major exploration of all manner of cultural and economic dimensions. Here Heasim Sul demonstrates how one Korean plant product became a major area of fascination for its medical and biological properties, thus promoting considerable trade and many articles and notices in the Western press and other publications. Consequently, the study of the reception of ginseng helps to expose the character of a whole variety of relationships between the East and the West, thereby contributing to the major study of cultural Orientalism which has been such a major source of scholarly fascination in recent decades. In these ways, microhistory can make a major contribution to a much wider scholarly debate, opening up wider discussions of considerable significance.

—**John M. MacKenzie**, Emeritus Professor of Imperial History, Lancaster University

A GLOBAL HISTORY OF GINSENG

Sul's history of the international ginseng trade reveals the cultural aspects of international capitalism and the impact of this single commodity on relations between the East and the West.

Ginseng emerged as a major international commodity in the seventeenth century, when the East India Company began trading it westward. Europeans were drawn to the plant's efficacy as a medicine, but their attempts to transplant it for mass production were unsuccessful. Also, due to a failure of extracting its active ingredients, Western pharmacology disparaged ginseng in the process of modernization. In the meantime, ginseng was discovered on the American continent and became one of the United States' key exports to Asia and particularly China, but never cultivated a significant domestic market. As such, historicizing the ginseng trade provides a unique perspective on the impact of both culture and economics on international trade.

A compelling interdisciplinary history of over five centuries of East–West trade and cultural exchange, this book will be invaluable to students and scholars of transnational history and a fascinating read for anyone interested in the history of international trade.

Heasim Sul is Professor in the Department of History at Yonsei University, Seoul, South Korea.

A GLOBAL HISTORY OF GINSENG

Imperialism, Modernity and Orientalism

Heasim Sul

Translated by Youngjae Josephine Bae

Routledge
Taylor & Francis Group
LONDON AND NEW YORK

Cover image: Getty Images

First published 2023
by Routledge
4 Park Square, Milton Park, Abingdon, Oxon OX14 4RN

and by Routledge
605 Third Avenue, New York, NY 10158

Routledge is an imprint of the Taylor & Francis Group, an Informa business

British Library Cataloguing-in-Publication Data
A catalogue record for this book is available from the British Library

Library of Congress Cataloguing-in-Publication Data
A catalog record has been requested for this book

ISBN: 978-1-032-26142-3 (hbk)
ISBN: 978-1-032-26141-6 (pbk)
ISBN: 978-1-003-28669-1 (ebk)

DOI: 10.4324/9781003286691

Typeset in Bembo
by Deanta Global Publishing Services, Chennai, India

CONTENTS

FIGURES

TABLES

PREFACE

The beginnings of this book can be traced back to one summer day in 1995. At the time, shops like GNC sprouted up everywhere as a dietary supplement craze swept across the United States. That day I happened to witness the "American Ginseng Festival" being held at a GNC store in a shopping mall in Newport Beach, California. I felt as though I'd been hit on the head. American ginseng? Wasn't ginseng a product native to East Asia?

Since then, "American ginseng" turned into a mystery for me. I tried asking my American friends about it, but none of them were able to offer an explanation. Ginseng never appeared in the countless Western history books I encountered thereafter. Then, in the winter of 2013, an American academic database provider sent me a promotional voucher to try out their new historical database for ten days. The database granted access to a collection of nineteenth-century local newspaper articles from small British cities. The collection seemed quite appealing to me since I was interested in microhistory. After logging in, I thought for a moment about what to search for and then entered "ginseng + Corea" (the once-prevalent spelling of Korea) just to indulge my curiosity.

The results took me by surprise. The key words retrieved as many as 200 articles! How could there be so many articles involving Korean ginseng in local newspapers circulated in small nineteenth-century British cities? Why on earth were people in the West so interested in Korean ginseng back then? Why was there no mention of ginseng in history books? Charged with a dose of curiosity, a tinge of exasperation, and a dash of stubbornness, I jumped into the search for references to ginseng in Western historical records. I collected anything I could get my hands on that included even a single mention of ginseng, from the reports of various East India companies to tariff charts, all sorts of pharmacopoeia and materia medica, as well as meeting minutes of the Ginseng Growers Association of America. It was no easy task, but each discovery felt that much more rewarding. Through the process, I realized that by the seventeenth century, ginseng had already emerged as an important commodity in the massive trade network between the East and the West. That filled me with a sense of mission; I had to determine why a commodity like ginseng hadn't been more deeply investigated in Western historical studies.

After reviewing the literature to a certain extent, I felt the need to conduct field investigations. I began with Korea, visiting ginseng farms, ginseng factories in Puyŏ and Wŏnju, and the Insam Museum in Yŏngju. I also went to Hoengsŏng to observe the digging of ginseng. Over the summer of 2015, I headed to Marathon County, Wisconsin, to tour the largest ginseng farm and factory in the United States. I also visited the archive and museum in Wausau, Wisconsin, as well as smaller farms to meet farmers and learn about their experience of growing ginseng.

It was also necessary to hold interviews with American ginseng diggers. I interviewed diggers who traveled deep into the Appalachians in search of ginseng. I was able to talk at length with a woman who dug ginseng in Minnesota and Wisconsin. When I went to present a paper in France in 2016, I roamed about Nantes in search of the site where the royal medicinal garden once was. Friends and students of mine who traveled to Hong Kong, San Francisco, and Singapore shared photos of various dried ginseng stacked up at herbal shops in Chinatown. It's a shame that I haven't been able to include all of them in this book.

As materials piled up, I began to worry about how to arrange them into a solid, pacey narrative. Time went by as the enormity of the topic made it difficult to decide on where to start. I tend to stumble upon an epiphany at the point where I can no longer put off writing. For this book, the epiphany came from the great botanist Carl von Linné. Von Linné gave ginseng its scientific name, which gained authority and recognition, but I always wondered whether he had personally encountered ginseng. One spring day in 2019, I discovered a record of von Linné's encounter with ginseng and decided it was time to start writing.

Using ginseng as a medium to delve into world history felt like peering into a different world that lay hidden underneath the thick epidermis of history. The place where Chŏngnimsa Temple once stood in Puyŏ is commonly associated with the ancient Korean kingdom of Paekche, but I have come to remember it as the site where seeds of Kaesŏng ginseng were supposedly buried during the Korean War. Mincing Lane in the City of London is historically known as a center where tea and spices used to be traded, but the street's name makes me picture stacked barrels of American ginseng seized after failure to pay storage fees. It was an exhilarating experience to learn that the facts beneath the skin of history were interconnected to form a vast global network.

This book covers a time and space more extensive than any other study I have thus far conducted. As such, I could not have done it without the help of others. Above all, I am deeply grateful to Professor Kenneth Pomeranz, who was my advisor in graduate school. He allowed me to serve as the teaching assistant for his newly created "World Economy" course in 1993, an experience that opened my eyes to a global perspective on history, or a world history free from the confines of national borders. The contents of the course would go on to form the basis for *The Great Divergence*, a book that proved to be a sensation worldwide. When Professor Pomeranz visited Yonsei University in November 2014 as Shinhan Distinguished Professor, I presented my idea for this book and asked him whether it seemed to be a feasible project. He told me it was a great topic and encouraged me to pursue it by introducing me to a professor in Hong Kong who had similar research interests.

While studying the history of ginseng from a global perspective, I sensed that I was grounded more firmly than ever in the present. Once I began writing, I suffered from the anxiety of having to cover unfamiliar areas beyond my realm of expertise in British history. The willing help of many distinguished experts in Korean, Asian, and Western history as well as pharmacology is why I have been able to make it this far. Of course, the greatest support came from family. So, I lovingly dedicate this book to Hyuk Lee, who hauled materials and laundry back and forth from Seoul every weekend while I retreated to the countryside over summer and winter breaks to chart the outline and write the manuscript for this book.

NOTES

1. The main types of ginseng covered in this book are *Panax ginseng* and *Panax quinquefolius*.

   Panax genus

Scientific name	*Alternative names*
Panax ginseng	ginseng, Korean ginseng, Asian ginseng
Panax notoginseng	sanchi, notoginseng, Chinese ginseng
Panax quinquefolius	American ginseng
Panax vietnamensis	Vietnamese ginseng
Panax japonicus	Japanese ginseng

   For the most part, this book does not draw a distinction between the Korean ginseng and the American ginseng and refers to them both as ginseng, especially when they are simply marked as "ginseng" in primary sources.
2. The word "ginseng" is often misunderstood to have originated from Japan, but it actually came from *xiangshen* (祥蔘), an old Chinese name that morphed into *shinseng* and then *ginseng* as it crossed over to the West. In Japan, ginseng is called *ninjin* (にんじん), while the Korean ginseng is called *Korai ninjin* (こうらいにんじん). *Korai* means Koryŏ (高麗), referring to the Koryŏ kingdom of Korea (935–1392), and *ninjin* means carrot or ginseng. In Europe, Japanese ginseng has been called *ninzin*, *ningine*, or *ninsi* since the seventeenth century and *ninzin* has sometimes been used to refer to ginseng in general, regardless of its type or origin.

PROLOGUE[1]

Have you ever come across writings on Western history featuring ginseng? Ginseng was already introduced to Europe by the early seventeenth century and since then it became a global commodity traded between the East and West. The process through which ginseng was made known to Western society is similar to how spices like cinnamon, pepper, clove, or nutmeg were introduced. Moreover, ginseng once enjoyed a degree of attention similar to sugar, coffee, or tobacco that spread across the world alongside Western colonialism, each of which was regarded as a panacea at some point. Yet, it is nearly impossible to encounter mentions of ginseng in Western historical writings. A global approach to history is growing prominent thanks to Timothy H. Breen's attempt to project the early modern economy as a global economy, Maxin Berg's perspective that emphasizes the Asian initiative in the Industrial Revolution, and Pratik Chakrabarti's study that highlights how material circumstances in colonies served as a prerequisite to the development of botany and medicine in the eighteenth century,[2] but none of these approaches or studies mention ginseng.

This absence originates foremost from the extreme imbalance in the study of ginseng. Studies on ginseng began to gain traction at a global level in the 1950s, resulting in nearly 8,000 publications so far. The problem is that more than 95 percent of such studies have focused on ginseng's pharmacological effects, which falls under the natural sciences. This dearth of research on ginseng from

1 The book's translation into English has been funded by the Korean Ginseng Corporation.

2 Timothy H. Breen, "An Empire of Goods: The Anglicization of Colonial America, 1690-1776," *Journal of British Studies* 25, no. 4 (1986): 467–99; Maxine Berg, "In Pursuit of Luxury, Global History and British Consumer Goods in the Eighteenth Century," *Past and Present* 182 (2004): 85–142; Pratik Chakrabarti, *Materials and Medicine: Trade, Conquest and Therapeutics in the Eighteenth Century* (Manchester: Manchester University Press, 2010).

the perspective of the humanities has resulted in an imbalance in ginseng studies.[3] Another imbalance lies in the fact that studies are primarily conducted on ginseng produced in East Asia by East Asian scholars. As such, it remains difficult to grasp how ginseng has been perceived or what status it has occupied in the United States or Europe, where ginseng-based products are being widely consumed nowadays.

At present, Korea is where studies on ginseng in the humanities and social sciences are being conducted most actively. Only after the 1970s did Korean scholars begin to engage in full-scale research on ginseng, initially led by those in the natural sciences and later joined by those in the humanities and social sciences. It took particularly long for historical research on ginseng to make any sort of progress, most likely because of the lack of historical sources. Nevertheless, the growing interest in studying ginseng since the 2000s managed to spur historical approaches. Scholars specializing in Korean history have actively investigated the history of ginseng-related policies and trade, such as the export of Korean ginseng to China or the development of the ginseng industry in Kaesong.[4] This is because the production, trade, regulation, and even exploitation of ginseng have been closely connected to metadiscourses or major historical events in Korea that date back as far as the days of the Three Ancient Kingdoms.

3 The ginseng varieties now commonly used are Korean ginseng (Panax ginseng) and American ginseng (Panax quinquefolius). Their main active ingredient is a complex carbohydrate (a compound of sugar and alcohol or phenol) called ginsenoside. Ginseng studies in the natural sciences have mainly been conducted in Korea, China, and Japan on the effects of ginsenosides, the anticancer effects of ginseng, and its contribution to accelerating protein and DNA synthesis in the body.

4 Yang Chŏng-p'il 양정필 and Yŏ In-sŏk 여인석, "Samguk-Shilla t'ongilgi insam saengsan kwa taeoegyoyŏk" 삼국-신라통일기 인삼 생산과 대외교역 [The Ginseng Growing District, Taxation and Trade in Ancient Korea], *Ŭisahak* 의사학 13, no. 2 (2004): 177–97; Park Pyeong-sik 박평식, "Sŏnjojo ŭi taemyŏng insam muyŏk kwa insam sangin" 宣祖朝의 對明 인삼무역과 인삼상인 [Ginseng Trade with Ming and Ginseng Merchants during the Years of King Sônjo], *Yŏksagyoyuk* 역사교육 108 (2008): 127–58; Park Pyeong-sik 박평식, "Chosŏn chŏn'gi ŭi insam chŏngch'aek kwa insam yut'ong" 조선전기의 인삼정책과 인삼유통 [Ginseng Policy and Its Distribution in the Early Choson Dynasty], *Han'guksa yŏn'gu* 한국사연구 143 (2008): 201–41; Moon Kwang-kyun 문광균, "18 segi kanggye chiyŏk kongsamje ŭi unyŏng kwa pyŏnhwa" 18세기 강계지역 공삼제의 운영과 변화 [18th Century Practice of the Taxation System in Ginseng and Its Change in Kanggye], *Chosŏn shidaesa hakpo* 조선시대사학보 57 (2011): 161–206; Yang Chŏng-p'il 양정필, "Taehanjegukki Kaesŏng chiyŏk samŏp pyŏndong kwa samp'omin ŭi taeŭng" 대한제국기 개성지역 삼업 변동과 삼포민의 대응 [A Crisis of Ginseng Capital and the Countermeasures of the Ginseng-Cultivating People during Daehan Empire], *Ŭisahak* 의사학 18, no. 2 (2009): 133–55; Yang Chŏng-p'il 양정필, "1910 nyŏndae ilche ŭi samŏp chŏngch'aek kwa Kaesŏng samp'oju ŭi hwaltong" 1910년대 일제의 삼업정책과 개성 삼포주의 활동 [Japanese Imperial Authorities' Policy Regarding Jinseng Production during the 1910s, and the Activities of the Jinseng Farm Owners in the Gaeseong Region], *Yŏksamunje yŏn'gu* 역사문제연구 24, no. 2 (2010): 265–97; Yang Chŏng-p'il 양정필, "1910-20 nyŏndae kaesŏng sangin ŭi paeksam sangp'umhwa wa p'anmae hwaktae hwaltong" 1910-20년대 개성상인의 백삼 상품화와 판매 활동 [White Ginseng Commercialization and Sales Expansion Activities of Gaesung Merchants in the 1910s and 1920s], *Ŭisahak* 의사학 20, no. 1 (2011): 83–118.

Recently, however, research topics in the history of Korean ginseng seem to be growing more diverse. Yoon Seon-ja's research focusing on how merchants in Kaesong formed a guild to protect their market under Japanese colonial rule and Kim Kwang-jae's research that reconstructs the activities of ginseng merchants in Shanghai are noteworthy for attempting a transition from institutional, economic history to cultural history.[5] Yŏ In-sŏk and Yang Chŏng-p'il reviewed the arguments in Imamura Tomo's *History of Ginseng* (人蔘史), considered a canonical book in ginseng studies by the Japanese, to point out the underlying colonialist biases and distortions. Adopting an interdisciplinary perspective, Yŏ and Yang brought up flaws in the theory that ginseng originated from China, raising the possibility that Korean ginseng could have flowed into China on the one hand, and on the other hand suggesting that the substance of Chinese ginseng may be a plant different from the present Panax ginseng (眞人蔘).[6]

Like Korea, ginseng studies in China have been preoccupied with either an economic approach of examining developments and policies in the ginseng industry, an approach focusing on agricultural technologies to cultivate, improve, and process ginseng, or a medical approach investigating the clinical, pharmacological effects of ginseng. As of late, research interest in ginseng has been growing rapidly in the field of Chinese history, which appears to be a result of the Chinese government's active promotion of ginseng since the mid-1990s. Song Chengji (宋承吉), a graduate of Harbin Medical University, is well known for studying the history of ginseng from the perspective of Chinese medicine. Song attempted to trace the history of ginseng's utilization back to its origins through *Shennong bencaojing* (神農本草經), a Chinese pharmacopeia presumably authored during the period of the Qin and Han dynasties and the earliest of its kind to catalogue ginseng. Song's literature-based research stressed that in ancient China ginseng was produced in the areas of Shangdang (上黨) and Liaodong (遼東), squarely refuting the suggestion that ginseng from that period was *dangshen* (黨蔘, a similar plant to ginseng, commonly known as "poor man's ginseng").[7]

5 Yun Sŏn-cha 윤선자, "Ilche ŭi kyŏngje sut'al kwa kaesŏng ŭi samŏp" 일제의 경제수탈과 개성의 삼업 [The Economic Plundering of Japanese Colonial Rule and the Ginseng Industry of Gaesung], *Han'guk kŭnhyŏndaesa yŏn'gu* 한국근현대사연구, no. 35 (2005): 92–123; Kim Kwang-jae 김광재, "Ilcheshigi sanghae koryŏ insam sangindŭl ŭi hwaltong" 일제시기 상해 고려인삼 상인들의 활동 [The Activities of Korean Ginseng Dealers in Shanghai During the Japanese Colonial Period], *Han'guk tongnibundongsa yŏn'gu* 한국독립운동사연구 40 (2011): 221–64.

6 Yang Chŏng-p'il 양정필 and Yŏ In-sŏk 여인석, "'Chungguk insam' ŭi shilch'e e taehan pip'anjŏk koch'al" '중국인삼'의 실체에 대한 비판적 고찰: 이마무라 토모의 학설을 중심으로 [A Study on the True Nature of 'Chinese Jinseng'], *Ŭisahak* 의사학 12, no. 2 (2003): 144–166; Yang Chŏng-p'il 양정필 and Yŏ In-sŏk 여인석, "'Chosŏn insam' ŭi kiwŏn e taehayŏ" '조선인삼'의 기원에 대하여 [A Study on the Origins of 'Korean Ginseng'], *Ŭisahak* 의사학 13, no. 1 (2004): 1–19.

7 Song Chengji 宋承吉, "Shilun Zhongguo Guadi Renshen de Zhuchanqu" 試論中國古代人蔘的主産區 [A Study of Major Ginseng Producing Areas in Ancient China], *Zhongguo nongshi* 中國農史 3 (1986): 56–59 Song Chengji 宋承吉 and Zhan Xiujuan 張秀娟, "Zhongguo yaoyong renshen shigang" 中國藥用人参史綱 [A Historical Outline of Chinese Medicinal Ginseng], *Renshen yanjiu* 人蔘研究 1 (1993): 41–44.

Nevertheless, the most eagerly investigated aspect of ginseng through Korean and Chinese historical research is the history of its trade. Notable studies that fall under this theme have so far examined the triangular trade of Ming silk, Korean ginseng, and Japanese silver during the eighteenth century;[8] the role ginseng played when the Later Jin (Shi Jin 石晉) was building its economic strength and influence through border trade in Liaodong;[9] the conflicts that arose with surrounding states as the Qing dynasty attempted to close off its Manchurian territories;[10] the issues pertaining to the system of managing ginseng production during the Ming and Qing dynasties;[11] and Western ginseng's influx into Qing China and its trade in ginseng with America.[12] Meanwhile, the Korean scholar

8 Fei Chi 費馳, "17 shijimo 18 shijichu de dongya shanglu jiqi yingxiang" 17世紀末18世紀初的東亞商路及其影響 [East Asian Trade Routes and Their Impact Between the Late Seventeenth to Early Eighteenth Century], *Zhongguo bianjiang shidi yanjiu* 中國邊疆史地研究 21, no. 4 (2011): 95–101; Hou Fuzhong 侯馥中, "Mingdai zhongguo yu chaoxian maoyi yanjiu" 明代中國與朝鮮貿易研究 [A Study of the Sino-Korea Trade in the Ming Dynasty] (Doctoral dissertation, Shandong University, 2010).

9 Long Wu 龍武, "Mingmo liaodong mashi maoyizhan he nuzhen" 明末遼東馬市貿易戰和女真諸部興衰 [Trade War at Horse Markets in Late Ming China and the Rise and Fall of Jurchen Ministries] (Master's Thesis, Graduate School of Chinese Academy of Social Sciences, 2014).

10 Zhang Jie 張傑, "Qing qianqi dui yalujiang fengjinqu de guanxia" 清前期對鴨綠江封禁區的管轄 [A Study of Closed Off Areas Near the Yalu River in Early Qing China], *Zhongguo bianjiang shidi yanjiu* 中國邊疆史地研究 4 (2004): 52–61; Zhang Jie 張傑, "Liutiaobian, yinpiao yu qingchao dongbei fengjin xinlun" 柳條邊, 印票與清朝東北封禁新論 [A Reexamination of the Willow Palisades, the Yinpiao System, and Qing China's Fengjin Policy Toward Its Northeastern Areas], *Zhongguo bianjiang shidi yanjiu* 中國邊疆史地研究 1 (1999): 78–85; Piao Fulan 朴福蘭, "Qingchao fengjin shiqi chaoxianren fanyue shili yanjiu" 清朝封禁时期朝鲜人犯越事例研究 [A Study of Border Violations by Chosŏn People During Qing China's Practice of the Fengjin Policy] (Master's Thesis, Yanbian University, 2013).

11 Lin Zhongfan 林仲凡, "Ming Qing shidai woguo dongbei gedi renshen de kaicai yu jingying" 明清時代我國東北各地人蔘的開採與經營 [The Collection and Management of Ginseng in Different Areas of Northeastern China During the Ming-Qing Dynasties], *Zhongguo nongshi* 中國農史 4 (1988): 33–40; Zhao Yunan 趙郁楠, "Qingdai dongbei shenwu guanli kaoshu" 清代東北蔘務管理考述 [A Study of the Qing Dynasty's Management of Ginseng-Related Affairs in Northeastern China] (Master's Thesis, Minzu University of China, 2007); Yu Lei 于磊, "Lun qingdai qianqi dongbei shenwe guanlitizhi de yanbian ji yingxiang" 論清代前期東北蔘務管理體制的演變及影響 [Changes and Effects of the Northeastern Ginseng Management System in Early Qing China] (Bachelor's Thesis, Liaoning University, 2009).

12 Lan Weiji 藍偉吉, "18 shijimo Zhongguo xiyangshenre yuanyin qianxi" 18世紀末中國西洋蔘热原因淺析 [An Analysis of the Craze for Western Ginseng in Late Eighteenth Century China], *Heilongjiang shizhi* 黑龍江史志 23 (2013): 21–24; Guo Weidong 郭衛東, "Xiyangshen: Zhongmei zaoqi maoyi zhong de zhongyao huopin" 西洋蔘:中美早期貿易中的重要貨品 [Western Ginseng: A Major Commodity in the Early Trade Between China and America], *Guangdong shehuikexue* 廣東社會科學 2 (2013): 122–32; Song Junling 宋軍令, "Ming Qing shiqi meizhou nongzuowu zaizhongguo de chuanzhong jiqi yingxiang yanjiu" 明清時期美洲农作物在中國的傳種及其影響研究 [A Study of American Crops Bred in Ming and Qing China and Their Impact] (Doctoral dissertation, Henan University, 2007).

Kim Sun-min's research appears to be at the forefront of studies around the world involving Manchuria and ginseng.[13]

Compared to East Asia, Western research on ginseng in the humanities and social sciences still seems to be taking its first steps. General publications on the history and culture of ginseng began to appear around 1900 in the United States, but they did not carry much academic merit since they were mostly supplementary to manuals on ginseng cultivation.[14] Ginseng-related studies and publications went through a lengthy static phase until a rising interest in alternative medicine and health foods in the 1980s served as a spur to its revival.[15] Only then did historical studies surface on the discovery and cultivation of ginseng in North America as well as the export of American ginseng to China.[16] Yet, ginseng continues to be a generally neglected crop in Western historical research.

This book is the outcome of an attempt to bring ginseng back into the realm of global history. The goal is to uncover Western sources on ginseng that shed light on its neglected presence in Western historical research and at the same time determine why a global commodity like ginseng failed to garner attention from scholars of history. It is an attempt to rectify the worldview based on Eurocentric diffusionism and create a rough sketch of the early modern times during which multiple world-systems may have existed. Such an attempt also serves as an opportunity to find out why consumers of ginseng remained limited to East Asia until the end of the twentieth century.

13 Kim Seon-min, *Ginseng and Borderland: Territorial Boundaries and Political Relations Between Qing China and Choson Korea, 1636-1912* (Oakland, CA: University of California Press, 2017); Kim Seon-min 김선민, "Insam kwa kangyŏk: Hugŭm-Ch'ŏng ŭi kangyŏk inshik kwa taeoegwan'gye ŭi pyŏnhwa" 人蔘과 疆域: 후금-청의 강역인식과 대외관계의 변화 [The State Development from the Later Jin to the Qing and the Boundary Making in the Early Seventeenth Century], *Myŏngch'ŏngsa yŏn'gu* 명청사연구 30 (2008): 227–57; Kim Seonmin 김선민, "17-18 segi ch'ŏngdae insam chŏngch'aek ŭi pyŏnhwa" 17-18세기 청대 인삼정책의 변화 [Qing Ginseng Monopoly During the 17th to 18th Century], *Chungguk'akpo* 중국학보 74 (2015): 405–24.

14 George V. Nash, *American Ginseng: Its Commercial History, Protection and Cultivation*, Revised (Washington, DC: Government Printing Office, 1898); Maurice Grenville Kains, *Ginseng: Its Cultivation, Harvesting, Marketing and Market Value, With a Short Account of Its History and Botany* (New York: Orange Judd Company, 1901); Charles Marvin Root, *What Is Ginseng: An Account of the History and Cultivation of Ginseng* (Omaha, NE: J. M. Roucek, 1905); John Henry Koehler, *Ginseng and Goldenseal Growers' Handbook* (Wausau, WI: P. F. Stolze, 1912).

15 Len C. Polczinski, "Ginseng (Panax Quinquefolius L.) Culture in Marathon County, Wisconsin: Historical Growth, Distribution, and Soils Inventory" (Master's Thesis, University of Wisconsin, 1982); Sharon Wai-Seung Lee, "Evolution of the 'Shang' (American Ginseng) Industry in Marathon County" (Master's Thesis, University of Wisconsin, Madison, 1998).

16 Brian L. Evans, "Ginseng: Root of Chinese-Canadian Relations," *The Canadian Historical Review* 66, no. 1 (1985): 1–26; Alvar W. Carlson, "Ginseng: America's Botanical Drug Connection to the Orient," *Economic Botany* 40, no. 2 (1986): 233–49; Paul E. Fontenoy, "Ginseng, Otter Skins, and Sandalwood: The Conundrum of the China Trade," *The Northern Mariner* 7, no. 1 (1997): 1–16; Dave Wang, "Chinese Civilization and the United States: Tea, Ginseng, Porcelain Ware and Silk in Colonial America," *Virginia Review of Asian Studies* 13 (2011): 113–31; Luke Manget, "Ginseng, China, and the Transformation of the Ohio Valley, 1783–1840," *Ohio Valley History* 17, no. 3 (2017): 3–23.

With the aforementioned purposes in mind, Part 1 focuses on botany in order to outline the intellectual exchange between the East and West from the early seventeenth century to the eighteenth century, during which time ginseng was introduced to the West. The Jesuits contributed substantially to introducing Korean ginseng to the Western knowledge system after it was delivered to the London headquarters of the East India Company in 1617. A Jesuit missionary's report about witnessing ginseng in Manchuria led to the discovery of a different variety of ginseng (Panax quinquefolius) in North America. Meanwhile, under the banner of mercantilism, European elites recognized ginseng as a valuable resource, thereby prompting efforts from the British Royal Society and French Royal Academy to study it. As a result, ginseng gained a scientific name and instances of its medical application emerged in Europe.

Part 2 examines ginseng as a global commodity that traveled across a dual structure with East Asia at the center and Europe and North America at the periphery. Since antiquity, ginseng had been distributed throughout China, Korea, and Japan as a tributary or trade item. Britain set foot in the periphery of that distribution network in the early seventeenth century and eventually obtained hegemony over it, only to lose it to America once it gained independence and made its own incursion into the ginseng trade. Ginseng thereby became the first and best export commodity for America at a time when the country had nothing to trade with China. Despite being the hegemon of the world during the nineteenth century, Britain lost its control over the trade network of ginseng but never lost interest in the plant itself. After all, ginseng was a major resource of Korea as competition between powers was growing intense on the peninsula.

Part 3 reviews the crises faced in the history of ginseng and how they were handled. In Western medical circles, ginseng was used to treat various symptoms and was distributed as a proprietary medicine. Since the late eighteenth century, however, such circles began to disparage the medicinal properties of ginseng and seemed to be working on its dismissal from pharmacopeias. The reason was the failure to extract active components from ginseng at a time when such components and chemical formulae were shaping the foundation of "modern" medicine and pharmacy. While considering why Western medical circles' attempts at extraction failed, Part 3 also traces ginseng's extremely stagnant entry into the modern system of pharmacology. In the meantime, ginseng was driven to the brink of extinction in East Asia and North America. In response to the near depletion of wild ginseng, efforts were launched to cultivate the plant. With the spread of cultivation, the nationality of ginseng has been growing increasingly meaningless.

Part 4 adopts a cultural approach to determine why ginseng has been neglected in Western historical research. Ginseng was defined as an exclusive property of the East in the West and was further associated with negative attributes such as extravagance, dissipation, autocracy, and irrationality. Despite being deeply involved in the production and export of ginseng, the West eventually otherized ginseng due to a sense of inferiority that they may never catch up with East

Asia in terms of techniques for processing ginseng and also due to economic interests that were preoccupied with its export, instead of the developing of a domestic market for ginseng. This Orientalist labeling of ginseng was pinned on professional ginseng diggers as well, creating an antisocial, backward impression of them in the United States. Even today, ginseng diggers whose livelihood depends on a mysterious Eastern object like ginseng are ascribed with a negative identity and experience a stigma akin to internal colonialism.

As previously mentioned, the foremost purpose of this book is to bring ginseng back into the realm of global history. That realm is largely divided in two, with East Asia occupying the core and the rest of the world outside the core. However, the parts covering Korea, China, and Japan in this book are mostly dedicated to merely outlining the major policies regarding ginseng and the circumstances of its trade. This is because such areas are beyond my field of expertise, but also because others have already conducted outstanding research in those areas. To me, uncovering traces of ginseng in the West, so that they may take root in the history of that part of the world, seemed a more important and urgent task. This is why such a diverse range of sources were considered, from medical tracts and pharmacopeias to economic papers and East India Company reports, not to mention botany books, atlases, travelogues, natural histories, newspaper articles, correspondences, dictionaries, novels, poems, and advertisements. As many direct quotes from such sources as possible have been included to create a vivid narrative. After all, from the beginning of this study, my motto has been to allow the sources themselves to testify to the presence of ginseng in Western history.

PART I

Ginseng Meets the West

1

THE ARRIVAL OF KOREAN GINSENG IN EUROPE

Korean Ginseng's Arrival in London

In 1617, Richard Cocks (1566–1624), the head of the East India Company's factory in Hirado, Japan, enclosed a letter in a small package sent to the company's headquarters in London. That very letter became the earliest "official" record of the arrival of Korean ginseng in Europe.

> I received a box by the advice with a certain root in it which came from Cape Bona Speranza, but it proveth here worth nothing, it being dried, that no substance remaineth in it. Herewithal I send your Worships some of it, with another piece of that which is good and cometh out of Corea. It is here worth the weight in silver, but very little to be had in any common man's hands, for that all is taken up for the Emperor by the King of Tushma, who only hath licence to trade with the Coreans; and all the tribute he payeth to the Emperor is of this root. It is held here for the most precious thing for physic that is in the world and is sufficient to put life into any man.[1]

The long journey that the package of ginseng embarked on from Korea, to Japan, and on to London was an outcome of Europe's expansion overseas during the Age of Discovery. Cocks' letter also revealed the existence of a different plant, similar to ginseng, at the southern tip of Africa, where the package of ginseng stopped by on its way to London. In fact, an East India Company record from 1611 indicates that an employee named Peter was instructed to bring back a root called *ningine* from the Cape of Good Hope in South Africa.[2]

The Peter in that record was referring to the Dutch merchant Peter Floris (Pieter Willemsz). After joining the East India Company in his thirties, Floris

DOI: 10.4324/9781003286691-2

came across the good fortune of boarding the *Globe*, which sailed to as far as the Bay of Bengal, the Strait of Malacca, and the Strait of Singapore. The four-and-a-half-year voyage turned out to be a lucrative success, yielding a three-for-one profit, and Floris would go on to publish an account of the expedition as a book. In the book was the following description about the ship's arrival at the Cape of Good Hope.

> Being by Gods grace here [Table Bay] arrived, we presently fell to the ordering of the ship, and hoping of our cask to fill fresh water, for much refreshing was not here to be had at this time of the year, by the great quantitie of rain, being now in the chiefest of winter so that the mountains lay covered with snow: during which time we used great diligence in seeking of the root Ningimm according to our instruction, the above mentioned 2 Holland ships being expressly come there for the same purpose, being one of Japan that first discovered the secret; but, being winter time, there was for this time no more to be done but to go away as wise as we came, for the old roots being decayed and rotten, the new leaves began only to come forth, so that had it not been by reason of some information which was gotten of one who here shall be nameless for divers considerations sake, we should have bene fayne to have departed without any notice thereof, the right time of gathering the same being in December, January, and February, being called of these inhabitants Canna.[3]

Another interesting bit of information that can be gleaned from the above description is that a Japanese crewman was aboard a Dutch East India Company ship. There is no way of knowing whether he became a crewman of his own accord, or whether he had been sold to, or was held hostage on, the ship. Yet the description indicates that the Japanese crewman was aware of ginseng and could recognize it. This was probably why ginseng was marked as "Ningimm," which sounds similar to the Japanese pronunciation of ginseng. As a matter of fact, the terms *ninzin* (*ningine*) or *ninsi* were commonly used to refer to the Japanese ginseng or ginseng in general in seventeenth- and eighteenth-century Europe. The use of *ninzin* is therefore an example of a foreign word introduced to Europe from coming into contact with Japan.

The aforementioned letter and book show that European merchants regarded the plant South African natives called *canna* (or *kanna*) as identical or similar to ginseng. Canna is nowadays distinguished from ginseng, but back then Europeans believed that it had "come from China."[4] The plant was a valued herb known for its excellent invigorating effect and hence available only to the upper class of native African societies. This is how a source from 1735 described the circumstances at the time.

> There is a root also in this country [Cape of Good Hope], which the Hottentots call Kanna, and will give almost any thing to purchase it, a

> little of it raising the spirits to a very high degree, and is compared to the ginseng of the Chinese.[5]

For a while, this root made the Cape of Good Hope bustle. Whenever a ship arrived, natives swarmed in to sell canna to its crew. East India Company employees offered pieces of copper in exchange for canna or even hiked up mountains to dig it for themselves. However, they would often be disappointed to find that the roots they uncovered were not as large or ripe as the canna made available through the natives. Records of such incidents show that at the time, the East India Company regarded canna as an attractive commodity identical to ginseng and therefore invested considerable efforts to secure the root. The records also suggest that some sort of criteria existed in distinguishing the quality of canna. Then, instead of the relatively inferior canna, Korean ginseng surfaced as the true archetype of premium ginseng, and Cocks was the first to present it to the East India Company's London headquarters.

Cocks was born in Staffordshire as the son of a farmer. He stepped into the clothing business, and after completing an apprenticeship with a clothmaker in London, he joined the Clothworkers Guild. Yet even while working as a clothmaker the mercenary instinct in Cocks enticed him to engage in trade on the side. Cocks later went to France where he worked as a factor in charge of purchasing goods to be shipped to England on behalf of merchants, which kindled his interest in trading overseas. Armed with experience and confidence, Cocks headed to Japan at the relatively late age of forty-seven to oversee the East India Company factory in Hirado. As the first port where Japan initiated trade with European countries in 1550, Hirado functioned as the primary point of trade in East Asia until the rise of Nagasaki in 1636. Despite banning Christianity in 1614, the Japanese shogun permitted trade with the Dutch and English only because they were interested in trade and had little regard for mission work or religious conversion.

As head of the East India Company factory in Hirado, Cocks exhibited exemplary performance and passionately engaged in trade. While managing a staff of a dozen, Cocks established branches of the factory in Osaka, Kyoto, and Edo. Through branches in those cities, he traveled extensively to meet and grow acquainted with prominent figures in Japan. His marriage to Matinga, the daughter of a Japanese nobleman, is known to have been a great help to his business as well as his acquisition of the Japanese language. In addition to a house and five servants, Cocks showered Matinga with money, rice, and all sorts of expensive gifts. Alas, in 1621, Cocks discovered that his wife was having an affair with seven different men. One of them happened to be a subordinate of his named William Nelson.[6] Out of despair, Cocks ended his relationship with Matinga and the factory in Hirado was soon forced to shut down due to bankruptcy. Cocks returned to England in a wretched state of mind and died shortly afterward. Nevertheless, the detailed logs he kept during his stay in Japan survived to become an invaluable source revealing various aspects of the early stages of trade between Britain and Japan.[7]

Since his time in France, Cocks had served as an informal spy for the English government. In fact, it was not uncommon for factors of any East India Company to act as a spy for their own government. However, Cocks' true worth as a spy materialized after his arrival in Japan. He continued to pass on information about the circumstances in East Asia and the movements of European competitors such as Spain or the Netherlands. And to gather information, entertainment was a must. Cocks sent generous gifts to the Japanese wives and children of Europeans staying in Japan and earned a reputation for hosting extravagant, interesting parties.

Cocks' efforts did not end there. He persistently tried to be aware of the tastes and preferences of his Japanese friends, guests from Europe and other countries, as well as potential clients and patrons. And he used the information he gathered to keep a detailed list of items that seemed to have sales potential, showing that he continued to be dictated by his mercantilist disposition.[8] This is probably how Cocks learned of ginseng and determined that its commercial value was great enough to bring it to the attention of the company's London headquarters. It most likely was not a coincidence that he developed the ability to tell the difference between high- and low-quality ginseng. Hence, his dual identity as a merchant and spy may have been what caused Cocks to regard ginseng as an unheard-of commodity that might have been able to contribute to England's national interests.

However, with the shutdown of the factory in Hirado, ginseng disappeared for a while from English records of overseas trade. It was nevertheless destined to be introduced to Europe through a different channel: the Jesuits.

The Jesuits and East–West Exchange

The Jesuits played a decisive role in making ginseng known to the world. Seaways found during the Age of Discovery furnished the physical conditions for Jesuit missionaries to travel abroad more frequently.[9] They accompanied merchants on their journeys to Central and East Asia. If the East India Company transported ginseng from the East to the West, Jesuit missionaries contributed to the Western accumulation of knowledge about ginseng and provided key information that led to the discovery of a different kind of ginseng in North America.

Just as the European expansion overseas was carried out at national levels, missionary work also required government support at the time. Missionary work thus turned into an arena of fierce competition. Portugal had been at the forefront of overseas missions, but Spain and France soon joined the race. Pope Paul V rescinded his permission for Portugal to exclusively proselytize in Asia and began to exercise more direct control by founding the Sacred Congregation for the Propagation of the Faith in June 1622. The Jesuits practically dominated evangelization efforts in Asia for a while until other orders such as the Dominicans and Franciscans sought to join them and began to send their own missionaries to China.

From a post-colonialist perspective, the Jesuits' activities were part of a religious, scholarly "colonialist program" executed with a bible in one hand and a compass in the other, instead of guns and swords. However, apart from the strategy aimed at evangelizing all Chinese, starting with the Chinese emperor, the nature of the Jesuits' activities early on leaned toward cultural exchange out of curiosity rather than a display of the West's unilateral superiority. Early modern Europe knew almost nothing about China, which is why seventeenth-century European intellectuals responded enthusiastically to the Jesuits' knowledge of China and tended to regard China as a frame of reference with which they had to become quickly familiar.

Even in the battle between ancients and moderns triggered mostly by English and French scholars, China was cited as a model that Europe should follow. Defenders of the ancients argued that because China had a history far longer than Europe and a highly efficient ruling system, it was worthy enough to serve as an exemplar for Europe. Historical records from ancient China appeared to be far more solid and empirical compared to biblical descriptions, leading to the suggestion that such Chinese records should be taken into consideration to rewrite ancient Western history.

John James Clarke once mentioned that "there is indeed something deeply ambivalent about the West's attitude towards the East."[10] According to Clarke, the West attempted to integrate Oriental ideas into their intellectual interests, even though such ideas could not be fully grasped through the concepts of power or rule that they were familiar with, and, ultimately, those attempts enriched the European Enlightenment. The notion that the West unilaterally disseminated knowledge and technologies to the East was formed only after Western imperialism seized worldwide hegemony.

The Jesuits played a key role in introducing knowledge and technologies from abroad to European societies and in facilitating cultural exchange between the East and the West. They also established educational institutes all over the world, thereby contributing greatly to the development of interdisciplinary, multiethnic scholarship. In particular, Jesuit missionaries are considered to have made significant contributions in the fields of astronomy, cartography, geography, natural history, ethnography, botany, and materia medica. This is most likely why Steven J. Harris mentioned that "Jesuit missionary naturalists represent an obvious point of intersection of natural theology, colonial natural histories, and Enlightenment epistemologies."[11] What set Jesuit missionaries apart from the merchants they traveled with was that they submitted highly accurate and intellectual reports to their respective home countries. Those reports were circulated among intellectual societies and thus changed the contours of knowledge in Europe. The Jesuits' reports about China, India, and East Indies tremendously broadened the European worldview and aroused among European scholars a great interest in China.[12]

Among the academic activities of the Jesuits, this book will focus on those in the field of materia medica. The Jesuits' approach to materia medica was quite different from their approach to other fields of study such as astronomy. Despite relying on a basic set of equipment, astronomy was a field that only Jesuit missionaries with expertise individually took part in, whereas even ordinary brothers engaged themselves in materia medica without possessing any expertise in the field.[13] The Jesuits set up an apothecary at each major base of operations, which allowed missionaries to collect all sorts of prescriptions to satisfy their personal curiosity or be prepared in case they fell ill.[14] Missionaries sent to China were especially eager to absorb knowledge on Chinese materia medica, medicine, and pharmacology.

In reverse, the Jesuits also introduced Western medicine to China. French and Portuguese Jesuit missionaries who stayed in Beijing and Macao brought medical books from Europe to stock the libraries they opened in those cities and supplied medications from the West to the Chinese imperial family.[15] In the 1680s and 1690s, French Jesuits brought items such as snakestones, theriac, and cinchona to Beijing as per the Chinese emperor's orders and such items actually did offer a great deal of assistance.[16]

In 1692, Jean de Fontaney (1643–1710), who led a group of French Jesuits to China, was summoned to the palace of the Kangxi Emperor (r. 1662–1723). The emperor had been interested in Western technologies and medicine and wished to try using cinchona to treat his high fever. Before the emperor could take the cinchona brought by the Jesuit missionaries, its safety had to be clinically tested against three other patients with similar symptoms and four nobles in charge of looking after the emperor's health. The Kangxi Emperor was thus completely cured of malaria, and as a reward he permitted the construction of the Beitang (北堂, "Northern Church") in Beijing for the French Jesuits to use as their missionary headquarters.[17] Nevertheless, Europe definitely sought more knowledge and information from China than the other way around.

Ginseng in Chinese Materia Medica Books

Ever since it began to come into contact with China, Europe desired information about Chinese herbs and other plants. The European countries' encounter with the New World had an enormous impact on botany, expanding its scope tremendously. The Spanish set out in search of gold, but when they reached the new continent, they discovered that it was a cornucopia of useful, valuable herbs, in addition to gold, silver, and other precious stones. In 1518, Paolo Riccio (1480–1541), the doctor of the Holy Roman Emperor Maximilian I, discovered that Guaiacum officinale from South America was effective in treating syphilis, a fact that soon became published in Germany. Tobacco, which was discovered during the first voyage of Christopher Columbus, started to be used to treat skin irritations when it was first brought to Portugal in 1548.[18]

The European expansion overseas is commonly regarded to have been triggered by the spice trade. While the category of spices included a wide range of items, from indulgent foods to medicinal plants and drugs, many were interchangeable. However, most such medicinal plants or foods were produced only in certain regions outside Europe. For instance, arabica coffee, originally from Ethiopia, turned into a crop when it reached Yemen and was grown only in Yemen for quite some time. Cacao was grown only in Mexico, coca only in the Andes, tea only in China, and tobacco only in the Americas.

Non-European states like China, the Ottoman Empire, the Aztec Empire, and the Inca Empire that exported the aforementioned crops banned their seeds or saplings from being transported outside their territory. To break their monopoly, European imperialism employed conciliatory and aggressive measures forcing such states open up or colonized regions that were natural habitats for such crops. Soon most medicinal foods were produced in faraway, unfamiliar colonies. According to Kenneth Pomeranz and Steven Topik, "botanical gardens that nurtured exotic seedlings became the advance guard of empire." In Pomeranz and Topik's opinion, European empires were built on "drug deals" and the tariffs imposed on tea, sugar, and tobacco supplied the foundation for such empires to sustain their bureaucratic systems and armed forces.[19]

There is no knowing whether Jesuit missionaries were aware at the time of such a heartless colonialist mechanism. At least on the surface, most missionaries who studied the flora and fauna native to the region they were sent to defended their cause as the exploration of knowledge that would benefit mankind. Michael Boym (c. 1612–1659) was a Jesuit missionary from Poland who became a leading figure in the dissemination of knowledge about Chinese plants and medicine to the West. Boym sent the specimens and seeds he collected from China to the Royal Botanical Garden in France. He expressed his wish to "make the treasure of Chinese medical knowledge accessible to Europeans as well as the whole world."[20] While studying Chinese materia medica, Boym grew fascinated by the 1596 compendium *Bencao gangmu* (本草綱目), compiled by a Ming dynasty Chinese scholar of materia medica named Li Shizhen (李時珍, 1518–1593). Boym eventually published *Flora Sinensis* (1656) in Europe, which covered twenty-two of the medicinal plants listed in *Bencao gangmu.*

Among Chinese medicinal herbs, ginseng particularly captured the attention of Europeans. Ginseng was known as a "panacea against all sickness" with surprising healing power, which made it destined to be a most appealing subject of research.[21] After all, ginseng had been used in East Asia for thousands of years. The first known record of ginseng was in *Jijiuzhang* (急就章), written by Shi You (史遊) during the reign of Emperor Yuan (元帝) of the Former Han (前漢, 48–33 BC). Various medicinal herbs are listed in the book, and *can* (參), which means ginseng, was among them.[22] The term ginseng (人參) appeared in multiple later books, including *Chunqiu wei yundou shu* (春秋緯運斗樞), a guide to *Chunqiu* (春秋, the Spring and Autumn Annals), and *Liwei douwei* (禮緯斗威儀), a guide to *Liji* (禮記, the Book of Rites). The first source known to describe ginseng as a medical substance is *Shanghanlun* (傷寒論) compiled by Zhang Zhongjing (張仲景, 150–219), a physician of the Eastern Han dynasty.[23]

Shennong bencaojing (神農本草經) is the first historical source to mention the efficacy of ginseng in detail.[24] Published during the Former Han period, the book is known as the oldest record on pharmacology, and although the original edition no longer exists, its content has been passed down through numerous medical and pharmacological books such as *Bencao gangmu*. The book classified 365 kinds of drugs into three grades—high, medium, and low—and describes each of their characteristics and efficacies. A high-grade drug contains no poisonous elements, inflicts no harm on the human body regardless of the amount of intake, and extends a person's lifespan. A medium-grade drug is a tonic taken as a prophylaxis, which can be poisonous depending on an individual's physical condition. A low-grade drug is used to cure an ill person and must be prescribed by an expert since long-term use can be harmful.[25]

Ginseng was classified as a high-grade drug "used as a main ingredient to boost the function of the five viscera and to help stabilize the mind, remove pathogens trying to enter the intestines, brighten vision, ease the heart, instill wisdom, and when taken long-term, it allows a person to feel physically lighter and enjoy longevity."[26] Chinese scholars have appraised that *Shennong bencaojing* is proof that a complete, organized degree of knowledge about ginseng's medicinal value had already been formed by the time the book was published.[27]

Among the publications that came after *Shennong bencaojing*, *Bencao gangmu* offers by far the most detailed record of ginseng. This compendium by the Ming scholar Li Shizhen is considered a masterpiece comprising all the knowledge China had thus far amassed on materia medica and pharmacology. What is worth noting is that the longest and most detailed descriptions throughout several chapters in the book are devoted to ginseng. The appendix chapter on treatment methods includes sixty-seven methods that use ginseng as an ingredient and prescribes how they can be administered to treat fifteen different types of symptoms.[28] Almost thirty years were required until this massive compilation of fifty-two volumes could finally be published in 1592, which was around the time a greater number of Jesuit missionaries began coming to China. The book thereafter became introduced to the West through Jesuit scholars like the aforementioned Michael Boym. Although its extensive content was not translated in its entirety, its descriptions of medicinal herbs managed to be translated into various languages including Latin, French, German, English, Japanese, Russian, and Spanish to be distributed all across Europe.

Álvaro Semedo (1585–1658), a Portuguese Jesuit missionary who spent twenty years in China, is known as the first person in Europe to have written about ginseng. Semedo had been acquainted with Boym, well enough to send him to the court of the Yongli Emperor (r. 1649–1662), the last emperor of the Southern Ming dynasty. Semedo's own missionary work was riddled with turbulence. At one point, he was imprisoned due to the Chinese persecution of Christianity. He was also blacklisted for remaining loyal to the Ming dynasty during the transition from Ming to Qing in China. Nevertheless, Semedo earned his fame through his book *Relatione della grande monarchia della Cina* (1643).[29] This introduction to China, covering a diversity of Asian products including ginseng, gained enormous popularity in Europe where it was translated and distributed in several different languages.

Through his book, Semedo described that the Chinese considered ginseng the finest among tonics and that it grew near the Liaodong region. He added that ginseng grew in Korea as well, where it was offered as tribute to China, and that Korea had been invaded by the Japanese between 1592 and 1598. Ginseng later made an appearance in *Bellum Tartaricum*, a book published in 1654 on the history of the wars of the Tartars in China by an Italian Jesuit missionary named Martino Martini (1614–1661).[30] Hence, until the mid-seventeenth century, Jesuit missionaries, mainly from Portugal and Italy, were responsible for disseminating information involving China and ginseng. Then, as a larger number of French Jesuit missionaries started to be sent abroad, several incidents prompted a more detailed interest in ginseng.

In 1687, the French emperor Louis XIV gained permission from the Vatican to proselytize in China and dispatched five Jesuit priests to Qing China. At the palace of the Kangxi Emperor, the priests were able to explore various disciplines such as astronomy, mathematics, physics, geography, zoology, botany, and medicine. And for reasons that remain obscure, ginseng emerged as a major subject of research for them. While introducing the external characteristics of ginseng as well as its intake methods, Louis Daniel Le Comte (1655–1728) commented that ginseng was an excellent tonic appreciated as a panacea in China.[31] Antoine Thomas (1644–1709) enjoyed the privilege of personally taking ginseng. He left a gloating description of how he benefited from two intakes of ginseng the Kangxi Emperor had bestowed upon him when he fell ill in 1691.[32] It was indeed an experience worth gloating about since the bestowal of ginseng was considered the greatest gesture of affection a Chinese emperor could show to his subjects.

Pierre Jartoux's Report on Ginseng

In 1713, the French Jesuit missionary Pierre Jartoux (1668–1720) wrote a report which eventually brought about the most groundbreaking change in the Western history of ginseng.[33] Out of his interest in alarm clocks, the Wanli Emperor invited Matteo Ricci (1552–1610) to serve as an adviser in 1601, and from then on Jesuit priests started to be increasingly involved in many of the scientific research projects in China. They worked at the Imperial Astronomical Bureau in Beijing and simultaneously sent a massive amount of geographical information back to Europe.[34] The cartography project carried out under the Kangxi Emperor's orders was one of the most important projects in which Jesuit priests were involved. For his talents in mathematical theory and machine manufacturing, Jartoux was selected by the emperor to assist in making maps of China. In 1708, Jartoux embarked on an exploration of the Manchurian region with Joachim Bouvet (1656–1730) and Jean-Baptiste Régis (1664–1738) (Figures 1.1 and 1.2).

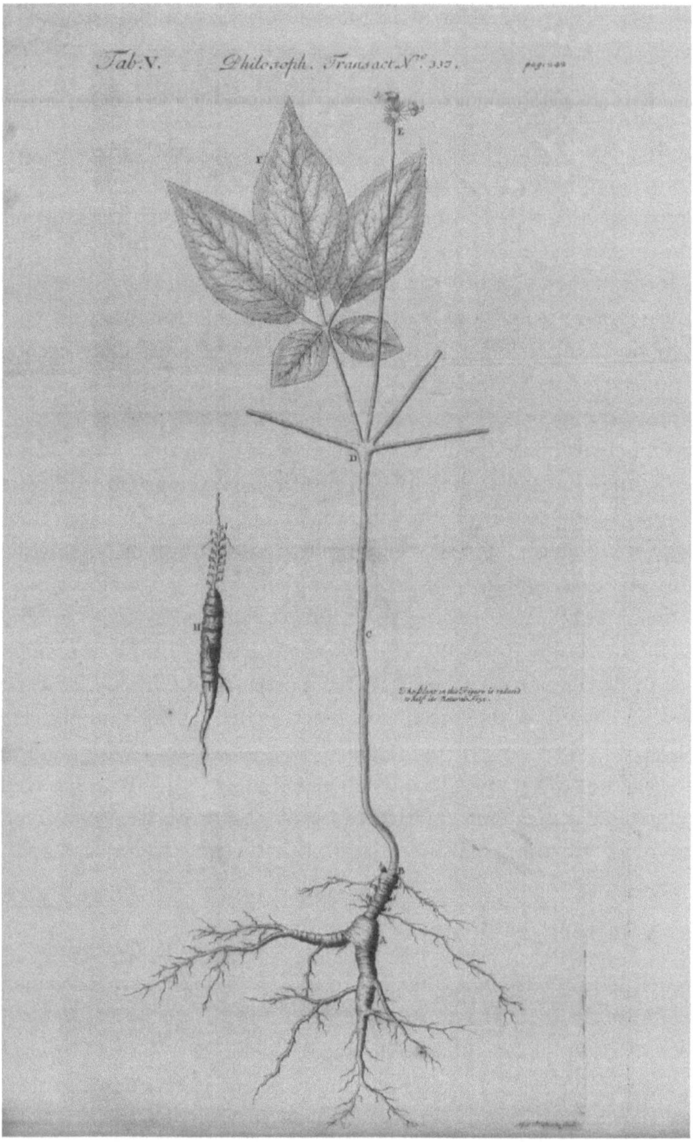

FIGURE 1.1 Ginseng witnessed near the Korean border.

In late July 1709, Jartoux witnessed ginseng near the Chinese border with Korea. He later began his 1711 report with the following line: "The map of Tartary, which we made by Order of the Emperor of China, gave us an Opportunity of seeing the famous Plant Gin-seng, so much esteem'd in China, and so little known in Europe."[35] Jartoux's description reflected his awe upon encountering ginseng. He noted that the root was valued immeasurably by the

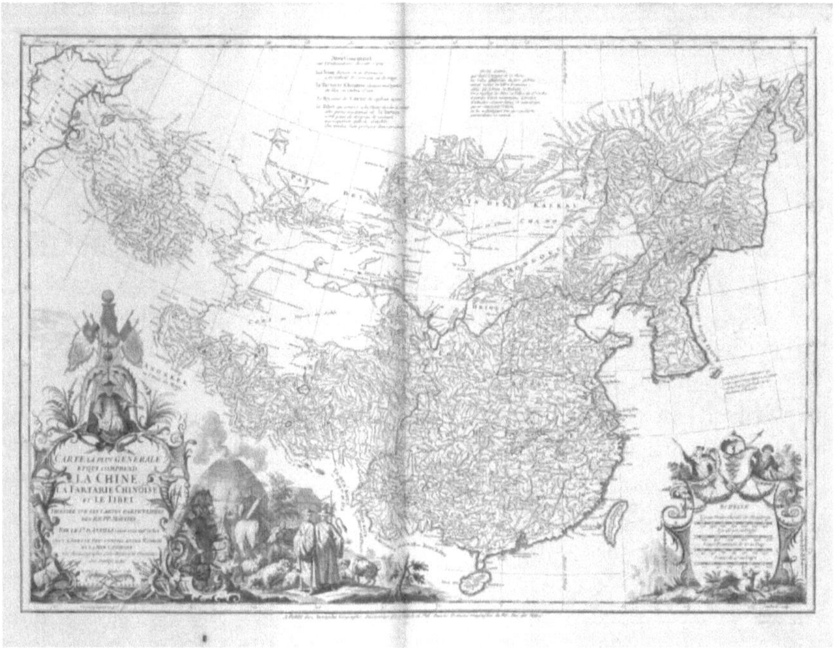

FIGURE 1.2 Carte la plus generale et qui comprend La Chine.

Chinese and Manchurians, more so than anyone could ever imagine. Below is a recollection of the experience from Jartoux's report.

> The most eminent Physicians in China have writ whole Volumes upon the Virtues and Qualities of this Plant; and make it an Ingredient in almost all Remedies which they give to their chief Nobility; for it is of too high a Price for the common People. They affirm, that it is Sovereign Remedy for all Weaknesses occasion'd by excessive Fatigues either of Body or Mind; that it dissolves Pituitous Humours; that it cures Weakness of the Lungs and the Pleurisy; that it stops Vomitings; that it strengthens the Stomach and helps the Appetite; that it disperses Fumes or Vapours; that it fortifies the Breast, and is a Remedy for short and weak Breathing; that it strengthens the Vital Spirits, and increases Lymph in the Blood; in short, that it is good against Dizziness of the Head and Dimness of Sight, and that it prolongs Life in old Age.
>
> No Body can imagine that the Chinese and Tartars would set so high a Value upon this Root, if it did not constantly produce a good Effect. Those that are in Health often make use of it to render themselves more vigorous and strong; And I am perswaded that it would prove an excellent Medicine in the Hands of any European who understands Pharmacy, if he had but

> a sufficient quantity of it to make such Tryals as are necessary, to examine the Nature of it Chymically, and to apply it in a proper quantity according to the Nature of Disease for which it may be beneficial.
>
> It is certain that it subtilizes, increases the motion of, and warms the Blood; that it helps Digestion, and invigorates in a very sensible manner. After I had designed the Root, which I shall hereafter describe, I observed the state of my Pulse, and then took half of the Root, raw as it was and unprepar'd; In an Hour after I found my Pulse much fuller and quicker; I had an Appetite, and found my self much more vigorous, and could bear Labour much better and easier than before.
>
> But I did not rely on this Trial alone, imagining that this Alteration might proceed from the Rest that we had that Day; But four Days after, finding myself so fatigued and weary that I could scarce set on Horse back, a Mandarin who was in company with us perceiving it, gave me one of these Roots; I took half of it immediately, and an Hour after I was not the least sensible of any weariness. I have often made use of it since, and always with the same success I have observed also, that the green Leaves, and especially the Fibrous part of them chewed, would produce nearly the same effect.[36]

What followed the above recollection was a detailed botanical description of ginseng along with a drawing of it. According to Jartoux's description, ginseng only grew in shady spots in mountains amid thousands of other plants at a latitude of thirty-nine to forty-seven degrees and a longitude of ten to twenty degrees. He also included details about what the five leaves, head, and root of the plant looked like. Jartoux confessed that he had never seen the flower of ginseng and was therefore quite curious, although some said ginseng had no flower or that the flower was very small and white. The only part the Manchurians valued was the root, which they either kept buried in the ground for ten to fifteen days or prepared for storage by washing, brushing, and steaming the root. Jartoux added that physicians in Europe would surely benefit from ginseng if they knew exactly what its components were and how much should be prescribed.[37]

The Matter of Ginseng's Habitat

In Jartoux's report, the comments he made about the natural habitat of ginseng warrant consideration. Jartoux claimed that ginseng could be discovered in Manchuria but not inner China. This was a direct refutation of what Martino Martini, the author of *De Bello Tartarico Historia*, mentioned in his description that ginseng "grows on the Mountains of Yong-pinfou in the Province of Peking." Jartoux believed that Father Martini had misunderstood Yongpingfu (永平府), today's Lulong County (盧龍縣) in Hebei Province (河北省), as a natural habitat of ginseng when it was actually the first stop on trade routes bringing ginseng to inner China after being dug up in Manchuria.[38]

Jartoux's claim was significant because it made his report the first Western record to squarely contradict the near mythic belief that premium ginseng was being produced at the heart of China. The location of ginseng's natural habitat later turned into a topic with major cultural and economic repercussions. Until the late nineteenth century, ginseng from the Liaodong region or Korea had to endure second-rate status because of "ginseng from inner China" such as Shangdang ginseng (上黨蔘); this ginseng of "inner China," however, no longer existed. And such a mythic belief was perpetuated at least in the West by texts like the works of Martini. Where then did this misunderstanding about ginseng's habitat originate from?

Records indicating that ginseng grew in Shangdang, today's Changzhi County (長治縣) in Shanxi Province (山西省), can be traced back to as early as the Later Han dynasty (後漢, 25–220). *Shuowen jiezi* (說文解字) by Xu Shen (許慎) is a Chinese character dictionary from 121 that includes a detailed entry for the character *shen* (蔘), noting that ginseng was produced in the Shangdang area. *Bencaojing jizhu* (本草經集注) by Tao Hongjing (陶弘景, 456–536) also notes that ginseng "grows in Shangdang and Liaodong" (生上黨及遼東).[39] This detail also made its way into *Bencao gangmu* since it was a compilation of contents from previous medical books, including the one by Tao Hongjing.[40] As *Bencao gangmu* was distributed in Europe, it served as a definitive source for Europeans on determining the natural habitat of ginseng. While quoting from *Mingyi bielu* (名醫別錄) by Tao Hongjing,[41] Li Shizhen added the following comment in *Bencao gangmu* about ginseng from the ancient Korean kingdoms of Paekche and Koguryŏ.

> The thin, solid, and white ginseng from Paekche is valued. It's potency and taste, however, are weaker than the ginseng from Shangdang. Ginseng from Koguryŏ is essentially from Liaodong, but it is less valued than that from Paekche for being less potent despite its larger size. Paekche is now a vassal of Koguryŏ so that two kinds of ginseng are being presented from Koguryŏ. It is simply a matter of choosing one over the other, but they are both inferior to the ginseng from Shangdang.[42]

Although the above description appeared in *Bencao gangmu* from the late sixteenth century, it was excerpted from *Mingyi bielu*, meaning it reflected circumstances that dated back to the sixth century when Tao Hongjing was alive. In that sense, *Mingyi bielu* demonstrates that Koguryŏ and Paekche produced ginseng around the time the three ancient Korean kingdoms were being established and that ginseng was being distributed as a major medicinal herb in China.[43] Another point worth considering is that Paekche ginseng is deemed as inferior to Shangdang ginseng in *Bencao gangmu*. In actuality, scholars have been divided on whether Shangdang ginseng was genuinely ginseng, instead of *manshen* (蔓蔘), or *Codonopsis pilosula*.[44]

Even if genuine ginseng was being produced in Shangdang and had been of premium quality, it was nearly extinct by the time Li Shizhen was authoring

Bencao gangmu. And this was a fact Li Shizhen was well aware of despite stating in his book that "ginseng grows in Shangdang and Liaodong." This is because he added in the same book that "The ginseng used nowadays is all from Liaodong. The three kingdoms of Koguryŏ, Paekche, and Shilla are now all part of Chosŏn, which continues to export ginseng to China today."[45]

What can be surmised from above is that ginseng no longer grew in inner China and the ginseng distributed in China during the Ming dynasty all came from Liaodong or Korea. Chinese books on medicine and pharmacology such as *Bencao gangmu* contained anachronistic information gathered from classics that were published centuries earlier. This context to Chinese medical literature was unknown in Europe, which is why *Bencao gangmu* was introduced as the sole creation of Li Shizhen from the late sixteenth century. The book thus contributed to spreading in Europe the belief that Paekche ginseng was inferior to Shangdang ginseng, even when the latter no longer existed. Although Martini and Jartoux both spent time in China, Martini committed the error of relying only on classical books to understand ginseng, while Jartoux was able to achieve greater insight by personally witnessing ginseng. Nevertheless, anachronistic information continued to be established as fact as translations of Oriental classics kept being introduced to the West.

Another book that contributed significantly to the tendency to establish anachronistic information as fact was the *General History of China* published in 1735. This book, which rose to fame among eighteenth-century intellectuals, was authored by a French Jesuit priest named Jean-Baptiste Du Halde (1674–1743). Du Halde had never been to China, but he enjoyed a reputation as an expert on China from collating the extensive amount of information his missionary colleagues sent his way. Its comprehensive coverage of Chinese history and geography made the *General History of China* a popular introductory book to China and it would go on to be translated and distributed across Europe.[46] A second edition was ordered as soon as the book was published in France in 1735, and after the publication of its English translation in 1738, other translations in German and Russian followed suit. While the outcome of the studies French Jesuit priests conducted on China were welcomed all over Europe, the *General History of China* contributed the most to arousing in European intellectuals a general, if genuine, interest in China.[47]

The *General History of China* devoted three chapters to Chinese medicinal herbs and their content certainly seems to have relied heavily on *Bencao gangmu*. Among the medicinal herbs mentioned in the *General History of China*, ginseng was covered in detail with descriptions ranging from its botanical features to the Chinese appraisal of it as well as myths and legends involving ginseng. However, many of the details were inaccurate because they had been gathered from disparate, outdated sources. For instance, Du Halde's ignorance was exposed in his describing of Petsi (Paekche) and Corea (Korea) as completely different states. Paekche was an ancient kingdom that occupied the midwestern region of the Korean peninsula until its fall in 660, while the name Corea originated from the kingdom of Koryŏ that lasted between 918 and 1392 and which was thereafter used to refer to the Korean peninsula. When Du Halde was writing the book, the state on the Korean peninsula was called Chosŏn. The description below evinces a temporal mismatch of states when it was unlikely that the Korean kingdom of Shilla paid tribute to China.

> The Gin Seng which the Kingdom of Sinro pays Tribute of has Feet and Hands, and resembles a Man, and is above a Foot high; it is kept pressed between the Planks of the Wood of a Tree called Cha mou, which is a kind of Fir, bound and wrapt up with red Silk.[48]

The above description originally appeared in the Chinese pharmacopoeia *Haiyao bencao* (海藥本草) written by Li Xun (李珣) during the reign of Emperor Suzong (肅宗) of Tang (r. 756–762), which thereafter made its way into *Bencao gangmu*[49] and was later excerpted by Du Halde.[50]

Du Halde also offered a lengthy introduction on ginseng's medical efficacy. He listed the use cases of ginseng to treat seventy-seven different symptoms related to the stomach, heart, lungs, blood circulation, thirst, high fever, sleep disorders such as nightmares or epic dreaming, vermin eradication, sexual disabilities, and pre- and post-pregnancy issues. He even added that although it can be called a panacea, ginseng needs to be taken for a considerable period of time in order to ensure its efficacy.[51] The book also advised that while ginseng was often prescribed as a decoction, it could be very tricky to use because dosages were not standardized and the type of illness as well as the patient's age and constitution had to be taken into consideration.[52] The quotation below shows how Du Halde ended his introduction to ginseng.

> At present the Ginseng pays a great duty to the Emperor, and 'tis death to defraud him of any part of it. Ginseng comes to Peking from various places, as Lea tong, Corea, and Northern Tartary; it comes likewise from Japan, but I believe that is not so much esteemed; This plant if good is at present very dear, and is sold at least for six times its weight in silver, and there is some of it at Peking that sells for eight times its weight in silver, and often more.[53]

As publishing flourished in Europe, Du Halde's introduction of ginseng came to be quoted constantly in travelogues, botanical books, pharmacopoeias, and even newspapers. The incorrect information in his introduction thus continued to survive and made a considerable impact on the forming of a stereotypical image of East Asian ginseng in the West.

Leibniz and Ginseng

What sort of influence did the information Jesuits conveyed about China, especially about ginseng, have on European intellectuals at the time? It will be near impossible to find a precise answer to this question. Nevertheless, how European intellectuals regarded ginseng back then can be gleaned from the way ginseng was described by a few leading scholars.

One of them was the English philosopher John Locke (1632–1704). Locke is widely known as a political thinker, but he was also a physician and scientist with a broad range of interests. His compulsion to keep records left a meticulous household ledger and diary, which happened to include mentions of ginseng. During his exile in the Netherlands (1683–1688), he apparently grew familiar with ginseng from reading *Specimen Medicinae Sinicae* (1682) authored by Michael Boym.[54] Locke noted in his diary that ginseng was used to treat fevers and venereal diseases and could also be taken as a tonic.[55]

Gottfried Wilhelm Leibniz (1646–1716) is someone who can shed further light on the connection between the Jesuits, China, and ginseng. In a letter he sent to the Jesuit priest Claudio Filippo Grimaldi (1638–1712) in 1689, Leibniz asked, "do the virtues of ginseng roots truly live up to their reputation?"[56] Considering the intellectual terrain of Europe at the time, it was perhaps only natural for Leibniz, a great philosopher and mathematician well known for inventing differential and integral calculus, to develop an interest in ginseng.

At the early age of fourteen, Leibniz enrolled at Leipzig University and received a doctoral degree in 1667 for his dissertation "On the Art of Combinations." He thereafter spent the rest of his life serving as an administrator, political adviser, and historian at one German court after another. Leibniz was well versed in various fields of study and deeply interested in China. His knowledge of and interests in all things Chinese, ranging from the classical Chinese texts known as the "Four Books" to Chinese morality and philosophy as well as scientific techniques, were formed through books published by Jesuit missionaries. At the age of twenty, he even wrote that "the Chinese may appear to be foolish and contradictory in general when it comes to medicine, but their medicine is still better than ours."[57]

Leibinz's desire to learn more about China coincided with the interests of the German princes who employed him. European rulers highly interested in economic independence sought to learn the secrets of Chinese agriculture and handicraft and aspired to compete more efficiently by producing goods that could rival those of China. What Europeans therefore craved from China was mostly practical, scientific information that could be developed into techniques. In this sense, Leibniz was bound to become interested in a herb like ginseng, as Jesuit missionaries had introduced it through their books as a panacea and a resource quintessential to China.

Leibniz's interest in ginseng grew more detailed after meeting Jesuit priests who had been to China in Italy. In 1689, Leibniz was commissioned to compile the history of the House of Hanover. Claiming that he had to gather sources for research, he headed to Rome. During his time in Italy, Leibniz continued to write as he traveled to different cities and communicated with scientific societies. He also became acquainted with Jesuit priests, especially Grimaldi, with whom he met almost every day over the summer of 1689. Originally from Piedmont, Grimaldi joined the Jesuits in 1658 and was sent to China in 1666. He taught astronomy and science at the court of the Kangxi Emperor before returning to Europe in 1686 and was scheduled to leave for China again shortly.[58]

When Grimaldi was about to set sail for China, Leibniz sent him a letter to express his gratitude for Grimaldi's generous sharing of information. In the letter, Leibniz reflected that "[we in Europe] have engaged in exchange with the Indies[59] in various ways so far but not so much in terms of science" and revealed his hope that "a greater amount of information about China can be offered from an observant person such as yourself."[60] Leibniz sought to collect information from people like Grimaldi who were intimately familiar with the local circumstances in China and then pass necessary data on to craftsmen, scientists, and scholars in Europe. Through his letter, Leibniz listed a series of thirty specific questions about the manufacture of metal, tea, paper, silk and "real" chinaware, dyes, the blades of Japanese swords, glass, and, of course, ginseng. Leibniz asked about ginseng in Latin: "An Radix Ginseng magnarum virtutum, ut vulgò praedicatur" (Do the virtues of ginseng roots truly live up to their reputation?)[61] Leibniz later summarized the answer Grimaldi gave as follows.

> One pound of ginseng roots is sold for approximately forty scudi (Italian silver coins) in China. The root of ginseng has a particularly great effect on the aged. It is brewed in water and drunk like tea, except that ginseng roots are submerged in water to be decocted instead of pouring boiling water on tea to brew it. Its taste is insipid and bears no other extraordinary characteristics. Grimaldi brought some ginseng roots to Florence and presented it to the grand duke.[62]

Out of the thirty questions Leibniz posed, the first was about the firepower of China and the second was about ginseng. The fact that ginseng was ranked second shows just how curious he was about it. Through the next question, Leibniz asked about the possibility of transplanting medicinal herbs from China to Europe. As did Locke, Leibniz had also read Boym's *Specimen Medicinae Sinicae* (1656),[63] but was likely in search of more practical, precise information that Boym's book failed to offer. In fact, Leibniz's interest in the circumstances of China was great enough that he would go on to publish *Novissima Sinica* (1697) based on information he gathered from Jesuit missionaries.

Leibniz also made inquiries about ginseng to Joachim Bouvet, one of the first French Jesuit missionaries sent to China by Louis XIV. Before leaving for China, Bouvet was elected a member of the French Royal Academy of Sciences, and from 1687 he began teaching astronomy, medicine, and chemistry as a royal tutor to the Kangxi Emperor. Leibniz asked Bouvet what French items he brought to China and what Chinese items he brought to France.[64] Ginseng was at the top of the list of Chinese items Bouvet brought back to France.[65] This is what Bouvet told Leibniz about ginseng.

> Ginseng roots specifically grow in Korea and Liaodong. The ginseng from Liaodong is the best. The best of Liaodong ginseng is presented to the emperor. There are other areas in China where ginseng grows, but their quality is inferior to that of Korean ginseng.[66]

Nearly ten years after his letter to Leibniz in 1699, Bouvet came to lead the Kangxi Emperor's cartography project in Manchuria. This was the very project that involved the survey Jartoux took part in and led to his vivid description of ginseng growing near the Chinese border with Korea.

Notes

1 "Richard Cocks to the Company, Firando, January 1 & 14, 1616–1617," in William Foyster, ed., *Letters Received by the East India Company*, vol. 5 (London: Sampson Low, Marston & Co., 1901), 17–18.
2 "Richard Cocks to the Company, Firando, January 1 & 14, 1616–1617," in Foyster, *Letters Received by the East India Company*, 5: 18.
3 Peter Floris, *Peter Floris, His Voyage to the East Indies in the Globe, 1611–1615: The Contemporary Translation of His Journal*, ed. William Harrison Moreland (London: Hakluyt Society, 1934), 4–5.
4 Thomas Salmon, *Modern History: Or, the Present State of All Nations*, vol. 27 (London, 1735), 133.
5 Salmon, *Modern History*, 133.
6 Gary P. Leupp, *Interracial Intimacy in Japan: Western Men and Japanese Women, 1543–1900* (London: Continuum, 2003), 60.
7 See Richard Cocks, *Diary of Richard Cocks* (London: Hakluyt Society, 1883).
8 See also Alison Games, *The Web of Empire: English Cosmopolitans in an Age of Expansion, 1560–1660* (New York: Oxford University Press, 2008), 88.
9 By the mid-sixteenth century, the Netherlands had encroached on Spain's and Portugal's domination over the trade system, later to be joined by Britain and France. Around that time, travelogues featuring journeys to Asia and information about China like *L'Ambassade de la Compagnie Orientale des Provinces Unies vers l'Empereur de la Chine* (1665) by Jan Nieuhoff (1618–1672) were published and translated into various European languages, thereby fanning the China craze. Johannes Nieuhof, *L'Ambassade de la Compagnie Orientale des Provinces Unies vers l'Empereur de la Chine, ou Grand Cam de Tartarie* (Leyde, 1665).
10 John James Clarke, *Oriental Enlightenment: The Encounter between Asian and Western Thought* (London: Routledge, 2002), 7.
11 Steven J. Harris, "Jesuit Scientific Activity in the Overseas Missions, 1540–1773," *Isis* 96, no. 1 (2005): 76.
12 Donald F. Lach, "China and the Era of the Enlightenment," *The Journal of Modern History* 14, no. 2 (1942): 209.
13 Harris, "Jesuit Scientific Activity in the Overseas Missions, 1540–1773," 73.
14 Marta Hanson and Gianna Pomata, "Medicinal Formulas and Experiential Knowledge in the Seventeenth-Century Epistemic Exchange between China and Europe," *Isis* 108, no. 1 (2017): 7.
15 Linda L. Barnes, *Needles, Herbs, Gods, and Ghosts: China, Healing, and the West to 1848* (Cambridge, MA: Harvard University Press, 2005), 179.
16 Hanson and Pomata, "Medicinal Formulas and Experiential Knowledge in the Seventeenth-Century Epistemic Exchange between China and Europe," 6.
17 Harold J. Cook, "Testing the Effects of Jesuit's Bark in the Chinese Emperor's Court," *Journal of the Royal Society of Medicine* 107, no. 8 (2014): 326–327.

18 Alain Touwaide, “Nature’s Medicine Cabinet: Notes on Botanical Therapeutics at the Birth of the New World,” *Journal of the Washington Academy of Sciences* 89, no. 3/4 (2003): 146.
19 Kenneth Pomeranz and Steven Topik, *The World That Trade Created: Society, Culture, and the World Economy, 1400 to the Present* (Armonk, NY: M.E. Sharpe, 2006), 72.
20 Hanson and Pomata, “Medicinal Formulas and Experiential Knowledge in the Seventeenth-Century Epistemic Exchange between China and Europe,” 13.
21 Alexandra Cook, “Linnaeus and Chinese Plants: A Test of the Linguistic Imperialism Thesis,” *Notes and Records of the Royal Society of London* 64, no. 2 (2010): 122.
22 Chinese characters referring to ginseng in ancient Chinese literature include *can* (參), *shen* (蔘), *jin* (浸), *qin* (侵), and *qin* (寑). *Insam* (人參) signified ginseng in ancient Korean literature, and beyond the Joseon dynasty, *insam* (人蔘) was uniformly used to denote ginseng.
23 Kwak Yi-seong 곽이성, “Koryŏ insam ŭi yurae mit hyonŭng ŭi sŏjihakchŏk koch’al” 고려인삼의 유래 및 효능의 서지학적 고찰 [Bibliographic Consideration on the Efficacy and the Origin of Korean Ginseng], *Insam Munhwa* 인삼문화 1 (2019): 45.
24 While the original edition of *Shennong bencaojing* is lost, its content partially survived from being relayed in *Bencaojing jizhu* (本草經集注) by the Liang period scholar Tao Hongjing (陶弘景), *Xinxiu bencao* (新修本草) by the Tang period scholar Su Jing (蘇敬), *Jingshi zhenglei beiji bencao* (經史證類備急本草) by the Song period scholar Tang Shenwei (唐愼微), and *Bencao gangmu* (本草綱目) by the Ming period scholar Li Shizhen (李時珍). During the Ming and Qing dynasties, several scholars of materia medica restored the content of *Shennong bencaojing* into several different editions.
25 Li Shizhen 李時珍, *Shinjuhae ponch’o kangmok* 新註解 本草綱目 [Newly Annotated Bencao gangmu], trans. Kim Chong-ha 김종하, vol. 1 (Seoul: Yŏil ch’ulp’ansa 여일출판사, 2007), 62–63.
26 “主補五臟 安精神 定魂魄 止驚悸 除邪氣 明目 開心益智 久服 輕身 延年.” Li Shizhen 李時珍, *Shinjuhae ponch’o kangmok* 新註解 本草綱目 [Newly Annotated Bencao gangmu], trans. Kim Chong-ha 김종하, vol. 4 (Seoul: Yŏil ch’ulp’ansa 여일출판사, 2007), 49; Ko Sungkwon 고성권 et al., *Uri insam ui ihae* 우리 인삼의 이해 [An Understanding of Korean Ginseng] (Seoul: Chung-Ang University Press 중앙대학교 출판부, 2005), 13.
27 Wang Tiesheng 王鐵生, ed., *Zhongguo renshen* 中國人蔘 (Shenyang: Liaoning kexue jishu chubanshe 遼寧科學技術出版社, 2001), 9–10.
28 Li, *Shinjuhae ponch’o kangmok*, 4: 42–66.
29 Alvaro Semedo, *Relatione della grande monarchia della Cina* (Rome, 1643).
30 Martino Martini, *Bellum Tartaricum, or The Conquest of the Great and Most Renowned Empire of China, by the Invasion of the Tartars* (London, 1654).
31 Louis Daniel le Comte, *Nouveau Mémoire Sur l’état Présent de La Chine*, Tome 1 (Paris, 1696), 377.
32 “Mémorial du père Thomas,” in Évariste-Régis Huc, ed., *Le christianisme en Chine, en Tartarie et au Tibet*, Tome 3 (Paris, 1857–1858), 409.
33 *Lettres édifiantes et curieuses, écrites des missions étrangères, par quelques missionnaires de la Compagnie de Jésus*, X. recueil (Paris, 1713), 159–185.
34 Harris, “Jesuit Scientific Activity in the Overseas Missions, 1540–1773,” 74.
35 Not long after Jartoux issued his report, the Royal Society excerpted the section on ginseng from the report and published in its journal *Philosophical Transactions* in 1713. Pierre Jartoux, “The Description of a Tartarian Plant, Call’d Gin-Seng; with an Account of Its Virtues. In a Letter from Father Jartoux, to the Procurator General of the Missions of India and China.,” *Philosophical Transactions* 28 (1713): 237.
36 Jartoux, “The Description of a Tartarian Plant, Call’d Gin-Seng,” 238–239.
37 Jartoux, “The Description of a Tartarian Plant, Call’d Gin-Seng,” 238–239.
38 Jartoux, “The Description of a Tartarian Plant, Call’d Gin-Seng,” 246.
39 Requoted from Wang, *Zhongguo renshen*, 1–2.

40 Li, *Shinjuhae ponch'o kangmok*, 4:43. The county of Shangdang was later renamed as Luzhou (潞州), which is why Shangdang ginseng was sometimes referred to as Luzhou ginseng.

41 In *Bencao gangmu*, Li Shizhen noted that the quote came from Tao Hongjing's *Mingyi bielu*, but later bibliographic scholars believe that it came from a different work by Tao Hongjing titled *Shennong bencao jing jizhu* (神農本草經集註). Li, *Shinjuhae ponch'o kangmok*, 1:63. The attribution to *Mingyi bielu* here reflects what is stated about the quote in *Bencao gangmu*.

42 Li, *Shinjuhae ponch'o kangmok*, 4:44.

43 Yang and Yŏ, "Samguk-Shilla t'ongilgi insam saengsan kwa taeoegyoyŏk," 179–180.

44 Refer to Ch'oryu insam (草類 人參) mentioned in *Haedong yŏksa* (海東繹史) by Han Ch'i-yun (韓致奫). Requoted from Yang and Yŏ, "Samguk-Shilla t'ongilgi insam saengsan kwa taeoegyoyŏk," 179. Yang Chŏng-p'il and Yŏ In-sŏk argue that although ancient Chinese materia medica named Shangdang ginseng as the best ginseng, it was in fact a variety of *manshen* of the Campanula genus, according to today's historical research findings.

45 Li, *Shinjuhae ponch'o kangmok*, 4:46–47.

46 Jean-Baptiste Du Halde, *Description Géographique, Historique, Chronologique, Politique, et Physique de l'empire de La Chine et de La Tartarie Chinoise*, vol. 4 (Paris, 1735). This book is better known as *The General History of China*.

47 Zhu Qianzhi 朱謙之, *Chungguk i mandŭn yurŏp ŭi kŭndae: Kŭndae yurŏp ŭi chungguk munhwa yŏlp'ung* 중국이 만든 유럽의 근대: 근대 유럽의 중국문화 열풍 [China's Influence on the Formation of Modern Europe: The Chinoiserie Craze], trans. Chŏn Hong-sŏk 전홍석 (P'aju: Ch'ŏnggye 청계, 2003), 89–90.

48 Jean-Baptiste Du Halde, *The General History of China: Containing a Geographical, Historical, Chronological, Political and Physical Description of the Empire of China, Chinese-Tartary, Corea and Thibet, Including an Extract and Particular Account of Their Customs, Manners, Ceremonies, Religion, Arts and Sciences*, vol. 4 (London, 1736), 3.

49 Li, *Shinjuhae ponch'o kangmok*, 4: 45.

50 Du Halde, *The General History of China*, 4: 2–3.

51 Du Halde, *The General History of China*, 4: 7–8.

52 Du Halde, *The General History of China*, 4: 20.

53 Du Halde, *The General History of China*, 4: 19–20.

54 *Specimen Medicinae Sinicae* (1682) was actually authored by the Polish Jesuit missionary Michel Boym, but due to a difference of opinion over its publication between the Jesuits and the Dutch East India Company, the book's author was printed as Andreas Cleyer, a physician who worked for the Dutch East India Company. John H. Appleby, "Ginseng and the Royal Society," *Notes and Records of the Royal Society of London* 37, no. 2 (1983): 126; Barnes, *Needles, Herbs, Gods, and Ghosts*, 105.

55 Kenneth Dewhurst, *John Locke (1632–1704), Physician and Philosopher: A Medical Bibliography with an Edition of the Medical Notes in His Journals* (London: The Wellcome Historical Medical Library, 1963), 277.

56 Rome, July 19, 1689. Gottfried Wilhelm Leibniz, *Der Briefwechsel Mit Den Jesuiten in China (1689–1714)*, eds. Rita Widmaier and Malte L. Babin (Hamburg: Felix Meiner Verlag, 2006), 10.

57 Preussische Akademie der Wissenschaften, eds., "Gottfried Wilhelm Leibniz: Politische Schriften," in Gottfried Wilhelm Leibniz, *Sämtliche Schriften und Briefe: Politische Schriften, 1667–1676*, IV (Darmstad: Otto Reichl Verlag, 1931), 552.

58 Grimaldi was a leading member of the Jesuit mission in China and served as rector of the Jesuit college in Beijing until he passed away there in 1712.

59 This refers to the East Indies, a term Europeans used since the sixteenth century to refer to the Indian subcontinent, Southeast Asia, Oceania, and the Southeast Asian waters.

60 Donald Frederick Lach, *The Preface to Leibniz' Novissima Sinica: Commentary, Translation, Text* (Honolulu, HI: University of Hawai'i Press, 1957), 29.

61 Rome, July 19, 1689. Leibniz, *Der Briefwechsel Mit Den Jesuiten in China*, 10.
62 Rome, Summer 1689. Leibniz, *Der Briefwechsel Mit Den Jesuiten in China*, 16.
63 Lach, *The Preface to Leibniz' Novissima Sinica*, 29.
64 La Rochelle, February 28, 1698. Leibniz, *Der Briefwechsel Mit Den Jesuiten in China*, 64.
65 Peking, September, 19, 1699. Leibniz, *Der Briefwechsel Mit Den Jesuiten in China*, 234–236.
66 Peking, September, 19, 1699. Leibniz, *Der Briefwechsel Mit Den Jesuiten in China*, 238.

2

GINSENG STUDIES BY THE ENGLISH ROYAL SOCIETY AND FRENCH ROYAL ACADEMY OF SCIENCES

The English Royal Society and Ginseng

One of the major impetuses that brought the West into the modern era was the "Scientific Revolution." And the driving forces behind that revolution were the English Royal Society and the French Royal Academy of Sciences. Launched in 1662 with approval from Charles II, the English Royal Society built a system that would serve as the foundation of modern science by publishing the world's first "scientific journal," developing a scientific language, introducing a peer review system, and standardizing experimentation methods. A few years later, the French Royal Academy of Sciences was established at the suggestion of the French statesman Jean-Baptiste Colbert. Unlike the English Royal Society that was open to civilians, the French Royal Academy of Sciences consisted of scientists who were also bureaucrats who directly served the king and promoted mercantilism. Despite these differences between the two organizations, they both played a leading role in the historical change in which science began to confront divinity.

The English Royal Society launched the journal *Philosophical Transactions* in 1665. Particularly interesting is that a paper about ginseng was included in the journal's first volume,[1] demonstrating the tremendous amount of interest leading English scientists had in ginseng. The paper featured a translated excerpt about ginseng from the travelogue *Relation de divers voyages curieux* by Melchisédech Thévenot (1620–1692). As a scientist, inventor, writer, and diplomat, Thévenot also worked for the Dutch East India Company at one point. In response to the mercantilist government policy, Thévenot led a group of scholars interested in introducing foreign natural resources and cultures. The vision of this group formed with Colbert's support ultimately led to the establishment of the French Royal Academy of Sciences.

DOI: 10.4324/9781003286691-3

Through his paper in *Philosophical Transactions*, Thévenot discussed the uniqueness of Chinese medicine for using "herbs, branches, and stones," before explaining the effects of ginseng, the herb the Chinese practically worshipped. He did not forget to mention that ginseng, which was valuable enough to be traded for three pounds of silver per pound, was a remarkable tonic often referred to as a cure-all. The reason the English Royal Society took note of ginseng and published a paper about it in its journal had to do with the demands of the times. The development of botany was deeply related to the desire of royalty and elites to retain power and survive in seventeenth-century Europe amid wars and the outbreak of plagues and epidemics like syphilis.[2] Ginseng had begun to make the list of major collectibles for botanical gardens and cabinets of curiosities that started to grow popular in Europe at the time.[3]

Records of the English Royal Society include many accounts of scientists personally bringing ginseng in from East Asia and testing its efficacy. In 1679, Sir Thomas Browne (1605–1682), a philosopher and physician with a great interest in medicinal herbs, mentioned in a letter to his son Dr. Edward Browne (1644–1708), a member of the English Royal Society, that, "I carefully observed ginseng." Sir Thomas Browne also mentioned the writings about ginseng by the Jesuit scholar Athanasius Kircher (1602–1680).[4] On June 26, 1679, a physician named Andrew Clench (?–1692) showed ginseng wrapped in Chinese paper at an English Royal Society meeting and reported the outcome of his experiment. As vice president of the society at the time, Sir Christopher Wren (1632–1723), well known for designing Saint Paul's Cathedral, took part in Clench's experiment and documented its procedure.[5]

Ginseng was becoming a familiar topic among the most prominent English scholars. Known as the father of English natural history, John Ray (1627–1705) included an illustration of ginseng in *Historia Plantarum* with a note that "this illustrious drawing [referring to an accompanying illustration of ginseng] was sent to the English Royal Society from China."[6] The extent of scholarly enthusiasm over ginseng is made evident by the fact that "the root Ninzin, corruptly called Gensing," was included in the *Catalogue and Description of the Natural and Artificial Rarities Belonging to the Royal Society* (1681). The catalogue explained that the root had been inside a package sent by a Chinese physician along with the following description.

> Not stringy, as that in Piso, but divided, as often the Mandrake and some other roots, into two legs. Of a sweetish taste, as Piso. But this here is also bitter; sweet in the first or lowest degree, and bitter in the second.
>
> This root is not known to grow (wild) anywhere, but in the Kingdom of Corea. In which place, as also in Tunquin, China, and Japan. It is much used, and relied upon in Epilepsy, Fevers, and other both Chronick and Acute diseases; either alone, or in composition as the basis.[7]

Hans Sloane, Ginseng, and Cocoa

When discussing the English Royal Society's relationship with ginseng, it is impossible to do so without mentioning Hans Sloane (1660–1753). Although known today as the collector responsible for providing the foundation of the British Museum's collection and for introducing cocoa to Europe, Sloane was also a renowned physician who served as president of the Royal College of Physicians as well as a scientist who succeeded Isaac Newton as the president of the English Royal Society. His hobby since youth was to collect specimens of various plants and other extraordinary objects, which allowed him to engage in in-depth communication with the likes of John Ray and Robert Boyle (1627–1691), best known for Boyle's Law.

In 1687, Sloane was ordered by the king to serve as the personal physician of the viceroy of Jamaica. Although his stay only lasted for fifteen months, he enthusiastically gathered specimens of animals and plants in Jamaica and islands nearby that amounted to a collection of more than 800 plant specimens alone.[8] At the time, Jamaica was an area of pressing interest for England as it began to practice imperialism. While Spain dominated the sea as a maritime power, England established plantations here and there to create more stable sources of revenue over the long term. Upon sending his collection of animal and plant specimens back home, Sloane expressed his wish for them to be used for medical purposes. Still, he was ultimately an imperialist who took a prominent role in the expansion of England's imperial plantation network.

After examining a substantial number of plant specimens from Spain, Portugal, Guinea in Africa, and the East Indies, Sloane concluded that many of them were common to Spain, Portugal, and Jamaica and that they grew more prolifically in Jamaica and Guinea than the East Indies. He thus claimed that Jamaica was a far more advantageous location to establish plantations.[9] Of course, Sloane's personal interests may have had a hand in making such a claim. Sloane used to work with Fulke Rose (1644–1694) who owned an enormous amount of land in Jamaica and engaged in the slave trade. After Rose suddenly died in 1694, Sloane married his widow and became a massive landowner in Jamaica. Sloane thereafter used his fortune to amass the extensive collection which he later donated to the British Museum and to create the Apothecaries' Garden in Chelsea, London (today known as the Chelsea Physic Garden).

Sloane's Apothecaries' Garden inspired the creation of other physic gardens across England where attempts were made to grow ginseng. His own interest in the plant also led to an attempt to grow it, one that ended in utter failure. Among Sloane's collection, there were more than thirteen samples of ginseng, including the seeds and leaves of Japanese ginseng, which he had collected around 1691–1692. Thanks to this, Sloane enjoyed an unrivaled status as an expert on ginseng, particularly Japanese ginseng.[10] Some of his samples had been gifts of esteem from high-ranking bureaucrats, indicating that ginseng was exchanged as a gift among dignitaries in England at the time.

Due to his reputation as a ginseng expert, Sloane was regarded as an authority to be consulted on all matters pertaining to the plant. When jumping into the trade in American ginseng, William Byrd II (1674–1744), a member of the English Royal Society and a plantation owner in colonial America, asked Sloane for a letter of recommendation on the medicinal effects of ginseng. Despite his tremendous interest in the plant, Sloane cynically replied that ginseng was useless as a medicinal herb. Piqued, Byrd sarcastically remarked in a letter to Sloane that, "I fancy you have been nibbleing of ginseng ever since you received that box from my good Lord Pembroke, by the vertue of which you have mended all the flaws which Jamaica had made in your constitution."[11]

The historian Christopher P. Iannini suspects that Sloane may have downplayed the efficacy of ginseng because economic interests were at stake. After his first encounter with cocoa in Jamaica, Sloane decided to turn it into a commodity that would yield huge profits in Europe. To do so, he had to present cocoa as a panacea and therefore tried to discredit ginseng as it had the potential to form a rivalry with cocoa.[12] Sloane had already attempted and failed to grow ginseng in Jamaica, so regardless of his reputation as a ginseng expert, it was impossible for him to turn it into a profitable business. To Sloane, ginseng had become nothing more than sour grapes.

Louis XIV and Ginseng

While Melchisédech Thévenot's assessment of ginseng emerged in the 1660s, research on ginseng began at the French Royal Academy of Sciences in the 1690s, much later than in England.[13] Previously, ginseng was mainly introduced through travelogues or reports authored by merchants, explorers, and missionaries. In fact, France had been far behind the Netherlands and England in terms of overseas trade. To catch up with its competitors, Jean-Baptiste Colbert (1619–1683), the French Controller-General of Finances at the time, promoted a strongly mercantilist policy and established the French East India Company (Compagnie royale des Indes) in 1664. Colbert also had Thévenot play a central role in forming a group of scholars to amass a broad range of information that could support France's mercantilist policy, from marine navigation techniques to the geography, customs, animals, plants, and herbs of foreign countries. As a result, an introduction of the mysterious Oriental herb ginseng was included in Thévenot's travelogue and thereafter made its way into the first issue of the English Royal Society's journal.

Based on Thévenot's group of scholars, Colbert established the French Royal Academy of Sciences (Académie Royale des Sciences) in 1666 to carry out the policy to promote science. One of the Academy's missions was to study plants and herbs brought from abroad. The key figures taking charge of this mission were Denis Dodart (1634–1717), a member of the medical faculty at the University of Paris, Claude Bourdelain (1621–1699), a physician and chemist, and Nicolas Marchand (?–1687), who was in charge of the king's gardens.

Decades after Thévenot mentioned ginseng, the Academy met a turning point for delving further into the study of ginseng when the plant was "officially" presented to Louis XIV. On September 1, 1686, a grand reception was held at the Hall of Mirrors inside the Palace of Versailles where the "Sun King" Louis XIV (r. 1643–1715) welcomed a Siamese embassy (Figure 2.1). Around that time, France was a latecomer to overseas trade, which made establishing a bridgehead in the East a matter of urgency for France. Hence, the French government sought to develop intimate relations with Siam (Thailand), known as a power in the East alongside China and India, in order to keep the Netherlands in check. Meanwhile, the King of Siam Phra Narai (r. 1656–1688) had grown tired of being hassled by foreign powers, and France happened to be the solution to his search for a European ally.

Siam sent its first embassy to France in 1681 and its second in 1684. Louis XIV welcomed the embassies with lavish receptions and in return sent a French embassy to Siam in 1685. The embassy's mission was as much cultural as political, which is why a large number of religious figures and scientists were on the list of ambassadors. Such ambassadors observed the cultures and products of Asia and reported their observations back to France. Most of the French ambassadors encountered ginseng for the first time during their visit to Siam. The priest François-Timoléon de Choisy (1644–1724) and the Jesuit missionary Guy Tachard (1651–1712) sent back to France detailed accounts of their encounter with ginseng.

In 1686, another Siamese embassy arrived at the Palace of Versailles. Despite suffering from high fever and infection due to an anal fistula caused by horseback riding, Louis XIV hosted a most elaborate welcoming and reception for the embassy. Items of furniture made of silver were placed in the Hall of Mirrors and the Sun King offered the Siamese ambassadors a tour of his private chambers, rooms for keeping treasures, and the Versailles gardens. At the reception attended by 1,500 dignitaries, an incident worthy of going down in the history of ginseng occurred: a Siamese ambassador presented Louis XIV with ginseng to wish him a long, healthy life. Records of this incident marked ginseng as "Jancam" and noted that the package of ginseng also included a silver kettle and Chinese teacups to "boil water to brew tea and decoct ginseng."[14]

It remains uncertain as to whether Louis XIV actually took ginseng. However, it is certain that his personal physicians committed to preserving his health took great interest in ginseng, which was known as a panacea in the East, because soon afterward in the 1690s, the French Royal Academy of Sciences delved into the study of ginseng. Some of the ginseng gifted by the Siamese embassy was kept as a valuable component of the Academy's collection for decades after the incident.

FIGURE 2.1 The Siamese embassy in France.

The First Doctoral Dissertation on Ginseng in the West

Claude Bourdelain is regarded as the first member of the French Royal Academy of Sciences to conduct an academic study on ginseng. On November 27, 1697, Bourdelain gave a presentation at the Academy on a plant highly valued in China called "Sin…sem." Bourdelain reported that the name of this foreign plant was a combination of the words man (*hominem*) and plant (*plantam*), suggesting that the Chinese plant's root resembled the shape of a human being. Bourdelain's presentation focused on the botanical characteristics of ginseng. It also mentioned that ginseng primarily grew in Liaodong, a region in the eastern parts of the Chinese Tartary, and was helpful in rejuvenating the elderly or patients severely enervated by an illness.[15]

Bourdelain's study was considered the beginning of French research on ginseng, according to the *Histoire de l'Académie royale des sciences* published in 1718. This publication on the Academy's history also included a paper titled "Sur le Gin-Seng" that summarized all the knowledge thus far collected or discovered about ginseng. The paper noted that "Jesuit missionaries were the first to mention ginseng as an herb esteemed in China, and thanks to them, Europe has been able to find out a bit about ginseng." According to the paper, a couple of ships brought back small amounts of ginseng, but "only enough to count as rare samples since it is such a prized, incredibly valued medicinal herb."[16]

On February 9, 1736, the University of Paris Faculty of Medicine held a screening for the first European doctoral dissertation on ginseng:[17] "An infirmis à morbo viribus reparandis Gin Seng?"[18] by Lucas Augustin Folliot de Saint-Vast.[19] Originally from Normandy in northern France, Folliot de Saint-Vast did not study sinology and had never been to China or anywhere else in Asia. However, Professor Jacques-François Vendermonde (?–1746), the head of the screening committee for the thesis, had extensive experience in Asia, having lived in Macao for more than a decade before obtaining Portuguese citizenship and then a doctoral degree from the University of Paris Faculty of Medicine (Figure 2.2).[20]

Through his thesis investigating ginseng's suitability as a tonic, Folliot de Saint-Vast offered a botanical overview of ginseng based on existing research outcomes, including those of Jartoux. He then argued that ginseng was useful in treating diarrhea, dysentery, pains in the stomach and intestines, fainting, paralysis, lethargy, and cramps and was exceptionally effective in rejuvenating enervated constitutions. He also argued that ginseng was just as effective as simarouba and ipecacuanha (ipecac) from the Americas. To support his argument, Folliot de Saint-Vast quoted from *Bencao gangmu*.[21]

Folliot de Saint-Vast's thesis also pointed out precautions associated with the intake of ginseng. Epicures and drunkards were unlikely to benefit from ginseng and its intake was to be prohibited in cases with fevers caused by an infection or epidemic or cases that involved dog or snake bites.[22] Folliot de Saint-Vast stressed that pairing ginseng properly with other medicinal herbs could amplify the efficacy of ginseng. Apart from being used to treat illnesses, he explained that ginseng had properties capable of offering gradual health benefits, which almost seems to predict how ginseng is used today. The thesis, concluding that ginseng was suitable as a tonic, attracted attention as it passed the screening and went down in history as the first doctoral thesis about ginseng in the West.

I V.

MEDICAMENTORUM vires experientia imprimis confirmat, quas à certis principiis dimanantes ex analyſi Chymicâ judicaveris, ſæpiùs errori obnoxias experimentis patebit; eadem chymicus ignis extorquet principia è plantâ eduli, quæ ſuppeditat planta toxicalis: nec ſemper ſapori & odori nimium crede, ſaporem amygdalaceum refert genuinum ſcammonium quod ſummâ virtute pollet catharticâ, dum amygdala in alimoniam cedit. Certa ineſt principiorum cujuſlibet mixti compages, è quâ exurgit virtus, quâ ſolutâ aut adulteratâ, nova naſcitur proles, à nativâ ſic degener, ut ipſi prorſùs contrarios promat effectus. Mixtum ideò quale natura edidit, exhibe, ipſimet manda naturæ, & tibi ſecundos votiſque conſentaneos edet effectus. Quæ novus Orbis ſeu America nuper in Medicinâ miniſtravit medicamina, rei ſtabiliunt argumentum. Cortex Peruvianus nullâ paratus arte, febris intermittentis verum & nunquam laudandum ſatis remedium. Sima-rouba nuperrimè ad nos advectum, diarrhœæ, dyſenteriæ, aliorum quorumvis remediorum, quin & ipſiuſmet Ipecacuanhæ virtutem eludentis, preſentiſſimum, quotidiana declarat experientia, medicamen. Num ſapor aut odor, num analyſis Chymica, tantas tamque ſtupendas in hiſce vegetalibus latentes indicavêre virtutes? Cortex Peruvianus odoris inops ſaporem amarum atque ſtypticum exhibet. Sima-rouba nec odoris nec ſaporis aut tantummodò modicæ amaritiei dives. Nonne innumera vegetabilia eaſdem ſenſibus exhibent dotes, quas tamen utriuſque viribus, non ſolùm inferiores, at ſæpiùs contrarias agnoveris. Undenam in his Americanis vegetabilibus virtutes? niſi in ipſorum nativo contextu, ventriculi fibras languidiores atque laxiores ad tonum revocante, hinc fibrarum reſtitutum robur, coctiones læſas redintegrando, ſecretiones ac præcipuè Diaphoreſim juvat. Sic in febribus intermittentibus, ſic in diarrhœâ & dyſenteriâ ad tonum reſtitutæ ventriculi ac inteſtinorum fibræ alimenta firmiùs retinendo atque ſubigendo, maſſam alimentorum comminuunt; nec uberior & aquoſior è glandulis affluit ſuccus, at ſtillando irrorat, undè genuina ingeſtorum coctio & redundantium excretio. A plantâ *Sinenſi* nec diverſas nec minores obtinendi ſpes, ſi ſapori credendum & odori: hic fragrantem etſi levem vim refert aromaticam; ille amaritiem dulcedine temperatam exhibet, ſalis eſſentialis, tantiſper volatilis, partiumque ſulphurearum reſinoſarumque ſigna & effectus, quorum conſortio & amico fœdere, nervis & ſpiritibus recreandis, ut & fibrarum nimis laxatarum elaſticitati reſtituendæ, aut tenſarum nimis elateri relaxando, non impar. At quæ iiſdem principiis gaudent, non eoſdem ſemper ſed & contrarios edunt effectus? Eſto. Non in his eadem principiorum miſcela, quam ſola detegit experientia. At, inquies, ubinam, à quibus gentibus veritas accipienda? *Sinas*, *Tartaros*, *Tunkinos*, *Japonenſes* alioſque Aſiaticos ſub diverſo Sole degentes conſule, apud quos poſt hominum memoriam uſus *Gin Seng* ſic invaluit, ut cuilibet ferè morbo, vel tanquam therapeuticum, vel prophylacticum, vel ſaltem viribus refocillandis aptum, cuilibet ætati, ſexui atque temperamento exhibeant. Non apud tot tamque diverſas gentes, novitatis amor; imò antiquitatis, id eſt per ſæculorum ſeriem comprobati remedii meretur encomium. Si viatoribus quædam habenda fides, quotquot qui haſce immenſas peragraverunt regiones, ad ſummas laudes in Medicinâ plantam evehunt, nec de laudibus quas Aſiatici huic radici tribuunt, detrahunt quicquam. Quonam fundamento tantoperè decantetur, ab ipſomet textu Sinenſi accipe. * In diarrhœis, dyſenteriis, ventriculi & inteſtinorum de- » bilitate aut depravatione, ſicuti in ſyncope, lipothymiâ, paralyſi, ſtuporibus & » convulſionibus prodeſt: mirum in modum refocillat nimiâ venere exhauſtos: ho- » minibus à morbis vel acutioribus vel chronicis enervatis, nullum huic æquiparan- » dum medicamentum: ubi poſt eruptionem fractis jam viribus, ſubſidunt variolæ, » felici cum ſucceſſu in largâ doſi propinatur: tandem repetitis vicibus, vires admo- » dum debilitatas reficit, & mirificè reſtaurat, perſpirationem auget, blando calore » ſenum corpora perfundit, medullam in oſſibus & totam artuum compagem ve-

* 本草綱目 李時珍

PEN SAU KAN MOU LI TCHI SIN

FIGURE 2.2 The first European doctoral dissertation on ginseng.

Notes

1 "Of Some Books Lately Publish't : Relations of Divers Curious Voyages," *Philosophical Transactions* 1 (1665–1666): 249.

2 Eugene Flaumenhaft and Carol Flaumenhaft, "Asian Medicinal Plants in Seventeenth Century French Literature," *Economic Botany* 36 (1982): 147.

3 William Curtis, *A Catalogue of the British, Medicinal, Culinary, and Agricultural Plants, Cultivated in the London Botanic Garden* (London, 1783), 44; Anon, *A Companion to Every Place of Curiosity and Enjoyment in and about London and Westminster* (London, 1767), 93; Lady Charlotte Murray, *The British Garden: A Descriptive Catalogue of Hardy Plants, Indigenous, or Cultivated in the Climate of Great Britain* (Bath, 1799), 241.

4 BM. Dept. of MSS., Sloane MS 1847, f. 68. 2 April [1679].

5 Thomas Birch, *The History of the Royal Society of London* (London, 1737), 490. The sample Clench showed has been described by Nehemiah Grew. Nehemiah Grew, *Musaeum Regalis Societatis* (London, 1681), 227.

6 John Ray, *Historia Plantarum*, vol. 2 (London, 1688), 1338.

7 Grew, *Musaeum Regalis Societatis*, 227.

8 Hans Sloane, *A Voyage to the Islands Madera, Barbadoes, Nieves, St Christophers, and Jamaica*, 2 vols. (London, 1707).

9 Pratik Chakrabarti, *Materials and Medicine: Trade, Conquest and Therapeutics in the Eighteenth Century* (Manchester: Manchester University Press, 2010), 144–146.

10 Nat. Hist. Museum (BM), Botany Library, Sir Hans Sloane-Vegetables and vegetable substances, nos. 887, 12140, 12141.

11 William Byrd II, "Byrd to Sloane, Aug. 20, 1738," in Marion Tinling, ed., *The Correspondence of the Three William Byrds of Westover, Virginia, 1684–1776*, vol. 2 (Charlottesville, VA: Virginia Historical Society Documents, 1977), 528–529.

12 Christopher P. Iannini, *Fatal Revolutions: Natural History, West Indian Slavery, and the Routes of American Literature* (Chapel Hill, NC: University of North Carolina Press, 2013), 116–117.

13 Lee Hye-min 이혜민, "Rui 14se ŭi insam: 17segi mal - 18segi ch'o p'ŭrangsŭ ŭi ponch'ohak chishik hyŏngsŏng" 루이 14세의 인삼: 17세기 말~18세기 초 프랑스의 본초학 지식 형성 [Louis XIV's Ginseng: Shaping of Knowledge on an Herbal Medicine in the Late 17th and the Early 18th Century France], *Ŭisahak* 의사학 25, no. 1 (2016): 111–145.

14 Michael Smithies, *The Discourses at Versailles of the First Siamese Ambassadors to France, 1686–1687* (Bangkok: Siam Society, 1986), 84–87.

15 Jean-Baptiste Du Hamel, *Regiae scientiarum academiae historia*, Revised (Paris, 1701), 451.

16 L'Académie royale des sciences, "Sur le Gin-Seng," in *Histoire de l'Académie royale des sciences* (Paris, 1718), 41–45.

17 See Lee, "Rui 14se ŭi insam," 127–137.

18 Lucas Augustin Folliot de Saint-Vast, "Resp. Quaestio medica, An infirmis à morbo viribus reparandis Gin Seng? Praes. F. Vandermonde" (Paris: University of Paris, 1736).

19 The exact year of Folliot de Saint-Vast's birth remains unknown, but according to the yearbook for 1737, he received his degree from the University of Paris and served as a professor in the university's Faculty of Medicine.

20 Antoine Laurent Jessé Bayle, *Encyclopédie des sciences médicales*, Sixième Division, Biographie médicale, II (Paris, 1841), 522.

21 Folliot de Saint-Vast, "Resp. Quaestio Medica, An Infirmis à Morbo Viribus Reparandis Gin Seng?," 3.

22 Folliot de Saint-Vast, "Resp. Quaestio Medica, An Infirmis à Morbo Viribus Reparandis Gin Seng?," 3.

3

THE DISCOVERY OF GINSENG IN NORTH AMERICA

The Discovery of North American Ginseng

In 1716, an incident that would revolutionize world history occurred: ginseng (*Panax quinquefolius*) was discovered in North America. As previously mentioned, the Jesuit missionary Jartoux's report about personally witnessing ginseng in Manchuria became widely distributed across Europe through publications such as the English Royal Society's journal. Joseph François Lafitau (1681–1746) was a French Jesuit missionary who encountered Jartoux's report through his order's newsletter ahead of discovering a plant similar to ginseng in Canada. Jartoux actually spent some time in Canada himself, and being aware of the country's ecology, he once speculated that if a plant as picky about its habitat as ginseng could be grown outside China, the only candidate was Canada.[1] And Lafitau indeed discovered a plant similar to ginseng in an area between Montreal and Ottawa at a latitude of forty-five degrees north.

Lafitau was not, however, the first to discover ginseng in North America. As a member of the French Royal Academy of Sciences, Michel Sarrazin (1659–1734) was sent to French Canada (Quebec) as a physician appointed by the king. Once there, Sarrazin collected a plant that seemed similar to Chinese ginseng around 1700 and referred to it as "aralia" when he sent it to the Royal Botanical Garden in France along with a note saying that the sample might be *ninzin* or a species of ginseng. Sarrazin's discovery, however, garnered little attention, and the credit for discovering American ginseng went to Lafitau. Considering the way conventional scientists in Europe tended to disregard scientific achievements made by the Jesuits at the time, it is difficult to understand how Lafitau could be remembered as the discoverer of American ginseng while a contribution by a recognized scholar like Sarrazin went unnoticed.[2]

DOI: 10.4324/9781003286691-4

The various explanations that have emerged for the recognition of Lafitau's discovery are therefore unlikely to be a coincidence. One explanation suggested that Sarrazin's discovery went unnoticed due to technical reasons, namely the inferior means of transportation at the time that caused most plant samples to rot before their arrival and the exorbitant number of plants shipped from the New Continent that led to a delay in processing them on time.[3] Meanwhile, scholars including Christopher M. Parsons have suggested that Jesuit priests may have been recognized for their openness to the traditional knowledge of indigenous peoples unlike European scientists like Sarrazin, who were authoritarian and inert. Indeed, Lafitau stayed for about five years in the area where he made his discovery and was keen to learn the indigenous language and culture. He treated indigenous peoples with respect, which in turn allowed them to trust and respect him. Such mutual trust and respect are likely to have facilitated the discovery and identification of ginseng. Sarrazin, on the other hand, paid no heed to the experience and knowledge of indigenous peoples and only focused on describing a discovered plant within the traditional European botanical framework, which prevented him from noticing the extraordinary value of ginseng.[4]

Lafitau was not, however, the one who actually "discovered" American ginseng. Once he realized that the location where he was staying in Canada was at a latitude similar to the habitat of ginseng in China, Lafitau asked a Mohawk medicine woman skilled in botany to look for a plant similar to ginseng.[5] With the help of indigenous peoples of the Mohawk tribe, Lafitau searched for ginseng, and when it was found three months later, he "carried it joyfully to a *Sauvagesse*," according to his account of the discovery.[6] Lafitau stressed in his report on the discovery that "I only report what I learned from my *sauvages*,"[7] which was both a demonstration of his respect for the knowledge of indigenous peoples and a clever attempt to avoid any potential controversies in the realm of science.

Indigenous Knowledge versus Academic Authoritarianism

When Lafitau returned to Paris a year after discovering ginseng in Canada, he published the discovery through *Journal de Trévoux* in 1717.[8] The French journal was fairly popular among intellectuals at the time and most of its contributors belonged to the Society of Jesus. Through his contribution to the journal, Lafitau reported that the indigenous peoples of the Canadian region where the plant was found had been successfully using it to treat various diseases. Latifau also donated an American ginseng root immersed in alcohol, a stalk of ginseng, ginseng seeds, and several sketches of ginseng to the French Royal Academy of Sciences. The Academy, however, heavily criticized Lafitau's discovery for lacking a scientific basis. Botanists in particular expressed their discontent toward Jartoux and Lafitau's unsystematic research methods and logic and declared that allowing amateurs like Jesuit priests to assign academic names to new plants was unacceptable.

After fierce discussions, the French Royal Academy of Sciences concluded that the German physician Engelbert Kaempfer (1651–1716) was a more reliable authority on ginseng. Having traveled to West Asian regions and all the way to Japan via Russia, Kaempfer was known for bringing the ginkgo tree to Europe. While working for the Dutch East India Company, Kaempfer stayed in Nagasaki for two years, beginning in 1690, during which time he enthusiastically began to collect material and write about the culture, history, and flora of Japan. Upon his return to Europe, Kaempfer published *Amoenitatum exoticarum* in 1712. The chapter titled "*Plantarum Japonicarum*" in this Latin publication included a fairly detailed description of ginseng. Kaempfer explained that there were various kinds of ginseng, such as between Tartar ginseng, Korean ginseng, and Japanese ginseng (ninjin).[9] Based on this explanation, scholars criticized that it made no sense for the Canadian ginseng that Lafitau discovered to be identical to Tartar ginseng when ginseng varied by region even in East Asia (Figure 3.1).

Lafitau countered that it was inadequate to make such a criticism based on knowledge gained solely from books and without actually having visited the growing region of his American ginseng, collected samples, or inquired with indigenous peoples about their usage of the plant. Nevertheless, most scholars in France sided with Kaempfer because his logic had been formed "under the botanist's knife" and therefore reflected the conventions and traditions of European botany.[10]

Amid such controversy, Sarrazin, who discovered American ginseng sixteen years earlier than Lafitau, sent a letter to the director of the Royal Academy of Sciences in November 1717. Through the letter, Sarrazin confessed his mistake

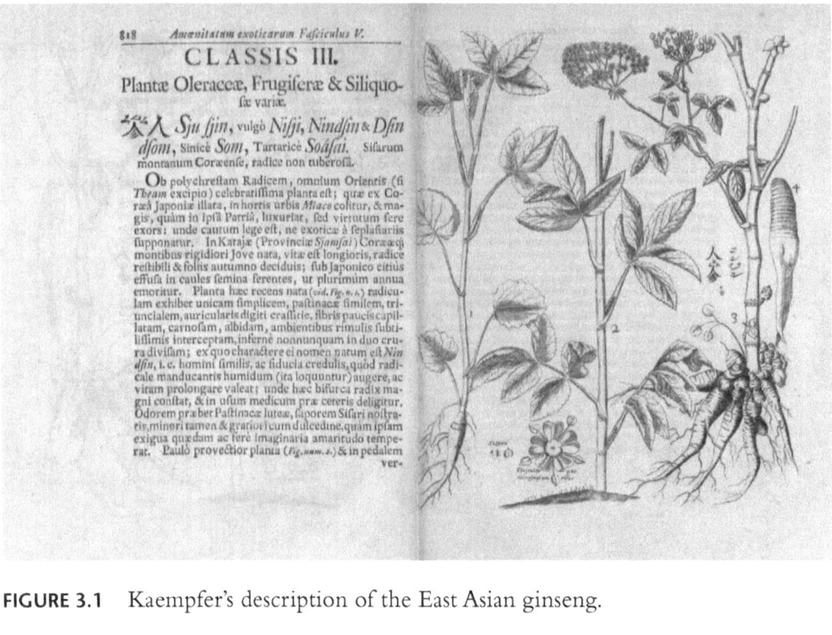

FIGURE 3.1 Kaempfer's description of the East Asian ginseng.

for failing to recognize that the plant he had discovered was ginseng. In contrast to Kaempfer, he too believed that Canadian ginseng was the same in kind as Asian ginseng. Sarrazin also admitted his lack of understanding toward indigenous cultures and languages. Despite staying in French Canada for two decades, the botanist blamed himself for allowing ginseng to "escape" him.[11]

The Royal Academy of Sciences still undermined Lafitau and put an end to the situation by concluding that the sample Sarrazin had sent years ago was identical to that of Lafitau. This conclusion was as good as a declaration that Sarrazin discovered Canadian ginseng earlier than Lafitau. At a meeting on February 9, 1718, the Royal Academy of Sciences announced that American ginseng belonged to a new genus of plants called *Araliastrum*, based on the name Aralia assigned by Sarrazin.

Lafitua must have been dejected, but he still observed the custom of officially submitting a paper about his discovery to the Royal Academy of Sciences on March 12, 1718, under the title "Sur le Gin-seng."[12] Meanwhile, he arranged for a complete version of his report to be separately published in Paris. That publication, *Mémoire presenté a son altesse royale Monseigneur le duc d'Orléans*, came to be referred to as the *Mémoire* (Figure 3.2)[13]

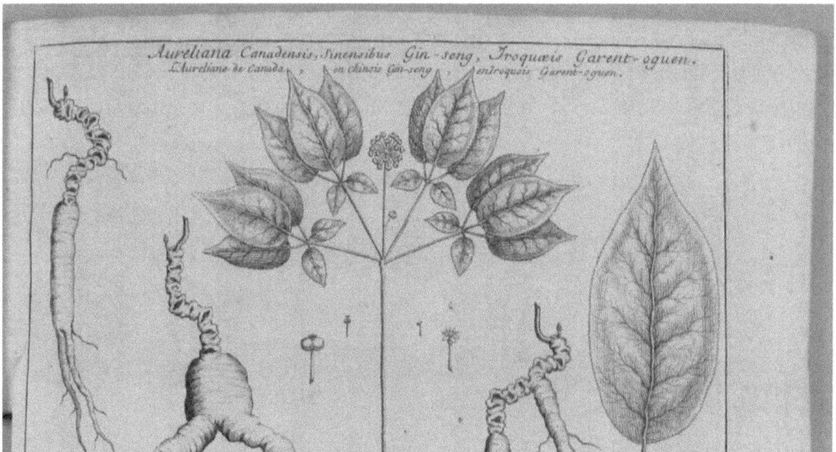

FIGURE 3.2 Lafitau's discovery of ginseng in Canada.

Lafitau was convinced that the plant he discovered in Canada was identical to the Tartar ginseng (Korean ginseng) Jartoux witnessed in Manchuria. He even claimed that the fact had already been proved through the trading of ginseng by French and Dutch merchants. Recalling that Sarrazin named Canadian ginseng Aralia, Lafitau pointed out that Sarrazin was unlikely to have been certain the plant he collected was ginseng because Jartoux's report had not yet been published nor had a name been established for the classification of ginseng at the time. Lafitau's argument appeared to be sympathetic toward Sarrazin's situation yet also seemed to underline the error Sarrazin committed.

Lafitau did not seem ready to hand Sarrazin the credit for having discovered ginseng. In the *Mémoire*, Lafitau explained at length the process he went through with indigenous peoples to find ginseng and revealed the excellence of indigenous remedies. While such remedies using natural medications were simple enough to be regarded as know-how, Lafitau argued that Jesuit missionaries were the only ones capable of disseminating such know-how for everyone's benefit since Jesuit missionaries communicated with indigenous peoples in their language and were trusted by them. In fact, what set Lafitau's report apart from others involving ginseng was that it documented how indigenous Americans used ginseng. Below is an excerpt from Lafitau's report about the indigenous use of ginseng.

> I first asked the *sauvages* how they used ginseng. They replied that ginseng was used as a purgative for children. They said ginseng wasn't strong enough to be used as a purgative for older people. For this reason, some seem to refer to it as children's medication. The *sauvages* were also using it to boost their appetite. However, lack of appetite is very uncommon among the *sauvages* here. The Hurons and Abenaki were each skillfully using it in their own ways. They said ginseng was used to treat dysentery, but in mixtures with other plants. All that I knew when I sent ginseng from Canada to Paris, where Père le Blanc had the honor of presenting it to your royal highness, was what a *Sauvagesse* told me about her experience of being cured three times of fever, which I have already mentioned. I experimented with ginseng on myself and found that its use cured the rheumatism that had been wearing me down, leaving me convinced that I may no longer suffer from the pain.[14]

Lafitau also introduced an episode about healing someone with ginseng. A lady he was well acquainted with had been suffering from a stomach disorder for nineteen months, which was accompanied by a fever, insomnia, and lack of appetite. She ingested cinchona bark, but it only helped lower her fever and left a scorching pain down her throat. However, after ingesting the ginseng Lafitau sent her for seven straight days, her appetite returned, and she was able to sleep. Within a month, the lady sent a letter informing that she was entirely rid of the fever and pain (Figure 3.2).[15]

Ginseng as Evidence of Continental Separation

Lafitau learned that the Iroquois in Canada referred to ginseng as "*Garent-oguen*." The term meant a man's legs or thighs, which was similar to the Chinese term for ginseng that meant a "plant resembling man." Lafitau claimed that the word *nisi* used in Japan to refer to ginseng was identical to the meaning of *Garent-oguen*.[16] To Lafitau, this etymological similarity was more than a simple coincidence. It could serve as a key motive for persistently promoting his discovery through the French Jesuit journal and Royal Academy of Sciences. In other words, ginseng could serve as clear evidence in proving that the indigenous peoples of the American continent had originated from the Old World.

With confidence, Lafitau stated that "ginseng proves that the American continent was originally one with Asia." Ginseng represented the homogeneity of people who once resided on the same land, and who, despite drifting apart due to continental separation, had managed to retain cultural and linguistic similarities. What Lafitau ultimately tried to demonstrate from a single root was that the history of humanity could be traced back to the days of Eden.[17] He thus believed that the sole origin of man could be found in Christianity.

At the time, such a belief was in fact widely shared among Jesuit missionaries. Missionaries sent to China argued that Chinese classics actually acknowledged the Christian God or that the shape of some Chinese characters proved that the cultures of China and Europe were born from the same origin.[18] In a similar sense, Lafitau suspected that ginseng and the indigenous of America both originated from somewhere other than North America. He believed that ginseng was once present across Western Europe and was known as a mandrake at one point. Yet, unlike Europeans, the indigenous in America were experiencing the efficacy of ginseng, which prompted Lafitau to further speculate that European ginseng must have gone extinct a very long time ago.[19]

After Lafitau's discovery, indigenous use of ginseng from all over the American continent was reported. A fellow missionary of Lafitau noted the use of ginseng by the Miami in the Great Lakes region: "The *Sauvages*, who have always been more concerned with medicine than others, are very fond of ginseng and are convinced that this plant has the virtue of making women fertile."[20] James Adair (c. 1709–1783), an Irish merchant who maintained close contact with indigenous Americans when he went to North America, noted that indigenous Americans used ginseng on religious occasions, as he wrote about in his history of the Chickasaw who resided in Mississippi and Alabama.[21] A publication released in Philadelphia in 1830 mentioned that indigenous Americans used ginseng to treat "asthma, weak stomach, debility, pains in the bones, excessive venery, gravelly complaints."[22] The Cherokee referred to ginseng as *a'tli-guli*, which meant "the mountain climber," because every time people moved to its vicinity, the plant seemed to retreat and climb further up the mountain.[23]

What is important here is that some people eagerly accepted and cited Lafitau's theory on continental separation developed from the etymology of ginseng. Below is what a French captain wrote in his travelogue.

> You know that ginseng is originally a native of the Mancheoux Tartary, the Chinese or Tartarian name of it signifies, the thighs of a man. The Americans, who were long acquainted with it, and made use of it, called it garelonguen, which has the same signification. If America did not join to Tartary, or if the latter had not peopled the first, how could their respective inhabitants give names of the same signification to the same plant?[24]

Some, however, dismissed Lafitau's argument as completely groundless. One of them was the great writer François-Marie Arouet Voltaire (1694–1778). Regarding articles circulating claims that the Tartars of Manchuria were the ancestors of Peruvians, or that the presence of plants similar to ginseng in Canada was proof that the great sailors of the Chinese past had been there before conquering the Chinese Tartary, Voltaire scoffed "what could I possibly say to such people or such rumors."[25] Despite his sarcastic tone, Voltaire's reaction proved that intellectuals did take Lafitau's argument seriously at the time.

Botanical Discussion on Two Kinds of Ginseng

As news of ginseng's discovery in North America reached Europe, a vibrant discussion ensued between Britain and France over the botanical features of the two different kinds of ginseng. North Americans claimed that their ginseng was as effective as that from China, but many in Britain believed the opposite.[26] Some in London were skeptical as to whether the North American ginseng they purchased was as effective as the Chinese ginseng.[27] One source went as far as to note that "The ginseng of Canada is deficient not only in colour, smell, and transparency, but also in its virtue and properties."[28]

The early stages of discussion in Britain surrounding ginseng from two different continents were led by the "ginseng expert" Hans Sloane and a naturalist named Peter Collinson (1694–1768). Collinson had entered into a partnership to export ginseng with William Byrd II, who felt betrayed by Sloane's enthusiastic promotion of cocoa. Collinson frequently exchanged information with Byrd, which triggered a discussion about ginseng among the literate in America.

Collinson also happened to be the first to bring North American ginseng to Britain, in 1740. He asked a botanist in the American colony named John Bartram (1699–1777) to send North American ginseng to Britain. Upon receiving the ginseng that Bartram personally collected from eastern Philadelphia, Collinson planted it in a shady spot with light soil he had carefully selected. Unfortunately, the plant never bloomed or bore fruit. The botanist Philip Miller (1691–1771) also tasted failure with ginseng from Maryland he had been growing at the Chelsea Physic Garden. The ginseng that Miller planted bloomed and formed seeds, but he failed to make the seeds germinate even though he waited three years without disturbing the ground.[29]

The British found North American ginseng attractive because they believed it could reap massive economic benefits. Those with interests in overseas trade were excited at the thought of being able to secure large amounts of precious ginseng. It did, however, remain uncertain as to whether the North American ginseng was identical to the Asian ginseng. Many claimed that the two were different despite appearing to be similar, but even more people wanted to believe that the two were alike. As a result, planting North American ginseng grew popular enough for it to be found in botanical and herb gardens across Britain less than half a century after it was first discovered in Canada.

Collinson grew the ginseng he received from Bartram at Peckham Garden in the outskirts of London.[30] However, he became frustrated when the plant didn't grow as well as he'd hoped. Meanwhile, the physician and collector John Fothergill (1712–1780) boasted in 1769 that the ginseng he too had received from Bartram was doing very well in his famed Upton Garden in Essex.[31] By that point, ginseng was being grown in botanical gardens in Oxford and Edinburgh. Ginseng appeared in the 1757 list of "plants now in blossom" at a pleasure garden in London.[32] In *The British Garden: A Descriptive Catalogue of Hardy Plants* (1799), "*Panax quinquefolium* Ginseng" was noted as a plant "native of China" that "leaves three-fold, in fives," "flowers in June," and was "introduced in 1740 by Peter Collinson."[33] As per this description, North American ginseng was commonly believed to have originated from China.

In Europe and America, there were divided views at the time as to whether North American and Chinese ginseng were identical. People who regarded them as identical thought North American ginseng was being discriminated against because of where it was grown. This belief was reflected in an overview of ginseng that appeared in the British Museum's 1762 catalogue of its collection. The overview began by introducing ginseng as a plant known in China and Japan for activating the brain, boosting stamina, and healing nerves and that had once traded at the price of gold in Europe and remained a commodity valued in India. Yet, the overview ended on a critical note by mentioning that ginseng was not as esteemed in Britain. It further added that the Chinese only recognized domestically grown ginseng and had little regard for the North American ginseng.[34] Meanwhile, after comparing the North American ginseng with a sample of ginseng from Nanjing, the British physician William Lewis (c. 1708–1781) concluded that the way they were each processed most likely determined the difference in their efficacy, since they exhibited no physical differences other than the fact that the Chinese sample had paler skin and was white on the inside. Yet Lewis also found it difficult to accept that inferior North American ginseng could be regarded as real ginseng even without having been processed.[35]

Ginseng and *Ninzin*

Another botanical discussion pertaining to ginseng arose regarding distinguishing the terms ginseng and *ninzin*. While numerous historical sources treated *ninzin* merely as an alternate name for ginseng, just as many attempts were made to establish that the two terms referred to two different plants. Among those who were preoccupied with the matter was John Hill (1714–1775). After beginning his career as a quack, Hill branched out into gardening, botany, and acting before making a name for himself through several books he authored at a time when the British publishing industry was expanding in the eighteenth century. Through the widely distributed *History of the Materia Medica* (1751), Hill explained that ginseng grew in shady, mountainous regions between a latitude of thirty-nine and forty-five degrees in not only Tartary but North America and Korea as well. However, he also claimed that "Ginseng of Corea is bigger but hollower" and "inferior in quality" than ginseng from other areas because "it is a different root called Ninzin."[36]

Hill's book reflected characteristics typical of his fame-seeking writer contemporaries. While building his argument about ginseng, Hill named all the renowned experts of the time, including John Ray, the father of English natural history, Engelbert Kaempfer, who was favored by the French Royal Academy of Sciences, and Carl von Linné, whom Hill personally regarded as his rival. Hill claimed that Europeans were incapable of distinguishing *ninzin* from ginseng and that the *ninzin* genuinely used for medicinal purposes could only be collected from the mountains of Korea. *Ninzin* was extremely challenging to cultivate in Japan, but despite such efforts, its quality could never match that of wild *ninzin*. Yet through a chapter devoted to *ninzin*, Hill identified it as an umbelliferous plant similar to ginseng, "much alike in their shape and colour, and yet more so in their virtues, which differ scarce at all except in degree."[37] The inaccuracy of Hill's knowledge became most apparent through his discussion of "true ginseng," as he claimed that only ginseng from the Korean kingdom of Paekche was worthy of the title (Figure 3.3).[38]

Meanwhile, some people were more convinced that *ninzin* was completely different from ginseng. In *A New Course of Chemistry* (1754), James Millar drew a distinction between *ninzin* and ginseng, noting that although the two roots were "not admitted into the Art of the *Materia Medica* of the College," they had to be mentioned because they were "so frequently spoken of."

> Ginseng is whitish Root, of the Length and Thickness of a Man's little Finger, rarely much more; commonly divided into two or more Parts toward the Bottom. It has a slight aromatick smell, and is of a bitter but pleasant Taste. The Plant which affords this Root is frequent in China. The Stalk is purplish, the Leaves grow five together, and are large and serrated. The Flowers are small, and are succeeded each by a single roundish Berry.
>
> Ninsi, or Ninzin is a larger Root, oblong, whitish on the outside and yellowish within, less firm than the Ginseng, and less bitter in the Taste.

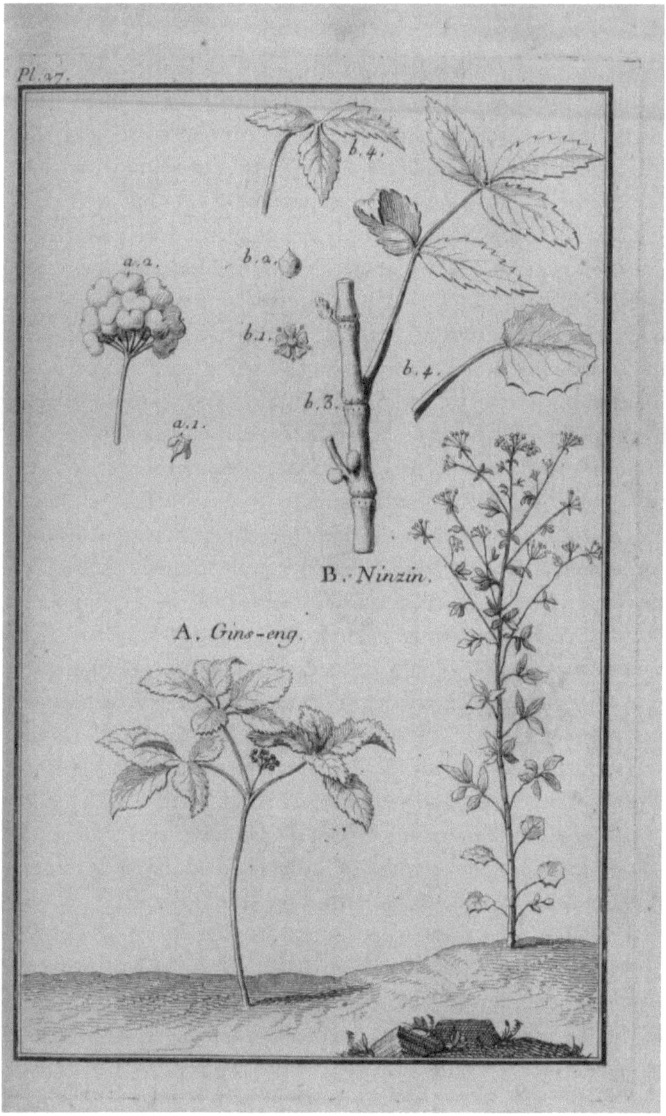

FIGURE 3.3 Ginseng and ninjin.

> The Plant which affords this is a Kind of Sisarum, or Skirret, an umbelliferous Herb, with two naked Seeds after each Flower.[39]

Discussions about distinguishing ginseng from *ninzin* tended to occur more often in the field of pharmacology, perhaps because it was a matter most pertinent to people who prepared and sold ginseng. This speculation is supported by Hill's remark that "the interest of the seller" caused the confusion between *ninzin* and ginseng, since apothecaries needed them both to be "understood as the same root" in order to profit from *ninzin* that was supplied at a "much smaller price than Ginseng."[40]

Notes

1 Jartoux, "The Description of a Tartarian Plant, Call'd Gin-Seng," 240.
2 Chakrabarti, *Materials and Medicine*, 116.
3 Chang Il-moo 장일무, *Han'guk insam sanŏpsa* 한국인삼산업사 [A History of the Korean Ginseng Industry], vol. 2 (Seoul: Korean Ginseng Corporation 한국인삼공사, 2018), 74. See note no. 27.
4 Christopher M. Parsons, "The Natural History of Colonial Science: Joseph-François Lafitau's Discovery of Ginseng and Its Afterlives," *The William and Mary Quarterly* 73, no. 1 (2016): 41, 45, 63. Jean Prat, a correspondent for the French Royal Academy of Sciences who was staying in Louisiana, secured a ginseng sample from Jesuit missionaries and sent it to the Royal Botanical Garden in 1736.
5 William N. Fenton, "Contacts between Iroquois Herbalism and Colonial Medicine," in *Annual Report of the Smithsonian Institute* (Washington, DC: Smithsonian Institute, 1941), 503–526. Refer in particular to pages 518–520.
6 Joseph-François Lafitau, *Mémoire presenté a son altesse royale Monseigneur le duc d'Orléans, regent du royaume de France: Concernant la précieuse plante du gin-seng de Tartarie, découverte en Canada par Le P. Joseph François Lafitau, de La Compagnie de Jesus, Missionnaire des Iroquois du Sault Saint Louis* (Paris, 1718), 14.
7 Lafitau, *Mémoire*, 61.
8 A journal issued monthly between 1702 and 1782. *Journal de Trévoux* was an abbreviation for the journal's original name, *Mémoires pour l'histoire des sciences et des beaux-arts*. The journal was first published in Trévoux, a commune near Lyon. Joseph-François Lafitau, "Le Genseng, Plante si précieuse à la Chine, découverte dans le Canada," *Mémoires pour l'histoire des sciences et des beaux-arts*, no. January (1717): 121–124.
9 Engelbert Kempfer, *Amoenitatum Exoticarum Politico-Physico-Medicarum Fasciculi V* (Lemgo, 1712), 818–821.
10 Parsons, "The Natural History of Colonial Science," 47–48.
11 "Michel Sarrazin to Jean-Paul Bignon, Nov. 5, 1717," in Arthur Vallée, ed., *Un biologiste canadien, Michel Sarrazin, 1659–1735: Sa vie, ses travaux et son temps* (Québec: Le Quotidien, 1927), 216.
12 "Académie Royale des Sciences," *Procès-verbaux* 37 (1718), 69.
13 Lafitau, *Mémoire*.
14 Lafitau, *Mémoire*, 49–50.
15 Lafitau, *Mémoire*, 51–52.
16 Lafitau, *Mémoire*, 17, 40–41.
17 Lafitau, *Mémoire*, 17–18.
18 Arnold H. Rowbotham, "The Jesuit Figurists and Eighteenth-Century Religious Thought," *Journal of the History of Ideas* 17, no. 4 (1956): 476–478.
19 Lafitau, *Mémoire*, 74–79, 82–83.
20 Pierre-François-Xavier de Charlevoix, *Journal d'un voyage fait par ordre du Roi dans l'Amérique septentrionale*, ed. Pierre Berthiaume, vol. 2 (Montréal: Les presses de l'Université de Montréal, 1994), 640.
21 James Adair, *The History of the American Indians* (London, 1775), 362.
22 *The Casket, Flowers of Literature, Wit and Sentiment*, vol. 5 (Philadelphia, PA: Samuel C. Atkinson, 1830), 236.
23 Luke Manget, "Sangin'io the Mountains: The Ginseng Economy of the Southern Appalachians, 1865–1900," *Appalachian Journal* 40, no. 1/2 (2012): 33.

24 Jean-Bernard Bossu, *Travels through That Part of North America Formerly Called Louisiana by Mr. Bossu, Captain in the French Marines*, trans. John Reinhold Forster, vol. 1 (London, 1771), 386.
25 Voltaire, *The Works of M. de Voltaire: Translated from the French with Notes, Historical and Critical*, trans. T. Smollet and T. Francklin, vol. 12 (London, 1761), 91.
26 John Payne, *Geographical Extracts, Forming a General View of Earth and Nature* (London, 1796), 336.
27 Tobias Smollett, *Humphry Clinker* (London: G. Routledge & Co., 1857), 31.
28 Alexis Rochon, *A Voyage to Madagascar and the East Indies*, trans. Joseph Trapp (London, 1792), 459.
29 James Akin, *Encyclopaedia: Or, a Dictionary of Arts, Sciences, and Miscellaneous Literature*, vol. 8 (Philadelphia, PA, 1798), 689–690.
30 Richard Hingston Fox, *Dr. John Fothergill and His Friends: Chapters in Eighteenth-Century Life* (London: Macmillan and Co. Ltd., 1919), 197.
31 William Darlington, ed., *Memorials of John Bartram and Humphry Marshall* (Philadelphia, PA: Lindsay & Blakiston, 1849), 339. [Fothergill to Bartram, London, 1 May 1769].
32 Philip Miller, *The Gardener's Kalendar*, 11th ed. (London, 1757), 215.
33 Murray, *The British Garden*, 241.
34 Robert Dodsley, *The General Contents of the British Museum: With Remarks Serving as a Directory in Viewing That Noble Cabinet* (London, 1762), 155–156.
35 William Lewis, *An Experimental History of the Materia Medica*, vol. 1 (Dublin, 1769), 393.
36 John Hill, *A History of the Materia Medica* (London, 1751), 590.
37 Hill, *A History of the Materia Medica*, 589–592; John Hill, *The Vegetable System*, vol. 5 (London, 1759), 25.
38 Hill, *A History of the Materia Medica*, 591–592.
39 James Millar, *A New Course of Chemistry* (London, 1754), 89.
40 Hill, *A History of the Materia Medica*, 589, 591.

4

THE CLASSIFICATION AND MEDICAL USE OF GINSENG

The Age of Classification

The discovery of a new kind of ginseng and other similar plants kept ginseng from being botanically classified at once. Hence, it took a considerable amount of time for ginseng to be established in the field of botany. As in the case of Lafitau's discovery, deciding where to place a plant like ginseng of non-European origin within a European botanical classification system was in fact an extremely complex and important matter.

Why, then, was classifying ginseng so important? Classification methods that emerged in Europe around the time were a major characteristic of the development of early modern science. The birth of classification was closely linked to the exponential growth of natural history in seventeenth-century Europe. Many scientists, including Francis Bacon, gathered a tremendous amount of data on the natural world and began to refer to it as "natural history." Thus emerged a new field of study that embraced both science expanding to an extent incomparable to the past and history reaching far back into the past.

The development of natural history could be partially attributed to the popularity of "the cabinet of curiosities" that exhibited extraordinary objects collected as part of a craze for the new and unusual dating back to the Renaissance. However, with so many things arriving from the New World, the need arose for a more systematic management of objects that went beyond simply collecting, exhibiting, and describing them. Ships transporting spices from the East Indies and sugar from the West Indies brought back plants, birds, shells, and insects as well. Classifying, arranging, and naming them became a task of importance. A collection was a means to display one's social status, so to the powerful, classifying and naming objects in their collection proved to be an essential project. Moreover, the practice of observing and experimenting with curious

DOI: 10.4324/9781003286691-5

objects from abroad emerged with the appearance of public museums and scientific research institutes since the mid-seventeenth century, further triggering the need to classify countless objects and assign a certain order to them.[1] This led to the beginning of an obsession with classification, which has been considered a major aspect of the Enlightenment.

To natural philosophers of the seventeenth century, classification was something of a mission. Even in botany, numerous scholars had been exploring diverse methods to classify plants since the early seventeenth century, more than a century before Carl von Linné suggested his classification system. The foundation for botanical classification was Gaspard Bauhin's (1560–1624) system for delineating botanical species and genera. Bauhin suggested a binomial system that identified the genus in the form of a noun in the first part of a name and the species in the form of an adjective in the second part of a name.

In Britain, John Ray earned the title of "the father of natural history" for his early contribution to the classification of plants. After compiling a catalogue of plants growing around Cambridge in 1660, Ray went on to publish *Historia Plantarum* (1686, 1688, 1704) through which he classified plants around the world based on multiple criteria. Interestingly enough, Ray adopted utility as a criterion for classifying plants. Based on their purpose, he sorted foreign plants into three different kinds: edible, medicinal, and decorative. While coffee, cocoa, tea, and banana were edible plants, ginseng was described as a medicinal plant alongside Peruvian quinine and the St. Ignatius bean, known for its use in treating hysteria and myoclonus. Decorative plants referred to wood that could be used to produce items like furniture.

In *Historia Plantarum*, Ray noted that "Ginseng or Ginsing" was a panacea that grew in Korea, China, and Japan.[2] According to Ray's description, ginseng was a root as thick as a finger, long and split at the end, brown on the outside, white on the inside, and having a fragrant yet spicy and bitter taste. The plant was rarely or never prescribed through apothecary's shops,[3] suggesting that the British father of natural history was referring to Asian ginseng because North American ginseng had not yet been discovered at that point.

The discovery of ginseng in Canada in the early eighteenth century posed a challenge to classifying the plant within the context of European botany. The French Royal Academy of Sciences and Sébastien Vaillant (1669–1722), a teacher at the king's gardens, became responsible for classifying the ginseng Michel Sarrazin sent from Canada in 1700. Sample no. 73 called "aralia" was labeled in what seemed to be Sarrazin's writing[4] as a "kind of ninzin or ginseng."[5] As he suggested a classification based on the structure of flowers in 1718, Vaillant proposed three new genera called "Araliastrum," "Sherardia," and "Boerhaavia."[6] Even after Lafitau submitted the *Mémoire* on his discoveries, Vaillant and his fellow botanists in France still recognized Sarrazin as the one who first discovered American ginseng and claimed that it belonged to a new genus called "Araliastrum" approximately three decades after Ray classified Asian ginseng.

Carl von Linné's Classification of Ginseng

Through *Species Plantarum* published in 1753, Carl von Linné (1707–1778) defined Canadian ginseng as a five-leaved (quinquefolius) species belonging to the *Panax* genus of the Araliaceae family.[7] This is known as the first binomial naming of ginseng. Yet, Jan Frederik Gronovius (1686–1762) placed ginseng under the *Panax* genus earlier than von Linné, in his *Flora Virginica* (1743). Gronovius's contribution, however, has barely been recognized in the history of botany. The reason von Linné came to occupy the spotlight today when it comes to the history of naming ginseng is probably because of his close relationship with Gronovius.

Born in Sweden, von Linné gave lectures on botany after graduating from Uppsala University. Unfortunately, discord with his colleagues led to dissatisfaction with his surroundings and prompted him to head to the Netherlands in 1735. The Netherlands was an optimal place to study natural history at the time, and to the Swedes, the best place to earn a doctoral degree. Von Linné went to Leiden in pursuit of a doctoral degree in medicine as well as an opportunity to publish his botanical manuscripts. Not only did the Netherlands share strong commercial and cultural ties with Sweden at the time, it offered the best chances of publishing manuscripts authored in Latin.

The international atmosphere of the Netherlands allowed von Linné to meet with people from various countries, some of whom became his lifelong patrons or academic companions. And the botanical garden in Leiden, with more than 5,000 species, fueled his passion to study botany. Yet, what surprised von Linné the most in the Netherlands was the fact that intellectuals were financially well off. The financially pressed young scholar then met Gronovius. As a physician and naturalist who came from a renowned family of classical scholars in Leiden, Gronovius possessed a massive collection of natural specimens, reflecting the remarkable achievements the Netherlands had achieved through overseas trade at the time. The collection was particularly well known for its vast number of plant specimens from North America that Gronovius had acquired through the Virginia-based botanist John Clayton (1694/5–1773). Gronovius showed von Linné his collection and consulted with him on how to classify it.

After examining a few plant specimens, von Linné came up with a quite simple, yet brilliant, classification method, which Gronovius immediately adopted and thereafter became a reliable patron of von Linné. Gronovius was the one who bore the expense of publishing von Linné's monumental work *Systema Naturae* (1735).[8] He also helped von Linné publish other works in Leiden including *Genera Plantarum* (1737), *Methodus Sexualis* (1737), and *Critica Botanica* (1737). Von Linné used his knowledge in anatomy and physiology to create a comprehensive classification system that covered the animal, vegetable, and mineral kingdoms. This system garnered tremendous acclaim across Europe by the 1750s and brought von Linné into celebrity status overnight.

Through the preface of *Species Plantarum* (1753), von Linné stated that "I have omitted here the plants not seen."[9] This revealed how much von Linné valued direct observation. And since von Linné gave ginseng a binomial name, it is safe to assume that he personally observed the plant as well. In fact, he left a record about witnessing ginseng at the garden of the Hartekamp,[10] a villa owned by George Clifford III (1685–1760), a wealthy Dutch financier who was also a director of the Dutch East India Company. Greatly impressed by von Linné's talent in botanical classification, Clifford invited von Linné to serve as his personal physician and look after his garden. So, von Linné worked at the Hartekamp in 1735, where he was able to study plants to his heart's content and travel to Britain during his stay.

Von Linné classified the ginseng he encountered at the Hartekamp as a plant of the genus Aralia, according to Sébastien Vaillant's classification. The ginseng he saw was most likely North American ginseng. However, von Linné's classification of ginseng was inconsistent. When describing ginseng in *Materia Medica* (1749), he quoted the name "Sinensibus Ginseng" by Joseph François Lafitau and associated ginseng with the genus *Panax*.[11] Could von Linné have observed Korean ginseng by the time he authored *Materia Medica*? If he was describing North American ginseng in the book, why did he quote Lafitau instead of Vaillant? More fundamentally, why did von Linné's naming of ginseng change?

One possible explanation is that von Linné was able to acquire knowledge about East Asia and Asian ginseng over time. After all, he lived in Europe during a period of fascination with China. His homeland Sweden was no exception to the Chinoiserie craze as it created Chinese gardens and imported Chinese porcelain through the Swedish East India Company, established in 1731. Von Linné agreed with his contemporary intellectuals who regarded China as a model Europe should follow. However, like most Europeans, he didn't even know exactly where China was located. In fact, most eighteenth-century Europeans were unable to distinguish China from India and sometimes bundled them together by referring to them as "India Orientalis."[12] Von Linné was no different, for he used the terms "India" or "Indies" to refer to not only India, but locations to its east and the West Indies as well.[13]

Under such circumstances, von Linné had friends who provided him with information about Asian plants. One of them who could have given him ginseng was Pehr Osbeck (1723–1805). Osbeck was a Swedish explorer and naturalist who served as chaplain on a commercial ship that sailed to China. Despite arriving in Guangzhou in 1751, Osbeck was unable to leave the ship due to the Chinese policy that forbade foreigners of religious affiliation from setting foot on its territory. Besides, he couldn't afford to travel far either. Compared to the activities Jesuit missionaries engaged in China at the time, Osbeck was extremely limited in terms of his range of movement and the information he could access. Nevertheless, he still managed to procure thirty-seven different Chinese plants and brought them back to von Linné in 1752. The extent of von Linné's gratitude can be glimpsed from the following passage.

> A Thousand thanks for the consignment, which was second to none, … Such a great collection of plants has never come from East India, except for that of Hermann who lived there [present-day Sri Lanka] for nine years. I

> cannot understand, Sir, how you were able to gather so much during such a short stay and under such awkward conditions, … Now I can compete with any other botanist as to the number of herbs.[14]

Could Chinese ginseng have been among the specimens Osbeck delivered to von Linné? There is no way of knowing at this point, but based on what Osbeck mentioned in his travelogue, he had certainly been aware of ginseng at the time.

> YAN-SAM, or Yan-som, is the Chinese name of a root, which is to be got in our apothercaries shops by the name of Ninsi (Panax quinque folia, Linn.), … it often divides into two stalks, in which the Chinese find the resemblance of a man, for which reason they have given it the aforementioned name.
>
> YAN-SAM, or, as we commonly say, Ginseng, is not allowed to be imported into China, because it grows wild in that country, … When Father Jartona undertook to make a map of Tartary, he described this plant; which is likewise, thoug seldom, found in Setchuen. In America it is called Garentouges, or human thighs.[15]

Osbeck's account, however, included numerous misconceptions. The most obvious among them was his firm belief that Chinese and American ginseng were one and the same. If a botanist like Osbeck was misinformed, expecting intellectuals in general to have been able to tell the difference between the two plants seems to be a remote possibility. Even the entry titled "Gin-seng" in the famed 1757 edition of *Encyclopédie* concluded that the two plants were identical. The rationale behind such a conclusion was that unless they were identical, French merchants would never have gotten away with selling 3,000 to 4,000 pounds of Canadian ginseng to China for years without being questioned about the authenticity of their goods.[16]

Carl Anton Meyer's Scientific Definition of "Real Ginseng"

By the 1780s, a time when von Linné's classification of ginseng remained inconsistent, British botanical publications began to make a distinction within the *Panax* genus between the five-leaved Canadian ginseng and the three-leaved Virginia ginseng.[17] An American encyclopedia published in 1798 subdivided *Panax* ginseng into five different kinds but considered American and Tartarian ginseng as the same.

> 1. Quinquefolium.
> 2. Trifolium.
> 3. Fruticosum.
> 4. Arborea.
> 5. Spinosa.

> The first and second are natives of North America. The quinquefolium is generally believed to be the same with the Tartarian ginseng.[18]

Amid such chaos, a German botanist and pharmacologist named Theodor Friedrich Ludwig Nees von Esenbeck (1787–1837)[19] became the first to distinguish the East Asian ginseng (Korean ginseng) through his book *Plantae medicinales*, published in 1833. He labeled Korean ginseng as "Panax Schin-seng var. Coraiensis T. Nees" after his own name.[20] Nees von Esenbeck was clearly aware that the East Asian ginseng was different from the American ginseng and thus added "Coraiensis," suggesting that Germans at least knew that Korea was a major producer of ginseng. "Schin-seng" appears to be a notation devised to resemble the Chinese word *xiangshen*.

After Nees von Esenbeck's contribution, the scientific name of Korean ginseng used to this day became determined in 1842. Based on the binomial naming system, Carl Anton Meyer (1795–1855) came up with the name "Panax ginseng C.A. Meyer."[21] As a naturalized Russian born in Germany, Meyer was a botanist who had served as director of the Imperial Botanic Garden at St. Petersburg.[22] Not only did Meyer distinguish the East Asian ginseng from the American ginseng, he named the East Asian ginseng after himself because he believed it to be the "true ginseng." According to Meyer, *Panax quinquefoliate* grew in North America, while *Panax ginseng* C.A. Meyer grew to the north of the Amur River, namely in Sakhalin and Japan in the east, and in the south, in the southern regions of Korea as well as the provinces of Shanxi and Hebei in China.[23]

What is interesting is that Meyer mentioned the provinces of Shanxi and Hebei as ginseng habitats. This indicates that although he was capable of distinguishing the Korean ginseng from the American ginseng, he had failed to move on from misinformation disseminated more than two centuries ago through Jean-Baptiste Du Halde's *General History of China*. Moreover, by the time the scientific name of ginseng was being determined, ginseng had already become extinct in China. The fact that the provinces of Shanxi and Hebei were still being cited as habitats of "true ginseng" proved that Europe remained limited in its knowledge of Chinese plants and that misinformation could be surprisingly persistent.

The West's Utilization of Ginseng

Not long after the English Royal Society began to observe ginseng, Robert Wittie (c. 1613–1684) published cases on the therapeutic use of ginseng in a 1680 pamphlet titled *Some Observations Made upon the Root called Nean, or Ninsing, imported from the East-Indies*.[24] As a physician in Yorkshire obsessed with making a name for himself, Wittie engaged in arguments over hydrotherapy with renowned physicians. He then developed an interest in medicinal drugs as a means other than hydrotherapy to attract affluent patients. Although Wittie's book featured excerpts from letters to a member of the Royal Society, it was closer to a promotional booklet and seemed to reveal Wittie's desire to take part in the latest discussions on ginseng among Royal Society members in London.

Through his pamphlet, Wittie admitted that he experienced "wonderful success" from treating a patient with a parcel of ginseng he had received as a gift.[25] He even went as far as to state that, apart from the mineral waters of Scarborough that he had long promoted, ginseng was among "the best medicines in the world" and that it was more effective than mineral waters in treating lung conditions. Wittie also listed several cases of having successfully prescribed ginseng, which are summarized in Table 4.1.

Wittie stressed in the pamphlet that ginseng was particularly effective in treating tuberculosis, regardless its cause.[26] Based on his statement that ginseng dramatically improved one patient's lung conditions, Wittie appears to have used ginseng mainly to treat lung diseases, general prostration, high fever, and pain.

The pamphlet included mention of several prominent figures, hinting at the author's ambitions and promotional intentions. One of those figures was a subject of Wittie's experimentation named Andrew Marvell (1621–1678). A poet from Yorkshire, Marvell was also a politician who gained a reputation for managing to preserve himself throughout the political conflicts between the Parliamentarians and Royalists during the English Civil War. Also mentioned in the pamphlet were the Pope and Robert Boyle, including Boyle's comment on ginseng: "it was a Medicine sent from Heaven, to save the Lives of Thousands of Men, Women and Children."[27]

Best known for Boyle's law, pertaining to the behavior of gases, Boyle also served as a director of the East India Company and was an avid supporter of the Jesuits' missionary work in China. It can therefore be presumed that he had a sufficient degree of knowledge about ginseng. He reportedly used Korean ginseng, which would have been costly but not difficult to acquire for someone like Boyle, who was the son of one of the wealthiest men in England at the time.

The ginseng Wittie experimented with was also from Korea. However, when ginseng was discovered in North America decades after his pamphlet was published, experimentations with American ginseng began to emerge. Even Sarrazin, who deprived Lafitau of his discovery, used American ginseng for treatment. Although he may not have been aware of the resemblance between the American ginseng and the East Asian ginseng, Sarrazin must have recognized that the American ginseng had medical properties. Through his correspondence with the French Royal Academy of Sciences, Sarrazin reported cases in which the American ginseng was used to treat patients, which later made their way into Sébastien Vaillant's paper.

In one case, Sarrazin treated a patient suffering from anasarca with a drink made of ginseng. He also witnessed excellent progress in treating a prolonged ulcer by boiling ginseng to use it as a cataplasm. Bathing in or injecting an extract of ginseng turned out to be highly effective in treating wounds.[28] Such cases featured a broader range of conditions like ulcers or wounds as well as a

TABLE 4.1 Successful cases of treatment using ginseng

Patient	*Symptoms or condition*	*Prescription and preparation of ginseng*	*Effect*
Mr. Andrew Marvel	The patient was much emaciated, and reduced to a perfect skeleton, a mere bag of bones, by a long hectic fever, joined with an ulcer of the lungs	Ginseng tincture in red cow milk every morning	His flesh came back again like that of a child, his lost appetite was restored, and his natural ruddy complexion was revived in his cheeks, to the amazement of his desponding relations
A very considerable person at Hull	The patient was very much pined away, had a cough and shortness of breath, a quick pulse, and an intense heat, at some certain times, with wandering pains in several parts of his body, and restless nights, and no appetite to food	The extract made with the ginseng root was prescribed every night in almond milk for a month	He grew fat and plump, and all his ill symptoms left him, and he is yet alive
The gentlewoman at Leeds in Yorkshire	The patient was catching cold in her lungs, was feeling very weak, with dry cough, stitches in her breast and sides, heat in her palms and feet, and pining away insensibly	The spirit made of this root, about ten drops at a time in a glass of Old Mallago after dinner, was given	In a short time, she gathered her flesh and had five children
Son of his good friend at Rippon	The patient fell into a deep consumption upon his breeding of teeth	Ginseng tincture, as a spirit and an extract	In six weeks' time, the child mended and grew strong and lusty and looked like a man
A friend at York	Buried six children	Ginseng was given in all their victuals and spoon-meat	Preserved the seventh child

more diverse application of ginseng as a cataplasm, bathing additive, or injectable extract, all of which were not mentioned in Wittie's booklet.

By the mid-eighteenth century, the types of conditions being treated with ginseng grew even more diverse. In the 1740s, Peter Kalm (Pehr Kalm, 1716–1779), a Swedish explorer and botanist well known as an apostle of von Linné, was commissioned by the Swedish Royal Academy of Sciences to collect plant specimens from North America. He thereby embarked on an expedition and came across Canadian ginseng in Quebec and Montreal but was shocked at how imprudently it was being collected for export. Still, Kalm was also able to notice that the French were using ginseng in Canada as a stomachic and other purposes such as treating asthma or improving fertility in women.[29]

The New Pharmacopoeia of the Royal College of Physicians of London, published in 1788, included a case in which a physician named "F. Dekker" successfully treated a patient suffering from convulsions by repeatedly injecting a scruple (twenty grains) of ginseng extract.[30] On the other hand, the book also conveyed cases that were unsuccessful in utilizing ginseng. A decoction of hemlock and ginseng was prescribed to a middle-aged man suffering from a genital ulcer, which ended up enlarging instead of reducing the ulcer.[31] Another middle-aged man infected with a venereal disease was prescribed with white vitriol and ginseng in addition to being subjected to a cold bath, but such measures proved to be ineffective.[32] Although the use of ginseng was unsuccessful in such cases, the cases still serve as proof that ginseng was in fact used to treat genital conditions.

Samuel Stearns (1741–1810), a physician who practiced in Massachusetts, stated that he often used ginseng to treat chronic coughs and lung conditions, all to great success. Stearns's recommendation was to brew pieces of ginseng or powdered ginseng and drink the decoction with a dash of sugar every morning and evening.[33] Ginseng also appeared in many pharmacopoeias and dispensatories published around the same time. For instance, ginseng was listed in a pharmacopoeia by Hermann Boerhaave (1668–1738)[34] who helped von Linné on numerous occasions, while other pharmacopoeias included a brief profile about ginseng like the one below.[35]

> Panax Quinquefolium. Linn. Ginseng: a small plant growing in Tartary, China, and North America
> Part Used: the root
> Sens. Prop: Mucilaginous, with sweetness, bitterishness, and some aromatic warmth
> Med. Virt: Tonic, obtunding
> M. Exhib: Power, Infusion, Extract

Ginseng even made an appearance in the work of a well-known novelist. Tobias Smollett (1721–1771), a novelist, critic, and physician of eighteenth-century

Britain, inserted a prescription for ginseng into one of his picaresque novels, *The Expedition of Humphry Clinker.* In the story, the protagonist, caught up in "clouds of mental chagrin," writes a letter to his doctor telling him that the prescribed "tincture of ginseng" was "exceedingly grateful to the stomach."[36]

It is nevertheless impossible to determine exactly how broad or frequent the use of ginseng was in the West at the time. After all, ginseng was used without prescription in many cases. For instance, when William Byrd II set out on a land survey to settle a long-standing border dispute between Virginia and North Carolina, he is known to have nibbled on ginseng roots to make it through the demanding journey on foot. He declared that ginseng could "chear the Heart even of a Man that has a bad Wife" but also complained about the fact that it grew "as sparingly as Truth & Public Spirit."[37]

The Supply and Intake of Korean Ginseng

Ginseng was not, however, available for common use in the eighteenth century, not even among physicians. Noteworthy clues as to the reason can be found among testimonies about how the shortage in the supply of ginseng made it difficult to procure. One such testimony was given by the British physician and chemist William Lewis (c. 1708–1781) in *The New Dispensatory.*

> The great value, there set upon it, has prevented its being exported from thence into other countries, and its discovery in North America is but of late date, so that among us it has hitherto been very rarely made use of; although, from what can be judged of it from the taste, it seems to deserve some regard.[38]

The above explanation proves that it was not easy to procure ginseng in Europe at the time. Other testimonies pointed out that ginseng was too expensive to readily prescribe. William Cullen (1710–1790), a renowned professor at the Edinburgh Medical School, once declared that although ginseng was well known to shops for quite some time, it was impossible to use because of "the great price put upon it."[39]

Another cause of frustration was the unstable price of ginseng, which had been subject to market circumstances. In the aforementioned novel by Smollett, the protagonist laments having to "live in a world of fraud and sophistication" upon finding out through a friend that the price of ginseng at the same shop had plummeted dramatically in a matter of six months.[40] The excerpt below from a medical article indicates that there were problems in retailing ginseng.

> Hence apothecaries are necessitated to sell plants which they have had by them many years, and which have lost all their vertues, … The root of ginseng, tho' a great restorative, being so very costly, is seldom prescribed; and when it is, it generally has lost its properties thro' age. For which reason

> we ought to contrive methods of cultivation it ourselves, … But we would not be understood as if in all cases we prefer the cultivated plants to the wild ones.[41]

Meanwhile, the prescription of ginseng in eighteenth-century Europe commonly came with two precautions. One was that no matter how effective ginseng may have been, taking overdoses could be fatal. This precaution remained a recurring topic in most discussions on ginseng after being mentioned in a report by Richard Cocks, who sent Korean ginseng to London in 1617.[42] In the same vein, some records featured recommendations on the best ways to take ginseng. One suggestion was to emulate the rich, who were "contented with taking, in the morning, a small quantity of it, equal in weight to about a grain of corn."[43] There were also suggestions that the intake of ginseng entailed twice as much danger because the root was so potent and effective.[44] In 1793, the *Edinburgh Magazine* published a detailed introduction to ginseng that ended with the specific warning that its excessive use could result in death. The other precaution was that although the elderly and weak may benefit from ginseng, it had to be used with care on youths or those with high body heat. This appears to coincide with the idea that Korean ginseng raises body temperature, which continues to be debated even to this day.

What is interesting is that in *Bencao gangmu*, Li Shizhen firmly negated both the danger of using ginseng on a person with high body heat and the belief that the excessive use of ginseng could lead to death.[45] Li Shizhen added that Ge Kejiu (葛可久, 葛乾孫, 1305–1353), a prominent physician before his time, never left ginseng out when making decoctions like *dushentang* (獨參湯) or *baozhentang* (保眞湯) and instead criticized physicians for avoiding the use of ginseng, even in cases where it was essential, simply because their remuneration was meager.[46] Considering that the content of *Bencao gangmu* had already been widely distributed across Europe by the eighteenth century, the blatant warning on the excessive use of ginseng makes one wonder whether Europeans had been selective in their acceptance of information about ginseng because it was a rarity to them.

Notes

1 Anna Marie Roos, "Naturalia: The History of Natural History and Medicine in the Seventeenth Century," *Notes and Records of the Royal Society of London* 66, no. 4 (2012): 317.
2 Ray, *Historia Plantarum*, 1338.
3 Ray, *Historia Plantarum*, 1338.
4 Bernard Boivin, "La Flore du Canada en 1708: Étude d'un manuscrit de Michel Sarrazin et Sébastien Vaillant," *Études Littéraires* 10, no. 1–2 (1977): 281.
5 It was documented as "Ninzin seu singin species" in Latin and "espèce de ninzin ou ginseng" in French.
6 Sébastien Vaillant, "A New Genus of Plants, Call'd Aralistrum, of Which the Famous Nin-Zin or Ginseng of the Chinese, Is a Species," *Philosophical Transactions* 30 (1717–1719): 705–707.

7 Caroli Linnæi, *Species Plantarum, exhibentes plantas rite cognitas ad genera relatas, cum differentiis specificis, nominibus trivialibus, synonymis selectis, locis natalibus, secundum systema sexuale digestas*, Tomus II (Holmiæ [Stockholm], 1753), 1058.
8 As with *Genera Plantarum* (Leyden, 1737) and *Methodus Sexualis* (Leyden, 1737), *Critica Botanica* (Leyden, 1737) was also published through the support of Gronovius. William T. Stearn, "The Influence of Leyden on Botany in the Seventeenth and Eighteenth Centuries," *The British Journal for the History of Science* 1, no. 2 (1962): 154–155.
9 Quoted from Cook, "Linnaeus and Chinese Plants," 123.
10 Carolus Linnaeus, *Hortus Cliffortianus* (Amsterdam, 1737), 113.
11 Carolus Linnaeus, *Materia Medica, Liber I. de Plantis* (Holmiæ [Stockholm], 1749), 39.
12 The term "East Indies" covered a broad geographical range that included today's India, Sri Lanka, Indonesia, the Philippines, the Marianas, China, Japan, and Vietnam, while the term "Indies" even encompassed the whole of North and South America as well.
13 Cook, "Linnaeus and Chinese Plants," 123.
14 "Linnaeus to Osbeck, 10 August and 7 September, 1752" requoted from Carlo Hansen and Anne Fox Maule, "Pehr Osbeck's Collections and Linnaeus's Species Plantarum (1753)," *Botanical Journal of the Linnaean Society* 67, no. 3 (1973): 203.
15 Pehr Osbeck, *A Voyage to China and the East Indies*, trans. John Reinhold Forster, vol. 2 (London, 1771), 222–224.
16 Denis Diderot and Jean le Rond d'Alembert, eds., *Encyclopédie, Ou Dictionnaire Raisonné Des Sciences, Des Arts et Des Métiers* (Chicago, IL: University of Chicago Press, 2008), s.v. "ginseng," Robert Morrissey, ed., ARTFL Encyclopédie Project, Winter 2008 edition, University of Chicago, http://encyclopedie.uchicago.edu.access.yonsei.ac.kr:8080/.
17 John Abercrombie, *The Propagation and Botanical Arrangements of Plants and Trees*, vol. 2 (London, 1784), 456; J. Gordon, T. Dermer, and A. Thomson, *A Catalogue of Trees, Shrubs, Plants, Flower Roots, Seeds, &c. Sold by Gorden, Dermer, and Thomson, Seed and Nurserymen, at Mile End, Near London* (London, 1783), 68.
18 Akin, *Encyclopaedia: Or, a Dictionary of Arts, Sciences, and Miscellaneous Literature*, 689–690, [s. v. "ginseng"].
19 He was the younger brother of Christian Gottfried Daniel Nees von Esenbeck (1776–1858), a renowned, botanist, physician, and natural philosopher.
20 Theodor Friedrich Ludwig Nees von Esenbeck, *Plantae Medicinales* (Düsseldorf: Arnz & Co., 1833), 70.
21 Meyer assigned a scientific name to Korean ginseng in the following papers: *Rep. Pharm. Prakt. Chem.* Russ. 7 (1842), 524; *Bull. Phys.-Math. Acad Sci.* St.-Petersb. 1 (1843), 340.
22 Ulrike Schwemmer, *Wunderdroge Ginseng: Vom Einzug einer mythischen Heilpflanze in die moderne Medizin* (Wien-München: Franz Deuticke Verlag, 1998), 64.
23 Appleby, "Ginseng and the Royal Society," 137.
24 Robert Wittie, *Some Observations Made Upon the Root Called Nean, or Ninsing, Imported from the East-Indies* (London, 1680).
25 Wittie, *Some Observations Made Upon the Root Called Nean*, 3.
26 Wittie, *Some Observations Made Upon the Root Called Nean*, 6.
27 Wittie, *Some Observations Made Upon the Root Called Nean*, 7.
28 Vaillant, "A New Genus of Plants, Call'd Aralistrum, of Which the Famous Nin-Zin or Ginseng of the Chinese, Is a Species," 707.
29 Peter Kalm, *Travels into North America*, trans. John Reinhold Forster, vol. 3 (London, 1770), 116.
30 The Royal College of Physicians of London, *The New Pharmacopoeia of the Royal College of Physicians of London*, trans. Thomas Healdes, 3rd ed. (London, 1788), 30.
31 Franz Schwediauer, *Practical Observations on the More Obstinate and Inveterate Venereal Complaints* (London, 1784), 98–99.

32 George Wallis, *Annual Oration, Delivered March 8th, 1790 before the Medical Society* (London, 1790), 53–54.
33 Samuel Stearns, *The American Oracle: Comprehending an Account of Recent Discoveries in the Arts and Sciences* (London, 1791), 584.
34 Herman Boerhaave, *Boerhaave's Treatise of the Materia Medica* (London, 1739), 41.
35 John Aikin, *A Manual of Materia Medica* (Yarmouth, 1785), 80.
36 Smollett, *Humphry Clinker*, 123.
37 William Byrd, *The Writings of Colonel William Byrd of Westover in Virginia Esqr.*, ed. John Spencer Bassett (New York: Doubleday, Page & Co., 1901), 211.
38 William Lewis, *The New Dispensatory* (Dublin, 1782), 147.
39 William Cullen, *A Treatise of the Materia Medica*, vol. 2 (Edinburgh, 1789), 161.
40 Smollett, *Humphry Clinker*, 31.
41 Carl von Linné, *Miscellaneous Tracts Relating to Natural History, Husbandry, and Physick*, trans. Benjamin Stillingfleet (London, 1759), 179.
42 Foyster, *Letters Received by the East India Company*, 17–18.
43 Rochon, *A Voyage to Madagascar and the East Indies*, 460.
44 Hill, *A History of the Materia Medica*, 591.
45 Li, *Shinjuhae ponch'o kangmok*, 4:53.
46 Li, *Shinjuhae ponch'o kangmok*, 4:55.

PART 2

The World-System of Ginseng

5

KOREAN, CHINESE, AND JAPANESE POLICIES AND THE GINSENG TRADE

Since the seventeenth century, ginseng was a global commodity. On a global scale, the ginseng trade operated under a dual structure consisting of a core and a periphery. At the core was a solid circuit formed between Korea, China, and Japan over a long time through tribute and trade. At the periphery was a massive trade network connecting Asia, Europe, and the Americans that began to grow active in the sixteenth century. This peripherical circuit traversing the East and West experienced significant change in the late eighteenth century. America emerged as a leading force, edging past Britain that had maintained its hegemony in the East–West ginseng trade since the sixteenth century.

Tribute and Trade

Throughout the history of East Asia, ginseng was a valued resource often utilized as a diplomatic gift to neighboring countries. Even before the birth of Christ, ginseng from the Korean peninsula made its way through the four Han commanderies and into China. By the Three Kingdoms Period of Korea, records began to mention specific instances of sending ginseng to China.[1] In April 513, the twelfth year of King Muryŏng's reign, the Kingdom of Baekje sent ginseng to Emperor Wu (武帝) of Liang (梁). In 627, the ninth year of King Chinp'yŏng's reign, the Kingdom of Shilla had an envoy deliver ginseng as a gift to Emperor Gaozu (高祖) of Tang (唐). In 662, King Munmu sent 120 kilograms of ginseng as a gift at a time when Shilla was seeking to combine forces with Tang China. In 929, the fourth year of Emperor Mingzong's reign, Koryŏ's founder Wang Kŏn had a high-ranking official (Kwangp'yŏngshirang) lead fifty-two men to deliver a large tribute of metalwork art, ginseng, and pine nuts to the Later Tang. Ginseng was also traded through the *gongshi* (貢市) system, specifically at markets called *hushi* (互市) formed for the exchange of goods between Chinese

DOI: 10.4324/9781003286691-7

merchants and foreign envoys visiting China to pay tribute.[2] Korean ginseng was sent to Japan as well. In 739, King Mun of Parhae is said to have sent eighteen kilograms of ginseng to the temple Todaiji in Japan.[3]

Other people in Northeast Asia engaged in tributary trade with China as well. Ginseng was included in the list of tributary items the Mohe (靺鞨) and Khitans (契丹) offered to the Chinese imperial family. In *Bencao tujing* (本草圖經), published in 1061 during the Song dynasty, there is a passage indicating which kinds of ginseng were traded in China.

> Ginseng grows in Liaodong and the mountain valleys of Shangdang. Nowadays, it also grows in several areas of Hedong and Mount Tai. The ginseng from *quechang* (榷場) markets in Hebei and Min (閩), also known as Fujian Province, is called Shilla ginseng, which is inferior than Shangdang ginseng.[4]

The content of this passage became widely known once it was relayed in *Bencao gangmu*. The *quechang* markets mentioned in the passage refer to *hushi* markets installed at frontier areas during the Song, Liao, Jin, and Yuan dynasties.[5] As previously mentioned in Part 1, the comment about ginseng being produced in Shangdang or Fujian Province has lately been a subject of controversy among scholars. The suggestion that the Chinese did not distinguish ginseng from *dangshen* (黨蔘) is pitted against the argument that these areas may have produced ginseng in the past, but that it had subsequently become extinct due to its indiscriminate collection.[6]

Meanwhile, the term "Shilla ginseng" stands out from the passage. Judging from the context, Shilla ginseng doesn't appear to refer to ginseng from the Kingdom of Shilla, but to Korean ginseng in general traded at *hushi* markets in the border areas of China. As the seaborne ginseng trade initiated during the Wei and Jin dynasties grew substantial by the early years of the Tang dynasty, ginseng shipped from Korea came to be called Shilla ginseng. The term the Chinese used to refer to Korean ginseng in general thereby settled down as the name of an international commodity without bearing any geographical or periodical relevance to the Korean kingdom of Shilla.[7]

As the political situation grew stable and the economy developed by the middle of the Ming dynasty, the Chinese imperial court and upper class increasingly indulged in extravagance. Such circumstances led to a surge in demand for luxury goods including fur and ginseng. However, ginseng from the inland regions of Ming China was nearing depletion. Demand for the root therefore had to be satisfied by Liaodong or Korean ginseng procured through horse markets or *hushi* markets along the frontier. It was no surprise that ginseng turned out to be one of the most frequently traded items at the horse market the Ming court installed at Liaodong as well as the districts of Datong and Xuanfu in 1406.

Horse trade in Liaodong thus formed a close connection to the economy of inland China and had a major impact on the Ming dynasty's economy. The head of each Jurchen tribe, Han Chinese merchants, and influential people in Liaodong became preoccupied with profiting from ginseng and sable fur. The ginseng trade guaranteed huge profits, implying that a tremendous amount of ginseng flowed into China.[8] Ginseng and fur ultimately helped Nurhaci and his successors build the economic foundation necessary for establishing the Later Jin and Qing dynasties.[9]

Qing's Policies toward Ginseng

After conquering the Central Plain, the Qing dynasty tried to maintain the Manchu traditions of hunting and gathering, because they were what distinguished the Manchus from other ethnicities. Only people with permission from the state were granted access to ginseng, pearls, and sable fur. Those items were symbolic to the Manchus and therefore had to be gathered from lawful areas by authorized people.[10] Manchurian ginseng in particular not only symbolized Manchu traditions and cultures but was strictly controlled as a major source of fiscal income for the Qing state and imperial family. Kim Seon-min took note of the fact that it wasn't until the Qing dynasty that polices involving the ginseng industry were revised for the first time. The revision "showed that Qing China was certainly aware of ginseng's economic value."[11]

After the Qing dynasty conquered Beijing in 1644, the Manchus left Manchuria to settle down in Inner China. However, they instituted a *fengjin* (封禁) policy which closed Manchuria off to the Han Chinese and banned them from settling down or cultivating land in the region.[12] Unlike Inner China, Manchuria was governed by the Eight Banners. As supreme commanders of the region, the generals of Shengjing (盛京將軍) and Jilin (吉林將軍) actively took part in governing ginseng habitats. Guard posts were installed in their respective jurisdictions to control access and Eight Banner troops were dispatched regularly to patrol and arrest anyone who illegally gathered ginseng. Until the early years of the Qing dynasty, such patrols were limited to Shengjing since that was where the government officially collected ginseng, but during the Kangxi Emperor's reign, the patrol range was widened to include Jilin (吉林), Ningguta (寧古塔), Ussuri (烏蘇里), Boduna (伯都訥), and Sanxing (三姓), most likely to overcome fiscal deficits.[13]

Until the end of the seventeenth century, ginseng collection in Manchuria was mostly overseen by the Supervising Office (uheri da yamun 總管衙門) of Hunting and Fishing (Butha Ula 打牲烏拉).[14] Established at Jilin in 1657, this office under the immediate control of the Imperial Household Department was responsible for procuring all sorts of goods for the Qing court. The Eight Banner district in Shengjing dispatched people to collect ginseng. And whenever the emperor requested, the three upper banners (上三旗) were obligated to offer ginseng as tribute. Members of the imperial household were also authorized to collect ginseng, although the quota on the amount of ginseng and the number of people that could be mobilized for its collection differed depending on rank.

Despite such regulations, imperial nobles sent too many people to indiscriminately gather ginseng so that all nobles were completely banned from collecting ginseng in 1699.[15]

By the 1730s, the Qing dynasty began to commission merchants for the collection of ginseng. In exchange for being responsible for hiring ginseng gatherers, a merchant received six *liang* of ginseng per certification label, which was issued for ginseng of a quality worthy of government approval. This policy proved to be quite effective in boosting the collected amount of ginseng and some merchants profited tremendously from taking part in the ginseng business. The supply the state was able to secure, however, dropped sharply as the number of merchants obtaining certification labels gradually decreased and the value of such labels fell. In 1745, the Qing court installed official ginseng bureau offices in Shengjing, Jilin, and Ningguta to directly and exclusively manage the collection and taxation of ginseng for the central government. Unfortunately, officials at the bureau ended up colluding with merchants, allowing corruption to prevail once more.[16]

Yet, the Qing dynasty's administration of ginseng was being threatened by more than illegal collection and corruption. In fact, its greatest concern was the depletion of wild ginseng. As wild ginseng grew rare, people increasingly began to plant and cultivate ginseng, which was strictly prohibited and punished as severely as the illegal collection of ginseng. Such a policy was maintained out of fear that the price of wild ginseng monopolized by the state might drop if cultivated ginseng were to be distributed. By the mid-nineteenth century, the Qing dynasty's rule rapidly lost its centripetal force due to crises at home and abroad such as the Opium War and the Taiping Rebellion. Such circumstances made it difficult for the Qing court to maintain its control over Manchuria and maintain a monopoly over the ginseng market. In 1853, the Qing dynasty finally decided to abandon its control over the collection of ginseng.[17]

The Chosŏn–China Ginseng Trade

Based on the inflow of Korean ginseng in China, ginseng is likely to have been collected by the government in Korea since at least the Three Kingdoms period. The details of related government practices remain unknown due to a lack of historical records, which gives reason to suspect that initially the amount of ginseng requisitioned by the state was not sufficient to warrant discussion as a matter of internal affairs. Ginseng began to make a more frequent appearance in official records from the Koryŏ dynasty. By then, the government requisitioned ginseng not only for the royal household and diplomatic occasions but for medical institutions as well.[18]

Korean policies on ginseng were devised with the establishment of the Kingdom of Chosŏn. Similar to the Koryŏ dynasty, ginseng was collected as tax paid in kind. Local counties and townships were supposed to supply ginseng as a tax in kind to central government agencies such as the Ministry of Taxation (Hojo), the Medical Bureau (Naeŭiwŏn), the State Council (Ŭijŏngbu), the Office of Royal Family Affairs (Chongch'inbu), the Royal Secretariat (Chungch'ubu), and the Office of Merit Awards (Ch'unghunbu). Ginseng supplied as tax in kind was referred to as *kongsam* (貢蔘). The Ministry of Taxation determined the amount of *kongsam* each county or township would supply based on their respective capacities and collected *kongsam* every spring, fall, and winter.

The Chosŏn government tried its best to prevent the outflow of ginseng by limiting its disbursement to diplomatic occasions when it had to be offered as a gift or bestowed as a reward.[19] There is no way of knowing how much Korean ginseng slipped out of the country. Yet, it can be estimated that a total of around 480 kilograms of ginseng made its way to China during the reign of King Sejong as gifts delivered through regular and irregular missions to the Ming dynasty or presented to Ming envoys who visited Chosŏn. Compared to the amount sent to China, only one-tenth of that was sent to Japan for diplomatic purposes.[20] When the Kingdom of Chosŏn was established, the total amount of ginseng collected as tax is estimated to have been approximately 900 kilograms. About eight decades later, in the reign of King Sejo, that amount had increased more than twofold. And by King Sŏngjong's reign, areas where ginseng didn't grow were still burdened with having to supply ginseng as tax in kind.[21]

According to the geographical appendix to the *Annals of King Sejong* (Sejong shillok chiriji 世宗實錄地理志), 112 out of a total of 329 counties and townships produced ginseng or supplied it as tax in Chosŏn.[22] The annual amount of ginseng collected as tax nationwide was anywhere between approximately 600 and 1,140 kilograms in total. Because ginseng was a major tributary item, central government agencies not only directly managed the collection of ginseng paid as tax in kind, but were extremely strict about holding magistrates and governors accountable for any issues pertaining to the taxation of ginseng. The Chosŏn government strived to smoothly secure quality ginseng even if it meant having to reinforce policies. *Kongsam* supplied to the government was in the form of sun-dried wild ginseng. The high concentration of moisture in ginseng made it difficult to be preserved in its natural state and therefore it had to be dried and processed to suffice as a tax in kind.[23]

By the sixteenth century, the Kingdom of Chosŏn's ginseng policies confronted new circumstances. Domestically, *kongsam* was increasingly being paid by proxy or through officials or merchants who acted as brokers, which in turn expanded the trade in ginseng in the private sector. In principle, ginseng had been strictly prohibited from being traded privately since the establishment of Chosŏn.[24] Nevertheless, the tremendous demand for ginseng in Ming China gave rise to rampant smuggling as well as the private trade in ginseng along the border.

Another circumstance that brought significant change to the ginseng trade was the Imjin War of 1592. Upon the outbreak of the war, Ming troops and merchants came to Chosŏn as the Ming dynasty joined the war. Although Ming merchants were operating under special circumstances to procure military supplies, they were highly interested in and preoccupied with acquiring ginseng. Furthermore, trade was allowed at Chunggang (中江) around that time. Alongside Sosŏgang (小西江) and Samgang (三江), Chunggang referred to one of the three channels created by the many islands in the Amnok River that ran along the Chosŏn–China border. A trade market named after Chunggang was established at an island called Ŏjŏkto (於赤島) on Chunggang.[25] The market's establishment was an exception made under emergency conditions to procure provisions from Liaodong. Yet, Ming China turned out to be more interested in trading silver and ginseng through the market. In any case, the Chunggang market came to play a significant role in Chosŏn's trade with China.[26] After the Ming dynasty's fall in 1644, the market was reopened in 1647, the twenty-fifth year of King Injo's reign, at the Qing dynasty's request, so that trade between Korean and Chinese merchants could take place on a daily basis almost all year around.[27]

Meanwhile, between the reigns of King Kwanghae and King Injo, Ming envoys brought large volumes of ginseng out of Chosŏn. Such a practice was an extension of the practice Ming merchants originally engaged in when they came to Chosŏn during the Imjin War. The problem was that the demand for Chosŏn ginseng continued to rise as the Ming dynasty drew to an end. One record noted that

> until the first half of King Sŏnjo's reign, Ming envoys visiting Chosŏn were not greedy, but those who visited near the end of the Ming dynasty grew increasingly greedy to the point where Chosŏn's coffers were nearly emptied and such envoys were particularly interested in ginseng.[28]

Moreover, apart from the ginseng official envoys were gifted with, Chosŏn ginseng dealers and translators frequently acquired ginseng from areas that produced them and exported them through missions heading to China. In such cases, merchants from Kaesŏng played a key role in dealing ginseng.[29]

During the transition from Ming to Qing, the ginseng trade between Chosŏn and China began to experience unprecedented changes. The most significant among them was the creation of a ginseng distribution channel between Later Jin and Chosŏn. Later Jin envoys brought ginseng from Manchuria to Chosŏn and asked to trade it for items they needed such as cotton fabric. For the first time, Chosŏn found itself in the position of having to import ginseng. However, because the demand for ginseng always exceeded its supply, such Manchurian ginseng failed to impact the market in Chosŏn or constrict the activities of its ginseng dealers. Chosŏn's export of ginseng nevertheless arrived at a major turning point when the Qing dynasty issued a ban on trading ginseng with Chosŏn.[30]

Qing China's Policy toward Chosŏn Ginseng

After the Qing invasion of Chosŏn in 1636 led to King Injo's surrender, the Qing dynasty issued a ban on Chosŏn ginseng in 1637. Emperor Hong Taiji regarded ginseng as a product symbolic of Later Jin territory and therefore refused to acknowledge it as a specialty of Chosŏn. Ginseng was even excluded from the list of tributary items Chosŏn was to offer to the Qing dynasty.[31] This was a notable change considering that Chosŏn ginseng had long been a representative tributary item presented to Chinese emperors, important enough to be mentioned in the collected statutes of the Ming dynasty, *Da Ming Huidian* (大明會典). Exclusion from the list blocked the channel for exporting Chosŏn ginseng to China, at least officially. Subsequently, the foothold of Chosŏn ginseng dealers grew weak and made it difficult for the Chosŏn government to raise tax revenue from them. Needless to say, people who made their living from gathering ginseng also took a blow.[32]

To overcome the hardship it faced, the Chosŏn government considered exporting ginseng to Japan.[33] Until then, ginseng had officially been prohibited from being sold to the Japanese through their trading post in Chosŏn called *Waegwan*. It was nevertheless traded in secret, but not at a fair price. According to Yang Chŏng-p'il, discussions on trading ginseng with Japan took place at the Chosŏn court, such a move was seen as a way out of the predicament caused by the cessation of the export of ginseng to China. When ginseng trade with Japan at *Waegwan* eventually did become allowed, the demand for ginseng surged in Japan.[34] Chosŏn ginseng was able to satisfy that demand and by the first half of the eighteenth century, trade with Japan came to constitute the majority of Chosŏn's ginseng exports.

From the mid-seventeenth century, Chosŏn's trade in ginseng with Qing China began to recover its former volume. The bilateral trade mainly occurred through diplomatic missions, the Chunggang market, and *hushi* markets. Trade through diplomatic missions took place three to four times a year at Zhamen (柵門), Shenyang (瀋陽), and Beijing as Chosŏn missions traveled back and forth to Beijing. Through such trade opportunities, Chosŏn merchants mainly acquired silk and white thread, paying for them with ginseng and silver coins.[35] The export of ginseng to China and Japan flourished between the 1650s and 1670s to the point where Chosŏn ran into a domestic shortage of ginseng. This led to a drop in the quality of domestically distributed ginseng, prompting the Chosŏn government to consider discontinuing the export of ginseng.

Yet, because of the ginseng trade's economic significance, the Chosŏn government concluded that it would be impossible to ban trade with both China and Japan. The government ultimately chose to continue trading with Japan but ban ginseng from being exported to Qing China.[36] The reason for this decision was that the Japanese came to Chosŏn to acquire ginseng at *Waegwan* in Tongnae (present-day Pusan), which carried far less risk than conducting trade in the distant markets of Beijing that heavily depended on whether merchants from southern China were able to make the journey to the capital city. Export to Qing China could not, however, be entirely discontinued because ginseng was persistently smuggled out of Chosŏn. Once a smuggler was caught traveling with a winter solstice mission in 1702. The smuggler was carrying about forty-five kilograms of ginseng and 268 sable furs, which the district of Ŭijubu confiscated.[37] As smuggling grew frequent, the ban on trading ginseng with Qing China was lifted completely in 1707.[38]

The Chosŏn–Japan Ginseng Trade

Panax japonicus, the ginseng indigenous to Japan, was far less effective than Korean ginseng but still used for medicinal purposes among Japanese commoners.[39] The Japanese royal family and nobles, on the other hand, used the pricier ginseng from Korea. Although for a long time, the Chosŏn government tried to preserve its dwindling source of national wealth by heavily restricting the export of ginseng to Japan, the root continued to make its way over to Japan through private trade and smuggling. And when the channel of export to China became blocked in the mid-seventeenth century, Chosŏn's export of ginseng to Japan thrived.

The trade routes linking Korea, China, and Japan may have been closed off from time to time, but they still maintained a certain degree of vigor from the sixteenth century on. And along the way, the role of Chosŏn grew far more important between the mid-seventeenth and mid-eighteenth centuries. While Japan's diplomatic relations with Qing China were severed after the Imjin War, Japan and Chosŏn were able to normalize their relations in 1609. At the time, Japan relied on imports procured through Tsushima Domain in order to obtain necessary goods. Among such goods, Qing silk proved to be a tremendously profitable item and Chosŏn ginseng enjoyed an equal degree of popularity.

The Japanese demand for ginseng surged as medicine settled down as a part of common culture in the seventeenth century.[40] After the Imjin War, Chosŏn medical books such as *Tongŭi pogam* (東醫寶鑑) were introduced to Japan, leading to a greater awareness of and demand for Chosŏn ginseng.[41] As a result, Chosŏn merchants emerged as key brokers in trade between Chosŏn, China, and Japan. They acquired silver from exporting ginseng to Japan and used that silver to acquire silk from China, which they distributed in Chosŏn or exported to Japan for profit.

In early eighteenth-century Japan, a special silver called *ninjindaiōkogin* (人蔘代往古銀) was minted for the purpose of purchasing Chosŏn ginseng. Previously, silver had been abundant in Japan so there was no problem in exchanging relatively pure silver for ginseng. However, as Japanese silver production fell from the eighteenth century, less pure silver started to be circulated. The least pure silver coins in Japanese history were distributed around 1710. In 1711, silver coins with a purity as low as 20 percent were minted. The magistrate of Tongnae and Chosŏn merchants vehemently refused to exchange ginseng for such debased silver coins.[42] They even refused to accept Genroku silver minted in 1697, which had a silver percentage of 64 percent. This was the alleged reason Japan had to separately mint a special silver to be exchanged for Chosŏn ginseng (Figure 5.1).[43]

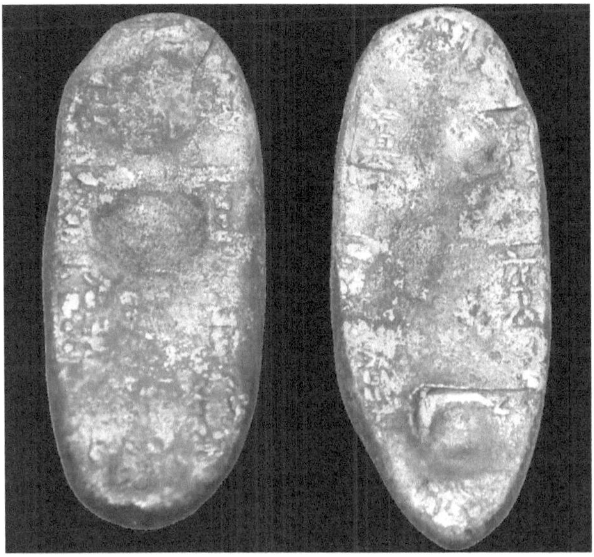

FIGURE 5.1 Ninjindaiōkogin.

Silver mined from all over Japan was assembled at Kyoto to mint *ninjindaiōkogin*, which passed through Tsushima Domain and became shipped to *Waegwan* in Tongnae where it was exchanged for Chosŏn ginseng and Chinese goods. Compared to the 30 percent pure silver coins circulated in Japan, *ninjindaiōkogin* had a purity of 80 percent, serving as a testament to how serious the Japanese were about importing Chosŏn ginseng.[44] On an annual basis, 5.3 tons of silver was required to mint *ninjindaiōkogin*, which was destined to stop by Chosŏn before heading to China alongside Chosŏn ginseng.[45] And missions typically served as opportunities to transport such silver to China and deliver Chinese goods to Tsushima Domain in Japan.

Winter solstice missions usually consisted of thirty-five official members; when including the number of merchants who accompanied them, the actual size of such missions amounted to nearly 300 people. Official members could take ginseng with them for private trade, and later on they were also allowed to carry 2,000–3,000 *taels* of silver per person. A thirty-five-member mission could therefore transport a total of 74,000 *taels* (2.8 tons) of silver. One such mission is known to have taken 80,000 *taels* (3 tons) of silver to China. Of course, a greater amount of silver than this was in fact circulated considering the amount exchanged through smuggling. Jou Kyung-chul has characterized such transfers of silver as "a massive current in which Chosŏn ginseng served as a medium between the world's greatest consumer of silver (China) and the second greatest consumer of silver (Japan)."[46]

Apart from what was consumed in Tsushima Domain, the ginseng imported from Chosŏn was mostly sent to Edo. Ginseng was commonly sold through a method called *yashiki uri* (屋敷売) which involved going door to door to target the privileged. *Ton'ya uri* (問屋売), or wholesale, was initiated in 1674 when Iseya Magohachi (伊勢屋孫八) became designated as a ginseng wholesaler. And the retail of ginseng began with the establishment of a ginseng guild called *ninjinza* (人参座).[47] When a shortage occurred in 1690 due to a drop in circulation over the previous year, people flocked to retailers' houses every morning to secure ginseng, which sometimes led to fights. This prompted the Edo bakufu to permit the processing and sale of Japanese ginseng. Apothecaries were allowed to sell Japanese ginseng but were prohibited from selling Chinese or Chosŏn ginseng.[48] While such measures showed just how high in demand ginseng was in Japan at the time, they were in fact adopted to prevent a mass outflow of silver.

By the reign of Tokugawa Ienobu (徳川家宣, r. 1709–1712), the sixth shogun of the Tokugawa shogunate, Japan was using 75 percent of its gold reserve and 25 percent of its silver reserve to import ginseng, thereby raising concerns of fiscal bankruptcy. To resolve the issue, the eighth shogun Tokugawa Yoshimune (徳川吉宗, r. 1716–1745) made up his mind to cultivate Chosŏn ginseng in Japan. He ordered the *daimyo* (feudal lord) of Tsushima Domain to bring ginseng seeds from Chosŏn and eventually succeeded in cultivating them, which will be covered in further detail in Part 3. This helped stabilize the supply and demand of ginseng by 1790, allowing Japan to deregulate the sales of ginseng and export Japanese-grown Chosŏn ginseng to China.[49] The volume of such export, however, remained limited.[50] For instance, 60 to 180 tons were exported in 1870, and the trade peaked at 300 tons around 1880, but plummeted to 36 tons the following year. The problem was that the Japanese had indiscriminately exported ginseng of inferior quality. As such, regardless of what was being cultivated domestically, ginseng from Chosŏn remained in constant demand among the Japanese.

Over the mid-to-late eighteenth century, the trade in ginseng between Chosŏn and Japan dwindled, mostly due to the depletion of their respective trade items. As ginseng grew scarce on the Korean peninsula beyond the mid-eighteenth century, Chosŏn struggled to satisfy its domestic demand. Around the same time, Japan ran out of silver, and copper emerged as its replacement. In the face of domestic shortages in their key export items, trade between Chosŏn and Japan naturally declined.

Overseas Trade of Red Ginseng

The method of boiling ginseng to process it was widely known in Chosŏn even before the seventeenth century. However, as ginseng started to be cultivated, the processing method changed to steaming instead of boiling ginseng before it was dried. This steam-processed ginseng came to be referred to as *hongsam* (紅蔘) or red ginseng. Because the Chosŏn government banned the export of ginseng, red ginseng was smuggled in small quantities. For official translators, red ginseng was an important means for them to cover their travel expenses on diplomatic missions to China. Instead of silver, the Chosŏn government had translators carry eight packets of ginseng referred to as *p'alp'o* (八包) on their way to Beijing to bear travel expenses and sell the rest for profit. Eight packets typically contained forty-eight kilograms of ginseng, which became replaced with red ginseng in 1797 during the twenty-first year of King Chŏngjo's reign. *P'alp'o* was also called *p'osam* (包蔘), which later came to refer to the processing and trade of red ginseng in general. As the volume of *p'osam* gradually increased, the right to deal it was granted not only to translators but to merchants in Kyŏngsŏng and Ŭiju as well.[51]

The rising volume of ginseng exports led to a surge in income and a subsequent increase in tax revenue. The Chosŏn government thereby began to recognize red ginseng as a major fiscal resource and officially approved its trade in 1797. Over the next two decades, the trade volume of red ginseng skyrocketed from 72 to 24,000 kilograms. In early nineteenth-century Chosŏn, the official price for 600 grams of red ginseng was 100 pieces of pure silver, enough to purchase 8,640–11,520 kilograms of rice. The same amount, however, was sold for at least 350 pieces to as much as 700 pieces of silver in China.[52]

In nineteenth-century Chosŏn, the trade of red ginseng was led by the merchants in Kaesŏng who dominated the cultivation and processing of red ginseng and the translators responsible for its export. Kaesŏng merchants and translators had to collaborate with merchants in Ŭiju who held the right to trade with Qing China. Since the 1850s, the annual amount of red ginseng Kaesŏng merchants exported to China was approximately 12,000 kilograms.[53] By then, Kaesŏng had turned into a bona fide center of ginseng farming. In 1896, 47 percent of ginseng farms in Chosŏn were located in the Kaesŏng area and that percentage rose to more than 92 percent by adding other farms in areas nearby such as Kŭmch'ŏn, Changdan, and P'ungdŏk.[54]

In the late nineteenth century, Western powers and Japan began to hasten their economic and political pillaging of Chosŏn. As a result, Chosŏn was half forced to sign treaties of trade with a number of countries and such treaties all included an article on red ginseng. The article would typically contain clauses that imposed a 15 percent tax on ginseng transactions and banned foreigners from purchasing and exporting red ginseng from Chosŏn. The 15 percent tax on red ginseng exports was an invaluable source of fiscal income for the Chosŏn government considering that the tariffs on imports and exports were between 5 and 6 percent at Chosŏn ports that gradually opened for trade like Pusan, Inch'ŏn, Mokp'o, and Yanghwajin.

In 1895, King Kojong established an office called *Naejangsa* (內臧司) to more efficiently manage the royal household's property. The office's name was changed to *Naejangwŏn* (內藏院) in 1899, and in December of that year a division called *Samjŏnggwa* (蔘政課) was newly created within the office to take charge of policies regarding ginseng and red ginseng. Since tributary missions to Qing China had been discontinued by then, *Naejangwŏn* turned into an organ preoccupied with collecting taxes on ginseng and processing and selling red ginseng. The domestic and overseas sale of red ginseng hence became a state enterprise run by *Naejangwŏn*. This change did not sit well with those in the ginseng business in Kaesŏng who had been expanding ginseng farms and supplying red ginseng to the government to build up capital. When they were paid far less than expected for the ginseng they had submitted to *Naejangwŏn*, they began to resist.[55] However, there was another problem at hand: the Japanese were coming after Chosŏn's ginseng.

The Japanese who came to Korea after it opened its ports were obsessed with acquiring ginseng so as to yield huge profits from its export to Qing China or Japan. At first, Japanese settlers smuggled small quantities of red ginseng through Inch'ŏn and exported them to China via retailers in Nagasaki. Once they had a taste of the profits from trading red ginseng, they began to scale up their operations by processing red ginseng themselves. However, when secretly processing small batches failed to satisfy their demand, they set out to plunder ginseng farms in Chosŏn.[56]

Some Japanese colluded with robbers to dig ginseng and afterward claimed they had paid for the stolen ginseng. Others had imposters pose as ginseng farm owners in order to acquire ginseng fields at cheap prices on their behalf. One of the worst cases was when nearly 100 armed Japanese ruffians joined forces to raid an entire ginseng farm of 3,300 square meters overnight. Ginseng growers in Kaesŏng demanded that the Japanese be punished for their illegalities, but government officials instead cast suspicion on ginseng growers who suffered damage and tried to arrest and punish them for secretly trading ginseng with the Japanese. This prompted ginseng growers in Kaesŏng to take action collectively, which developed into the so-called Kaesŏng Revolt.[57]

Such fierce resistance caused the *Naejangwŏn* director Yi Yong-ik to seek an agreement with ginseng growers. *Naejangwŏn* would offer loans to cover the cost of cultivating ginseng, grant the freedom to sell and trade white (dried) ginseng, and allow them to supply *Naejangwŏn* with fresh ginseng used to make red ginseng. The processing and sale of red ginseng, however, was to remain under *Naejangwŏn*'s strict supervision.[58] In 1900, Yi Yong-ik signed a seven-year contract with the unlimited partnership company Mitsui bussan (三井物産合名會社) in Japan to sell red ginseng on consignment. According to the contract, Mitsui bussan was to be paid a fee for storing and transporting red ginseng to be exported to China. However, Japan pressured *Naejangwŏn* into granting Mitsui bussan the right to exclusively handle all red ginseng exports.

In 1908, the second year of King Sunjong's reign, the Empire of Korea promulgated "Law No. 14" instituting a state monopoly on red ginseng. The license to produce red ginseng was thus transferred to the Division of Ginseng Policies within the Ministry of Finance's Taxation Bureau. Under the state monopoly system, the Korean government held a tight rein on the ginseng industry[59] as it sought to boost the production of ginseng by designating special zones for its cultivation.[60] After Japan's annexation of Korea in 1910, red ginseng was placed under the purview of the Japanese Government-General of Korea's Monopoly Bureau.[61] Mitsui bussan was granted the exclusive right to export red ginseng and after the 1930s, it traded the root of ginseng, red ginseng, and ginseng-based products manufactured by Kaesŏng merchants such as soap and red ginseng extract. Mitsui bussan's primary export item was red ginseng, which was exported mainly to China, and partly to Southeast Asian countries and the United States. While Mitsui bussan was assigned approximately 1,560 kilograms of ginseng in the 1910s, the amount jumped to approximately 36,000 kilograms by 1929, to be sold mostly in the Chinese market. In China, 600 grams of Korean ginseng was sold at around 150 yuan on average in 1916, whereas the same amount was sold at around 20 yuan for American ginseng, around 8 yuan for Manchurian Kwantung ginseng, and around 5 yuan for Japanese ginseng.[62]

Publication of Ninjinshi, *Liberation, and the Korean War*

In April 1931, the Japanese Government-General of Korea's Monopoly Bureau commissioned Imamura Tomo (今村鞆) to write a book about the history of ginseng.[63] A former police official who served in Japan after graduating from the Japanese National Police Academy, Imamura was originally hired by Governor-General Itō Hirobumi to serve as a police chief in the Korean provinces of North Ch'ungch'ŏng and Kangwŏn. Imamura went on to work as the governor of Jeju Island and retired after serving as a *Yiwangjik* secretary (head of general affairs) under the chief magistrate of Wŏnsan. During his time in public service, he developed an interest in the history and folklore of Chosŏn and authored a number of writings on these subjects. Apart from his intimate knowledge of Chosŏn's history, Imamura is likely to have been entrusted with the task of writing a history of ginseng partly because of his experience as an *Yiwangjik* secretary. *Yiwangjik* was an office created to handle all of Chosŏn's royal household affairs and therefore held a large collection of records involving ginseng.[64]

Beginning with the publication of volume 7, *Reflections on Ginseng Names* (Shin meii kō hen), in August 1934, Imamura authored the seven-volume series *Ninjinshi* over the course of nine years until volume 1, *Thoughts on Ginseng* (Ninjin shisōhen), was published in March 1940. *Ninjinshi* turned out to be a masterpiece, offering encyclopedic knowledge about Oriental ginseng based on records of Korean, Chinese, Japanese histories as well as botanical, medical, pharmacological, and agricultural sources and even covered myths and legends involving ginseng. The reason the Japanese Government-General of Korea launched a publication project of such magnitude was to build an intellectual basis for the efficient management of Korean ginseng, which was an important resource to Japan.

Ninjinshi therefore propounded arguments and interpretations that justified Japanese aggression as historically inevitable, suggesting that a resource as important as ginseng should be managed by Japan. For instance, it argued that "the 139 volumes of *Koryŏsa* [*History of Koryŏ*] and the annals of former Chosŏn kings amounting to nearly 1,300 volumes are records of sin showing how brutal their misrule was," adding that, "such exploitative tendencies have been heavily aimed at ginseng."[65] This lack of historical neutrality and objectivity is why *Ninjinshi* tends to be regarded as a collection of sources rather than an accurate historical account.

The year the Japanese Government-General of Korea commissioned Imamura to write *Ninjinshi* in 1931, Japanese aggression toward China took a more serious turn with the Mukden Incident (Manchurian Incident). Mitsui bussan's export of red ginseng to China had already begun to suffer around 1930 under the Great Depression, coupled with the anti-Japan movement in China. As red ginseng piled up in its warehouses, Mitsui bussan started to broaden its market to Korea, supplying red ginseng extract at low prices to its Korean factory workers. Once Manchukuo entered a period of stability in the mid-1930s, the company's red ginseng exports bounced back and by the late 1930s, Mitsui bussan directly exported 1,800 kilograms of white ginseng and 78 kilograms of red ginseng to the United States. The company's sale of red ginseng, however, met an abrupt end as the company withdrew from Korea upon its liberation, leaving behind a massive stock of red ginseng in Kaesŏng.[66]

Even while Korea was under American military rule after its liberation, a considerable amount of ginseng was grown in farms at Kaesŏng. However, the Korean War brought tremendous change to the domestic ginseng industry. Ginseng growers who fled south lost everything when Kaesŏng became North Korean territory. After relocating to Puyŏ in South Ch'ungch'ŏng Province in March 1951, the Kaesŏng Branch for Ginseng Monopoly sought for a way to sustain the cultivation of ginseng. The most urgent task at hand was to secure quality ginseng seeds. Seeds were available in South Korea from areas like P'unggi and Kŭmsan, but they were mainly white ginseng seeds, whereas experts considered Kaesŏng ginseng the best for producing red ginseng.

South Korean authorities obtained information that a large batch of seeds was being kept at Mangp'o, Kaep'ung County, under the North Korean Army's control. Three staff members of the Kaesŏng Branch for Ginseng Monopoly and three ginseng merchants formed a task force for the retrieval of the ginseng seeds. In late February 1952, South Korean marines covered the task force as it set off from Kanghwado and infiltrated Mangp'o. Despite the shots Chinese troops fired, they were able to escape without suffering any casualties. With four sacks of ginseng seeds, they boarded a ship at Kanghwado and stopped by Inch'ŏn before arriving at Puyŏ.[67] After the Korean War ended, a modern red ginseng factory called Koryŏ insamch'ang was built in 1956, right beside the spot where the Buddhist Chŏngnimsa Temple had once stood.[68]

Notes

1 Yang and Yŏ, "Samguk-Shilla t'ongilgi insam saengsan kwa taeoegyoyŏk," *Ŭisahak* 13, no. 2 (2004): 177–197.
2 Wang, ed., *Zhongguo renshen*, 32–33.

3 Imamura Tomo 今村鞆, *Insamsa* 人蔘史 [History of Ginseng], trans. Koh Seungtae 고승태, vol. 2: Insam chŏngch'ip'yŏn 인삼정치편 [Ginseng Politics] (Yŏngju: Dongyang University 동양대학교, 2015), 15–198.
4 Li Shizhen, *Shinjuhae ponch'o kangmok*, 4:45.
5 The *quechang* markets were created to facilitate trade between Koryŏ and northern peoples such as the Khitans or the Jurchens and merchants were required to pay tax in order to take part in external trade at such markets. Wang, *Zhongguo renshen*, 33.
6 Yang and Yŏ, "'Chungguk insam' ŭi shilch'e e taehan pip'anjŏk koch'al," *Ŭisahak* 12, no. 2 (2003): 144–166; Yang and Yŏ, "'Chosŏn insam' ŭi kiwŏn e taehayŏ," *Ŭisahak* 13, no. 1 (2004): 1–19; Song, "Shilun Zhongguo Guadi Renshen de Zhuchangu."; Song and Zhan, "Zhongguo yaoyong renshen shigang."
7 Wang, *Zhongguo renshen*, 33.
8 According to *Mingdai liaodong candang* (明遼東殘檔), the Haixi Jurchen made twenty-six trips to the passes of Guangshun and Zhenbei between July 1583 and March 1584 and engaged in trade at markets where they sold a total of 1,733.75 kilograms of ginseng.
9 Yang Chŏng-p'il 양정필, "17–18 segi chŏnban insam muyŏk ŭi pyŏndong kwa Kaesŏng sangin ŭi hwaltong" 17–18세기 전반 인삼무역의 변동과 개성상인의 활동 [Changes in the Ginseng Trade and Operations of Gaesung Merchants in the 17th to Early 18th Century], *T'amna munhwa* 탐라문화 55 (2017): 118–119.
10 Jonathan Schlesinger, "The Qing Invention of Nature: Environment and Identity in Northeast China and Mongolia, 1750–1850" (Doctoral dissertation, Harvard University, 2012).
11 Kim, "17–18 segi ch'ŏngdae insam chŏngch'aek ŭi pyŏnhwa," *Chungguk'akpo*, no. 74 (2015): 406.
12 Richard Edmonds, "The Willow Palisade," *Annals of the Association of American Geographers* 69, no. 4 (1979): 599–621.; Wang Jingze 王景澤, "Du Qingdai fengjin dongbei zhengce de zairenshi" 對淸代封禁東北政策的再認識 [A Reexamination of Qing China's Fengjin Policy toward Its Northeastern Areas], *Dongbei shida xuebao* 東北師大學報 166 (1997); Zhang, "Liutiaobian, yinpiao yu qingchao dongbei fengjin xinlun."
13 Imamura Tomo 今村鞆, *Insamsa* 人蔘史 [History of Ginseng], trans. Koh Seungtae 고승태, vol. 1: Insam sasangp'yŏn 인삼사상편 [Thoughts on Ginseng] (Yŏngju: Dongyang University 동양대학교, 2015), 82–83.
14 The Manchu word *butha* means to hunt and gather animals, fish, and herbs. *Ula* is the Manchurian name of a place near Jilin that was used during the Qing period. Butha Ula yamun therefore refers to the office that oversaw hunting and gathering in Jilin. Kim Seon-min 김선민, "Manjujok kwa insam" 만주족과 인삼 [The Manchus and Ginseng in the Qing Period], *Insam munhwa* 인삼문화 1 (2019): 20.
15 Tong Dong 佟冬, ed., *Zhongguo dongbeishi* 中國東北史 [A History of Northeastern China], vol. 4 (Changchun: Jilin wenshi chubanshe 吉林文史出版社, 1998), 1577–1578; Kim, "Manjujok kwa insam," 21–22.
16 Kim, "17–18 segi ch'ŏngdae insam chŏngch'aek ŭi pyŏnhwa," 414–415.
17 Kim, "17–18 segi ch'ŏngdae insam chŏngch'aek ŭi pyŏnhwa," 421.
18 Imamura, *Insamsa*, 2015, 2:326–329.
19 Park, "Sŏnjojo ŭi taemyŏng insam muyŏk kwa insam sangin," 127.
20 Park, "Chosŏn chŏn'gi ŭi insam chŏngch'aek kwa insam yut'ong," 226.
21 Imamura, *Insamsa*, 2015, 2:336–337.
22 Refer to Table 1 in Yang and Yŏ, "Samguk- Shilla t'ongilgi insam saengsan kwa taeoegyoyŏk," 185.
23 Park, "Chosŏn chŏn'gi ŭi insam chŏngch'aek kwa insam yut'ong," 205–208.
24 Park, "Chosŏn chŏn'gi ŭi insam chŏngch'aek kwa insam yut'ong," 233.

25 Lee Chul-sung 이철성, "Kaesŏng insam i wae yumyŏnghage toeŏssŭlkka" 개성 인삼이 왜 유명하게 되었을까? [How Did Kaesŏng Ginseng Earn Its Fame?], *Naeirŭl yŏnŭn yŏksa* 내일을 여는 역사 13 (2003): 89.
26 Yang, "17–18 segi chŏnban insam muyŏk ŭi pyŏndong kwa Kaesŏng sangin ŭi hwaltong," 112–14.
27 Park, "Sŏnjojo ŭi taemyŏng insam muyŏk kwa insam sangin," 137–138.
28 Imamura, *Insamsa*, 2015, 2:69–70.
29 Yang, "17–18 segi chŏnban insam muyŏk ŭi pyŏndong kwa Kaesŏng sangin ŭi hwaltong," 116.
30 Yang, "17–18 segi chŏnban insam muyŏk ŭi pyŏndong kwa Kaesŏng sangin ŭi hwaltong," 119–120.
31 Kim, "Insam kwa kangyŏk," 251.
32 Yang, "17–18 segi chŏnban insam muyŏk ŭi pyŏndong kwa Kaesŏng sangin ŭi hwaltong," 121.
33 Yang, "17–18 segi chŏnban insam muyŏk ŭi pyŏndong kwa Kaesŏng sangin ŭi hwaltong," 122.
34 Yang, "17–18 segi chŏnban insam muyŏk ŭi pyŏndong kwa Kaesŏng sangin ŭi hwaltong," 121–122.
35 Lee, "Kaesŏng insam i wae yumyŏnghage toeŏssŭlkka," 89–91.
36 Yang, "17–18 segi chŏnban insam muyŏk ŭi pyŏndong kwa Kaesŏng sangin ŭi hwaltong," 124.
37 Entry for March 9, 1702 in *Pibyŏnsa dŭngnok* (備邊司謄錄), or *Records of the Border Defense Council.* Yang, "17–18 segi chŏnban insam muyŏk ŭi pyŏndong kwa Kaesŏng sangin ŭi hwaltong," 128.
38 Yang, "17–18 segi chŏnban insam muyŏk ŭi pyŏndong kwa Kaesŏng sangin ŭi hwaltong," 130.
39 *Panax japonicus* has a thin, long, bamboo-shaped rhizome and its full scientific name is *Panax japonicum* C. A. Mey. f. typic-um Nakai.
40 Imamura Tomo 今村鞆, *Insamsa* 人蔘史 [History of Ginseng], trans. Koh Seungtae 고승태, vol. 3: Insam kyŏngjep'yŏn 인삼경제편 [Ginseng Economy] (Yŏngju: Dongyang University 동양대학교, 2012), 238.
41 Lee, "Kaesŏng insam i wae yumyŏnghage toeŏssŭlkka," 87–88.
42 Imamura, *Insamsa*, 2012, 3:324.
43 Prior to Genroku silver, Japan used Keicho coins, minted in 1601 with a silver percentage of 80 percent, in order to trade with Chosŏn. Because it proved to be tricky for Chosŏn officials to determine the exact percentage of silver in Genroku silver, they argued that the percentage was somewhere between 60 and 62 and eventually acknowledged the percentage as 63. The conversion ratio for Keicho coins to Genroku silver therefore became eighty to sixty-three instead of sixty-four, a disadvantage the Japanese had no choice but to accept since they couldn't afford to further delay their trade with Chosŏn. Jou Kyung-chul 주경철, *Taehanghae shidae: Haesang p'aengch'ang kwa kŭndae segye ŭi hyŏngsŏng* 대항해 시대: 해상팽창과 근대세계의 형성 [The Age of Discovery: Maritime Expansion and the Formation of the Modern World] (Seoul: Seoul National University Press 서울대학교 출판부, 2008), 269.
44 Lee, "Kaesŏng insam i wae yumyŏnghage toeŏssŭlkka," 88.
45 Tashiro Kazui, "Exports of Japan's Silver to China via Korea and Changes in the Tokugawa Monetary System during the Seventeenth and Eighteenth Centuries," in *Precious Metals, Coinage and the Changes of Monetary Structures in Latin-America, Europe and Asia*, ed. Eddy van Cauwenberghe (Leuven: Leuven University Press, 1989), 102–104.
46 Jou, *Taehanghae shidae*, 269–270.
47 Chung Ha-mie 정하미, "Pŏmnyŏngjip Ohure gaki shūsei e nat'anan Edo makpu ŭi insam chŏngch'aek" 법령집, '어촉서집성(御觸書集成)'에 나타난 에도막부의 '인삼' 정책 [The Edo Shogunate Policy about Ginseng Showed in Statute Ohuregaki Syusei], *Pigyo ilbonhak* 비교일본학 39 (2017): 179–196.

48 Imamura, *Insamsa*, 2015, 1:87.
49 Chang Il-moo, *Han'guk insam sanŏpsa*, 1:265–271.
50 Chang Il-moo, *Han'guk insam sanŏpsa*, 1:511.
51 Imamura, *Insamsa*, 2015, 2:440–442.
52 Lee, "Kaesŏng insam i wae yumyŏnghage toeŏssŭlkka," 96.
53 Yang, "Taehanjegukki Kaesŏng chiyŏk samŏp pyŏndong kwa samp'omin ŭi taeŭng," 134.
54 Lee, "Kaesŏng insam i wae yumyŏnghage toeŏssŭlkka," 96.
55 Han'guk insamsa p'yŏnch'an wiwŏnhoe 한국인삼사 편찬위원회, *Han'guk Insamsa* 한국인삼사 [History of Korean Ginseng], vol. 1 (Seoul: Han'guk insamsa p'yŏnch'an wiwŏnhoe 한국인삼사 편찬위원회, 2002), 447–448.
56 Imamura, *Insamsa*, 2015, 2:456–457.
57 Yang, "Taehanjegukki Kaesŏng chiyŏk samŏp pyŏndong kwa samp'omin ŭi taeŭng," 139–145.
58 Chang, *Han'guk insam sanŏpsa*, 2018, 1:448.
59 Yun, "Ilche ŭi kyŏngje sut'al kwa Kaesŏng ŭi samŏp," 96–98, 105–110.
60 A total of eight counties were designated as special zones for ginseng cultivation including Kaesŏng-gun, Changdan-gun, and P'ungdŏk-gun in Kyŏnggi Province, Kimch'ŏn-gun, T'osan-gun, P'yŏngsan-gun, Sŏhŭng-gun in Hwanghae Province as well as Pongsan-gun, which was included later on.
61 Chang, *Han'guk insam sanŏpsa*, 2018, 1:493.
62 Yun, "Ilche ŭi kyŏngje sut'al kwa Kaesŏng ŭi samŏp," 109.
63 Imamura Tomo 今村鞆, *Ninjinshi* 人蔘史 [History of Ginseng], 7 vols. (Keijō: Chōsen sōtokufu senbaikyoku 朝鮮總督府 專賣局, 1934).
64 Imamura Tomo 今村鞆, *Insam shinch'o, insamsa* [The Mystical Herb Ginseng and Its History], trans. Yang Chŏng-p'il 양정필, vol. 1, Han'guk kŭndae minsok illyuhak charyo taegye 21 한국근대 민속·인류학자료대계 21 (Seoul: Minsogwŏn 민속원, 2009), 6–10.
65 Imamura, *Insamsa*, 2012, 3:57.
66 Chang, *Han'guk insam sanŏpsa*, 2018, 1:461.
67 Im Hyŏn-yŏng 임현영, "Namgigo ship'ŭn iyagidŭl" 남기고 싶은 이야기들 [Stories Worth Preserving], *Joongang Ilbo* 중앙일보, June 24, 1974; Museum exhibits at the Puyŏ factory of Koryŏ insamch'ang.
68 Koryŏ insamch'ang relocated from Buyeo-eup to nearby Nae-ri of Gyuam-myeon in 1978. Today, Korea Ginseng Corporation's Koryŏ insamch'ang is the world's largest red ginseng factory, with its 72,727 square meter facility sprawled across a 185,124 square meter site.

6

THE EAST INDIA COMPANY'S PRIVATE TRADE IN GINSENG

An Item for "Country Trade"

After a Portuguese fleet led by Vasco da Gama (1469–1524) landed in Calicut along the western coast of India in 1498, others in Europe such as the Dutch and British began to venture across the Indian Ocean and into the waters of East Asia. Europeans thus formed a network of maritime trade that entailed adventure, exploration, and plunder. What they were after was Oriental spices that could bring them huge profits.[1] The range of spices at the time, however, was quite broad. Spices and medicinal herbs were interchangeable categories, and the distinction between food and medicine was so vague that even dye or wax could fall under either category. What they all had in common was that they were difficult to procure in Europe or were highly profitable items.

As much as long-distance trade offered tremendous profits, it also carried serious risks. To engage in long-distance trade more efficiently, British merchants were granted a charter from Queen Elizabeth I in 1600 to found the East India Company. Meanwhile, several Dutch companies were already engaged in trade in the East Indies, and in 1602, six of them merged to found the Dutch East India Company. The Danish East India Company was chartered in 1616, and in 1664 the French East India Company was chartered by King Louis XIV. Similar companies were subsequently established in Scotland, Germany, Sweden, and Prussia. Among the numerous companies, the Dutch and British East India companies were at the forefront of seventeenth-century trade in the East Indies.

As mentioned in Part 1, the East India Company began to bring East Asian ginseng into Europe from the early seventeenth century. Yet, the company seems to have considered ginseng an item of "country trade" than of long-distance trade. "Country trade" referred to transactions confined to Asia: purchasing an item from one region, selling it in a different region, and using the earnings to

DOI: 10.4324/9781003286691-8

purchase another local item to be resold elsewhere in Asia. This was a major mode of business unique to the East India Companies in the seventeenth century, which is why maintaining such a commercial network was most important. Unlike the Portuguese trading-port empire built upon plunder and duties, country trade proved to be key to the long-term commercial success the Dutch and British East India companies enjoyed overseas.

Scholars like Pratik Chakrabarti have recently criticized that the discussions on the European expansion overseas have been too preoccupied with its economic aspect and pointed out the need to explore the effects of empire in the realms of science, particularly medicine. Between the sixteenth and nineteenth centuries, the use of new medicinal ingredients surged in Europe and many of them had come from Asia or the Americas. In the seventeenth century alone, the import of medicinal ingredients increased at least twenty-five-fold in Europe and some of them, like the root of ipecacuanha, a South American plant belonging to the Rubiaceae family, gained tremendous popularity in Britain for its use as an emetic or purgative. Information on such new medicinal ingredients were typically obtained while conducting country trade.[2]

The East India Company recruited not only a massive number of sailors but also medical professionals.[3] Throughout the long voyages and sojourns abroad, physicians traveling with the crew, British soldiers stationed in India and other regions, and locally hired mercenaries often found themselves in situations where they had to use local ingredients to provide medical treatment. This naturally turned them into agents who introduced a diversity of new medicinal ingredients to the West. And the place where vast numbers of Eastern and Western medicinal ingredients and spices could usually be found were Asian markets called bazaars, which also happened to be key places of country trade for the East India Company.

These circumstances led to the emergence of "bazaar medicine," meaning medicine that could be procured locally by those engaging in colonial activities. Such medicines originated from all over the world: gum arabic from Egypt, aloe and camphor from East and Southeast Asia (to treat itching), licorice from West Asia, smilax glabra or China root from East Asia (to treat purulent inflammation), Columba root from Mozambique in southeast Africa, and dragon's blood from Java. Bazaar medicine was physical proof that East–West trade routes existed worldwide at the time. Physicians aboard East India Company ships even made quite a bit of extra income through country trade at bazaars in each region.[4] Ginseng was a precious commodity in country trade, which was highly popular at southeast Asian trade points during the seventeenth century.

There are records indicating that ginseng was traded through country trade routes. Carl Peter Thunberg (1743–1828) was a Swedish botanist who visited Japan while working as a physician for the Dutch East India Company. According to Thunberg, "unicorn's horn" and ginseng imported via private trade were particularly popular in Japan.

> Ninsi-root, called Som by the Chinese, likewise sells very high. It grows in the northern parts of China, particularly in Korea. A bastard kind, brought from America, perhaps the Ginseng root, is often brought hither by the Dutch; but this is strictly prohibited by government, lest it should be fraudulently sold for the genuine sort.[5]

The reference to American ginseng as a "bastard kind" hints at its reputation at the time in Europe. Thomas Maurice (1754–1824) was an Orientalist particularly knowledgeable in the history of India. In a book he wrote on Indian antiquities, Maurice mentioned that "they have always set a very high value on the invigorating root of ginseng, and other of similar quality, and have been but too happy in finding out a great variety."[6] This shows that the East India Companies transported various kinds of ginseng throughout Asia and that ginseng was widely known in India.

India was not alone in its desire for ginseng. A report published in Britain in 1793 expressed the dissatisfaction in having to rely on goods supplied by the Chinese after trade between Cochinchina (southern Vietnam) and Japan became discontinued and suggested that Britain actively develop new trade channels. Ginseng was among the major items Cochinchina imported, besides paper, silk, and copper.[7] Cochinchina was a major exporter of sea swallow nests used to make bird's nest soup, a world-famous delicacy that required ginseng as an ingredient. For this reason, ginseng often makes an appearance in mentions of bird's nests in historical sources.

Although the volume is likely to have been less than that exchanged through country trade, ginseng does seem to have been distributed in Europe. A Dutch record from the seventeenth century mentions that ginseng "was very dear, and sold in Holland for twenty-five florins a pound."[8] As aforementioned in Part 1, ginseng was a rare gift exchanged among dignitaries in Britain. In the *Annual Ledgers of the Inspector-General of the Customs*, which was a port book listing imported items for the purpose of imposing duties, the British classified ginseng as a medical item free of duty.[9] However, because ginseng was bought and sold through private trade, records from seventeenth-century Europe reveal no trace of exactly how much ginseng was imported.

The Private Trade in Ginseng

Among the items traded by the East India Company, ginseng was classified as an item of "private trade." At the time, private trade commonly referred to the privilege of being able to personally trade a certain amount of goods transported by a merchant vessel. While such a privilege was typically granted only to a ship's captain and the supercargo in charge of overseeing the cargo on behalf of the ship's owner, company officials and crewmen also engaged in private trade all the time to supplement their insufficient income. Some company officials stationed at trade posts went as far as to use their position to engage in larger volumes of private trade. One such official even managed to amass a sizable fortune not long after the company's establishment and abandoned his position to return home.[10] In 1628, the East India Company threatened to confiscate the cargo of any crewman who exceeded their shipping limit, but it failed to completely stop them from engaging in private trade. The company's board of directors eventually had to relent and partially allow private trade in 1635.

Goods allowed to be privately traded were expensive and rare items like jewels, musk, and ambergris that could deliver huge profits. Ginseng also fell under the same category. Another reason the East India Company allowed the private trade in ginseng was because it wasn't fit to be traded in large volumes. Not only was ginseng difficult to procure but trading it in large batches bore the risk of driving down its price. In this sense, the British were clever merchants who already knew the secret to trading ginseng. For its private trade, they selectively procured a small amount of the finest quality. This commercial principle stood in stark contrast to the practice of Americans who supplied China with far too much American ginseng, forcing them to accept bargain prices for their goods.

The East India Company was not, however, the only importer of ginseng in Europe. In Britain, ships other than those of the East India Company were banned from sailing between the Cape of Good Hope and Cape Horn for the purpose of trade. The Dutch government only allowed the Dutch East India Company to trade in areas between the east side of the Cape of Good Hope and the west side of the Strait of Magellan. These were typical cases in which the state granted exclusive rights to an individual company. The reason for doing so was to avoid excessive competition over Asian markets. When competition left traders on the brink of being ruined altogether, the state attempted to establish order by granting exclusive rights and patents.

Thanks to its exclusive rights, the East India Company's ships gained a reputation for their high freight charges. This often induced private traders to turn to ships from other European countries or America to export goods, which was referred to as 'clandestine trade' at the time. Such clandestine trade is also likely to have been involved in the importing of ginseng. Regardless of whether it was supplied through the East India Company or clandestine trade, the ginseng Europe imported around this time was Korean ginseng. Until the mid-to-late seventeenth century, Korean ginseng was shipped to Japan before arriving in Europe, and as China opened its ports in the late seventeenth century, European ships began to directly acquire ginseng in China.

Britain initiated trade with China in 1684. After quelling rebellions to restore the Ming dynasty led by Zheng Chenggong (鄭成功), the Qing dynasty issued an edict announcing that it would lift the ban on foreign trade and open its waters. Private ships were thereafter allowed to set sail from China to engage in trade overseas, and five ports, including those in Canton (Guangzhou), Amoy (Xiamen), and Ningbo, were opened to accept merchant ships from abroad. Britain obtained approval from the Qing dynasty to trade silk, tea, and chinaware in Canton. By the eighteenth century, a greater number of European ships came calling. The rising demand for tea was their foremost reason for coming to China. Throughout the seventeenth century, Europe mainly imported pepper and spices, and while its import of fabrics like calico and silk gradually increased, the import of coffee and tea particularly surged by the eighteenth century. On the other hand, Europe had little to export to China, at least until American ginseng became available.

As soon as ginseng was discovered on the North American continent in the early eighteenth century, British, French, and even Swedish vessels began to ship it to China. North American ginseng would be loaded in Montreal or Quebec and sent to European ports along the Atlantic coast where it would be handed over to the East India Company to be delivered to Canton. The reason such a long detour was necessary was because the East India Company held the exclusive right to trade along the routes to China. Despite the detour and cumbersome resale process, the Canadian export of ginseng supposedly raised profit margins as high as 3,000 percent in the mid-eighteenth century. Upon learning that ginseng could bring such tremendous profits, the French East India Company came to declare in 1751 that it would begin officially trading ginseng.[11] For ginseng from British colonies in North America to reach Asia, it had to be loaded in Philadelphia and sent to London where the East India Company would take over and privately trade it in China.

Upon its arrival in China, the imported ginseng was sold through the *cohong* (公行).[12] The *cohong* was a guild of Chinese merchants authorized to trade with foreigners. Since 1686, Qing China launched a company called the *yanghuo-hang* (洋貨行) to exclusively handle imports and exports and collect duties. This, however, didn't mean that Westerners were allowed to roam around and meet Chinese merchants as they pleased. As the appearance of Westerners grew frequent and missionaries like the Jesuits broadened their range of activities, the Chinese grew fearful that foreigners might threaten their world view and social order. As a result, Qing China opted for seclusion and issued a decree in 1757 which prohibited European ships from trading at all ports except for Canton. In 1759, *Fangfan waiyi guitiao* (防范外夷规条) was promulgated as a set of regulations against "foreign barbarians." From then on, trade along the coasts of Qing China was controlled under the "Canton System" for seven decades until the end of the Opium Wars in the 1840s.

During the trading season, Westerners had to remain in the approved area for foreigners along the Pearl River known as the "Thirteen Factories" and were therefore not allowed to step outside the area.[13] Once they finished their transactions, they had to reside in Macao until the next trading season. They were only allowed to trade with licensed Chinese merchants referred to as *hongs* (行). Under the Canton System, all ships seeking to dock at Canton had to be vouched for by the *cohong*. With the exclusive right to trade with and vouch for Western traders, the *cohong* was in control of the conditions of trade, which frustrated and hindered Westerners hoping to expand their trade in China. This clash of interests eventually became moot when the Treaty of Nanjing was signed in 1842 at the end of the First Opium War.

In the mid-eighteenth century, Britain emerged as the largest Western trade partner of Qing China and came to play a leading role in the trade of North American ginseng in Canton. Because North American ginseng was brought into China through Canton, it was often referred to as "Canton ginseng." Trading American ginseng for tea reaped the highest profit, although in principle this wasn't allowed by the East India Company. Nevertheless, ginseng was often traded for tea, and whenever that proved to be impossible, illicit deals with the *cohong* could always be arranged.[14] Furthermore, transactions that did not involve the East India Company, unaccounted for in statistics or records, could have taken place at any time.

The East India Company's reports indicate that the demand for ginseng always exceeded its supply and garnered massive profits for the company until America's independence was declared in 1776.[15] While pointing out how the main medicinal ingredients in Chinese treatments have barely changed over a long period of time, Linda L. Barnes notes that ginseng and opium "represented the largest shares of the China trade."[16] A report on trade practices around the time in the newspaper *Liverpool Mercury* classified "ginseng and other drugs" as an independent category of "exports to Asia, or East India and China for the Year 1800."[17]

Presumably, North American ginseng met the high demand for ginseng in China and was distributed without much resistance. Guo Weidong (郭衛東) remarks that the Chinese vaguely sensed that the ginseng was from abroad but were not quite aware of its origin.[18] At first, the imported ginseng was called *yangshen* (洋蔘), which meant "ginseng from overseas." This vague term that could be applied to ginseng from anywhere besides China stood in contrast to *dongyangshen* (東洋蔘) which referred to Japanese ginseng. The geographic range of such terms was gradually narrowed so that ginseng from the West was called *xiyangshen* (西洋蔘), which referred to "Canton ginseng."[19]

Meanwhile, Chinese medicine quickly began to make use of North American ginseng. It was used in ways similar to the existing use of ginseng or for emergency medications. However, its medicinal properties were generally regarded as milder than and inferior to Asian ginseng.[20] In *Bencao gangmu shiyi* (本草綱目拾遺, Supplement to *Bencao gangmu*),[21] compiled by Zhao Zuemin (趙學敏) in 1765, the section "Xiyangshen yaoxing kao" (西洋蔘藥性考) discusses the medicinal properties of foreign ginseng and notes that "*yangshen* is similar to *Liaoshen* [ginseng from Liaodong]" and "has cooling properties."[22] Scholars have interpreted this as an indication that American ginseng could be used to supplement "yin fluid" (陰液), but could not be used as a tonic like Korean ginseng. In other words, Korean ginseng could replenish energy, blood, and bodily fluids, whereas American ginseng was only capable of replenishing bodily fluids, and as such was similar in efficacy to *shashen* (沙蔘), referring to *Codonopsis lanceolata* or *Adenophora verticillate* utilized in traditional medicine.[23]

Forerunners in the Export of North American Ginseng

Through the *Mémoire* he published after discovering ginseng in Canada, Joseph François Lafitau urged the French government to take an interest in "this valuable resource" before it became dominated by competitors like Britain and the Netherlands. As a devoted Jesuit missionary, he seemed anxious at the thought that the French could be outrun by Protestants in gaining an advantage over such a valuable resource like ginseng.[24] Lafitau's *Mémoire* begins by mentioning that the French Ambassador to Canada especially ordered a search for ways to utilize the abundant plant resource.[25] This may be why Lafitau's writing reads like a record of botanical observations as well as a manual of sorts for ginseng traders. The *Mémoire* even included vocabulary from the indigenous language intended to be of use when digging ginseng with indigenous peoples. Lafitau added that "now everyone knows ginseng there, all in Montreal, where this summer the *Sauvages* have been selling it at the market at dear prices."[26]

The first to recognize North American ginseng's potential in the Chinese market were French fur traders. The most notable among them were the Desauniers sisters, who operated in Canada in the 1720s. Marguerite, Marie-Anne, and Marie-Madeleine Desauniers were the daughters of a successful merchant in Montreal. Despite being female, the sisters learned the mechanics of trade and maritime transport from their father and rose to prominence in the fur and ginseng businesses. The sisters moved to an Iroquois village and earned their trust by learning the Iroquois language and respecting their culture. The Iroquois thereafter helped the sisters secure large volumes of fur and ginseng. As their business grew, it attracted smugglers and led to various illicit practices that tarnished the family's reputation. In 1751, the French colonial government expelled the Desauniers sisters from Canada, forcing them to spend the rest of their lives in France.[27]

As word of the French fur traders' success spread, traders from other European countries such as the Netherlands jumped into the trade in ginseng. They employed indigenous peoples to search for ginseng in Canadian and American mountains. Indigenous peoples were the greatest source of labor at the time and European traders believed they were knowledgeable enough to distinguish ginseng from other plants. The rumor was that ginseng was worth eight times more than silver in the Chinese market, which drove Europeans in North America into a frenzy to grab such an enormous commercial opportunity.

The frenzy peaked by the late 1740s. Peter Kalm, one of the most well-known apostles of Carl von Linné, noted that indigenous peoples in particular roamed all over Canada in search of ginseng and sold what they gathered to merchants in Montreal.[28] Their pursuit of ginseng caused labor shortages for French farmers in Canada during the harvest season. The circumstances were similar in British colonies. A priest who visited an Iroquois village in 1752 reported that the village was completely deserted because men, women, and children were roaming in the woods in search of ginseng.[29]

The collection and sale of ginseng even blurred the border Britain and France had established between Canada and America. A Frenchman who visited a missionary headquarters in Quebec in 1752 was surprised to find that all the indigenous Americans had left for New England to collect or sell ginseng and reported that only those too old or infirm to walk had been left behind.[30] Some missionaries joined in the collection and sale of ginseng and accompanied indigenous Americans to New York. Ginseng helped indigenous Americans to earn enough money for necessities like blankets or food. Its sale, however, also entailed the predictable side effect of making liquor available to them. Hence, missionaries grew concerned that ginseng would give indigenous Americans a taste of money and ultimately deprave them.[31]

Moves to commercially benefit from ginseng occurred not only in Canada but also in British America. While fur traders in Montreal led the ginseng trade in Canada, Quakers were at the core of ginseng trade in the British colonies in America. The huge Quaker merchant community formed in Philadelphia over the eighteenth century turned the city into a North American hub for the wholesale and retail of medical goods.[32] The antiauthoritarian, egalitarian Quakers valued devotion to Christian communities and serving society. They cherished the lives of everyone blessed by the sacrifice of Christ and respected the right to life. This principle even applied to their political or religious enemies and thus agreed with the fields of medicine and pharmacology. Perhaps that was why many Quakers went to work in medicine and pharmacology and why Quaker immigrants ran many of the pharmacies in major American cities.

The Quaker Cartel along the Atlantic Coast

The export of North American ginseng to China was carried out through a well-established cartel of Quakers spanning London and Philadelphia. Members in London included Peter Collinson (1694–1768), a botanist and fellow of the British Royal Society; John Coakley Lettsom (1744–1815), one of the most successful, wealthiest physicians in London; and John Fothergill (1712–1780), a physician who grew ginseng in his lustrous botanic garden in Upton. Notable members on the North American continent included John Bartram (1699–1777), a first-generation botanist from the colonial period, and Humphry Marshall (1722–1801) who sent numerous samples of American plants to several botanic gardens in Britain.

This network of devout Quakers across Europe and the North American continent wasn't formed solely out of religious fervor. It was more of a partnership to pioneer a business model for exporting seeds and plants. In the eighteenth century, botany was an activity widely enjoyed in the West, enough to become part of school curriculums. The obsession over Enlightenment science and classification sparked a craze to collect and to classify one's collection. Collecting and studying plants became an accessible hobby recognized by society as entertaining and helpful in self-improvement.[33] Under these circumstances, exotic plants from the New World grew immensely popular in Europe, signaling that meeting such demands was bound to become an enormously profitable business. The one to pioneer such a business was none other than John Bartram.

Despite having never received higher education, Bartram was known as a genius during his time. His tremendous interest in nature and plants since child hood eventually established him as the most outstanding botanist in colonial America. Bartram was considered an expert second to Benjamin Franklin (1706–1790) within the American Philosophy Society, and King George III appointed him as a royal botanist and naturalist for the American colonies. Even Carl von Linné himself called Bartram "the world's greatest natural botanist."[34] Collinson in London asked Bartram in Philadelphia to send North American seeds and plants. Bartram responded with amazing vigor and skill, sending to Britain a massive number of items related to natural history, including ginseng he personally discovered in the east of Philadelphia.[35]

Exported as a plant indigenous to North America, ginseng started to be grown in botanic gardens in Britain. It was soon described as an interesting plant in British gardening books. *A Complete Body of Planting and Gardening* (1770), popular at the time for featuring gardening in diverse settings from kitchen gardens to botanic and orchid gardens, covered ginseng at length along with a few interesting episodes related to the plant. The book introduced ginseng as a plant originally from China that now grew in North America. It also suggested that ginseng's efficacy may have been exaggerated in light of social practices that abused ginseng for erroneous purposes (deviation and sexual arousal) under the pretense of improving one's health. The book even offered detailed advice on cultivating ginseng. The fruit had to be picked in the fall as soon as it ripened for the creating of a nursery with fresh but not too rich soil, which should be covered with a half-inch layer of fine moss. It added that a mat should be laid over the nursery during the icy winter months.[36]

By 1783, ginseng was already available for sale as a "Canadian five-leaf *Panax quinquefolium*" according to a catalog published by a seedling seller in Mile End, London.[37] Yet, John Coakley Lettsom was the cartel member who commercialized ginseng for its original, medicinal purpose. Lettsom earned his reputation from using ginseng tea to treat his patients. In the 1790s, advertisements about Lettsom's ginseng tea treatment could easily be spotted in many newspapers including *The Times*.

> The Ginseng Tea, which is so universally recommended by Dr. Coackley Lettsom, M.D. to be drank instead of Green and Bohea Tea, can only be had genuine at the Doctor's as above; at Mr. Randall's, Royal Exchange-gate, and at Mr. Salmon's, No. 49, between York-buildings and the Adelphi.[38]

This "botanic cartel" on both sides of the Atlantic was not about to remain satisfied with exporting American ginseng for the sale of seedlings and prescribing of ginseng tea in Britain. From the very beginning, the cartel was after a bigger market: China. The Quakers had been utterly convinced that far greater profits could be gained from selling ginseng in China. Peter Collinson shared with John Bartram his aspiration to export North American ginseng to China, telling Bartram that he believed ginseng could generate profit margins greater than any other item in the Chinese market.[39] Collinson even told Bartram that he compared the ginseng Bartram sent with Chinese ginseng and discovered that the two were one and the same.

Now for an interesting twist: although Collinson had been convinced that North American and Chinese ginseng were the same, he made his agent promise not to disclose the fact that the packet of ginseng being sent to China was actually from North America. He gave a sheepish excuse: "for if they know that it is American, they are so fanciful, it may not be so good as their own."[40] In 1739, Collinson sent ginseng to China and told Bartram to prepare another batch for the next shipment. Bartram continued to send ginseng to Collinson in the 1740s. Collinson appears to have raked in enormous profits from selling ginseng in China. At the time, Britain had the upper hand in trade with China so that American ginseng mostly arrived in Canton on British ships before being distributed throughout China. Since local ginseng was incredibly expensive, Chinese ginseng dealers seemed to have been willing to purchase American ginseng at ridiculous prices despite its inferior quality.

Yet no matter how high a price the Chinese charged for American ginseng it was certainly a bargain compared to the price of local ginseng. Robert Dodsley (1704–1764), a British poet and publisher, complained in 1762 that "the Chinese do not esteem that which grows in America, valuing only their own."[41] The quality of American ginseng was undeniably inferior and European merchants were aware of the fact. While conveying the good news that ginseng was being produced in North American colonies in 1753, *The Gentleman's Magazine* remarked that in order to yield more profit in the future, it would be necessary to be skilled at collecting ginseng at the proper time and curing it in the Chinese manner.[42]

The task of procuring large quantities of American ginseng was left to Humphry Marshall. Originally a stonemason, Marshall was passionate about collecting plants, and his efforts eventually led to his election as a member of the prestigious American Philosophical Society.[43] He jumped into the plant trade with Britain as he began helping John Fothergill procure American plants for his garden in Upton. Thanks to Fothergill's fame and his celebrated garden, Marshall was able to secure many clients from high society. One of them was Joseph Banks (1743–1820). Banks was a botanist who accompanied Captain James Cook (1728–1779) on his first Pacific voyage and later served as president of the British Royal Society. In 1788, Banks placed an order with Marshall for 200 pounds of fresh ginseng root.[44]

Marshall thus sent his nephew to western Pennsylvania to search for roots of adequate size. The ginseng there, however, had already been dug up for sale or consumed by hogs, leaving almost none in sight where people resided. Unable to find enough roots to satisfy the amount that had been ordered, Marshall was forced to report to Banks the circumstances his nephew was in.

> He was likewise obliged to hire a person, at a dollar a day, to assist him in digging said Ginseng, both of them being obliged to encamp in the mountains, strike up a fire and lie by it all night, in the morning take their hoes and knapsacks on their backs, and climb up the sides of the mountains, and dig till towards evening, and then bring what they had dug to their camp, and cook their morsel and eat it. It took him about twenty days, in going and coming home again, digging the roots, and packing up, &c., the expense of carriage being considerable … I expect thou'll be willing to pay a reasonable compensation, which would be, at least, an English crown a pound, I should apprehend.[45]

Banks agreed to pay the asked price.[46] Apart from the facts their correspondence reveal, the letters themselves are valuable historical sources for including vivid descriptions about how ginseng was collected at the time.

Ginseng Habitats in North America

Not long after Canadian fur traders began to actively collect and export ginseng with the help of indigenous peoples, ginseng started to be discovered in multiple places across North America.[47] In 1720, it was found in an area now part of Michigan as well as in Pennsylvania in 1738. When a large batch of wild ginseng was found in Sturbridge, Massachusetts, a rush to dig ginseng ensued all over the continent in a fashion much like the gold rush that took place later in the American West. The discovery of ginseng was big news to intellectuals in the American colonies. On July 27, 1738, Benjamin Franklin, one of the most talented individuals in American history, happily announced the discovery of ginseng in Pennsylvania through *The Pennsylvania Gazette*. The newspaper owned by Franklin was one of the most influential in North America until the American independence.

> We have the Pleasure of acquainting the World, that the famous Chinese or Tartarian Plant, called Gin seng, is now discovered in this Province, near Sasquehannah: From whence several whole Plants with a Quantity of the Root, have been lately sent to Town, and it appears to agree most exactly with the Description given of it in Chambers's Dictionary, and Pere du Halde's Account of China. The Virtues ascrib'd to this Plant are wonderful.[48]

Ginseng was also discovered in New York, Massachusetts, and Vermont in 1751. Soon, large amounts of ginseng were found in the southern Appalachian region, the west side of the Mississippi, as well as Wisconsin and Minnesota. As the ginseng rush spread east, some indigenous ginseng diggers faced a moral hazard. Ginseng collecting "kept them [the Indians] from public worship and when in Albany to sell the product, they were subjected to various vices."[49] The concerns Jesuit missionaries carried as they went searching for ginseng with indigenous Americans had turned into a reality.

Perhaps it was only natural for a streak of patriotism to be applied to ginseng at a time when many in America were on the hunt for it. Unbelievable as it may be, eighteenth-century American geographical books, travelogues, almanacs, and even textbooks mentioned the fact that ginseng could be found in several different regions, defining it as a local specialty and staple of American exports.[50] This was a climate completely different from that when Peter Collinson tried to keep the place of origin a secret as he explored the possibility of exporting American ginseng to China.

In the 1780s, British merchant ships that sailed along the American west coast were looking into the possibility of exporting ginseng collected from northwestern America and even Alaska.[51] There is no way of knowing whether ginseng was actually discovered in those regions, but some claimed that not only was the northwestern coast far closer to China, the quality of ginseng from those regions was better than that from the east.[52] This leads to the question of whether wild ginseng did in fact grow on the west side of North America, because the wild ginseng habitats listed in travelogues all belonged to nineteen states on the east side. Yet, considering the fact that ginseng is now being grown in western regions of the United States as well, it is difficult to completely exclude the possibility that ginseng, albeit in small amounts, did in fact grow wild in western areas of North America.

Alas, the eighteenth-century rush for American ginseng soon led to its indiscriminate collection. The wise voiced their concern that American ginseng might go extinct, but there was virtually no way to stop its collection. Ginseng indeed disappeared for good in many areas. The following is how Swedish botanist Peter Kalm described Canada's situation in the mid-eighteenth century.

> During my stay in Canada, all the merchants at Quebec and Montreal, received orders from their correspondents in France to send over a quantity of Ginseng, there being an uncommon demand for it this summer. The roots were accordingly collected in Canada with all possible diligence; the Indians especially travelled about the country in order to collect as much as they could together, and to sell it to the merchants at Montreal. The Indians in the neighbourhood of this town were likewise so much taken up with this business, that the French farmers were not able during that time to hire a single Indian, as they commonly do, to help them in the harvest. Many people feared lest by continuing for several successive years, to collect these plants without leaving one or two in each place to propagate their species, there would soon be very few of them left; which I think is very likely to happen, for by all accounts they formerly grew in abundance

> round Montreal, but at present there is not a single plant of it to be found, so effectually have they been rooted out. This obliged the Indians this summer to go far within the English boundaries to collect these roots.[53]

Another problem mass collection and exportation caused was a drop in prices. Chinese merchants earned enormous profit margins from selling mixtures of Asian ginseng and Canadian ginseng brought by French merchants. French merchants also enjoyed huge profits and exported excessive amounts of Canadian ginseng, which caused its price to plummet. While they earned 100,000 dollars in 1752, that number dropped to 6,500 dollars in just a matter of two years.[54]

In 1764, Collinson censured the greed of North Americans for exporting excessive amounts of ginseng to China and thus causing a tremendous depletion. While criticizing the American "rage after Ginseng," he bemoaned that, "I call it so, because all the mountains and uncultivated country was ransacked for this valuable root, and imported hither by hogshead full, and the market in China glutted with this root." He pointed out that the reason American ginseng was initially sold for high prices was because it "had been artfully concealed and prepared by the cunning Chinese, and sold under secrecy to the great people for true Chinese ginseng, but this great plenty soon discovered the cheat, and then it sank to nothing." Considering these circumstances, it was perhaps only natural for Collinson to call Americans "great losers."[55]

Notes

1 Harold J. Cook and Timothy D. Walker, "Circulation of Medicine in the Early Modern Atlantic World," *Social History of Medicine* 26, no. 3 (2013): 337–351.
2 Pratik Chakrabarti, "Medical Marketplaces beyond the West: Bazaar Medicine, Trade and the English Establishment in Eighteenth-Century India," in S. R. Mark Jenner and Patrick Wallis, eds. *Medicine and the Market in England and Its Colonies, c. 1450 –c. 1850* (Basingstoke: Palgrave Macmillan, 2007).
3 Chakrabarti, "Medical Marketplaces beyond the West," 196.
4 Chakrabarti, "Medical Marketplaces beyond the West," 202–203.
5 Charles Peter Thunberg, "Travels in Japan and Other Countries," in *Historical Account of the Most Celebrated Voyages, Travels, and Discoveries*, vol. 15 (London, 1797), 191–192.
6 Thomas Maurice, *Indian Antiquities*, vol. 7 (London, 1800), 635.
7 *The New Annual Register, or General Repository of History, Politics and Literature for the Year 1792* (London, 1793).
8 George Henry Loskiel, *History of the Mission of the United Brethren among the Indians in North America*, trans. Christian Ignatius La Trobe (London, 1794), 117.
9 Patrick Wallis, "Exotic Drugs and English Medicine: England's Drug Trade, c. 1550–c. 1800," *Social History of Medicine* 25, no. 1 (2012): 41.
10 Hamauzu Tetsuo 浜渦哲雄, *Taeyŏngjeguk ŭn Indo rŭl ŏttŏk'e t'ongch'i hayŏnnŭn'ga: Yŏngguk tongindo hoesa 1600–1858* 대영제국은 인도를 어떻게 통치하였는가: 영국 동인도 회사 1600–1858 [How the British Empire Ruled India: The British East India Company 1600–1858], trans. Kim Sŏng-tong 김성동 (Seoul: Shimsan 심산, 2004), 22.
11 Evans, "Ginseng: Root of Chinese-Canadian Relations," 12.

12 In 1726, six merchant households were designated to take charge of customs affairs on behalf of the government. Instead of paying the government a hefty commission, those households, called *baoshang* (保商), *baoxing* (保行), or *zongchang* (總商), managed and supervised foreign merchants coming into China.
13 Haneda, Masashi 永田雄三, *Tongindo hoesa wa asia ŭi pada* 동인도회사와 아시아의 바다 [The East India Company and the Waters of Asia], trans. Yi Su-yŏl 이수열 and Ku Chi-yŏng 구지영 (Seoul: Sŏnin 선인, 2012), 312–313.
14 Evans, "Ginseng: Root of Chinese-Canadian Relations," 19–20.
15 *Jordan's Parliamentary Journal, for the Year MDCCXCIII*, vol. 2 (London, 1793), 11–12, 80, 90–97.
16 Barnes, *Needles, Herbs, Gods, and Ghosts*, 173.
17 "Imports and Exports," *Liverpool Mercury*, April 3, 1812.
18 Guo, "Xiyangshen," 126–127.
19 The term "American ginseng" emerged after the United States gained independence and began to export its ginseng to China.
20 Guo, "Xiyangshen," 128. See footnote no. 53.
21 *Bencao gangmu shiyi* covers 921 herbs, including some that were missing from *Bencao gangmu*, and offers further explanations on some herbs that had previously been cataloged. The book classifies ginseng into twelve different types. Guo, "Xiyangshen," 127–128.
22 Guo, "Xiyangshen," 128. See footnote no. 58.
23 Ko et al., *Uri insam ui ihae*, 16–18.
24 Parsons, "The Natural History of Colonial Science," 61.
25 Lafitau, *Mémoire presenté a son altesse royale monseigneur le duc d'Orléans*, 4.
26 Lafitau, *Mémoire presenté a son altesse royale monseigneur le duc d'Orléans*, 52.
27 David L. Preston, *The Texture of Contact: European and Indian Settler Communities on the Frontiers of Iroquoia, 1667–1783* (Lincoln, NE: University of Nebraska Press, 2009), 58; John Demos, *The Unredeemed Captive: A Family Story from Early America* (New York: Alfred A. Knopf, 1994), 184–186.
28 Kalm, *Travels into North America*, 416.
29 Gail D. MacLeitch, "'Red' Labor: Iroquois Participation in the Atlantic Economy," *Labor: Studies in Working-Class History of the Americas* 1, no. 4 (2004): 81.
30 Louis Franquet, *Voyages et mémoires sur le Canada en 1752–1753* (Montréal: Editions Elysée, 1974), 99–100.
31 Timothy J. Shannon, "Dressing for Success on the Mohawk Frontier: Hendrick, William Johnson, and the Indian Fashion," *The William and Mary Quarterly* 53, no. 1 (1996): 13–42, esp. 19–20; Gail D. MacLeitch, *Imperial Entanglements: Iroquois Change and Persistence on the Frontiers of Empire* (Philadelphia, PA: University of Pennsylvania Press, 2011), 92–93.
32 Renate Wilson, "Trading in Drugs through Philadelphia in the Eighteenth Century: A Transatlantic Enterprise," *Social History of Medicine* 26, no. 3 (2013): 354.
33 Ann B. Shteir, "Gender and 'Modern' Botany in Victorian England," *Osiris* 12 (1997): 29.
34 Quoted from Christopher Hobbs, "The Medical Botany of John Bartram," *Pharmacy in History* 33, no. 4 (1991): 182.
35 Hobbs, "The Medical Botany of John Bartram," 182.
36 William Hanbury, *A Complete Body of Planting and Gardening*, vol. 1 (London, 1770), 690–691.
37 Gordon, Dermer, and Thomson, *A Catalogue of Trees, Shrubs, Plants, Flower Roots, Seeds, &c. Sold by Gorden, Dermer, and Thomson, Seed and Nurserymen, at Mile End, Near London*, 68.
38 "Advertisement," *The Times*, August 31, 1790.
39 William Darlington, ed., "Collinson to Bartram, February 24, 1738-9, London, Pennsylvania Coffeehouse," in *Memorials of John Bartram and Humphry Marshall* (Philadelphia, PA: Lindsay & Blakiston, 1849), 127.

40 Darlington, ed., "Collinson to Bartram, February 24, 1738-9, London, Pennsylvania Coffeehouse," in *Memorials of John Bartram and Humphry Marshall*, 127.
41 Dodsley, *The General Contents of the British Museum*, 155.
42 *The Gentleman's Magazine* 23 (1753), 209.
43 In 1768, Humphry Marshall became a member of the American Society, which later morphed into the American Philosophical Society.
44 Louise Conway Belden, "Humphry Marshall's Trade in Plants of the New World for Gardens and Forests of the Old World," *Winterthur Portfolio* 2 (1965): 115–117.
45 Darlington, ed., "Marshall to Banks, Nov. 14, 1786," in *Memorials of John Bartram and Humphry Marshall*, 561.
46 Darlington, ed., "Banks to Marshall, Mar. 2, 1791," in *Memorials of John Bartram and Humphry Marshall*, 564.
47 G. M. Hocking, "A Chronology of Ginseng," *Quarterly Journal of Crude Drug Research* 14 (1976): 168. With the exception of Florida, there have been reports of wild American ginseng having been discovered in nearly all the eastern states leading up to the west side of the Mississippi River and even in Texas. Jeanine Davis and W. Scott Persons, *Growing and Marketing Ginseng, Goldenseal and Other Woodland Medicinals* (Gabriola Island: New Society Publisher, 2014), 10–11.
48 *The Pennsylvania Gazette*, January 3 to December 28, 1738.
49 A. W. Schorger, "Ginseng: A Pioneer Resource," *Transactions of the Wisconsin Academy of Science, Art and Letters* 57 (1969): 67.
50 Peter Whitney, *The History of the County of Worcester in the Commonwealth of Massachusetts* (Worcester, MA, 1793), 98; J. F. D. Smyth, *A Tour in the United States of America*, vol. 1 (Dublin, 1784), 190; *Fleets Pocket Almanack for the Year of Our Lord 1790* (Boston, MA, 1789), 20–21; Jedidah Morse, *Geography Made Easy: Being an Abridgement of the American Universal Geography* (Boston, MA, 1790), 87; Mathew Carey, ed., *The American Museum, or, Universal Magazine*, vol. 7 (Philadelphia, PA, 1790), 15, 126–128, 295, 301.
51 John Adams, *Modern Voyages: Containing a Variety of Useful and Entertaining Facts*, vol. 2 (London, 1790), 164.
52 John Meares, *Voyages Made in the Years 1788 and 1789, from China to the North West Coast of America* (London, 1790), lxxi.
53 Kalm, *Travels into North America*, 116–117.
54 Kalm, *Travels into North America*, 116–117.
55 Lewis Weston Dillwyn, *Hortus Collinsonianus: An Account of the Plants Cultivated by the Late Peter Collinson* (Swansea: W. C. Murray and D. Rees, 1843), 37.

7

GINSENG, AMERICA'S FIRST EXPORT ITEM

Tea and Ginseng

The history of ginseng's discovery across the North American continent shared the same path white American settlements took as they spread westward. News of ginseng's discovery indicated that immigrants had begun to settle down in a given area. And as the number of settlers increased, the amount of ginseng tended to decrease rapidly. Nevertheless, the undying pursuit of ginseng obscured its depletion and made it seem as though the areas in which ginseng was available were increasing.[1] It is therefore safe to say that the history of ginseng collection in America reflected the process through which the country achieved economic independence. The relatively few merchants and entrepreneurs mentioned in records in relation to the ginseng trade in North American hired countless unnamed people to collect massive amounts of ginseng.

After declaring its independence from British rule on July 4, 1776, it took eight years of war until the United States was finally able to be acknowledged as an independent country through the Treaty of Paris, concluded on September 3, 1783. Prior to its independence, American ginseng was not exported directly to China, but to Britain or France before it was re-exported to China. Upon its independence, the United States began to seek ways to directly engage in trade with China. The reason it was desperate to trade with China was tea. As a commodity exclusively supplied by the East India Company, tea was sold at expensive prices to Americans. In fact, the importing of tea was the most discussed topic among merchants around the time America gained independence. To understand how the American ginseng industry came to be infused with capital, it is therefore necessary to understand the importance tea occupies in American history.

DOI: 10.4324/9781003286691-9

Tea was a daily necessity to Americans, but importing it directly from China was absolutely prohibited under the British colonial rule. All tea had to pass through Britain and had to be shipped to America only by East India Company vessels. Until the United States declared its independence in 1776 and became recognized as an independent country through the 1783 Treaty of Paris, the supply of tea to America had nearly been discontinued. To satisfy the surging demand for tea, American merchants searched desperately for a commodity to export to China. China was, however, self-sufficient for the most part, which left America with practically nothing worth selling to the Chinese.

The shortage of tea was so acute as to raise an interesting question: Since ginseng was discovered in America, wouldn't it be possible to discover or grow tea there as well? The question was discussed through the bulletin published by the American Philosophical Society, a group of prominent intellectuals at the time. Considering, the bulletin proposed, that the only place where ginseng (purported to originate from "eastern Beijing") was found outside China was the North American continent, the discussion arrived at the conclusion that the soil and ecology of America must be the most similar to those of China than other regions in the same latitude. Except for mistaking eastern Beijing as ginseng's place of origin, it was a fairly rational conclusion.[2]

Other arguments emerged, claiming that Chinese tea was toxic and should therefore have been replaced with tea made from American ginseng. Such arguments were based on an analogic view that the Chinese brewed ginseng tea the same way as any other tea, using leaves and roots; an economic view that ginseng tea was more efficient, requiring smaller amounts to brew; or a nationalist rhetoric of favoring what was local.[3] Some claimed that the Chinese actually favored ginseng tea over ordinary tea and even suspected that they may have created appealing names to help sell tea overseas even though they were aware that "eastern teas are slow, but sure poison."[4]

These arguments were, however, all unrealistic plots. Americans couldn't stop drinking tea and for economic reasons they desperately needed to import it without involving the British. As America's independence grew imminent, the colonists faced the task of initiating direct trade with East Asia. The problem was that, despite their strong desire to engage in direct trade, Americans lacked the necessary capital.

A round-trip between America and China costed ten times more than the equivalent journey between America and Europe.[5] Hence, Americans had to satisfy two conditions in order to trade directly with China. One was to find a commodity easily and cheaply available in America that could be sold at high prices in China and the other was that the commodity had to be available in quantities large enough to purchase tea and other Chinese goods without having to bring silver from America to help pay for them. The only commodities that fit the bill were fur and ginseng, which had been traditional export items since the American colonial period.

The Empress of China and US–China Trade

Soon after the Treaty of Paris was concluded, a group of investors led by Daniel Parker in New York and Robert Morris in Philadelphia decided to focus on exporting ginseng to China instead of fur, which was growing more and more difficult to procure. According to the information gathered from their sources in China, ginseng continued to be in demand in China. To the Americans, ginseng was a plant easily available at nearby mountains and a specialty that could provide them with a comparative advantage over European merchants in its trade.[6] American merchants were less experienced in choosing trade items likely to sell well, but they did have a certain degree of confidence in ginseng based on what they experienced under the British and French colonial rule. Hence, American ginseng (*Panax quinquefolius*) became America's first export commodity as an independent country. This is a fact that remains relatively unknown to historians and barely mentioned in descriptions of American history.

In 1784, the United States succeeded in exporting with a merchant ship of its own: the *Empress of China*. The vessel was originally built as a privateer during the American revolution but became converted into a merchant ship immediately after the conclusion of the Treaty of Paris. On August 23, 1784, it set sail on the historic voyage after being forced to wait when the bitter cold froze New York Harbor. The most valuable cargo on board was ginseng, worth 240,000 dollars out of the entire cargo which sold for a total of 270,000 dollars.[7] In terms of quantity, the ship was transporting half of the total amount of ginseng exported to China for that season.

After a long voyage, the *Empress of China* successfully lowered its anchor at Canton. The ship's captain was an Irishman named John Green and the supercargo was Samuel Shaw (1754–1794). The crew received a warm welcome from Europeans who arrived earlier from France, Denmark, and the Netherlands. Contrary to the expectation that the British would be hostile toward Americans, they also welcomed the American crew and shared their relief that the American Revolutionary War was over. The Chinese were unsure of what to call the people from the newly independent country. They eventually settled on "new people" and called the star-spangled banner hanging from the ship *huaqi* (花旗), which meant "flowery flag." This is where the Chinese name for American ginseng, *huaqishen* (花旗蔘), originated from (Figure 7.1).

In their trade with Westerners, the Chinese were more interested in selling rather than buying. Ginseng was, however, an exception. The *Empress of China* sold all the American ginseng, leather, and fur it brought and returned to New York Harbor in 1785 with 300 piculs (there are approximately 60.48 kilograms per picul) of Hyson green tea (熙春) and Bohea black tea (武夷), 20,000 sheets of cotton pants, and a massive amount of chinaware.[8] Investors traveled along the east coast to sell the goods from China and realized that was the way to make real profit. [9]

FIGURE 7.1 The Empress of China's arrival at the Canton port.

Dave Wang has pointed out that "it would be unthinkable for the journey of the *Empress of China* to Canton without ginseng."[10] This was precisely how the supercargo Samuel Shaw felt as someone who took part in the voyage from beginning to end. The experience led to Shaw's appointment as the first United States consul to China (1786–1789). Upon his arrival in Canton, Shaw, formerly a naval officer who served during the Revolutionary War, soon submitted a very detailed report about the historic voyage to China to John Jay (1745–1829), the first United States Secretary of Foreign Affairs.[11] The report was circulated in the parliament and the United States soon began to devise various ways to boost direct trade with China.

Shaw stressed the importance of trading with China and predicted that the demand for tea would continue to rise in the United States with the growth of its population. To secure the necessary tea from China, Shaw advised that Americans must use ginseng, as it was one of "the advantages peculiar to America."

> To the Honorable John Jay, Secretary of the United States for the Department of Foreign Affairs
>
> Canton in China, January, 1787
>
> The inhabitants of America must have tea, the consumption of which will necessarily increase with the increasing population of our country.

> And while the nations of Europe are, for the most part, obliged to purchase this commodity with ready money, it must be pleasing to an American to know that his country can have it upon easier terms; and that the otherwise useless produce of her mountains and forests will in a considerable degree supply her with this elegant luxury. The advantages peculiar to America in this instance are striking; and the manner in which her commerce has commenced, and is now going on, with this country, has not a little alarmed the Europeans. They have seen, the first year, a single ship, not on fifth part of whose funds consisted of ready money, procure a cargo of the same articles, and on equally good terms, as those of their own ships, purchased, as has been observed, for the most part, with specie. The have seen this ship again here, on her second voyage, and four others in addition. They see these ships depending, and that, too, with sufficient reason, upon the productions of their own country to supply them with the merchandise of this; and though a very small proportion of their funds consisted of specie, they see them all returning with full and valuable cargoes. Such are the advantages which America derives from her ginseng.
>
> With respect to the demand in this country for the ginseng of America, which might be rendered as beneficial to her citizens as her mines of silver and gold have been to the rest of mankind, the world has been much mistaken. Until the American flag appeared in this quarter, it had been generally supposed that forty of fifty piculs were equal to the annual consumption. But experience has proved the contrary. Upwards of four hundred and forty piculs were brought here by the first American ship, in 1784, which did not equal the quantity brought from Europe the same season, the greatest part of which must have been previously sent there by citizens of the United States. The present year more than eighteen hundred piculs have been sold, one half of which came in the American vessels. Notwithstanding this increased quantity since 1784, the sales have not been materially affected by it, and it is probable there will always be a sufficient demand for the article to make it equally valuable.[12]

From Britain's point of view, the *Empress of China*'s voyage was as good as an official declaration that the United States would compete with Britain. American vessels busily shipped ginseng to China. A total of 1,800 piculs of ginseng was exported to China in 1786, and one-fifth of that was transported by American vessels. In 1820, a magazine article openly boasted that "while Europe produces nothing which it can offer to the Chinese in exchange for their productions, America possesses in this remarkable plant an article peculiarly its own."[13]

The East India Company was bound to suffer a huge blow from America's direct export of ginseng. Ginseng had previously been a major export item for Britain and one that brought massive profits from China.[14] Britain foresaw the change in circumstances and desperately tried to stop the United States from directly trading with China. As a matter of fact, the *Empress of China* was not the first American vessel to sail to Canton. In late 1783, the *Harriet*, loaded with nothing but ginseng, set sail for Canton. However, it ran into an East India Company ship at the Cape of Good Hope. The British merchants immediately began to urge the Americans to sell them the ginseng on the *Harriet*, offering twice as much black tea as the weight of ginseng on board in exchange. It was an extremely tempting offer for the *Harriet*. The Americans quickly agreed and turned the ship back to New York.[15] Britain was willing to suffer such losses in order to stop American ships from heading to China. Based on its abundant experience in overseas trade, the East India Company was also able to predict that flooding the Chinese market with American ginseng would ultimately drive its price down.

> It is generally admitted that no Market varies more than that of China, the Prejudices of the Natives operating most powerfully upon their conduct. Of this, the Article of Ginseng is a striking Proof. The Moment it was offered in Quantities larger than usual, and by Persons from whom the Chinese were not accustomed to purchase, it became unsaleable; and your Committee are confident that American Ginseng will never be consumed in China as heretofore.[16]

The East India Company managers admitted that while ginseng used to bring enormous profits, the company was unable to supply enough of it. They noted that the overflow of ginseng since 1783 caused the Chinese to pretend that imported ginseng had no potency, rendering such ginseng unsellable.[17] The East India Company's concern was that such an immature export strategy would ultimately allow China to gain an upper hand in trade.[18]

The East India Company's assessment was in fact accurate. In 1783, Shaw reported that the price of American ginseng in China was around thirty dollars per pound. The *Empress of China* delivered such a massive amount of ginseng in 1784 that by the time the *Experiment* arrived in China two years later, the price of ginseng had dropped to a mere dollar per pound. This collapse in price, however, did not stop the United States from exporting ginseng. It shipped 142,000 pounds of ginseng to China in 1788, 274,000 pounds in 1789, and 53,000 pounds in 1790.[19]

The reason American merchants continued to export ginseng was because trade with China rewarded them with huge profits. After the *Empress of China*'s successful return, New England merchants accumulated tremendous wealth over the next six decades. One of them was the prominent industrialist John Jacob Astor (1763–1848). Astor is known to have made a fortune through the fur trade and real estate development, but the actual foundation of his wealth came from none other than ginseng. Once he made a great deal of money from trading fur, he headed to London. Astor's plan was to form connections that would help him sell fur at higher prices in major cities across Europe. In London, however, he learned the details of the East India Company's trade with China and realized the incredible commercial value of ginseng. Astor thereby invested all the capital he amassed from selling fur to buy ginseng. In 1800, he personally sent a ship to Canton and reaped enormous profits from trading ginseng. He also profited hugely from selling the Chinese tea, silk, and fine fabric the ship brought on its return to the United States.[20]

George Washington (1732–1799) also took a great interest in ginseng. In 1784, at the Cheat River basin in West Virginia, the future president of the United States came across a "number of persons and pack horses going in with ginseng; and for salt and other articles in the markets below."[21] Washington soon went searching for ginseng on his own property and even attempted to grow it himself.

Another well-known figure who actually jumped into the ginseng trade was the American pioneer and "frontier hero" Daniel Boone (1734–1820). After pioneering Kentucky beyond the Appalachian Mountains, Boone found out about ginseng in 1787 and made up his mind to take part in its trade. In 1788, Boone combed the mountains in Kentucky and West Virginia to collect ginseng and sent around twelve tons of it to Pittsburg. He loaded the rest of the ginseng on carriages to be sent to Philadelphia. However, he lost the ginseng destined for Philadelphia when the boat carrying it sank in the Ohio River.[22]

Despite such hardships, Boone continued to trade ginseng. He hired workers to dig ginseng and acquired more from others in order to sell ginseng in Ohio, thus making thousands of dollars in profit.[23] Needless to say, ginseng was an important source of income to the 200,000 or so people who settled down along the Kentucky route Boone pioneered. When people brought the ginseng they collected to a general store in the fall, the store owner would enter them in the books and provided goods at the store in exchange from the winter to the following summer.[24]

Investment tycoons initially relied on merchants in the northeast with ties to the Iroquois but gradually shifted their gaze to the south yet to be explored at the time. They sent reliable brokers to purchase ginseng from the south, upon which they raked in as much ginseng as possible before sending it to Philadelphia. The amassed ginseng would then be sent to New York Harbor where it would be shipped to China. One such broker who became "legendary" was a physician named Robert Johnston from Philadelphia. Johnston was hired to purchase ginseng for Daniel Parker, an investor in New York. With a large advance in his pocket, he toured the southern regions and rose to fame as a ginseng broker. Over the summer and fall alone, Johnston purchased more than 40,000 pounds of ginseng and sent it to New York Harbor where another 50,000 pounds of ginseng procured by others were waiting to be exported to China.[25]

According to a customs report issued in 1826, "the whole amount of domestic produce exported to China in 1826 was but 242,000 dollars, and of this more than half was ginseng, and the amount of cotton goods was less than 15,000 dollars."[26] What is interesting is that by the early nineteenth century, ginseng's share in American exports to China plunged to about 2–5 percent. The share of silver, on the other hand, surged to around 70 percent.[27] However, silver wasn't an "article of home production," which meant that American ginseng still amounted to more than half of the domestically produced goods exported to China.

The American Export of Ginseng in the Nineteenth Century

In the nineteenth century, ginseng remained a major domestically produced commodity and export item for the United States. The trade of American ginseng continued despite the ups and downs in its volume and price or factors like the Civil War. *The American Farmer's Encyclopedia*, published in 1860, recognized ginseng's tremendous commercial value and proudly listed by year its annual export volume. The list indicated that 70,202 dollars' worth of ginseng was exported in 1834, which jumped to 437,245 dollars by 1841.[28] In 1851, the United States exported 100,509 dollars' worth of ginseng, the third highest amount behind that of fur and timber.[29] Out of the one million dollars' worth of American goods exported in the first half of 1884, grains accounted for half a million dollars and ginseng accounted for about 250,000 dollars.[30]

By the late eighteenth century, thirteen states in America were engaged in the ginseng trade. While Philadelphia used to be the center of ginseng trade during the colonial period, Louisville and Cincinnati emerged as major trading centers in the nineteenth century.[31] The center of ginseng's trade overseas was New York where most ginseng brokers were based and most ships carrying exported goods set sail from.

From the early eighteenth century, when North American ginseng was discovered in Canada, the export of ginseng was primarily left to fur traders. That was why it became customary for the American Fur Company to trade ginseng.[32] Today, ginseng is cultivated by independent companies, but in many states wild ginseng still tends to be purchased by fur traders. Just like ginseng is economically and culturally tied to tobacco in Korea because both commodities used to be monopolized by the state, ginseng and fur are considered a pair in the United States. In China, ginseng tends to be paired with bird's nests. At a time when there was an association in Shanghai for the trade in ginseng and bird's nests,[33] the two were bundled as a pair in the compilation of price indexes,[34] and in 1928, the Kuomintang decided to tax ginseng and bird's nests as luxuries.[35]

Meanwhile, North American ginseng was suffering from being branded as cheap and inferior. While supplying the market with exorbitant amounts of it was partly to blame, other causes were explored by the National Institute for the Promotion of Science in 1846 as it was preparing a proposal on ways to boost the export of American ginseng. One of the more interesting causes discussed in the proposal had to do with crude packaging.

> No doubt much higher prices could be obtained, if more care was taken in the preparation and transporting it [American ginseng], as the American

> appears in the market in Canton as very inferior. The Tartar ginseng is carefully put up in boxes, made of pasteboard and handsomely gilt. The root is also enveloped in gilt paper stamped with the druggist's name who vends it, and other particulars, and the box is half filled with roasted ricc.[36]

In 1879, the United States consul in Amoy, A. B. Johnson, submitted a report proposing that America should be more proactive in its trade in ginseng. Titled "A Great Market for Ginseng," the report was a written appeal urging the United States to overtake Korean ginseng.

> I wish to call especial attention to an article now imported from the United States to a limited extent and from Korea – ginseng. It is a native of Colorado, Wyoming, Utah, as well as other mountainous districts of America, also of Korea and northern Asia. I do not exaggerate when I state that it is possible to market annually in China $20,000,000 worth of these roots. They are now being cultivated in the United States to a limited extent, and prices obtained by the grower are entirely out of proportion to these realized by the thrifty exporter. It sells in Amoy at a price from $25 to $35 (Mexican) per pound. It costs in America for $2 to $3 in gold or $4 to $6 in Mexican currency. Yet at these figures Amoy handled during 1896, 109,823 haikwan taels' (or $88,517.34 in United States gold) worth of these roots from America alone. From Korea the value of 54,867 haikwan tales, or $44,222.80 (United States gold) was imported. The Korean article is much higher priced and more skillfully cured, although not otherwise superior in quality to the American product. It seems to me that if our people realized that at least $3 in gold could be fairly demanded by the grower for every pound of well-cured roots, and that the market would be practically unlimited, a new mine of wealth, affording employment for a large population, would be opened.
>
> It [the ginseng] is used as an invigorating tea by all the wealthy Chinese and as a medicine by the native physicians. It enters largely into the list of presents sent by the wealthy to friends and the articles exchanged between high officials. It is bought by the middle classes throughout the entire Empire, and even the poor peasants give up their hard-earned silver for this national panacea.
>
> I hope that these facts will be brought to the attention of the chambers of commerce throughout the districts mentioned, in order not only that the possibilities maybe disclosed, but knowledge of the prices may be disseminated, to protect those who most need the benefits to be derived from the industry.[37]

Johnson's report is highly interesting for several reasons. One is that despite all the progress botanical approaches had made since the early eighteenth century to draw a distinction between North American and Asian ginseng, the two are regarded as one and the same in the report. Moreover, the report indicates that the difference in manufacturing method is the only reason Korean ginseng is regarded as far more superior. These assumptions seem to be aimed at deceiving readers into believing that North American and Asian ginseng were identical, most likely to boost the export of American ginseng, thereby yielding higher profits.

The fact that the report states that Utah and Colorado were ginseng habitats is also interesting. Considering that the wild ginseng was traditionally found in the eastern regions of the continent, naming western states as ginseng habitats gives reason to question whether there were any ulterior motives to the report. Another interesting fact is that the report predicts that a far greater volume of American ginseng would be exported to China in the future, since its share in the Chinese market was still low. This prediction hints at a confidence that only the United States would be capable of meeting China's near infinite demand for ginseng, possibly because competitors like Britain had already been eliminated from the worldwide distribution of the American ginseng (Table 7.1).

Britain Expelled from the Ginseng Trade?

Around 1800, a major change occurred in Britain's overseas trade. After the Dutch East India Company was dissolved in 1799, Britain took over all of its trade ports, and Mincing Lane in London emerged as the global hub of the spice trade. In terms of the ginseng trade, however, the nineteenth century was a dark age for Britain as it lost the upper hand in the ginseng trade in China.

From the moment the United States began to directly export ginseng to China, Britain lost its leverage in the ginseng trade. The difference in shipping cost left Britain at a severe disadvantage. Guo Weidong (**郭衛東**) explains that "the British were expelled from the trade since 1804."[38] Brian L. Evans, on the other hand, concludes that rather than being expelled, the British East India Company withdrew from the ginseng trade of its own accord. According to Evans, the company naturally moved on to opium as Britain began to promote its trade, which garnered even greater profits than ginseng.[39]

Britain did not, however, completely abandon the ginseng trade. Signs of its continued interest in the trade can be found foremost in records related to import duties. Britain was a proponent of free trade in the nineteenth century, which generally made import duties a matter of social interest. Despite many controversies, Britain kept lowering its import duties over the first half of the nineteenth century. This applied to ginseng as well.[40] According to the new duty rates approved by Parliament in 1832, the rate for 100 catty[41] of ginseng was lowered from eight pounds and eight shillings to four shillings.[42] The re-introduction of income tax by the Robert Peel (1788–1850) administration further drove the duty rate down to two shillings for ginseng.[43] By 1845, Britain removed duties on 430 imported items, including ginseng.[44]

According to a report on overseas trade submitted to Parliament, Britain exported 3,024 pounds of ginseng (worth 189 British pounds) to China in 1812

TABLE 7.1 United States' exports of domestic ginseng, 1821–1899 [Carlson, "Ginseng," 239]

	1821–1829	*1830–1839*	*1840–1849*	*1850–1859*	*1860–1869*	*1870–1879*	*1880–1889*	*1890–1899*	*Total*	*(%)*
Lb	3,871,765	3,192,375	3,915,129	1,999,999	4,149,445	4,041,727	6,771,830	2,163,302	30,105,572	
Metric tons	1,756	1,448	1,776	907	1,882	1,833	3,071	981	13,654	
Value $	1,432,524	1,108,010	1,637,340	987,462	3,902,218	4,537,008	3,457,294	7,639,859	24,692,715	
Average value/lb	0.37	0.35	0.42	0.49	0.94	1.12	0.51	3.53	0.97	
Destinations (lb)*										
Africa	–	–	–	–	6,747	–	–	–	6,747	(0.2)
Asia										
Far East	3.612,081	3,136,122	3,871,901	1,997,797	4,141,342	3,672,527	6,712,824	2,162,187	29,306,781	(97.35)
Southeast Asia	14,996	10,408	28,059	–	–	–	–	–	53,463	(0.18)
Europe										
Northern	97,072	15,031	13,443	-	1,356	366,187	58,946	–	552,035	(1.83)
Southern	127,891	16,955	–	–	–	–	–	–	144,846	(0.48)
Latin America										
South America	–	10,000	–	1,500	–	3,013	–	–	14,513	(0.05)
West Indies										(0.01)
Oceania										
Australia	–	–	1,036	–	–	–	–	–	1,036	–
Other Pacific	1,338	–	–	–	–	–	60	–	1,398	(0.01)
Canada	–	–	690	702	–	–	–	1,115	2,507	(0.01)
Other	18,317**	–	–	–	–	–	–	–	18,317	(0.06)

Source: United States Treasury Department, Statistics Bureau, Foreign Commerce and Navigation, Annual reports, 1821–1899.

*Pounds by country/area: Argentina (10,000), Australia (1,036), British American colonies (1,563), British East Indies (9,385), Canada (1,817), Chile (1,500), China (16,464,975), China, including Hong Kong and Singapore (474,310), China and Japan (1,356,656), Cisplatine Republic (presently Uruguay) (1,046), Colombia (3,013), Danish West Indies (2,986), Dutch East Indies (38,718), England/United Kingdom (548,151), Floridas (70), Germany (150), Gibraltar (144,567), Hanse Towns (122), Hawaiian Islands (60), Holland/Netherlands (1,360), Holland and Dutch colonial possessions (1,206), Hong Kong (10,947,459), Japan (63,381), Liberia and ports in Africa (6,747), Northwest coast of America (18,317), Philippine Islands (5,360), South Seas (1,338), and Spain (279).

and 1,837 pounds (worth 115 British pounds) in 1823.[45] What is interesting is that the East India Company was not responsible for importing some of the ginseng brought to Britain around the time. An act promulgated in 1812 specified that certain goods would be detained at warehouses at the port of London if they hadn't been imported by the East India Company and had outstanding duties. Among these goods was ginseng.[46] This indicates that although the East India Company had withdrawn from trading ginseng, other British merchants had continued to engage in the trade.

In 1834, the *Caledonian Mercury* published an article about two British ships that entered the port of Liverpool after their voyage to China. According to the article, "crude" ginseng was sold in Canton for thirty to thirty-four dollars per picul and fifty-five to sixty dollars per picul for "clarified" ginseng from Britain.[47] The ginseng Britain exported to China had been imported from the United States and Canada. Britain's trade with Canada increased significantly between 1800 and 1805, during which Canada exported fur, oil, timber, and ginseng. Ginseng was also included in the list of American goods unloaded at the London docks in 1810, and it must have been a considerable amount based on the note that its worth was 140,000 dollars.[48] Records of cargo unloaded at the port of Cardiff between 1873 and 1874 show that one J.B. Taylor in London ordered a total of 204 casks of ginseng.[49]

In London, a large auction of imported goods was held four times a year, which the East India Company had taken part in since the mid-seventeenth century. In 1788, *The Times* advertised that 2,650 pounds of nutmeg and 114 casks of ginseng would be auctioned off at a coffee house on Exchange Alley.[50] Other auctions were held at places like portside warehouses upon the arrival of a ship, which was why advertisements on the sale or auction of ginseng often appeared all over Britain, from Liverpool to Birmingham to Dublin.[51] Auctioned goods were distributed domestically or exported overseas. "Wine ginseng" would sometimes turn up on lists of auctioned goods, but it remains unknown as to whether the term was used to refer to ginseng pickled in wine or red ginseng that exhibited a wine-like hue.[52]

As of 1843, the Chinese tariff on imported ginseng is presented in Table 7.2.[53]

According to Table 7.2, tariff rates differed between the first and the second quality ginseng. The Chinese tariff on any kind of imported tea, on the other hand, was 2 taels, 5 maces, 3 candareens, and 47 cash per picul. This standard was

TABLE 7.2 Chinese tariff on imported ginseng in 1843

		per	*T.* (兩)	*M.* (錢)	*C.* (分)	*C.* (釐)	*D.* (毫)	*C.* (絲)
Ginseng	First quality	Picul	38	0	0	0	52	77
	Second quality or refuse		3	5	0	0	4	86

T(兩) = tael / M(錢) = mace (1/10 tael) / C(分) = candareen (1/100 tael) / C(釐) = cash (1/1,000 tael) / D(毫) = hao (1/10,000 tael) / C(絲) = si (1/100,000 tael)

different from that applied to goods including ginseng, which developed into an issue between China and its trade partners. In Britain's case, even after satisfying its demands through the Treaty of Nanjing, it craved more from China.

In 1843, *The Examiner* scrutinized detailed aspects of the treaty so as to openly criticize the shortcomings of Henry Pottinger (1789–1856) who negotiated the treaty's terms. It pointed out that the treaty failed to secure enough warehousing room and that the residential space for foreigners was extremely limited, which led to the suggestion of taking over the property monopolized by the *hong* merchants. It particularly complained about the switch to levying duty by weight, which increased the tax burden on tea, and claimed that the duty on tea should have been differentiated depending on quality, as was the case for other goods like ginseng, shark's fin, and nutmeg.[54]

The Chinese tariff on ginseng went through several adjustments. By 1860, the duty on crude American ginseng was six taels per catty and eight taels per catty on clarified American ginseng.[55] In terms of exports, an ad valorem tariff of 5 percent was imposed on Chinese ginseng, while five taels and three taels were each imposed on a catty of Korean or Japanese ginseng.[56] By 1866, all imported and exported ginseng were subject to an ad valorem tariff of 5 percent.[57]

Although Britain continued to engage in the ginseng trade, the United States had long outshined it in terms of volume. Nevertheless, the British press remained conscious of and kept reporting on the United States' ginseng exports throughout the nineteenth century. *The Manchester Guardian* pointed out that the main reason the United States' trade volume with China jumped between 1838 and 1839 was because its export of ginseng had quadrupled.[58] After the Treaty of Wanghia was concluded in 1844, *The Times* in London published a column complaining that China had granted the United States too many privileges, adding that American ginseng was likely to become a major item of export to China.[59]

The British press also provided constant updates on the price of American ginseng in China. It would report on the volume of ginseng available at markets in Canton, Shanghai, and Amoy, and on how well it was selling. One report stated that the demand for ginseng was so high[60] in Canton that the price of crude ginseng was 70 to 80 dollars and 130 to 140 dollars for clarified ginseng, although no sales were made at such prices.[61]

Britain's fear of the American expansion was what compelled it to remain conscious of the United States' export of ginseng. Once the American frontier reached the west coast and cities appeared along the coast, the United States gained a shortcut to China across the Pacific without having to make a detour around Africa. Britain not only foresaw such developments but grew deeply concerned about the changes they would bring to the hegemonic order in the world.

Since the mid-nineteenth century, approximately 85 percent of the North American ginseng exported to China departed from San Francisco. The times in which exporting ginseng to China required making a trip three-quarters of the way around the world had come to an end. Ginseng collected from eastern regions was transported by railway to the west coast where it was loaded on ships destined for China. Having anticipated this since the early nineteenth century, Britain had been on edge. As early as 1814, *The Times* predicted that America would ambitiously advance westward, dominating the Pacific as well as the South Sea, and sell fur and ginseng to China as well as to a quarter of the other countries around the world.[62] The concern was that the Pacific might turn into the United States' "backyard."

Britain's concern started to turn into reality as the United States planned to build military and commercial bases along its west coast. When a bill proposing that a port of entry to be built at the Columbia River basin in Oregon was discussed in Congress in 1825, *The Morning Chronicle* predicted that the United States was likely to profit greatly from exporting ginseng and fur to China since it was the country's most important market overseas.[63] One year later, a report in *The Times* bemoaned that British ships had been replaced by their American rivals on routes across the Pacific and predicted that the ginseng's share in American exports was likely to increase because fur-producing animals like beavers were on the brink of extinction.[64]

In 1843, a British newspaper article reported that the American west coast was brimming with expectations that ginseng exports might increase upon learning that China was to open its ports. The article was, of course, misleading in stating that American ginseng growing wild in western states was as good as Manchurian ginseng.[65] Even if ginseng had been growing in the western regions of North America, exportable ginseng was being procured entirely from the country's eastern parts. The journalist who wrote the article may have been compelled to say that ginseng grew in the west only to emphasize the importance of the American west coast and its potential to economically threaten Britain. In January 1850, an editorial in *The Morning Chronicle* mentioned that the steamer *Empire City*'s return to San Francisco from China was just a prelude to the colossal volume of transportation that was set to occur across the Pacific. In other words, America's greatest expansion had already begun.[66]

Notes

1 Manget, "Ginseng, China, and the Transformation of the Ohio Valley, 1783–1840," 17.
2 American Philosophical Society, *Transactions of the American Philosophical Society*, vol. 1 (Philadelphia, PA, 1771), v; Mathew Carey, ed., *The American Museum, or Repository of Ancient and Modern Fugitive Pieces, &c.*, vol. 2 (Philadelphia, PA, 1787), 177.
3 Jonathan Carver, *The New Universal Traveller* (London, 1779), 4–5.
4 Adair, *The History of the American Indians*, 361–363.
5 Fontenoy, "Ginseng, Otter Skins, and Sandalwood," 4.
6 Philip Chadwick Foster Smith, *The Empress of China* (Philadelphia, PA: Philadelphia Maritime Museum, 1984), 9–12, 28–34.
7 Fontenoy, "Ginseng, Otter Skins, and Sandalwood," 5.
8 Picul, also referred to as *dan* (擔), was a Chinese and Southeast Asian unit of weight used in maritime transport. It was defined as the maximum weight one person could carry, which was roughly 63.55 kilograms. One picul was equal to 100 *jin* (斤) or sixteen *guan* (貫) and fifteen piculs equaled one ton.

9 Wang, "Chinese Civilization and the United States," 119.
10 Wang, "Chinese Civilization and the United States," 119.
11 Samuel Shaw, *The Journals of Major Samuel Shaw* (Taipei: Ch'eng-Wen Publishing Co., 1968), 342–352.
12 Shaw, *The Journals of Major Samuel Shaw*, 342, 350–351.
13 *The Rural Magazine and Literary Evening Fire-Side* 1, no. 10 (1820): 381.
14 Hosea Ballou Morse, *The Chronicles of the East India Company Trading to China 1635–1834*, vol. 2 (Cambridge, MA: Harvard University Press, 1926), 174, 180; Board of Trade, *Tables of the Revenue, Population, Commerce of the United Kingdom, Part III* (London: William Clowes, 1834), C2.
15 "Estimate of Expenditure and Profits for the Voyage of the Empress of China," reel 15, folio 5888, L. C. John Holker Papers (JHP).
16 East India Company, *First, Second, and Third Reports of the Select Committee, Appointed by the Court of Directors of the East India Company* (London, 1793), 34.
17 Morse, *The Chronicles of the East India Company Trading to China 1635–1834*, 174–180.
18 East India Company, *First, Second, and Third Reports of the Select Committee, Appointed by the Court of Directors of the East India Company*, 32.
19 Fontenoy, "Ginseng, Otter Skins, and Sandalwood," 5.
20 Anna Youngman, "The Fortune of John Jacob Astor," *Journal of Political Economy* 16, no. 6 (1908): 350–352.
21 Donald Jackson and Dorothy Twohig, eds., *The Papers of George Washington, Diaries*, vol. 4 (Charlottesville, VA: University of Virginia Press, 1976), 20.
22 Barnes, *Needles, Herbs, Gods, and Ghosts*, 176.
23 Manget, "Ginseng, China, and the Transformation of the Ohio Valley, 1783–1840," 14.
24 Oren Frederic Morton, *A History of Monroe County, West Virginia* (Dayton, VA: Ruebush-Elkins, 1916), 191–194.
25 Smith, *The Empress of China*, 41–42.
26 Nathan Hale, *The American System, or the Effects of High Duties on Imports Designed for the Encouragement of Domestic Industry* (Boston, MA: Nathan Hale's Press, 1826), 77.
27 Fontenoy, "Ginseng, Otter Skins, and Sandalwood," 7.
28 $70,202 (1834); $94,970 (1835); $211,405 (1836); $109,368 (1837); $36,622 (1838); $118,904 (1839); $22,728 (1840); $437,245 (1841). *The American Farmer's Encyclopedia* (New York: A. O. Moore, Agricultural Book Publisher, 1860), 540.
29 "From Our American Correspondent," *Manchester Times*, January 28, 1852.
30 "Commercial Notes," *Glasgow Herald*, October 24, 1884.
31 "The United States," *The Morning Chronicle*, December 25, 1849; "America-Commercial Intelligence," *The Times*, October 5, 1850; "The United States," *The Morning Chronicle*, January 23, 1850; "The United States," *The Morning Chronicle*, March 5, 1850; "The United States," *The Morning Chronicle*, August 14, 1850; "The United States," *The Morning Chronicle*, August 27, 1850; "By Magnetic Telegraph, Philadelphia," *The Morning Chronicle*, December 18, 1850; "The United States," *The Morning Chronicle*, June 24, 1852.
32 Schorger, "Ginseng: A Pioneer Resource," 67.
33 "Tens of Thousands Line City Streets to Pay Last Tribute to Colonel Short," *The China Press*, April 25, 1932.
34 "Last Month's Price Index Number 16 Points Higher than for November 1925," *The China Press*, December 29, 1926.
35 "Message to Overseas Chinese," *The North China Herald and Supreme Court & Consular Gazette*, April 21, 1928.
36 The National Institute for the Promotion of Science, *Fourth Bulletin of the National Institute for the Promotion of Science, February 1845 to November 1846* (Washington, DC: W. Q. Force, 1846), 554.
37 "A Great Market for Ginseng, Annual Report of Consul Johnson, Dated Amoy, China, July 29, 1897," in *Consular Reports: Commerce, Manufactures, Etc.*, vol. 60 (Washington, DC: Government Printing Office, 1897), 473–474.

38 Guo, "Xiyangshen," 125–126.
39 Evans, "Ginseng," 22.
40 Britain's efforts to achieve free trade began to materialize in the form of lowering import duties. Through William Huskisson's limited reform in 1824/1825 and Robert Peel's reform in the 1840s, import duties became limited to a maximum of five percent on raw materials, twelve percent on semi-processed goods, and twenty percent on processed goods. In 1845, the import duties on raw cotton were abolished and after William Ewart Gladstone further lowered duties in the 1850s, nearly all protective duties and differential duties became abolished in the 1860s.
41 Catty, also known as *jin* (斤), is a unit of weight used in China and Southeast Asia. One catty is approximately 600 grams, although this conversion is known to have varied between countries as well as markets and public offices in China.
42 "Schedule of Duties," *The Hull Packet and Humber Mercury*, June 19, 1832.
43 "The New Tariff," *The Morning Chronicle*, March 14, 1842.
44 "The Proposed New Tariff," *The Morning Chronicle*, February 22, 1845; "Taxes Repealed," *The Leeds Mercury*, March 1, 1845; "The New Tariff," *The Manchester Times and Gazette*, March 1, 1845; "The Arsenic, Beef-Wood, and Tiger-Tall Tariff," *Liverpool Mercury*, February 28, 1845; "The Hangman's 'Moral Lessons'," *The Morning Chronicle*, April 3, 1845.
45 Britain's export of ginseng amounted to 1,792 pounds (worth 112 British pounds) in 1813, 5,992 pounds (worth 375 British pounds), and 1,904 pounds (worth 119 British pounds) in 1822. Board of Trade, *Tables of the Revenue, Population, Commerce of the United Kingdom, Part III*, 366–373.
46 "Gazette Issue 16573," *London Gazette*, February 8, 1812; "Gazette Issue 16574," *London Gazette*, February 11, 1812. Until the 1820s, ginseng appeared in trade statistics for ships hired by the East India Company.
47 "Foreign Intelligence," *Caledonian Mercury*, November 8, 1834.
48 The transport fee (landing charge) was 1s per cask. The storage fee per week was 1s per cask. William Anderson, *The London Commercial Dictionary and Sea-Port Gazetteer* (London: Printed for Effingham Wilson, 1819), 17, 212.
49 "District Intelligence," *Western Mail*, July 3, 1873; "Shipping Intelligence," *Western Mail*, February 12, 1874.
50 "Sales by Candle," *The Times*, February 6, 1788.
51 "Advertisements & Notices," *Liverpool Mercury*, June 1, 1860; "Advertisements & Notices," *Glasgow Herald*, March 27, 1882; "Advertisements & Notices," *Birmingham Daily Post*, June 28, 1883; "Advertisements & Notices," *Glasgow Herald*, August 1, 1883; "Advertisements & Notices," *The Era*, July 30, 1887; "Advertisements & Notices," *Freeman's Journal and Daily Commercial Advertiser*, September 6, 1889.
52 "Advertisements & Notices," *Glasgow Herald*, May 9, 1881.
53 "Foreign Intelligence," *The Manchester Times and Gazette*, October 14, 1843; "Schedule Tariff of Duties of the Foreign Trade with China," *Liverpool Mercury*, October 13, 1843; "Proclamation," *The Belfast News-Letter*, October 13, 1843.
54 "The Political Examiner," *The Examiner*, October 21, 1843.
55 "Gazette Issue 22465," *London Gazette*, December 28, 1860.
56 "Gazette Issue 22465," *London Gazette*, December 28, 1860.
57 "Gazette Issue 23160," *London Gazette*, September 7, 1866.
58 "Commerce of the United States," *The Manchester Guardian*, January 6, 1841.
59 "Our Foreign Trade with China," *The Times*, July 26, 1845.
60 "China," *The Morning Chronicle*, September 23, 1850.
61 "Canton Market Report, February 26," *The Morning Chronicle*, April 13, 1852.
62 "For The Times," *The Times*, November 5, 1814.
63 "American Papers," *The Morning Chronicle*, January 20, 1825.
64 "The American Fur and Sandal-Wood Trade," *The Times*, March 31, 1826.
65 "The American Markets," *The Morning Chronicle*, January 31, 1843.
66 "The United States," *The Morning Chronicle*, January 23, 1850.

8

GINSENG AND CIRCUMSTANCES IN EAST ASIA

Throughout the early-to-mid-nineteenth century, the British press continued to report about ginseng and the American expansion of production and export, until its focus shifted to East Asia in the late nineteenth century. As the most influential medium at the time, newspapers painted vivid descriptions of how the Western powers' economic and political desire to plunder East Asia was unfolding through ginseng. Although they included many inaccurate details and were founded on equally inaccurate preconceptions, newspaper articles still managed to lay bare the desires, interests, and intentions of the Western powers that were hidden in commercial treaties they half-forced their East Asian counterparts to sign.

The amount of attention newspapers paid to ginseng showed that it was considered to be a resource that was extremely useful to imperialist expansion. Even lesser-known or rural papers eagerly conveyed news about newly discovered ginseng. For instance, in 1828, *The Asiatic Journal*, circulated in London, reported that on October 10, 1827, the Medical and Physical Society of Calcutta had announced the discovery of ginseng in Nepal. According to the report, a surgeon named Nathaniel Wallich (1786–1854) found ginseng on a mountaintop in the Bengal plains at an altitude of between 9,000 and 10,000 feet.[1]

Wallich's report added that unlike the Chinese, the Nepalese didn't use ginseng, nor did they know anything about it. Wallich named the ginseng he discovered as "panax pseudo-ginseng" and concluded that it was related to "real ginseng" from Manchuria and North America.[2] Wallich's conclusion was quoted and disseminated through newspapers as well as other media channels. It hints not only at the hope that it might have been a valuable resource even though it might not have been "real ginseng" but also at the desire for the unregulated collection of a plant of little concern to the locals. The implicit imperialist ambition in the article was disseminated to readers in the West, causing them to share that ambition.

DOI: 10.4324/9781003286691-10

Interest in Manchuria

In 1867, *The Manchester Guardian* published an interesting article titled "Ginseng."[3] According to the article, China previously permitted only forty merchants to trade in ginseng only after they offered a certain amount from their collected stock to the government. Those merchants mainly hired outlaws who snuck into the rough wilderness, despite the risk of being "menaced by starvation, and by the wolf, the tiger and the leopard." Wild ginseng, however, had grown so scarce by the reign of the Daoguang Emperor (道光帝, r. 1820–1850) that a considerable amount had to be collected in Russian territories. The article added that although the Chinese government didn't encourage the cultivation of ginseng, a substantial amount was already being grown in Manchuria and Korea. Traditionally, Qing rulers had considered ginseng cultivated in the mountains, known as *yangshen* (秧蔘), as fake ginseng and banned it from being distributed for medicinal purposes. Upon the depletion of wild ginseng, however, there was no choice left but to lift the ban on cultivating ginseng.[4]

As powers increasingly competed in East Asia, the cultivation of ginseng turned into a sensitive issue. Like its competitors, Britain was keeping an eye on the moves Russia was making as it sought to pressure China from the north. As early as 1812, *The Observer* reported the fact that China and Russia had each attempted and failed to cultivate ginseng in their "respective territories." China managed to harvest ginseng but had to dispose of the entire batch because the quality turned out to be so poor. As a result, the shortage of ginseng grew so severe that Korean ginseng was worth five times more than silver in Beijing.[5]

Through the 1858 Treaty of Aigun and the 1860 Convention of Peking, China lost the lands north of the Amur River and east of the Ussuri River, which happened to be major areas of ginseng production. Having had its eye on ginseng, Russia began to take action as soon as the treaties were concluded. And Britain was on the alert as it kept track of Russia's every move. In 1860, *The Times* quoted a Russian newspaper article to report that the Siberia branch of the Imperial Russian Geographical Society launched an expedition to survey the Ussuri River and the valleys at the southeastern edge of Manchuria near Korea. *The Times* report added that the expedition had likely been fueled by the Russian desire to create a ginseng plantation near the Ussuri River.[6]

As Russia's aspiration to expand south grew evident, Manchuria surfaced as a subject of interest among the British, who wished to keep in check the Russian desire for an ice-free port.[7] British newspaper articles highlighted the fact that although Manchuria was a "colony of outlaws," it was a cornucopia of gold mines and ginseng.[8] In 1886, a group of British experts embarked on an expedition to Manchuria. *The Times* as well as other British papers also reported about the publication of *The Long White Mountain*, a travelogue of the expedition written by Henry Evan Murchison James (1846–1923).[9] Through the book, James, who was a member of the Indian Civil Service, offered detailed portrayals of hunters and ginseng diggers in Manchuria as well as ginseng growers who had migrated from Korea.[10]

Ginseng digging in Manchuria was also mentioned in a report about the 1873 World's Fair in Vienna. The report mentioned that China had displayed ginseng at the exhibition, despite the fact that the panacea had grown so rare in China that it had to be imported from the United States or Korea through the port of Yantai. Interestingly enough, the report noted that while the Manchus were very careful in digging up ginseng, they described it as a weed the Chinese coveted as medicine.[11] In 1898, *The Times* published a detailed introduction about the finances of Manchuria based on a report by an expert on China named Edward Harper Parker (1849–1926). According to the introduction, Manchuria was experiencing a shortage of ginseng because forest reclamation had made it difficult to secure the 1,000 to 2,000 taels worth of ginseng that used to be imported annually through border trade with Korea.[12] In an 1895 newspaper report on Japan's attack on Manchuria and its occupation of Niuzhuang, ginseng was mentioned as a major export item of Manchuria.[13]

Ginseng, Korea's Best Resource

In the late nineteenth century, Korea started to be mentioned far more frequently in Western newspapers. Britain showed a great interest in Korea because the peninsula had turned into an arena of heated competition for great powers. Korea appeared to be a potential trade partner and a country newly being discovered in Asia.[14] And, without fail, ginseng was mentioned in every introduction to Korea's politics, economy, geography, or culture. Alongside gold, ginseng was noted as one of Korea's most important export items.[15] Korea was a country with great potential for trade but did not require the dispatch of an ambassador or warship, and its major export items were gold and ginseng.[16]

In 1888, *The Manchester Guardian* published a very detailed introduction to Korea. While the "hermit kingdom" was a country with a vast history, having been established in "2235 BC" (likely a mistaken attempt at reporting the year 2333 BC, the generally accepted date of the founding of the Gojoseon kingdom), it had turned into a target of competition for China, Russia, and Japan, with the United States about to join the race. The introduction highlighted Korean ginseng as a valuable resource on par with gold in terms of value.[17]

Another article in 1887 quoted a report by the British consulate in Seoul to mention that the export of gold and large volumes of ginseng accounted for the significant gap between Korea's exports, worth 84,037 British pounds, and imports, worth 411,786 British pounds.[18] In 1890, the *Glasgow Herald* even remarked with pity that, "There does not exist in the world under a civilized Government a country poorer than Corea is at present."

> At present the Corean King and Government live from ginseng, a root which the Chinese consume for medicinal purposes, and in which they have the utmost faith. It is a monopoly of the Government, and on this little plant rests the whole fabric of Corean administration.[19]

The reason the Chosŏn government could sustain itself under strenuous economic circumstances was because ginseng was held in such high regard. At the time, Korean ginseng started to be cited as the best of its kind. This was contrary to how it was regarded in the West during the seventeenth and eighteenth centuries, when Korean ginseng was stigmatized as inferior, attributable largely to Du Halde's *General History of China*, which had been definitive in forming the European understanding of ginseng. While the book explained that ginseng could be found in Paekche and was used by the "Kingdom of Sin lo" as a tributary item, it ultimately considered Korean ginseng second-rate compared to Shangdang ginseng.[20] A geography book published in Britain in 1790 mentioned that thanks to the quality ginseng growing in the cold, northern parts of Korea, its people were able to profit from trading with the Japanese. Yet, the same book still described Korean ginseng as second-rate.[21]

Such treatment, however, showed signs of change by the late nineteenth century. British newspapers would often mention how the Chinese prized Korean ginseng, which was a major trade item for Korea.[22] In 1904, *The Times* quoted a report by the American consul in Korea to explain that Manchuria and Korea were native habitats of Manchurian ginseng.[23] What is interesting is that the article featured cultivated instead of wild ginseng and yet conveyed the widespread belief that cultivated ginseng was inferior to wild ginseng. Other newspaper reports went into further detail on how ginseng was cultivated and prepared for export: seeds were covered with moss and grown in the shade under canopies made of pine trees for five years until the plant's roots grew big enough to be dug up and sun-dried.[24] Such cultivated ginseng was still less effective than the famous wild ginseng found in forests near the Ussuri or Amur rivers, but was nevertheless highly valued on the Chinese market.[25]

Such high regard for Korean ginseng may have been attributable to Korea's advanced cultivation technique, but another factor likely at play was the fact that wild ginseng was on the verge of extinction in China. Ginseng was already nearing depletion during the Ming dynasty, a crisis the subsequent Qing dynasty also failed to avoid even after closing Manchuria off through the *fengjin* policy. In 1886, the *Glasgow Herald* remarked that while ginseng was a medicinal herb widely used in East Asia, it was almost entirely supplied by Korea.[26] This was consistent with the circumstances described in *What Is Ginseng?* (1905), one of the first books to impart information on how to grow ginseng. The book noted that, "Corea has been in the source of main supply of China for Ginseng roots" and that "when China thinks about Corea it is not about political status but the ginseng that comes from Corean mountains."[27]

As much as it was valued, Korean ginseng was placed under separate management. British newspapers reported that ginseng was monopolized by the king and only a select few farmers were authorized to cultivate it.[28] In 1885, *The Times* reported that Parliament had published a blue book based on a report by a diplomat who visited Korea. That diplomat was William R. Carles (1848–1929). Having served as a British Vice-Consul in China and Korea, Carles later relayed his experience in Korea through his book *Life in Corea* (1888), in which he discussed ginseng in detail, just has he had in his report that was the basis for the blue book.[29] According to Carles, ginseng was a staple product of Korea monopolized by the king and government and exported to China. It was mainly produced and processed in an area called Kaesŏng with a population of about 40,000. He added that while selling ginseng may be a tremendously profitable enterprise, it was bound to suffer from the trade of North American ginseng.[30]

The Western press now took an interest in Kaesŏng (Songdo), the main production area of ginseng. In a report about "Corean tobacco-pouches of oiled silk" popular among officers of her Majesty's navy, the London-based *Daily News* mentioned that Songdo was the very place where such pouches were produced. Songdo was primarily known for producing ginseng, a commodity for export like tobacco pouches. The report explained that while white or natural ginseng was grown in various places across the peninsula, red ginseng was produced only in Songdo by steaming ginseng in earthenware pots. It added that ginseng was widely recognized as a cure-all, although it was lately being replaced with quinine peddled by people who sold Bibles (Figure 8.1).[31]

Gradually, the Western press began to differentiate red ginseng from ordinary ginseng. Red ginseng was described as a tributary item Korean envoys traditionally offered only to the Chinese imperial family, the export of which, therefore, had been banned for a long time. Because it was so rare, Chinese officials employed various methods to smuggle red ginseng into China and were suspected of continuing to import it through illegal channels.[32] Newspapers would also report about the trade of red ginseng that took place at regular markets in Beijing as well as markets along the border through which Chinese as well as European merchants were able to acquire red ginseng by barter.[33]

Newspaper articles covering overseas trade in a more official capacity revealed how Korea was being deprived of its right to trade. One of them was "The Trade of Corea," published in *The Times* in 1889, which became widely circulated as other papers rushed to relay its content.[34] The article pointed out that although Korea's trade with European countries was increasing, it was being dictated by China and Japan so that European goods had to pass through Japan in order to reach Korea. Meanwhile, compiling statistics on Korea's external trade was challenging because the trade of major export items like ginseng and gold remained untraceable. As the Korean king's largest source of income, red ginseng was, in principle, prohibited from being exported, although there were reports of it being supplied to China under strict surveillance. Rumor had it that red ginseng was being smuggled out of Korea while opium was being smuggled into the country, but there was no way of knowing exactly how much trade was taking place along the border.[35]

WATCHMAN IN GINSENG GARDEN.

FIGURE 8.1 Korean ginseng garden.

Japan's Plundering of Korean Ginseng

British newspapers often exhibited an acute wariness of Japanese aspirations to plunder the Korean peninsula and advance into China. The British who visited Japan paid attention to its modernization efforts and observed mines and factories across the country. The intelligence thus gathered was delivered back to their homeland and sometimes shared nationwide through the press. In 1871, a British diplomat stationed in Niigata witnessed ginseng being processed at Wakamatsu Castle. The diplomat documented the process in detail, and the report he submitted became publicized through *The Times*.[36]

Immediately after the conclusion of the 1876 Treaty of Kanghwa, foreign newspapers began publishing articles pointing out the trade disparity between Korea and Japan.[37] Without fail, such articles mentioned ginseng to criticize how Japan was using the treaty to force Korea into exporting its ginseng. In 1877, *The Times* cited a report by Harry Smith Parkes (1828–1885), the British Consul General to Japan, to lambaste Japan for sending a ship to sell all kinds of foreign merchandise at a time when Korea was overflowing with corpses from severe famine. Parkes reported that "a Corean came to a Japanese merchant ship, and tried hard to sell a child of seven years old even for 5 cents." The article was brimming with pity for Korea's situation, having been left with nothing worth exporting to Japan except for ox hides, gold, and ginseng.[38]

In its coverage of Korea's imports and exports since it opened the port in Wŏnsan, the *London Gazette* reported that the ban the Korean government placed on the export of red ginseng was equally applied to the trade treaty Korea concluded with the United States in 1882. The coverage added that exclusive rights to red ginseng must have been awarded to Kaesŏng merchants because the item was in such high demand in China.[39] In the meantime, Japan depended on its capital strength to satisfy its desire for Kaesŏng ginseng. In 1899, detailed media coverage attributed the revolt in Kaesŏng to those in the ginseng industry.

> Trouble is on over the control of this crop. By treaty stipulation the Japanese may purchase the raw root and manufacture it into red ginseng, but they may not export it, and the Coreans are prohibited from buying it of them. The Japanese, however, laugh at this arrangement and deal in the drug extensively. They have been in the habit of advancing money on the crop while in the ground, and then, if the Corean tried to get out of the bargain, harvesting the crop by force. This has Occasioned some scandal, and recently a Commission in charge of the ginseng has been appointed with Mr. McLeavy Brown at its head, and troops (to the number of 900) put at the disposal of the Commission. They have established a guard over the farms at Songdo and this year propose to prevent a repetition of past experiences of violence. The profits in the trade are enormous and it is doubtful if Japan will allow the matter to rest where it is.[40]

A mere two years after the above coverage, an article in *The Times* reported in 1901 that Japan's plundering of Korea had worsened to the point where the railway and ginseng fields had all fallen into Japanese hands, such that the most valuable among Korean crops was being "farmed by the powerful Japanese company *Mitsu Bishi*."[41]

After Japan's annexation of Korea in 1910, the Monopoly Bureau within the Japanese Government-General of Korea's Department of Finance monopolized red ginseng in Korea. On June 10, 1911, *The North China Herald* reported that the Monopoly Bureau decided to utilize electrotropism to increase the production of Kaesŏng ginseng.[42] Scientists in the West had discovered that electrotropism caused certain plants to grow faster and larger. This discovery was successfully confirmed through experiments, and because the technique caused a considerable diffusion and dissipation of electricity, "authorities, always keen in the cultivation of ginseng" expected it would be suitable for the dry Korean atmosphere. Twice a day at two in the morning and the afternoon, current was to be "passed through the stem by means of wires supported by the covering frames of the fields."

The report added that electrotropism had been used to grow crops at an experimental farm in Japan. If the technique could be successfully applied in Kaesŏng, a 10 percent increase could be expected to the then harvest of 1,500 to 2,000 tons every five years, which would far exceed the cost of installing the equipment necessary for electrotropism. While it remains undetermined as to whether this technique was actually employed, it is certain that such scientific interests and experiments had been aimed at exploiting greater amounts of Korean ginseng.

Notes

1 Nathaniel Wallich was a Danish botanist who worked for the Danish East India Company and the British East India Company in Calcutta and contributed to the development of the Calcutta Botanical Garden.
2 "Medical and Physical Society of Calcutta," *The Asiatic Journal and Monthly Miscellany* 25 (1828): 493.
3 "Ginseng," *The Manchester Guardian*, April 24, 1867.
4 Wang, *Zhongguo renshen*, 34.
5 "Untitled Article," *The Observer*, January 19, 1812.
6 "Russian Exploring Expedition," *The Morning Chronicle*, January 6, 1860; "Foreign Intelligence," *The Times*, January 3, 1860.
7 "Turning the British Flank in Asia," *The Times*, January 26, 1888.
8 "Manchuria," *The Times*, November 11, 1875.
9 Henry Evan Murchison James, *The Long White Mountain, or, A Journey in Manchuria: With Some Account of the History, People, Administration and Religion of that Country* (London: Longmans, Green, and Company, 1888).
10 "A Journey in Manchuria," *The Times*, April 4, 1888; "Literature," *Glasgow Herald*, April 3, 1888.
11 "China and the Vienna Exhibition," *The North-China Herald and Supreme Court & Consular Gazette*, March 3, 1873; "China and the Vienna Exhibition," *The North-China Herald and Supreme Court & Consular Gazette*, May 24, 1873.
12 E.H. Parker, "The Finances of Manchuria," *The Times*, May 23, 1898.
13 "This Morning's News," *Daily News*, March 8, 1895.
14 "The Closed Markets of the East," *The Manchester Guardian*, May 16, 1873.
15 "The Trade of Corea," *The Manchester Guardian*, August 13, 1889.
16 "Untitled Article," *Glasgow Herald*, May 26, 1886. In 1883, Korea and Britain concluded a Treaty of Friendship, Commerce and Navigation, and in April of the following year, a British Consulate General was established in Seoul.
17 "Corea," *The Manchester Guardian*, July 14, 1882.
18 "Commercial and Financial Notes," *The Manchester Guardian*, September 14, 1887.
19 "Our London Correspondence," *Glasgow Herald*, June 11, 1890.
20 Du Halde, *The General History of China*, vol. 4, 2–3.
21 Thomas Bankes, Edward Warren Blake, and Alexander Cook, *A New Royal Authentic and Complete System of Universal Geography Antient and Modern* (London, 1790), 128.
22 "The Economical Condition of Korea," *The Times*, August 25, 1897; "The Trade of Korea Prior to the War," *The Times*, October 9, 1894.

23 "The Production of Ginseng in Manchuria," *The Times*, August 18, 1904.
24 "Corea," *Manchester Times*, November 2, 1872.
25 "Corea," *Manchester Times*, November 2, 1872.
26 "Wednesday Morning, May 26," *Glasgow Herald*, May 26, 1886.
27 Root, *What Is Ginseng: An Account of the History and Cultivation of Ginseng*, 25.
28 "Trade Prospects in Corea-Japanese versus Manchester Goods," *The Manchester Guardian*, August 26, 1897; "Travel and Adventure," *The Newcastle Weekly Courant*, November 22, 1890; "Corea from the Saddle," *The Pall Mall Gazette*, September 8, 1891.
29 William Richard Carles, *Life in Corea* (London: Macmillan, 1888). See also "Life in Corea," *Glasgow Herald*, March 15, 1888; "A Shamefaced People," *Hampshire Telegraph and Sussex Chronicle*, March 24, 1888.
30 "Parliamentary Summary-Leading Articles-Corea," *The Times*, April 23, 1885.
31 "This Morning's News," *Daily News*, October 9, 1897.
32 "Untitled Article," *The Manchester Guardian*, February 17, 1890; "The Trade of Corea," *The Times*, August 2, 1889.
33 "Corea," *Manchester Times*, November 2, 1872; "A Corean Envoy to China," *The Graphic*, December 23, 1882.
34 "The Trade of Corea," *The Times*, August 2, 1889.
35 "Ten Years of Corean Foreign Trade," *The Times*, July 3, 1893; "The Trade of Corea," *The Times*, August 2, 1889.
36 "Tour in Japan," *The Times*, March 7, 1871.
37 "Commercial and Financial Notes," *The Manchester Guardian*, November 10, 1883; "The Treaties with Corea," *The Manchester Guardian*, August 18, 1882; "The Japanese Commercial Treaty with Corea," *The Manchester Guardian*, December 13, 1883. According to the *Chae Chosŏn Ilbon inmin t'ongsang changjŏng* (在朝鮮國日本人民通商章程) on trade rules and detailed rules on maritime customs, concluded in June 1883 as a follow-up treaty to 1876 Treaty of Kanghwa, imports were classified into eight types and duties on Japanese daily necessities were 5 percent, 8–10 percent on general goods, and 25–30 percent on luxury goods. As for export duties, an ad valorem duty of 5percent was imposed on all items except for the duty-free items of gold and silver; a duty of 15 percent was levied on ginseng.
38 "The Japanese in Corea," *The Times*, November 3, 1877.
39 "Gazette Issue 25180," *London Gazette*, December 22, 1882. Reports on the treaty of commerce concluded in 1899 between the Korean Empire and the Qing Empire noted that the export of red ginseng had been completely banned so that any Chinese caught trying to secretly purchase or export it would suffer confiscation and be fined at double the market price of what was confiscated. "China and Korea," *The Times*, October 20, 1899.
40 "Ginseng," *The North China Herald and Supreme Court & Consular Gazette*, October 9, 1899.
41 In the article, "Mitsui" was misspelled as "Mitsu Bishi." "The Situation in Korea," *The Times*, September 20, 1901.
42 "Local and General News," *The North China Herald and Supreme Court & Consular Gazette*, June 10, 1911.

PART 3
Crisis and Response

Beginning in the mid-eighteenth century, two changes morphed into what can be dubbed a crisis in the history of ginseng. One of them was the movement in Western medical circles to disparage the medicinal value of ginseng and thereby expunge it from pharmacopoeias. The other was the near depletion of wild ginseng due to its indiscriminate collection. Unlike other medicinal herbs, ginseng was a tricky plant in terms of extracting active components. As a result, its entry into the scheme of modern pharmacology was extremely slow, but this was also why ginseng managed to survive in the age of Western chemical drugs. In response to the depletion of wild ginseng, full-blown efforts were made to artificially cultivate ginseng, such that today it is grown throughout the world. Various attempts and efforts to keep ginseng alive in the face of a crisis proved to be key to extending its life amid countless medicinal ingredients and health foods that appeared and disappeared over time.

DOI: 10.4324/9781003286691-11

9

EXPUNCTION FROM PHARMACOPOEIAS?

Ginseng was a medicinal plant and prescription far more familiar to early modern medical practitioners in Britain and the United States than it is today. By the late eighteenth century, however, its reputation began to dwindle compared to other foreign medicinal ingredients. Ginseng's efficacy had started to be depreciated in British and American pharmacopoeias and materia medica. What is worth noting is that rather than taking an absolute or objective approach, such depreciation tended to find fault with the exceptional esteem ginseng enjoyed in China. Descriptions would state that although the Chinese may have believed in the "extraordinary virtues" of ginseng, Europeans found it hard to share that belief.[1]

After ascribing significance to the merits of ginseng, why did British and American medical discourse later display cynicism toward ginseng? Several different circumstances are likely to have contributed to the sudden change of attitude. One of them involved the great difficulty Britain faced in procuring ginseng. As America began to directly trade ginseng, not only did the price of ginseng in Britain skyrocket by the late eighteenth century, it grew increasingly difficult to procure. Through his materia medica, John Hill mentioned that "ginseng is a root lately brought into Europe, and extolled with immoderate praise, but its great price has prevented its hitherto coming into general use."[2] William Cullen (1710–1790), a renowned professor at the Edinburgh Medical School, went as far as to say that "while ginseng has now for many years been well known in our shops, the great price put upon it by them, would ever have engaged our attention to it as a medicine."[3] Such difficulties in gaining access to ginseng may have prompted British medical practitioners to depreciate its efficacy and exclude it from their list of applicable medicinal ingredients. Perhaps the British did so to restore their self-esteem after losing the upper hand in ginseng trade to the Americans.

DOI: 10.4324/9781003286691-12

Why, then, did similar remarks appear in American pharmacopoeias when America was mass producing and exporting ginseng? The foremost reason was because Americans simply accepted British pharmacopoeias without incorporating their domestic circumstances into them. American medical professionals were not yet capable of publishing their own pharmacopoeias and the American publishing industry was still in its inchoate stage. For expertise in fields like medicine, American immigrants therefore had to rely on publications from their homeland in Europe such as Britain or Germany. In a similar sense, they also relied heavily on European medical books published long ago in the seventeenth century. Some American medical practitioners appended to pharmacopoeias prescriptions based on "indigenous" herbs such as ginseng, senega root, and snakeroot, but only sporadically.[4]

Moreover, Americans were less eager to use ginseng medicinally since it was such a common domestic herb that could be found in abundance. In fact, John Redman Coxe (1773–1864), a professor of medicine at the University of Pennsylvania, mentioned in the *American Dispensatory* (1818) that although ginseng enjoyed an absolute prestige like silver in China, "the Americans, on the contrary, disregard it, because it is found plentifully in their woods."[5] This criticism was shared by another professor of medicine who insisted that American medical professionals should take a greater interest in using the root for medicinal purposes instead of neglecting it simply because it was so cheap and common.[6]

No Longer Covered in Pharmacopoeias?

What was most responsible for jeopardizing ginseng's stature was the claim that ginseng had been expunged from Western pharmacopoeias. For a botanic catalogue published in 1783, William Curtis (1746–1799), a renowned British botanist, classified ginseng and scores of other plants under the category of "Medicinal Plants not contained in the London and Edinburgh Dispensatories."[7] In eighteenth-century Britain, botany grew popular enough to settle down as a subject of liberal arts education and Curtis's publications on botany enjoyed its share of popularity at the forefront of this trend.

Curtis's remarks therefore gained impact and authority as they became relayed in numerous sources and even became accepted, to a certain extent, as established views. Materia medica published in the early nineteenth century often stated that ginseng "had formerly a place in the British materia medica, but which now, perhaps, is justly discarded" or that ginseng was a "superfluous article of the materia medica."[8] Ainslie Whitelaw (1767–1837), a British surgeon and writer on materia medica, even speculated that the reason ginseng disappeared from British pharmacopoeias but survived in French pharmacopoeias was probably to uphold the authority of the French Jesuit missionaries who authored them.[9]

These claims Curtis made, however, were not entirely true. *The New Pharmacopoeia of the Royal College of Physicians of London* (1788), published later than Curtis's botany books, included a detailed description of ginseng as a highly effective herb,[10] and the 1797 edition of *The Edinburgh New Dispensatory* retained its entry about ginseng.[11] An American botany book published in 1887 mentioned that ginseng "was dismissed from the U.S. Pharmacopeia at the last revision, and is simply mentioned in the Eclectic Materia Medica."[12]

These examples show that many pharmacopoeia editions published until 1882, and even as they were being revised in 1887, continued to cover ginseng.[13] What, then, caused the claim that ginseng had been expunged from pharmacopoeias? Part of the answer seemingly has to do with how pharmacopoeias were defined at the time. Today, pharmacopoeias serve as guides that suggest specific standards regarding the manufacture, description, efficacy, quality, and storage of medicines in order to ensure their homogeneity. Until the first half of the nineteenth century, however, pharmacopoeia was a term referring to a broad range of publications that involved medications. Without any legally binding guidelines to abide by, such publications were mostly published by physicians instead of apothecaries and therefore tended to be locally produced and circulated.

Hence, the claim that ginseng was expunged from Western pharmacopoeias in the late eighteenth century was not true because ginseng continued to appear in them for at least another century. Furthermore, Western medicine at the time was struggling to identify the specific efficacies of ginseng rather than disregard it entirely. It was in the process of attempting to catch up with the East Asian tradition of analyzing ginseng's medicinal effects that had begun at least a thousand years earlier. Thus, it seems necessary at this point to examine the Chinese tradition of using ginseng for medicinal purposes prior to the West's encounter with ginseng.

China's Historical Use of Ginseng

As mentioned in Part 1, ginseng's efficacy was offered with detail from the oldest Chinese pharmacopoeia, *Shennong bencaojing* (神農本草經). According to the book, ginseng was the main ingredient for medications that sought to reinforce the five internal organs, calm the mind, stop heart palpitations, rectify the soul, clear up vision, soothe the heart, and even provide wisdom. When taken long term, ginseng was expected to help one's body feel lighter and bring longevity.[14] By the Han dynasty, pharmacopoeias began to include more detailed suggestions on how ginseng could be used to treat patients. One of them was *Shanghanlun* (傷寒論), which was based on the earlier publications *Wuwei Handai yijian* (武威漢代醫簡) and *Shanghan zabing lun* (傷寒雜病論). All three have been recognized as academically significant for compiling individual medical cases dating back to antiquity and systematically theorizing them.[15]

Wuwei Handai yijian is thought to have been authored early in the Later Han period (25–220) and published on strips of bamboo at a time when paper was unavailable. Known as the earliest source to mention the medicinal use of ginseng, the book stated that ginseng could be used to treat a broad range of illnesses and listed certain rules regarding its medicinal application. Ginseng was especially used to relieve pain or symptoms of a cold. It was also used to treat epilepsy, hematochezia, bloody discharge, and leprosy, or to discharge toxins. Compared to the description in *Shennong bencaojing*, *Wuwei Handai yijian* offered more specific instructions on how to use ginseng to treat a broader range of symptoms or illnesses.[16]

Shanghan zabing lun, authored by the "wizard of medicine" Zhang Zhongjing, presented the essence of Chinese medicine's past and present. For encompassing such an abundance of medical traditions and even incorporating clinical experience into its descriptions, the book is recognized as a major contribution to the foundation of Chinese medicine and pharmacy.[17] After the original edition became lost, the book was divided into two parts and passed down as *Shanghan* (傷寒)[18] and *Zabing* (雜病). Among the 114 prescriptions included in *Shanghanlun*, twenty-one, or 18.58 percent of them, involved ginseng. According to a modern method of classification, the prescriptions involving ginseng can be classified into the following six categories:[19]

1. Antipyretic formulas (淸熱劑).
2. Harmonizing formulas (和解劑).
3. *Qi*-regulating formulas (理氣劑).[20]
4. Internal-warming formulas (溫里劑).
5. Replenishing formulas (補益劑).
6. Worm-expelling formulas (驅蟲劑).

Rather than the contemporary understanding of ginseng as a restorative, *Shanghanlun* served as specific proof that ginseng had been clinically used as a major medicinal ingredient in treatment and emergencies.[21]

Ginseng's medical application is considered to have reached its pinnacle during the Tang dynasty. *Beiji qianjin yaofang* (備急千金要方, 652) and its supplement *Qianjin yifang* (千金翼方), authored by the "king of medicine" Sun Simiao (孫思邈, 581–682), who refused government posts and instead devoted his entire life to medicine, are known as works demonstrating that ginseng had established itself as the most highly regarded medicinal herb in Chinese medicine. This is because no less than 445 prescriptions in *Beiji qianjin yaofang* involved ginseng, not to mention 310 prescriptions in *Qianjin yifang*. As the Tang culture spread overseas, Chinese medicine and pharmacy also became known internationally, which helped disseminate ginseng's esteem beyond China.[22]

When the Tang traditions of utilizing ginseng reached the Ming dynasty, two exceptional texts emerged. One was *Renshenchuan* (人蔘傳) by Li Yanwen (李言聞, 1483–?), the father of Li Shizhen who compiled *Bencao gangmu*. Through *Renshenchuan*, Li summarized and analyzed how ginseng was medically used prior to the Ming dynasty, endorsing good prescriptions and confronting errors to form a legitimate theory. This served as the basis for the content on ginseng in his son Li Shizhen's work *Bencao gangmu*, an extensive compilation of

Chinese knowledge and experience in botany and materia medica prior to the sixteenth century.

Among all the medicinal herbs discussed in *Bencao gangmu*, ginseng was covered more extensively than any other herb. Also, the appendix chapter on treatment methods included sixty-seven prescriptions utilizing ginseng to treat fifteen different types of symptoms.[23] Soon, parts of *Bencao gangmu* were translated and disseminated in various languages such as Latin, French, German, English, and Japanese, which unfortunately helped spread chronological errors related to ginseng habitats as well. And around the same time, ginseng became delivered to the West and made its way into the Western knowledge system, allowing Western medicine to determine its own methods of utilizing ginseng.

Notes

1 Richard Brookes, *The General Dispensatory* (London, 1773), 42; William Rhind, *A History of the Vegetable Kingdom* (Glasgow: Blackie & Son, 1841), 529.
2 Hill, *A History of the Materia Medica*, 589.
3 Cullen, *A Treatise of the Materia Medica*, 161.
4 Renate Wilson, "The Traffic in Eighteenth-Century Medicines and Medical Ideas and the 'Medicina Pennsylvania' of George de Benneville," *Pharmacy in History* 44, no. 4 (2002): 147.
5 John Redman Coxe, *The American Dispensatory* (Philadelphia, PA: Thomas Dobson, 1818), 406.
6 Constantine Samuel Rafinesque, *Medical Flora; or Manual of the Medical Botany of the United States of North America*, vol. 2 (Philadelphia, PA: S. C. Atkinson, 1830), 54.
7 Curtis, *A Catalogue of the British, Medicinal, Culinary, and Agricultural Plants, Cultivated in the London Botanic Garden*, 44.
8 Whitelaw Ainslie, *Materia Indica*, vol. 1 (London, 1826), 154; Richard Pearson, *A Practical Synopsis of the Materia Medica*, vol. 2 (London: C. and R. Baldwin, n.d.), 125.
9 Ainslie, *Materia Indica*, 154.
10 The Royal College of Physicians of London, *The New Pharmacopoeia of the Royal College of Physicians of London*, 30.
11 William Lewis, *The Edinburgh New Dispensatory*, 5th ed. (Edinburgh, 1797), 165.
12 Charles F. Millspaugh, *American Medicinal Plants* (Philadelphia, PA: Boericke & Tafle, 1887), 70.
13 Ginseng is not covered in *The Pharmacopœia of the United States of America*, Sixth Decennial Revision (New York: William Wood & Company, 1882).
14 See Li, *Shinjuhae ponch'o kangmok*, 4:49.
15 Wang, *Zhongguo renshen*, 10.
16 In November 1972, a pile of wooden slips holding medical prescriptions from the Han dynasty was discovered in Wuwei County, Gansu Province, and has come to be known as *Wuwei Handai yijian* (武威漢代醫簡). Seventy-eight out of the ninety-two slips were bamboo slips and fourteen were slips made of other wood. One bamboo slip and two slips made of other wood displayed ginseng-based prescriptions. *Wuwei Handai yijian*'s significance in the history of ginseng lies in the fact that it is the earliest record of mankind's clinical application of ginseng, not only in China but the world.
17 Wang Shuhe was the Chinese physician who pieced the book back together and divided it into two parts, which was later revised by the Bureau for Revising Medical Texts (*Jiaozheng yishuju* 校正醫書局) of the Northern Song dynasty in 1065. The book has been since passed down in three variations: the ten-volume *Shanghanlun*

(傷寒論), the three-volume *Jingui yaolue fanglun* (金匱要略方論), and the eight-volume *Jingui yuhan jing* (金匱玉函經).

18 In a broader sense, *shanghan* refers to diseases triggered by changes in the weather such as colds, strokes, and other febrile diseases.

19 Song Chengji 宋承吉, "Gu shangdang renshen shi jin zhi yaoyong renshen" 古上黨人蔘是今之藥用人蔘 [Yesterday's Shangdang Ginseng Is Today's Medicinal Ginseng], *Mingbao yuekan* 明報月刊, no. 9 (1984): 83–84; Wang, *Zhongguo renshen*, 12.

20 This formula was used to treat symptoms due to weak vital energy (*qixu* 氣虛) or when the flow of vital energy became congested (*qizhi* 氣滯) or reversed (*qini* 氣逆).

21 Wang, *Zhongguo renshen*, 12.

22 Wang, *Zhongguo renshen*, 13–14.

23 Li, *Shinjuhae ponch'o kangmok*, 4:44–66.

10

WESTERN MEDICINE'S VIEW OF GINSENG'S EFFICACY

Beginning in the seventeenth century, Europe began to overflow with medicinal ingredients from Asia, North America, and Africa. According to an analysis by Pratik Chakrabarti, the volume of inflow was at least twenty-five times greater than it had been in the past, which not only caused a rapid enlargement of European materia medica but fundamentally changed its nature.[1] In other words, imported medicinal ingredients exponentially expanded the knowledge of Europeans and spurred the publication of pharmacopoeias and medicinal plant catalogues.

European materia medica placed foreign medicinal ingredients under a category called "native tradition." Ginseng was a plant typically placed in this category within the European discourse of materia medica. Without fail, books introduced ginseng as a medicinal herb extremely revered in China, monopolized by the emperor, and used to make panaceas. This was an inaccurate description from the viewpoint of Oriental medicine. Shiu-Ying Hu has stressed that while most accounts of ginseng in English portray it as a cure-all, it was in fact used in a very limited capacity.[2] Within the category of native tradition, the discourse surrounding ginseng was nevertheless focused on its property as a panacea, and more importantly, made no distinction between Asian and American ginseng, considering them to have all originated from China. In the *Philadelphia Medical Dictionary*, ginseng was noted as "Ginseng of Tartary and North America; a species of all heal."[3]

Ginseng Formulas

Western medical practitioners used ginseng root to make medicine in the forms of powder, infusion, decoction, or extract. Pharmacopoeias published in the eighteenth and nineteenth centuries recommended that powdered ginseng be

DOI: 10.4324/9781003286691-13

prescribed at a minimum dosage of ten to twenty grains (64.799 milligrams per grain),[4] which could be increased to twenty to thirty grains[5] or up to as much as sixty grains when necessary.[6] Physicians who used powdered ginseng sometimes mixed it with honey, sugar, ginger, licorice, cinnamon, or peach pits. An American physician suggested that the prescription of powdered ginseng mixed with honey or sugar was effective as a tonic or as treatment for stomach disorders and issues related to the nervous system.[7] When administered as an infusion, dosages between one or two drams (one-eighth of an ounce per dram) and one pint could be prescribed.[8] Some physicians would occasionally use ginseng leaves to make medical tea, especially in areas where ginseng could be found in abundance, such as Canada or Philadelphia, Kentucky, and Virginia in the United States.[9]

Ginseng was, however, commonly prescribed as a decoction or extract because those two forms were believed to be the most effective.[10] William Woodville (1752–1805), a physician and botanist based in London, claimed that decocting ginseng root was the most recommended formula for medicinal purposes, for like extraction, it retained enough moisture to preserve all the beneficial properties of ginseng.[11] Because decoction was the preferred formula, the process tended to be covered in detail in pharmacopoeias and books on botany.[12]

> A dram of the ginseng root may be sliced and boiled in a quarter of a pint of water to about two ounces; then a little sugar being added, it may be drunk as soon as it is cool enough. The dose must be repeated morning and evening; but the second dose may be prepared from the same portion of root which was use at first, for it will always admit of being twice boiled.[13]

Ginseng was also made into a tincture, which was the formula European medicinal traditions had long favored. Below is the recipe for ginseng tincture suggested by the American botanist Charles F. Millspaugh (1854–1923).

> The genuine Chinese or the American root, dried and coarsely powdered, is covered with five times its weight of alcohol, and allowed to stand eight days, in a well-stoppered bottle, in a dark, cool place, being shaken twice a day. The tincture, poured off and filtered, has a clear, light-lemon color by transmitted light, an odor like the root, a taste at first bitter then dulcamarous, and an acid reaction.[14]

As a skilled botanist, Millspaugh must have been aware of the difference between Chinese and American ginseng. Yet, curiously enough, he did not make a distinction between the two when producing tinctures.

Stimulant or Demulcent?

In the mid-eighteenth century, a movement arose within Western medical circles to further pinpoint ginseng's medical efficacies. Rather than simply describing it as a panacea, efforts were made to specify which symptoms could be treated with ginseng. Samuel Stearns (1741–1810) was an American physician and astronomer who suffered severe hardships after the Revolutionary War for being a British loyalist. Stearns happened to be greatly interested in treatments based on medicinal herbs. After mentioning that, "the Radix Ginseng was formerly imported from China, and sold at Boston, in New-England, for guinea an ounce; but of late great quantities of it have been found in Canada, Vermont, and Pennsylvania," he documented his clinical experience of using ginseng as follows.

> The Chinese esteem this root as a general restorative and corroborant, and excellent in all decays of age, intemperance, or disease. It is a mucilage, sweet to the taste, with a slight degree of bitterness, and an aromatic warmth. I have frequently used it for coughs and other disorders of the lungs with success. A drachm, in slices or powder, may be boiled in a gill of water, and the decoction sweetened with sugar, and drank as soon as it is cool enough. This is for one dose; it should be repeated night and morning.[15]

In some cases, ginseng would be mixed with other drugs or used as a supplement. *The London Practice of Physic* published in 1769 prescribed antimony to treat rheumatism,[16] and if it caused diarrhea, recommended ginseng as a remedy.[17] There was also a case in which ginseng was used to facilitate digestion while treating hydrops.[18]

These records demonstrate that Western medical practitioners used ginseng to treat a variety of symptoms. Opinions were mixed, however, on the matter of which properties fundamentally belonged to ginseng. John Elliot (1736–1786), an affluent, renowned physician who served the Prince of Wales and was better known as the husband of Grace Dalrymple Elliott,[19] classified ginseng as a stimulant in *The Medical Pocket-Book* (1791), which was popular in Britain and the United States. Due to its stimulating properties, Elliot described that ginseng was used as a tonic, pain reliever, and antispasmodic.[20] Yet, other physicians argued that such pain-relieving, antispasmodic properties were the very reasons why ginseng should be classified as a demulcent rather than a stimulant.[21]

Despite such mixed opinions on whether ginseng was primarily a stimulant or antispasmodic, there was a consensus that the herb was particularly effective in stimulating the stomach and offering general revitalization.[22] Hill defined ginseng as an excellent medicine used by European physicians to treat spasms, vertigo, and all nerve disorders, and recommended it as one of the most effective among all the known restoratives.[23] Hill's book was so popular that the statement he made in it kept resurfacing in materia medica books authored by others later on.[24] The British physician J.A. Cope declared that ginseng was a "sovereign remedy for all weaknesses" and highly effective in treating a wide range of symptoms, specifically that,

> it dissolves pituitous humours; that it cures weakness of the lungs and pleurisy; that it stops vomitings; it strengthens the stomach, and helps the appetite; that it disperses fumes or vapours; that it fortifies the breast, and is a remedy for short and weak breathing; that it strengthens the vital spirits, and increases lymph in the blood; in short, that it is good against dizziness of the head, and dimness of the sight; and that it prolongs life in old age.[25]

Cope's claim suggests that ginseng was recommended mostly to improve numerous symptoms related to asthenia. At a broader scale, however, ginseng was often prescribed to either boost a patient's stamina before undergoing the main treatment or to restore someone who regularly underwent purgation to maintain one's health.[26]

American Prescriptions after the Nineteenth Century

By the nineteenth century, Americans came to utilize ginseng far more than the British, at least on record. A manual for botany published in 1830 in Philadelphia noted that American physicians found ginseng to be very effective in treating "asthma, weak stomach, debility, pains in the bones, gravelly complaints."[27] One of the more intriguing cases involved the use of ginseng tincture to treat alcoholism. A "Dr. Culter" and "Dr. Greenway" reportedly had long used ginseng to successfully treat alcoholics. The two physicians stressed that ginseng was also an excellent treatment for convulsions, vertigoes, nervous affections, palsy, dysentery, and even with dosages as low as ten to twenty grains, marked improvement could be witnessed. "Dr. Hales," who practiced in Troy, Michigan, used ginseng as "a good analeptic and restorative in fevers." Dr. Hales was rather unique for making frequent use of the leaves of ginseng in addition to its root.[28]

J.Q.A. Clowes (1845–1938) who practiced in Shelby, Ohio, authored a clinical paper based on a case in which ginseng was prescribed to treat rheumatism. A middle-aged man suffering from an extreme case of rheumatism came to Clowes after consulting several other physicians to no avail. Clowes treated the man for weeks only to find that instead of showing progress, pain newly developed in the patient's lower back and stomach. He then prescribed ginseng and the following is his description of the outcome.

> After using the medicine [ginseng], he returned, saying the last bottle had served him so well that he wanted it filled with the same medicine as before. I attribute the curative properties of ginseng in rheumatism to stimulating the healthy action of the gastric juices, causing a healthy flow of the digestive fluids of the stomach, thereby neutralizing the extra secretion of acid that is carried to the nervous membranes of the body joints, causing the inflammatory condition incident to rheumatism.[29]

Clowes claimed that the effect of ginseng could be boosted significantly by administering it with ripe pineapple juice. That way, the secretion of pepsin could be bolstered to help prevent indigestion Americans commonly experienced. In a similar sense, he also mentioned that pairing fixed dosages of ginseng with fine wine could help soothe severe stomachaches. He added that, "[to the] 'Sang grower' [ginseng grower] who is troubled with dyspepsia or foul stomach, I would tell him to 'take some of your own medicine and don't be selling it all to the Chinaman.'"[30]

The above cases suggest that while ginseng was used to treat various symptoms, Western medical discourse took particular note of its usage as an antidote, as a substitute to other foreign medicinal ingredients, and as a tonic.

Ginseng as an Antidote

Ginseng was defined as an antidote in Western medicine, just as it was used as an antidote to opium in the East. As such, an American botany book published in 1811 classified ginseng as an antidote.[31] A book published in 1830 mentioned a case of treating an alcoholic with a tincture made from ginseng.[32] A research paper published in 1841 stated that ginseng could relieve side effects from the habitual intake of tea and opium.[33] In addition to tea, opium, and alcohol, tobacco was another intoxicant that required detoxification. James Ewell (1773–1832), famous for his pioneering book *The Medical Companion, or Family Physician*, described ginseng as a plant not only capable of restoring the constitution ruined by tobacco but of serving as an excellent substitute to tobacco.[34]

In fact, ginseng was, like tobacco, a favored masticatory at the time in several North American regions. And since it improved one's health, nineteenth-century American physicians advised that ginseng "forms an excellent substitute for tobacco."[35] In order to maximize the benefits of ginseng as a masticatory, physicians stressed the importance of swallowing the saliva secreted from chewing ginseng.[36]

To make a name for himself, the aforementioned J.A. Cope created an imaginary character called "Count Belchingen." Cope would sometimes impersonate Count Belchingen or name the Count as a co-author of his book. Count Belchingen was listed as co-author of *Essay on the Virtue and Properties of the Ginseng Tea* (1786), which turned out to be a sensation in both Britain and the United States.[37] The two countries both happened to be troubled by the trade imbalance they were each experiencing from the import of tea. Cope's suggestion to replace tea with ginseng tea was therefore particularly welcomed at a time when patriotic sentiments were prevalent.[38] The ginseng tea Cope suggested was to be made with American ginseng.

Through the book, Cope described vividly the side effects of tea and argued that ginseng was a worthy replacement that could cure all symptoms of frailty and prevent scurvy often suffered by sailors. He also attached detailed accounts of twelve cases that were treated with ginseng tea. A summary of those cases can be found in the table below (Table 10.1).

A particularly interesting case was that involving a lady living on New Ormond Street. After she drank ginseng tea, "a large worm above four inches long" and "one hundred and thirty four more worms of different sizes" apparently came out of the lady's nose. In European medicine, worms were considered a major cause of physical debilitation. However, accounts of ginseng's efficacy as an anthelmintic are extremely rare, which makes this a noteworthy case.

Regarding the antidotal effect of ginseng, it seems necessary to review a recent argument made by Shigehisa Kuriyama, a historian of medicine at Harvard University. Kuriyama argues that due to the high domestic demand for ginseng, Japan began to grow ginseng with seeds brought from China and Chosŏn and eventually joined the ranks of ginseng producing countries by the mid-eighteenth century.[39] According to Kuriyama, Japan thereafter started to export ginseng to China so that by the late nineteenth century, the demand for Japanese ginseng in the Chinese market exceeded that for American ginseng. Kuriyama explains that the reason Chinese demand for Japanese ginseng rose sharply was not only because of its low price but because of its antidotal effect, which was something Manchurian and Korean ginseng lacked. Fresh Japanese ginseng turned out to be the solution the Chinese society had desperately been seeking against the grave problem of opium addiction.

Kuriyama's argument needs to be scrutinized from two viewpoints. One is whether China's demand for Japanese ginseng did in fact rise sharply. While the demand for ginseng did indeed surge in China when it was wrestling with opium addiction, there is no proof that such demand was specifically for Japanese ginseng. What is more problematic is the claim that only Japanese ginseng had an antidotal effect. This effect was noted in aforementioned Western pharmacopoeias, but such texts made no distinction between Manchurian, Korean, and American ginseng.

Besides, Korean ginseng was already known in China for its efficacy as an antidote. The volume of Korean red ginseng exported to China peaked in the 1840s and 1850s, especially because red ginseng was regarded as an excellent antidote to opium. The demand for red ginseng persisted into the late nineteenth century, enough for it to be frequently traded in secret with foreign ships in the Yellow Sea.[40] Korean red ginseng was, however, very expensive and was rarely affordable for lower-class Qing Chinese laborers. Under such circumstances, cheaper American ginseng was the best option left for Chinese commoners.

The antidotal effect of American ginseng started to be discussed in Chinese literature from the mid-eighteenth century. In 1765, Zhao Xuemin (趙學敏) supplemented and made corrections to Li Shizhen's *Bencao gangmu* to publish *Bencao gangmu shiyi*(本草綱目拾遺), which included a section on the efficacy of Western or American ginseng titled "Xiyangshen yaoxing kao (西洋蔘藥性考)." This demonstrates that Chinese medical practitioners processed Western ginseng to produce an excellent solution for the removal of toxins from opium smoke.

TABLE 10.1 Cases Treated with Ginseng by J.A. Cope

	Patient	*Symptom or illness*
1	The honorable Edward Benham, L.L.D	storpidity, great trembling in all his joints, was seized with a kind of storpidity, and a great trembling in all his joints, general lethargy lasting 4–5 hours, terribly frightened when he awoke
2	The honorable George Gore	was in such a debilitated state and he was as helpless as a new-born infant, had taken such a quantity of medicines he could not take more, a frenzy or melancholy seized his brain, his countenance grew wan, his eyes quite hollow, his breath affected, and his whole frame was quite emaciated
3	The honorable Richard Stafford	he used to be seized, as he was walking along, with such a terrible dizziness in his head, has fallen down in the street and on the floor, and laid insensible for some time
4	George Collier, Esq.	having been some years in a declining state, his whole frame was entirely debilitated, He went abroad for the benefit of his health, drank the different waters, tried all the medicines he heard of, and never mended in the least
5	A noble lord	whole frame was debilitated, and greatly relaxed, little or no appetite, inclinable to the wind dropsy and yellow jaundice, his sight greatly affected, great tremblings in his nerve, could get no rest at night, the agonies he was continually in almost tempted him to commit suicide
6	John Cliffton, Esq.	terrible gouty pains in his limbs for above twenty-five years, a general storpidity seized him, and a violent headache, frightened at the sudden opening and shutting of the door, has been troubled from his infancy with a terrible flux, which brought him to a perfect skeleton
7	The Rev. James Floyd	nervous disorder from an infant. went abroad for the benefit of his health, drank the different waters, but to little or no effect, and was reduced to a perfect shadow
8	Miss Harriot Moulton, daughter of Edward Moulton, Esq.	has been constantly afflicted with laughing and crying hysterics, rising in the throat, continual pain in her stomach, violent pain in her head, bad sight, and great tenesmus
9	A Lady who lives in New Ormond Street	has been afflicted for a number of years with a dreadful nervous complaint, which lately affected her head, and obstructed her hearing to a most alarming degree
10	Miss Lucy Clark, daughter of Sir Edmond Clark	has been constantly afflicted with laughing and crying hysterics, rising in the throat, continual pain in her stomach, violent pain in her head, depression and lowness of spirits, despair and melancholy, walking in her sleep, terrible agitation in her stomach and bowels, wind, and sour belchings
11	The right honorable Viscount B——n's daughter	has been afflicted from her infancy with a dreadful nervous disorder, attended with laughing and crying hysteric fits, strong convulsions in her bowels, and foaming at her mouth; after these dreadful fits are over, she is scarcely able to move herself in bed for a fortnight together
12	Miss Louisa Collins, daughter of John Collins, Esq.	was afflicted with a bleeding from her lungs and nose, tremblings all over her, sudden startings in her sleep, a general storpidity all over, violent headache, continual spasms, and at times loss of her speech and memory; she has been afflicted these ten years

Chinese medicine traditionally drew a connection between toxin and fever or the elimination of toxins and the removal of fever, which is why some explain that Western ginseng with cooling properties was considered suitable for the purpose of detoxifying opium poison.[41]

As opium addiction developed into a social hazard in China, the then Viceroy of Huguang (湖廣總督) Lin Zexu (林則徐, 1785–1850) ordered the confiscation of opium and announced a prescription to help quit opium consumption. *Sheng yangshen* (生洋蔘), or American ginseng, happened to be an ingredient of this prescription, called *jisuan wanfang* (忌酸丸方) or *buzheng wanfang* (補正丸方). American ginseng was recommended not only because of its antidotal effect, but also because it was cheaper and easier for ordinary people to procure compared to Korean ginseng. Opium addicts benefited markedly from the intake of American ginseng, and although it helped save a considerable number of addicts and their families, the increase in sales caused the market price of American ginseng to multiply severalfold in China.[42]

As such, any kind of ginseng was widely known to possess an antidotal effect, although red ginseng was thought to be especially effective. And while Japan may have succeeded in artificially growing ginseng, its seeds had originally been stolen from Chosŏn and Manchuria, which makes it impossible for "Japanese ginseng" to be a different kind of ginseng particularly effective as an antidote as per Kuriyama's claim. Furthermore, the volume of ginseng Japan managed to produce was too small to be actively exported to China.[43] This leaves no choice but to conclude that the claim Kuriyama made about Japanese ginseng's exclusive antidotal effect and the surge in its export was farfetched due to a lack of information or his nationalistic viewpoint.

Substitute for Foreign Drugs

Ginseng was often recognized in the West as a substitute for other drugs. Like today, substitute drugs, especially medicinal herbs from abroad, carried significant meaning in early modern Europe. Discovering substitute drugs was important to mercantile Europe at a time when spices and medicines were as valuable as jewels and relevant to building a foundation for the continued advancement of medicine. Well-known apothecaries in London kept vast collections of plants from all over the world and strove to identify medicinal herbs that had similar effects.[44]

Ginseng was first named as a substitute for licorice. Its taste and properties were considered more similar to licorice than any other drug, making it a viable substitute for licorice extract or pills.[45] Multiple descriptions came to mention that the medicinal properties and effects of fennel were similar to those of ginseng, hinting a desire to replace expensive ginseng with fennel that commonly grew along the Mediterranean coast.[46]

What was more important was the fact that ginseng was defined as a substitute for cinchona (Peruvian bark). As an ingredient of quinine, cinchona was brought to Europe from South America by Jesuit missionaries in the late sixteenth century and soon became widely known to be effective in treating diarrhea and malaria. Although it was already being used in Europe to treat malaria since the seventeenth century, Puritans who seized power during the English Civil War dismissed cinchona as a "Catholic conspiracy." The demand for cinchona nevertheless rose in the eighteenth century as it became known to be especially effective in treating the "emperor's disease," gout, a widespread chronic disease among upper class Europeans. When cinchona proved difficult to procure, physicians would recommend ginseng as a substitute, claiming that if used correctly, ginseng could be far more effective than cinchona.[47]

Aphrodisiac

An aspect inseparable when discussing the efficacy of ginseng is its purported property as an aphrodisiac and tonic. In fact, ginseng was famous in Europe for enhancing sex drive and physicians were aware of the herb's reputation.[48] "An infirmis à morbo viribus reparandis Gin Seng?" (1736), the first doctoral dissertation on ginseng in Europe, explored the efficacy of ginseng as a tonic and noted that it could help make a surprising recovery from exhaustion due to sexual excess.[49] This statement, according to the dissertation's author Lucas Augustin Folliot de Saint-Vast, could be substantiated through *Bencao gangmu*, which included detailed accounts of several cases where ginseng was used to treat exhausted lechers or internal injuries caused by drinking and womanizing.[50]

In the *History of the Materia Medica*, Hill mentioned that ginseng was "famous in the East for giving strength and spirit to persons who have disabled themselves by too free a use of women."[51] Yet, by the time the book was being circulated in Europe, ginseng's reputation as an aphrodisiac was already public knowledge. Even William Hanbury warned through his book on gardening that ginseng should not be used for "bad purposes" under the pretense of improving one's health.[52]

Unexpected among those who contributed to characterizing ginseng as an aphrodisiac was the great thinker Jean Jacques Rousseau (1712–1778). Rousseau tends to be named as a habitual user of ginseng but when or where he first encountered the herb remains a mystery. Since he traveled around Europe and was acquainted with members of the British Royal Society and French Royal Academy of Sciences, he most likely learned about ginseng through such acquaintances.

There is, however, record of an episode that proves Rousseau enjoyed ginseng enough to keep it within reach. In June 1772, Bernardin de Saint-Pierre (1737–1814), a writer, botanist, and pupil of Rousseau, sent his teacher a sack of expensive coffee beans after learning that Rousseau was fond of the scent of coffee. At first, Rousseau refused to accept the beans, but when Saint-Pierre suggested he was welcome to offer something in return, Rousseau presented Saint-Pierre with a book and a ginseng root.[53]

While Rousseau is now known as a great philosopher, he was an international celebrity with countless female fans during his time. His fame was such that a "Rousseau tour" appeared after his death for those who wished to retrace his footsteps. Rousseau's fame and popularity were largely attributed to the romantic novels he wrote but his sexual appeal also attracted many women. Rousseau was, in fact, an inveterate womanizer. The sight of Rousseau meeting with prostitutes at Café Florian in Venice was already legendary among his contemporaries. As a result, Rousseau was riddled with syphilis. Nevertheless, rumors of his untiring energy and the fact that he enjoyed taking ginseng are likely to have spread the belief that ginseng was good for potency.[54]

Pharmacopoeias or materia medica books did not, however, devote much attention to ginseng's efficacy as an aphrodisiac. Rather, some of the surviving documentation is pessimistic about its aphrodisiac property. William Cullen (1710–1790), well known as a professor at the Edinburgh Medical School and as David Hume's physician, cast doubt on ginseng's aphrodisiac property in *Lectures on the Materia Medica* and supported his view by referring to a case he personally witnessed.[55] According to Cullen, a middle-aged gentleman he was well acquainted with chewed on ginseng every day for years but failed to see even the slightest improvement in his venereal faculties.[56] This case seems significant for demonstrating the gap that existed between popular belief and medical opinions about ginseng.

In the United States, studies on ginseng as an aphrodisiac emerged in the early twentieth century. A group of researchers at the Homeopathic Department of the University of Michigan published a report in 1905 about an interesting experiment.[57] The Homoeopathic Medical College of the University of Michigan and the Hahnemann College of the Pacific in San Francisco conducted a joint experiment aimed at proving that ginseng, a tonic highly regarded in China, was especially effective in improving the deterioration of faculties from aging. In the early twentieth century, ginseng-related collaborations between industry and academia actively took place in Michigan because it was the American center of ginseng cultivation and collection. The reason the Hahnemann College of the Pacific joined the experiment had to do with the college's area of specialization. Named after the founder of homeopathy, Christian Friedrich Samuel Hahnemann (1755–1843), the college was highly interested in practicing homeopathy and employed experimental treatment at several medical schools and hospitals in the United States. Since the research trend on homeopathy was preoccupied with crude drugs at the time, perhaps it was only natural for the college to develop an interest in an herb known as a cure-all like ginseng.

Although the details of the experiment's procedures remain unknown, it was conducted by nine participants from Michigan and eight from San Francisco. Among seventeen test subjects, the results of seven were excluded for being inaccurate or incomplete. Despite acknowledging that "it is sometimes said that ginseng possesses no medicinal merits, that the value placed upon it by the Chinese is fanciful or based upon superstition," Dr. W.A. Dewey, a participant from the

University of Michigan, remarked that, "we of the Homoeopathic school will not be astonished to find that the employment of Ginseng in the past rests purely upon a scientific basis."[58] This indicates that Dewey was aware that ginseng was generally used to improve enervation and boost libido, and discovered that even from the perspective of homeopathy, ginseng was certainly effective as an aphrodisiac. Dewey was convinced that ginseng was particularly effective in treating sexual disabilities.

> Ginseng is evidently a cerebro-spinal depressant and will do its best work in those cases of depression where the nervous element predominates and is so pronounced that the mental sphere is involved. We know how intimately the mind and sexual sphere are correlated and it is in the disorders of the sexual mind that the drug will find its best action. We consider this proving, while not all that could be wished for, places the drug on a more scientific basis than it has ever rested on before.[59]

The tendency to associate ginseng with sexual competence seems to have already grown prevalent within twentieth-century American culture. An example of this would be the following line from the Pulitzer-winning novel *The Keepers of the House* (1964) by Shirley Ann Grau (1929–2020): "The ginseng with its tiny purple flower, whose root, people said, was good for making love."[60] Ginseng also made an appearance in the novel *Hollywood Wives* (1983) by Jackie Collins, who became a best-selling author from writing about the rich and famous in Los Angeles since the 1980s. After listing the various nutritional supplements her husband was taking, the protagonist of *Hollywood Wives* adds, "Plus ginseng, which was said to jazz up your sex drive. But it didn't seem to have done him any good."[61] This indicates that ginseng was known as an aphrodisiac among the American upper class. Yet, such knowledge was not exclusive to the upper class. America's most well-known hermit, Kenny Salwey (1943), noted in an autobiographical account that ginseng could "naturally, turn you into a love machine."[62]

Patent Medicine Containing Ginseng

In Britain, medicine made from ginseng was available on the market in the form of finished products from at least the mid-eighteenth century. Such drugs were distributed for sale and did not require a physician's prescription. They were also called "patent medicines," with various parties seeking protection for their exclusive rights to trademarks registered under the patent system that had existed since the late Middle Ages. By the eighteenth century, patent medicines were so abundant in Britain and America that they were peddled by quacks and widely promoted through newspaper advertisements and leaflets. One such drug was Dr. Anthony's Irish Pills, which was advertised extensively as using ginseng as an ingredient and therefore as especially effective in treating stomach disorders.[63]

In 1787, *The Times* published an advertisement for ginseng tea prescribed by "renowned physicians" that was capable of curing serious cases of hysteria. Another widely advertised product was a treatment for the eyes that contained ginseng extract.[64] An advertisement published in 1790 claimed that the intake of ginseng tea alone had helped alleviate symptoms of neurosis for 50,000 patients over the past five years.[65] In the mid-nineteenth century, a surgeon based in London named Dr. Morace Goss released a unique product called "ginseng ointment" which was heavily advertised as effective in treating infertility, anxiety, and sexual dysfunction.[66]

In the mid-nineteenth century, fancy pamphlets to advertise ginseng products were circulated in the United States. One of them was the *Interesting History of the Panax: Quinquefolium*, created by a pharmaceutical firm in Boston to promote Dr. Conine's Ginseng and Mallow Syrup.[67] The pamphlet introduced Conine as a doctor who traveled to several countries including China and offered a detailed summary on the reputation ginseng enjoyed in the East as well as the history of ginseng's discovery. At the beginning, the pamphlet explained how the Ginseng and Mallow Syrup was likely to be more effective than any other drug people had experienced thus far and that it was particularly effective in treating all functional disorders of the stomach and lungs. Personal accounts of having used the syrup appeared near the back of the pamphlet, testifying to how effective the syrup was in relieving and treating violent coughs, seizures, hemoptysis, and phlegm coughed up from the throat or stomach.[68] Such a broad scope of application and its reputation as a panacea, however, eventually worked against ginseng's capacity as a medication.

Notes

1 Chakrabarti, *Materials and Medicine*, 171.
2 Shiu Ying Hu, "The Genus Panax (Ginseng) in Chinese Medicine," *Economic Botany* 30 (1976): 11–28.
3 John Redman Coxe, *The Philadelphia Medical Dictionary* (Philadelphia, PA: Thomas Dobson, 1808).
4 Hill, *A History of the Materia Medica*, 591.
5 William Buchan and Joseph Granville Norwood, *Domestic Medicine: A Treatise on the Prevention and Cure of Diseases* (Cincinnati, OH: U. P. James, 1838), 677.
6 Anthony Florian Madinger Willich and James Mease, *The Domestic Encyclopaedia; or, A Dictionary of Facts, and Useful Knowledge*, vol. 3 (Philadelphia, PA: William Young Birch, 1804), 157.
7 Rafinesque, *Medical Flora*, 56–57.
8 Hill, *A History of the Materia Medica*, 591.
9 Rafinesque, *Medical Flora*, 57.
10 Aikin, *A Manual of Materia Medica*, 80.
11 William Woodville, *Medical Botany*, vol. 1 (London: William Phillips, 1810), 151.
12 James Alleyne, *A New English Dispensatory* (London, 1733), 72; John Nott, *A Posologic Companion to the London Pharmacopoeia* (London, 1794), 41–42; Pierre Pomet, *A Complete History of Drugs* (London, 1748), 195; Thomas Curtis, ed., *A London Encyclopaedia, or Universal Dictionary of Science, Art, Literature, and Practical Mechanics*, vol. 16 (London: Thomas Tegg, 1829), 531.

13 Oliver Goldsmith and G. F. Shaw, *A History of the Earth and Animated Nature, Together with the Elements of Botany* (London: R. Edwards, 1819), 792.
14 Millspaugh, *American Medicinal Plants*, 70–72.
15 Stearns, *The American Oracle*, 583–584.
16 Antimony was used as an emetic or anthelmintic, or to treat all sorts of protozoan diseases.
17 *The London Practice of Physic* (London, 1769), 84.
18 George Wallis, ed., *The Works of Thomas Sydenham, M. D., on Acute and Chronic Diseases*, vol. 2 (London, 1778), 293.
19 Grace Dalrymple Elliott (1754–1823) was a Scottish woman educated in France. She married John Elliott in 1771 but divorced three years later and became a courtesan. She was famous for having been mistress to the Duke of Orléans and to the future King George IV and secretly worked for the British government in Paris during the French Revolution. A memoir about her life in France, *Journal of My Life during the French Revolution*, was published in 1859 and her life was also dramatized into the film *The Lady and The Duke* (*L'Anglaise Et Le Duc*), released in 2001.
20 John Elliot, *The Medical Pocket-Book* (London, 1791), 12–13, 78, 91.
21 James Ewell, *The Medical Companion, or Family Physician* (Washington, DC, 1827), 673; Jacob Bigelow, *American Medical Botany*, vol. 2 (Boston, MA: Cummings and Hilliard, 1818), 94; William P. C. Barton, *Compendium Florae Philadelphicae*, vol. 2 (Philadelphia, PA: M. Carey and Son, 1818), 201.
22 Pomet, *A Complete History of Drugs*, 194; Rafinesque, *Medical Flora*, 57; *The Quarterly Journal of Agriculture* 11 (1840–1841): 131.
23 Hill, *A History of the Materia Medica*, 591.
24 For instance, see Temple Henry Croker, Thomas Williams, and Samuel Clark, *The Complete Dictionary of Arts and Sciences*, vol. 2 (London, 1765), s.v. "foeniculum" and "ginseng."
25 Count Belchingen and J.A. Cope, *An Essay on the Virtues and Properties of the Ginseng Tea* (London, 1786), 7.
26 *The London Practice of Physic*, 84, 126.
27 Rafinesque, *Medical Flora*, 57.
28 Rafinesque, *Medical Flora*, 57.
29 J.Q.A. Clowes, "By J.Q.A. Clowes, M.D.," in Koehler, *Ginseng and Goldenseal Growers' Handbook*, 13.
30 Clowes, "By J.Q.A. Clowes, M.D.," 14.
31 W.J. Titford, *Hortus Botanicus Americanus* (London: C. Stower, 1811), 25.
32 Rafinesque, *Medical Flora*, 57.
33 "Miscellaneous Notices," *The Quarterly Journal of Agriculture* 11 (1840–1841), 131.
34 Ewell, *The Medical Companion, or Family Physician*, 674.
35 Rafinesque, *Medical Flora*, 57; Ewell, *The Medical Companion, or Family Physician*, 674; Barton, *Compendium Florae Philadelphicae*, 201; Bigelow, *American Medical Botany*, 95.
36 Ewell, *The Medical Companion, or Family Physician*, 674.
37 Belchingen and Cope, *An Essay on the Virtues and Properties of the Ginseng Tea.*
38 Mathew Carey, "Remarks on the Commerce of America with China," in Carey, ed., *The American Museum, or, Universal Magazine*, 7:126–27; Adair, *The History of the American Indians*, 362; Carver, *The New Universal Traveller*, 4–5; The Royal College of Physicians of London, *Medical Transactions*, vol. 3 (London, 1775), 9–20.
39 Shigehisa Kuriyama, "The Geography of Ginseng and the Strange Alchemy of Needs," in Yota Batsaki, Sarah Burke Cahalan, and Anatole Tchikine, eds., *The Botany of Empire in the Long Eighteenth Century* (Washington, DC: Dumbarton Oaks, 2017), 61–72.
40 Lee, "Kaesŏng insam i wae yumyŏnghage toeŏssŭlkka?," 97.
41 Guo, "Xiyangshen," 128.
42 Lin Zexu quanji bianji weiyuanhui **林則徐全集編輯委員會**, *Lin Zexu Quanji* **林則徐全集** [The Complete Works of Lin Zexu], vol. 3 (Fuzhou: Haixia

wenyi chubanshe 海峡文藝出版社, 2002), 1165, 1200. See note 61 in Guo, "Xiyangshen," 128.
43 Chang, *Han'guk insam sanŏpsa*, 1:439–440.
44 Chakrabarti, *Materials and Medicine*, 171.
45 Bigelow, *American Medical Botany*, 94; Coxe, *The American Dispensatory*, 406.
46 Lewis, *The New Dispensatory*, 142; John Quincy, *Pharmacopoeia Officinalis, or a Complete English Dispensatory* (London, 1782), 64; John Rutty, *Observations on the London and Edinburgh Dispensatories* (London, 1776), 56–57.
47 Wallis, *The Works of Thomas Sydenham, M. D., on Acute and Chronic Diseases*, 2:213.
48 William Cullen, *Lectures on the Materia Medica* (London, 1772), 276; William Byrd, *The Prose Works of William Byrd of Westover*, ed. Louis B. Wright (Cambridge, MA: Harvard University Press, 1966), 292; Hill, *A History of the Materia Medica*, 591; Hanbury, *A Complete Body of Planting and Gardening*, 1:690.
49 Folliot de Saint-Vast, "Resp. Quaestio Medica, An Infirmis à Morbo Viribus Reparandis Gin Seng? Praes. F. Vandermonde," 3.
50 Li, *Shinjuhae ponch'o kangmok*, 4:54, 62.
51 Hill, *A History of the Materia Medica*, 591.
52 Hanbury, *A Complete Body of Planting and Gardening*, 1:690.
53 Leo Damrosch, *Jean-Jacques Rousseau: Restless Genius* (Boston, MA: Houghton Mifflin Company, 2007), 470.
54 Heasim Sul, *Grand Tour: Elite kyoyuk ŭi ch'oejong tan'gye* [Grand Tour: The Final Stage of Elite Education] (Seoul, Humanist, 2020), 340, 366–368.
55 Cullen, *Lectures on the Materia Medica*, 276.
56 Cullen, *A Treatise of the Materia Medica*, 2:161.
57 A.E. Ibershoff, "An Original Proving of the Drug by the University of Michigan Society of Drug Provers (1905)," in Koehler, *Ginseng and Goldenseal Growers' Handbook*, 9–11.
58 Ibershoff, "An Original Proving of the Drug by the University of Michigan Society of Drug Provers (1905)," 9–10.
59 Ibershoff, "An Original Proving of the Drug by the University of Michigan Society of Drug Provers (1905)," 10.
60 Shirley Ann Grau, *The Keepers of the House* (Baton Rouge, LA: Louisiana State University Press, 1995), 111.
61 Jackie Collins, *Hollywood Wives* (New York: Pocket Books, 1994), 87.
62 Kenny Salwey and J. Scott Bestul, *The Last River Rat: Kenny Salwey's Life in the Wild* (Stillwater, MN: Voyageur Press, 2001), 124–125.
63 Michael Devlin, *Pillula Salutaris; Or, the Justly Celebrated Dr. Anthony's Irish Pills* (London, 1790).
64 "Case, 719th," *The Times*, April 25, 1787.
65 "Advertisement," *The Times*, August 31, 1790.
66 "Advertisements & Notices," *Reynold's Newspaper*, May 13, 1855; May 20, 1855; May 27, 1855; June 3, 1855.
67 Wilson, Fairbank, & Co., *Interesting History of the Panax (Quinquefolium) of Linnaeus: The Ginseng of the Chinese from the Archives of History and Medical Science* (Boston, MA: White & Potter, 1851).
68 Wilson, Fairbank, & Co., *Interesting History of the Panax (Quinquefolium) of Linnaeus*, 14–16.

11

REFORM OF PHARMACOPOEIAS AND CHALLENGES TO EXTRACTING ACTIVE INGREDIENTS

The Reform of Pharmacopoeias

As reviewed in Chapter 1, the claim that ginseng was dismissed from Western pharmacopoeias in the late eighteenth century was not entirely true. Yet, there is no denying that ginseng's prominence began to diminish significantly around that time. The main cause was the reform of pharmacopoeias. In the late eighteenth century, several European countries started to combine the various pharmacopoeias in circulation to create an officially approved national pharmacopoeia, a process which came to be referred to as the "reform of pharmacopoeias."

At the forefront of the reform was Britain. In the 1780s, the Royal College of Physicians of Edinburgh began to combine the steadily and widely consulted pharmacopoeias published in London and Edinburgh. In 1818, *Codex Medicamentarius Sive Pharmacopoeia Gallica* became officially approved in France. Such moves involved royal mandates to merge the academic field of medicine with the popular practice of concocting medications, so as to impose joint responsibility. The United States used the national pharmacopoeia of France as a reference to publish the *Pharmacopoeia of the United States of America* in 1820. In Britain, pharmacopoeias circulated in London, Edinburgh, and Dublin were combined to launch the *British Pharmacopoeia* in 1864.[1]

These efforts were part of a process to establish official criteria for pharmacopoeias that used to be compiled haphazardly. Standardization prompted several changes in the nature of pharmacopoeias. To satisfy the criterion of avoiding the irrational, pharmacopoeias excluded many medications passed down since antiquity, and theriaca formulas based on a mixture of honey and dozens of herbs were simplified or eventually removed. This consolidation and standardization were strictly an outcome of the medical, scientific paradigm dominant at the time, which medical professionals approved of.[2] The botanical theory of von

DOI: 10.4324/9781003286691-14

Linné and the chemical theory of Antoine Laurent de Lavoisier (1743–1794) were the two strands of scientific theory that contributed the most to the reform of pharmacopoeias.

At a time when most medicinal ingredients were still herbal, it may come as no surprise that von Linné was a pioneer who influenced the reform of pharmacopoeias. For the purpose of standardization, however, concentrating on active ingredients alone would have been far more effective and exact since the efficacy of herbs differed depending on their stage of growth and methods to prepare them were so diverse.[3] This was when the "father of modern chemistry" Lavoisier entered the picture. Lavoisier contributed to the improvement of botanical nomenclature and the specific identification of active ingredients.[4] By the 1790s, British pharmacopoeias began to list Lavoisier as a co-author and pharmacopoeias reformed according to his chemical methodology publicized the fact.

Revised pharmacopoeias excluded many plants that were previously included, and instead of offering a botanical profile of each plant, they increasingly tended to document only the active ingredients of each plant. To medical professionals, stipulating only the active ingredients instead of listing all the characteristics of each plant seemed quite efficient and progressive.[5] Moreover, major active ingredients became discovered one after the other in the early nineteenth century. Quinine was extracted from cinchona, caffeine from coffee, emetine from ipecacuanha, morphine from opium, and nicotine from tobacco. And these discoveries proved to be crucial to the pharmaceutical industry's development.

Challenges to Extracting Active Ingredients

In the process of reforming pharmacopoeias, ginseng tended to be excluded from major pharmacopoeias, and although it continued to appear in pharmacopoeias in the broader sense, its efficacy kept being discredited. The foremost reason was because Western scientists had failed to discover enough active ingredients in ginseng. At a time when objective, scientific methods of experimentation were yet to be developed, identifying active ingredients in a plant proved to be an extremely complex and technically challenging task.[6]

The molecular structure of saponin, the main ingredient of ginseng, contains both polar and non-polar components responsible for creating soap-like foam. Isolating and refining such components was extremely complicated, such that it required a special technique called chromatography. In other words, saponin was a compound difficult to isolate at a time when chromatography was not yet fully developed, which was one of the main reasons for the slow progress in researching the ingredients of ginseng.

Despite all the interest Western medical professionals took in ginseng, the extraction of active ingredients from it turned out to be extremely slow and unsuccessful compared to other plants. It is therefore necessary to consider other factors that may have hindered extraction aside from the fact that chromatography was not yet available.

The most likely reason Western medical professionals failed to extract active ingredients from ginseng was because of problems with the samples used as test subjects. The quality of the ginseng samples was inconsistent, or in many cases, the researchers were unaware of exactly what they were testing. With expectations of coming across cure-all efficacy, researchers experimented with American ginseng or plants similar to ginseng instead of the legendary plant from Asia. The first ginseng to be introduced to Europe in the early seventeenth century was Korean ginseng, and until the early eighteenth century, scientific discussions about ginseng were centered around East Asian ginseng. And once American ginseng arrived in Europe in the early eighteenth century, Western botanists channeled their efforts into distinguishing different kinds of ginseng. Many botanists including von Linné identified various kinds of ginseng and were at least aware of the fact that ginseng from America and Asia were different.

Western literature seeking to medically utilize ginseng, however, assumed or argued that ginseng from Asia and America was identical or at least possessed the same efficacy even though they were different kinds of ginseng.[7] In *An Experimental History of the Materia Medica* (1769), the British chemist and physician William Lewis (1708–1781) even remarked that "on comparing the American roots with some specimens received from Nankin, no material difference could be observed between them, either in their external appearance or in their quality."[8] Also, claims were frequently made that American ginseng was being accepted as authentic local ginseng in China or that its efficacy was being recognized even without undergoing the skilled Chinese curing process.

An American encyclopedia published in 1798 identified five different kinds of Panax ginseng and considered American and Manchurian ginseng identical.[9] The Bulletin of the National Institution for the Promotion of Science, published in 1846, noted Manchuria and America as the origins of American ginseng.[10] There were even rumors that, as with ginseng, North America and China were the origin of Southeast Asian *ninzin*, believed to be a plant similar to ginseng but inferior in terms of efficacy.[11] Circumstances were worse in the medical market; apothecaries would mix *Siam ninsi* with ginseng or even pass *Siam ninsi* off as ginseng.[12] In the same vein, one record indicated that *ninsi*, believed to be from Manchuria or Korea when it was actually grown in Japan, was mistaken for genuine ginseng in Europe.

These claims could have been intentional distortions to equate Asian ginseng with American ginseng. The motive was very much economic. American ginseng had to be equated with Asian ginseng in order to have market value and be exported. As previously mentioned, ever since ginseng was discovered on the North American continent, a considerable amount of research was carried out on how it was different from Asian ginseng. Some research findings even included detailed descriptions about differences between various kinds of Asian ginseng.

> The officinal part of the plant is the root; it varies with the country from which it has been collected; in Korea and in China it is white, wrinkled in a dried state, and covered externally with a pulverulent mass which resembles starch; in Manschuria and Dauria it is yellow, and resembles amber; when dried it is even and smooth.[13]

The following description of ginseng imported from Britain in the early nineteenth century implies that it was in fact Asian ginseng.

> The dried root of ginseng, as imported here, is scarcely the thickness of the little finger, about three or four inches long, frequently forked, transversely wrinkled, of a horny texture, and both internally and externally of a yellowish white colour. On the top are commonly one or more little knots.[14]

There were, however, conscientious scientists who criticized the attempts to regard Asian and American ginseng as identical. The American botanist Constantine Samuel Rafinesque (1783–1840) argued that while most of his contemporaries may have claimed that Chinese and American ginseng belonged to the same species, closer examination revealed that not only were they different, but American ginseng varied in itself.[15] Rafinesque declared that Chinese medical writers could distinguish at least ten different kinds of Chinese ginseng, and because there were so many kinds of ginseng, it was inevitable that medical professionals would have different opinions about the plant's value and efficacy. This implies that ginseng's efficacy was being depreciated because researchers had each been experimenting with different kinds of ginseng. The British botanist and physician John Sims (1749–1831) pointed out that the efficacy of imported ginseng was undervalued in Europe because "*Siam ninsi*" grown in Japan was being passed off as "true ginseng."[16]

Another reason that extracting active ingredients from ginseng was challenging was that the quality of the samples was terrible. Many records note that the ginseng used in experiments was too unripe or of bad quality. Such complaints were most often directed at expensive and therefore sparsely sold Korean ginseng that had grown stale at apothecaries.[17]

Experiments conducted with American ginseng alone, however, equally suffered from criticism over the quality of test samples. Experts capable of distinguishing American ginseng would criticize the prevalent practice of using bad roots, or low-quality ginseng, in clinical tests or experiments. What they meant by "low quality" was mainly ginseng collected at an inappropriate time.[18] This was in fact an issue several had been raising for a while. The rule in China was to harvest ginseng in the fall. On the correlation between the harvesting season and the quality of ginseng, *Bencao gangmu* stipulated that ginseng harvested in the fall and winter was wholesome while that harvested in the spring and summer was empty and weak.[19] Even in the United States, it became common knowledge among late eighteenth-century intellectuals that fall was the appropriate season to harvest ginseng.

To stress that ginseng had to be harvested during the driest days of October, the American economist Matthew Carey (1760–1839) mentioned an incident in which American ginseng exported to China had to be disposed for very little return because the whole stock had become rotten. To retain its efficacy, ginseng had to be dug up on days when there was no scorching sunshine and heat and immediately stored carefully without being washed.[20] Other records were also critical about the practice of prematurely digging up ginseng in the summer. Some warned that digging up wild ginseng seedlings before they could take root in the soil would eventually lead to ginseng's extinction. Moreover, summer was a season when ginseng roots were still growing and therefore required an abundant supply of nutrients, which implied that prematurely harvested roots would lack efficacy.[21]

Some scholars, however, thought the efficacy of American ginseng was inherently weak. Rafinesque once blatantly remarked that, "our American ginseng is so mild that it may be used in pretty large doses as far as an ounce."[22]

> The best Chinese kinds may contain other active substances, and although their high price precludes our using them, we ought, instead of laughing at the Chinese for paying once $100 the LB. for them (as we did for Quinine and other drugs) to try how far our own kinds may be equivalents.[23]

Yet a greater number of scholars claimed that the difference between Asian and American ginseng was not intrinsic but depended on the conditions of their growth and development, particularly the soil and manufacturing method, especially on how the root was dried.

> There is great similarity in the American and Chinese individuals of this species, but the place of growth or mode of drying seems to more or less affect the properties of the roots, especially if the accounts of the usefulness of the Oriental produce can be credited.[24]

To support such a claim, some even quoted Chinese "testimonies." At a seminar held at the Royal College of Physicians in London in November 1773, William Heberden (1710–1801), once physician to King George III, presented on "The Method of Preparing the Ginseng Root in China." Through this presentation, Heberden argued that based on correspondence with a Chinese who used to reside in Manchuria, Chinese and American ginseng originally had little difference in virtue, but a tremendous difference could be made depending on how they were cured.[25]

Many had in fact been interested in curing ginseng since it was a matter directly connected to the export of American ginseng. Americans firmly believed that the reason their ginseng was distributed at meager prices in China was because of inferior curing. Ginseng was one of the most profitable export items to the United States, so Americans were bound to be highly interested in curing methods.

Since the 1790s, Americans began to emulate the curing process used in China, the main producer of ginseng. The Chinese preferred to steam and dry ginseng, a process they referred to as clarification. The process would involve boiling and then skinning ginseng roots to make them transparent. There is, however, record that only one out of twelve roots could be clarified successfully.[26] When exported, clarified ginseng was worth far more than crude ginseng,[27] so that in the early 1830s, clarified ginseng was traded for fifty-five to sixty dollars per picul,[28] while crude ginseng was traded for thirty to thirty-four dollars per picul.[29]

In the history of processing American ginseng, the Philadelphian physician Isaac Heylin is a notable figure. Heylin apparently learned how to clarify ginseng while traveling around China in the 1790s. He thereafter headed to an area in Kentucky where ginseng was being grown and invested 1,000 dollars into building a factory. The ginseng processed in the Chinese style at the factory was sold for six to seven dollars per pound, which was ten times higher than the price for crude ginseng, so Heylin is said to have raised 24,000 dollars in profit within a matter of years.[30]

By the early nineteenth century, factories like the one Heylin built had become the standard layout for ginseng processing. Such factories would normally consist of two large rooms, one for steaming and the other for drying ginseng. Once freshly harvested ginseng arrived, workers would wash the roots outside the building, gently scrape them with the back of a knife, brush them first with a shoe brush and then with a toothbrush. The roots would thereafter be brought into the steaming room to be placed on a linen cloth suspended above boiling water in an iron kettle at least eighteen inches in diameter. Once the roots turned semi-translucent from an hour of steaming, they would be wrapped in the linen and cooled in cold water for a few minutes ahead of the drying process. In the airy, warm drying room, ginseng roots would be laid out on shelves until their color turned into "a beautiful amber."[31]

Ginseng factories were closed spaces to which access was restricted and the process of clarification was kept strictly secret. In 1793, the French botanist François André Michaux (1770–1855) mentioned that to those in Kentucky who desired to know the secret was available for 400 dollars.[32] Instructions on how to clarify ginseng soon spread beyond the boundaries of the state. Robert Wellford, physician to George Washington, built Virginia's first factory in Scott County, and soon thereafter similar facilities cropped up everywhere from New York to North Carolina.[33] Ginseng exports seem to have jumped as clarifying methods were refined. While the annual export volume was approximately 30,000 pounds in the 1790s, it surged to 280,000 pounds around 1800.[34]

However, no matter how technically developed American clarification became, it was rudimentary compared to that of East Asia, and American and

British medical experts were well aware of the fact. After all, the clarification of ginseng had been a process handed down in East Asia for nearly 1,000 years. From the way Xu Jing (徐兢, 1091–1153) distinguished processed ginseng, noted as *shushen* (熟蔘), from raw ginseng, noted as *shengshen* (生蔘), in *Gaoli tujing* (高麗圖經), a report to the Chinese emperor about a diplomatic mission to Korea, ginseng already seems to have been steamed to produce red ginseng at the time.[35] Steaming to make red ginseng allowed it to be stored long term, implying that there was enough demand for such ginseng and enough supply to meet that demand.

In China, ginseng is said to have been processed since at least the Liu-Song dynasty. This is how the process was described in *Jilin jiuwenlu* (鷄林舊聞錄) compiled during the late Qing dynasty:

> Ginseng is placed in boiling water, cleansed with a small, angled brush, and the bowstring of a white bow is used to remove any residual dirt on the surface. The root is then immersed in liquefied ice and sugar for a day or two before being steamed, boiled, and baked again.[36]

By the later years of the reign of the Qianlong Emperor (乾隆帝, r. 1736–1795), more types of ginseng processing were in use. And documentation of various ways to process ginseng appeared in the 1778 publication *Renshenkao* (唐秉鈞), authored by the Qing dynasty doctor Tang Bingjun (唐秉鈞). In the book, Tang listed nearly forty different finished products made from ginseng, which hints at the variety of ginseng products available during the Qing dynasty and the level of sophistication the Chinese had achieved by then.[37]

Western medical professionals were well aware of how complex and refined Chinese methods were when it came to processing ginseng. From the moment ginseng started to be discussed at the British Royal Society and the French Royal Academy of Sciences in the late seventeenth century, the Chinese method of processing ginseng was a hot topic of discussion. Members were already familiar with stories about how Manchurians kept ginseng buried in soil for ten to fifteen days after harvesting, or washed and brushed it clean before it was cured. There were, of course, records describing further details related to processing ginseng. One explained that in China, cleansed ginseng roots were immersed in decoctions of rice or sorghum and then exposed to the steam produced from boiling such decoctions. That was how the Chinese made ginseng roots become much firmer and transparent.[38]

In 1787, Matthew Carey wrote the editorial "Chinese Manner of Curing Ginseng" for *The American Museum*, a magazine that voiced various suggestions on how the fledgling United States could achieve economic prosperity.

> They gather the root sound and good (not in the season when the plant is in flower); and gently wash it from the earth, being careful not to break the skin. Then they take an iron torch (that is, a very flat kind of stew-pan,

> used in China over a charcoal fire) boil therein water; put in the root, and let it lie three or four minutes, but not so long as to injure or break off the skin, when, on cutting the root, the inside will appear of a light straw colour. They then take a clean linen cloth, and having wiped the ginseng clean and dry, place the torch over the gentlest fire, and lay in it a row of ginseng. Here they let it dry gradually, turning it leisurely, till it is something elastic, but not too dry; afterwards they take a damp clean cloth, in which they roll up the longest pieces in parallel lines, and wrap them up very tight, binding them hard round with thread; after being dried a day or two by a very slow fire, they unpack the same, and repeat the packages of the inside and moist part, until it is all like the outside, and the whole dry enough to sound like a piece of wood, when dropped upon a table. The heaviest pieces, of a straw, or light brown colour, are much the best. They take a box well lined with lead, and put it into a larger one with quick-lime (to prevent vermin) and close the whole against air and weather.[39]

Although this Chinese method of curing Carey mentioned through his editorial was widely talked about, it was far too elaborate for the Americans to attempt. In 1758, John Hill self-deprecatingly remarked that "we cannot preserve any root as [the Chinese] do Ginseng."[40] Factories were built in the United States to cure American ginseng, but their methods were notably unrefined compared to those of China. Rather than improving their curing techniques, Americans had in fact been more preoccupied with exporting as much ginseng as possible. The difference in processing method was therefore a convenient explanation as to why the price of American ginseng was so low in China. It was easier to blame mediocre techniques than to admit that American ginseng was inferior to Korean ginseng.

These circumstances made it challenging for Western medical professionals to even secure samples of uniform quality for the purpose of extracting active ingredients from ginseng. Rafinesque admitted that, "we are ignorant in Botany, have never properly analyzed this root, and have even none but an inferior kind to try."[41] This admission proved that no progress had been made in realizing the proposition the British Royal Society discussed nearly a hundred years ago in 1713, that, "if European doctors could closely examine its ingredients, and prescribe the right amount, ginseng would bring about a huge medical advantage."[42] Since their encounter with ginseng in the seventeenth century, Europeans may have medically utilized the root in a variety of ways but the failure to extract active ingredients from it ultimately became a key factor in discouraging its use.

Notes

1 Glenn Sonnedecker, "The Founding Period of the U.S. Pharmacopeia: I. European Antecedents," *Pharmacy in History* 35, no. 4 (1993): 151.

2 Stuart Anderson, "Pharmacy and Empire: The 'British Pharmacopoeia' as an Instrument of Imperialism 1864 to 1932," *Pharmacy in History* 52, no. 3 (2010): 112–116.

3 "The 'British Pharmacopœia,'" *The British Medical Journal* 2 (1885): 1026.
4 John P. Swann, "The Evolution of the American Pharmaceutical Industry," *Pharmacy in History* 37, no. 2 (1995): 77.
5 "The 'British Pharmacopœia,'" 1025–1026.
6 Sonnedecker, "The Founding Period of the U.S. Pharmacopeia: I. European Antecedents," 158.
7 Ewell, *The Medical Companion, or Family Physician*, 672; Goldsmith and Shaw, *A History of the Earth and Animated Nature, Together with the Elements of Botany*, 791; Bigelow, *American Medical Botany*, 93; The National Institute for the Promotion of Science, *Fourth Bulletin of the National Institute for the Promotion of Science, February 1845 to November 1846*, 554.
8 Lewis, *An Experimental History of the Materia Medica*, 1:393.
9 Akin, *Encyclopaedia: Or, a Dictionary of Arts, Sciences, and Miscellaneous Literature*, 8:689–690.
10 The National Institute for the Promotion of Science, *Fourth Bulletin of the National Institute for the Promotion of Science, February 1845 to November 1846*, 554.
11 Lewis, *An Experimental History of the Materia Medica*, 1:393.
12 Edward Balfour, ed., *Cyclopaedia of India and of Eastern and Southern Asia* (Madras: The Scottish Press, 1857), 1401.
13 *The Chemical Gazette, or, Journal of Practical Chemistry* 1 (1843): 237.
14 Goldsmith and Shaw, *A History of the Earth and Animated Nature, Together with the Elements of Botany*, 791–792.
15 Rafinesque, *Medical Flora*, 53.
16 John Sims, *Curtis's Botanical Magazine, or, Flower-Garden Displayed* 33 (1811).
17 von Linné, *Miscellaneous Tracts Relating to Natural History, Husbandry, and Physick*, 179.
18 Rafinesque, *Medical Flora*, 57.
19 Li, *Shinjuhae ponch'o kangmok*, 2007, 47.
20 Mathew Carey, "Remarks on the Commerce of America with China," in Carey, ed., *The American Museum, or, Universal Magazine*, vol. 7 (Philadelphia, PA, 1790), 576–577.
21 Nash, *American Ginseng*, 9.
22 Rafinesque, *Medical Flora*, 57.
23 Rafinesque, *Medical Flora*, 54.
24 Millspaugh, *American Medicinal Plants*, 70.
25 The Royal College of Physicians of London, *Medical Transactions*, 3:34; Edward Smedley, Hugh James Rose, and Henry John Rose, eds., *Encyclopaedia Metropolitana*, vol. 19 (London, 1845), 583.
26 Willich and Mease, *The Domestic Encyclopaedia; or, A Dictionary of Facts, and Useful Knowledge*, 3:158.
27 Heasim Sul 설혜심, "19 segi Yŏngguk shinmun e nat'anan insam" 19세기 영국신문에 나타난 인삼 [Ginseng as It Appeared in 19th-Century British Newspapers], *Yŏngguk yŏn'gu* 영국연구 34 (2015): 13.
28 "Foreign Intelligence," *Caledonian Mercury*, November 8, 1834.
29 One picul was equal to one hundred *jin* (斤) or sixteen *guan* (貫), which weighed approximately 63.55 kilograms.
30 "Ginseng," *Wilmington Daily Herald*, March 6, 1860. Exactly when Heylin traveled to China, however, has been debated. See note 17 on Manget, "Ginseng, China, and the Transformation of the Ohio Valley, 1783–1840," 22.
31 Qi Lian-Wen, Wang Chong-Zhi, and Yuan Chun-Su, "Ginsenosides from American Ginseng: Chemical and Pharmacological Diversity," *Phytochemistry* 72, no. 8 (2011): 693.
32 François André Michaux, *Travels to the West of the Alleghany Mountains* (London, 1805), 233.
33 Manget, "Ginseng, China, and the Transformation of the Ohio Valley, 1783–1840," 12.

34 Manget, "Ginseng, China, and the Transformation of the Ohio Valley, 1783–1840," 13.
35 *Gaoli tujing* (高麗圖經), 23 juan (卷), 2 zasu (雜俗).
36 Wang, *Zhongguo renshen*, 27.
37 Wang, *Zhongguo renshen*, 27.
38 Rhind, *A History of the Vegetable Kingdom*, 529.
39 Carey, *The American Museum, or Repository of Ancient and Modern Fugitive Pieces, & c*, 448.
40 John Hill, *The Valerian or, the Virtues of That Root in Nervous Disorders; and the Characters Which Distinguish the True from the False* (London, 1758), 17.
41 Rafinesque, *Medical Flora*, 54.
42 Jartoux, "The Description of a Tartarian Plant, Call'd Gin-Seng; with an Account of Its Virtues," 237–247.

12

GINSENG'S SLOW ENTRY INTO THE MODERN PHARMACEUTICAL SYSTEM

In Europe, the flames of the Chinoiserie craze died down quickly by the late eighteenth century. This coincided with the beginning of the reform of pharmacopoeias, the use of chemical nomenclature, and the extraction of active ingredients from plants. The overflowing admiration European intellectuals had for China and the attempts to study the Chinese system as a model for Europe waned significantly. Compared to the progressive West, China and the East were increasingly seen as stagnant areas in need of enlightenment. Jean-Baptiste Du Halde, who introduced China and ginseng to Europe through the *General History of China*, seems to have foreseen this change in perception when he remarked that, "the Chinese have made discoveries in all the sciences, but have not brought to perfection any of those we call speculative."[1]

A distinct shift in approach emerged in the medical realm as well. Whether intended or not, Europeans encountered non-European medicine and pharmacy since the seventeenth century. A countless diversity of foreign plants made their way into the European medicinal market, and pulse diagnosis, moxabustion, and acupuncture were introduced. Up until that point, Chinese medicine was considered capable of refined treatment based on personal instinct and centuries of accumulated know-how. However, as the West increasingly aimed for the professionalization of orthodox medicine, it came to reject experiential, subjective knowledge.[2] Even those who held Chinese medicine in high regard began to remark that it was falling behind.[3] Chinese medicine thus faced criticism for having been "long, but most imperfectly, practiced by the Chinese."[4]

Until the mid-to-late eighteenth century, Enlightenment medicine operated under syncretism, but upon the threshold of the nineteenth century, medical sects engaged in fierce competition, each with its own theory to claim a monopoly on knowledge about the human body and diseases.[5] This was how Western society established "modern" medicine and pharmacy, and created a category

DOI: 10.4324/9781003286691-15

called alternative and orthodox medicine. The road to modern medicine and pharmacy involved several steps. The first was to acquire "indigenous traditions," medicinal ingredients and medical knowledge from non-Western regions the West gained access to through its expansion overseas. The next step was to internalize such knowledge yet disparage or even reject non-Western traditions. The fate of "China root" serves as a typical example of this process.

China root came into the limelight in Europe as a remedy for syphilis. Regarding syphilis, which had become rife in Europe since the Renaissance, the theory that it originated from the American continent was pitted against another theory that it was native to Europe since the days of the Roman Empire and spread rapidly as people began to travel more frequently in the early modern period. Whatever its origin, Europe had been troubled by the surge in syphilis infections since the Age of Discovery. It was only by chance that Europeans found out China root was excellent for treating syphilis, which of course boosted the European demand for the plant. According to one scholar, the root was "more representative of the miraculous panaceas China offered the world than ginseng, ginger or rhubarb."[6] Then, as China root grew challenging to secure, European countries scrambled to find an alternative that could satisfy the demand for it.

A quest for an alternative usually involved several steps. Like discovering American ginseng to substitute for expensive Chinese ginseng, Europe found a plant similar to China root on the American continent: American sarsaparilla. Once the plant's medicinal efficacy was confirmed, it would soon be transplanted to plantations in Jamaica for mass production. The next step involved ruthless competition. At first, China root competed with American sarsaparilla in Western markets, but its popularity soon began to wane. By using slave labor at plantations, larger volumes of American sarsaparilla could be grown and supplied stably at cheaper prices. Drug companies with the right to produce and sell American sarsaparilla marketed the plant so that it would spread worldwide.

Such quests were accompanied by stories of discovery surrounding "miraculous plants" like China root. However, memories related to Europe's discovery of China root were gradually forgotten and the "discovery" of American sarsaparilla was instead glorified as a great discovery of mankind or a moment of innovation. The esteem China root held as a medicinal herb was erased from the history of conquering syphilis, a disease that once terrified Europe. Europe thus excluded China while monopolizing the history of medicinal ingredients and their administration.

What is more is that European botany and medicine began to refer to sarsaparilla from Jamaica as the "true" sarsaparilla. Instead of the ambiguous medicinal efficacy assigned to China root, this true sarsaparilla became acknowledged as a truly medicinal ingredient with "standard" active ingredients. In 1914, the British General Medical Council identified China root as a "completely inert drug" and excluded it from its pharmacopoeia after failing to isolate parillin from the plant.[7]

Ginseng met a fate similar to that of China root. Ginseng and China root were both known as Chinese plants when they were actually from East Asia. Both were once considered panaceas capable of curing all sorts of diseases. As in the case of China root, a plant similar to ginseng was discovered on the American continent and both eventually became excluded from pharmacopoeias. Yet, unlike China root, ginseng did not disappear entirely despite its demotion. Ironically, the West's failure to extract active ingredients from ginseng is likely to have contributed to its survival.

Nowadays saponin or ginsenosides may be named as typical natural products of ginseng, but only after the mid-twentieth century did the root's active ingredients start to be properly identified. As such, the West could not completely disregard China's authority on the efficacy of ginseng when it was in the position of having to export it to China since the early eighteenth century. Without precise knowledge of ginseng's medicinal properties, the West was incapable of challenging the Chinese knowledge system that had long admired ginseng. Unlike China root's exclusion for being a "completely inert drug," Western medical professionals therefore had no choice but to keep arguing that American ginseng was as effective as Asian ginseng or pretend that American ginseng was from China.

Even so, the West was not convinced that American ginseng could be a perfect substitute to Korean ginseng. As previously mentioned, Western scientists were already aware of the difference in efficacy between the two. Although uncertain as to whether the difference was intrinsic or caused by processing methods, merchants, economists, physicians, and chemists were all aware that the two plants were treated differently. So, although American ginseng surfaced as a substitute like Jamaican sarsaparilla, it could never be a true, perfect substitute to Korean ginseng.

What also made it challenging to find a substitute for ginseng was the fact that ginseng could not become a plantation crop. Colonial plantations were mostly established in hot regions where it was impossible to grow ginseng, which required cooler climates. Even if it could be planted at cooler locations such as the foot of a mountain, ginseng was too sensitive to be grown at scales large enough to necessitate slave labor. These circumstances were the reason why the West failed to artificially grow ginseng until the late nineteenth century or declare it a "Western innovation."

Meanwhile, ginseng's fame as a panacea contributed to its survival. Globally known wonder drugs at the time were concocted with active ingredients chemically extracted from different plants. A typical example was quinine.[8] Cinchona or quinquina bark gained immense popularity in Europe as it became known to be highly effective in treating fevers in Spanish Peru (today's Columbia), where it was discovered in the mid-seventeenth century. The tree was also referred to as Peruvian bark or Jesuit's bark from having been traded by the Jesuits. And when an alkaloid called quinine was extracted from the bark in the early nineteenth century, it became the quintessential cure for malaria.[9]

Quinine settled down as an indispensable prophylactic among Western imperialists advancing into tropical areas, and as it came to be globally known as a malaria remedy, the name Peruvian bark was forgotten. In other words, the name of this natural product from Peru was replaced by the name quinine, an active ingredient extracted in the West, and the name of the disease it specifically attacked. Unlike quinine, ginseng had a powerful reputation for being effective against many diseases, which made it impossible to narrow down its range of application. So, even if the West had succeeded in extracting ginsenosides from ginseng sooner, it would have still faced the issue of having to identify which disease ginsenosides are especially effective in treating. That is, of course, not to say that efforts to chemically extract active ingredients from ginseng were not made in the West.

Chemical Analysis of Ginseng

The nineteenth century saw attempts to analyze the chemical constituents of ginseng. Western scientists had moved on from the stage of observing, tasting, and smelling ginseng into the stage of active experimentation by analyzing the mucus generated from water or alcohol infused with ginseng or burning the oil extracted from infusions.[10]

The first person to chemically analyze ginseng was Constantine Samuel Rafinesque. Born in Istanbul, Turkey, Rafinesque spent his youth gaining experience in various regions of Europe. Since 1808, he began working in the medicine trade in Sicily and was not only successful but had opportunities to interact with renowned physicians at the time. Once he settled down in the United States, Rafinesque lectured at Transylvania University in Lexington, Kentucky, for seven years beginning in 1819 and made a name for himself as a botanist and zoologist. Rafinesque was also well versed in medicine. Nevertheless, his botanical contemporaries did not hesitate to call Rafinesque "crack-brained" or a quack. The reason he became a target of criticism was because he was too experimental and interdisciplinary for his time. Rafinesque was, after all, a pioneer in a movement of sorts for herbal medicine.[11]

Regarding ginseng, Rafinesque once remarked that "this is one of the plants upon which I have made many experiments."[12] He explained that he grew interested in the root because he was curious as to whether the efficacy of American ginseng was identical to that of Chinese ginseng, a panacea verified through 2,000 years of experimentation. Rafinesque thus attempted cutting-edge chemical experimentation and analysis of ginseng.

> The roots have a pleasant camphorated smell; the taste is sweet and pungent, with a slight degree of aromatic bitterness. They are a fine gentle and agreeable stimulant, both fresh and dry; also nervine, cordial, restorative, analeptic, demulcent, edulcorant, expectorant, stomachic, attenuant, deobstruent, &c. They owe their active properties to peculiar substance,

very similar to camphor, which I call Panacine, white, pungent, soluble in alcohol and water, and more fixed than camphor; they contain also a volatile oil, sugar, mucilage, resin, &c.[13]

However, a mere two decades later, Rafinesque's analysis of ginseng was denounced as insufficient by Samuel S. Garrigues (1828–1898). The son of a Philadelphian pharmacist, Garrigues learned the family trade and then went to study in Germany, where he earned a doctoral degree from the University of Göttingen through his dissertation "Chemical Investigations on Radix Ginseng Americana."[14]

Garrigues's dissertation was practically the world's first research paper to chemically analyze ginseng. The first thesis on ginseng to be produced through the Western university system was, as mentioned in Part 1, Lucas Augustin Folliot de Saint-Vast's thesis "An infirmis à morbo viribus reparandis Gin Seng?" from 1736, submitted for his doctoral degree from the University of Paris.[15] However, from a modern point of view, Folliot de Saint-Vast's thesis did not involve a chemical analysis of ginseng. Despite placing an emphasis on the premise that medically useful ingredients could be extracted from medicinal herbs, ingredients were not prominently discussed because chemical formulae had yet to be adopted, which is why evidence of ginseng's efficacy tended to be sought from *Bencao gangmu*. Garrigues's dissertation, on the other hand, took a "modern approach" at a time when great strides were being made in chemical formulae and chemical analysis.

In the introduction to his dissertation, Garrigues acknowledged that Rafinesque identified as ginseng's constituents "a volatile oil, starch, sugar, gum, slime, rasin, and a substance resembling camphor to which he gave the name Panacin." Yet, Rafinesque had failed to identify a more crucial constituent and the "incompleteness" of his study was what Garrigues revealed as his own motivation for delving deeper into the matter.[16] After experimenting with the traditional method of infusing cold water with ginseng, Garrigues claimed that instead of sugar, he found a considerable amount of albumen in the infusion. And through the application of various chemical techniques and solutions, he also claimed that he was able to extract two new constituents, which he named "panaquilon" and "panacon."[17]

The panaquilon Garrigues extracted from American ginseng was an amorphous saponin compound ($C_{24}H_{25}O_{18}$). Garrigues's discovery has since been recognized as the origin of studies on saponin compounds in ginseng. In 1889, the same compound was extracted from Korean ginseng collected at the Ussuri River valley in eastern Siberia. In 1906, Japanese scientist Y. Asahina and his colleagues managed to isolate saponin and sapogenin from Korean ginseng but failed to identify their chemical structure.[18] In the 1930s, H. Kodake and his colleagues reported that they were able to isolate panaxin and prosapogenin from ginseng. However, such studies on the constituents of ginseng had to be temporarily suspended with the Great Depression and World War II.[19] Still, studies on Korean ginseng were actively conducted in Korea while it was under Japan's colonial rule.

Ginseng Studies Under Japanese Colonial Rule

As soon as it forcibly occupied Korea, Japan established the Rules for Medical Practitioners, which defined doctors of traditional Korean medicine as medical practitioners with less authority than physicians. The Japanese Government-General of Korea nevertheless regarded traditional Korean medicine as an invaluable resource and was highly interested in utilizing that resource during wars. In fact, Japan had been interested in Korean medicinal herbs and begun to study them long before its colonial rule of Korea. As briefly mentioned earlier, the Japanese even smuggled Korean ginseng out of the country in an attempt to grow it back home. With the Japanese Government-General of Korea's establishment, an extensive investigation was launched into medicinal herbs on the Korean peninsula through the Food Production Bureau under the Government-General's Ministry of Agriculture, Commerce, and Industry. The Government-General's Department of Police Affairs also conducted a field survey of medicinal plants for the purpose of collecting powerful, poisonous drugs, growing poppies, and producing opium. Meanwhile, the Government-General's Central Laboratory conducted research and experiments to meet the need to develop alternative medications. The data gathered from these large-scale investigations and experiments was used for research at the Sugihara Laboratory of the Keijo Imperial University.[20]

Sugihara Noriyuki (杉原德行) was a professor of pharmacology at the Keijo Imperial University's medical school. The school's pharmacology program had two tracks. One track focused on Western medicine while the other, headed by Sugihara, focused on natural, herbal medicine, including traditional Korean medicine. The laboratory Sugihara ran was key to researching traditional Korean medications and analyzing their ingredients and pharmacological effects. Min Pyŏng-ki and Kim Ha-sik were among those who took part in many early studies on the pharmacological effects of Korean ginseng.[21] Min and Kim went beyond the boundaries of traditional Korean medicine and attempted to analyze and test the root from the viewpoint of Western medicine. From 1929, Min fed ginseng to rats to study whether the root was addictive, whether it triggered convulsion or paralysis, and to determine its lethal dosage.[22]

In 1939, Sugihara began to additionally serve as director of the Keijo Imperial University's Herbal Medicine Research Institute. The fact that the research institute was established in Kaesŏng indicates just how interested the Government-General and the Keijo Imperial University were in Korean ginseng. To live up to their expectations, Sugihara published research papers about studies on Korean ginseng, the effect white and red ginseng had on glucose regulation, the difference between Korean and American ginseng, and ginseng's effect in neutralizing neurotoxins. He also led the institute's development of various products including liquid ginseng extract, powdered ginseng tea, and ginseng soap.[23] Japanese research on ginseng was thus conducted through close cooperation between the Government-General, the Keijo Imperial University, and Mitsui bussan.[24]

Meanwhile, another doctoral dissertation about Korean ginseng was approved at the University of Berlin's medical school. The author of the dissertation "Über die echte Ginsengwurzel: Panax Ginseng, Song-Sam" (On the Real Ginseng Root: Panax Ginseng, Song-Sam) was a Korean named Sun In-su.[25] The dissertation began by defining Korean ginseng as the "real" ginseng among the various kinds available on the market. The ginseng studied for the dissertation was white ginseng from Songdo referred to as *Song-sam*. The author states that the *Song-sam* used for the study was procured through his childhood friend from the "Kong family"[26] that was apparently well known for its generations of ginseng growers, which gives reason to suspect that the friend was related to the famous merchant in Kaesŏng named Kong Sŏng-hak.[27]

Through the dissertation, Sun argues that ginseng should be mixed with other medicinal ingredients instead of being used independently. If used as a concoction, it could be effective in treating fevers due to tuberculosis, bronchitis, laryngitis, puerperalism, bleeding due to hemoptysis, nasal hemorrhage, hematuria, dysentery, as well as anemia, postpartum weakness, and syphilis. Such concoctions made with ginseng could also be used as a sedative or an aphrodisiac. The dissertation also discusses the tendency to consider ginseng as a tonic to replenish stamina depleted by various illnesses. Yet, according to the dissertation, ginseng is especially effective in treating symptoms related to disruptions in the nervous system such as depression. In the case of opium addicts, the intake of ginseng after smoking opium could have a detoxifying effect.[28]

The dissertation states that Sun tested the effects of ginseng on animals such as rats, pigeons, amphibians, and fish. The tests were conducted under the assumption that the root's efficacy is different from that of the rootlets of ginseng. While it was difficult to distinguish Panax acid in ether extracted from ginseng, Sun concluded that growth-stimulating substances were concentrated in the root of ginseng. Sun also confirmed ginseng's potential as a remedy for sexual dysfunction after experimenting with castrated rats and fish.[29] Sun's dissertation stands out not for its originality or innovativeness but for the fact that it refers heavily to Korean and Japanese pharmacological research on Korean ginseng, especially studies done by Sugihara Noriyuki and Min Pyŏng-ki.[30] Pharmacological studies on ginseng in Korea had thus served as a foundation to German pharmacological research on ginseng.

Around the time, a number of interesting studies were being conducted in Korea and Japan on the botanical characteristics of ginseng, the root's medicinal properties, cultivation methods, and the diseases it was prone to.[31] Between the 1910s and early 1930s, research was focused on analyzing the constituents of ginseng and their pharmacological actions, and since the mid-1930s, a more diverse range of topics were academically explored such as the natural crossing of Korean ginseng and its prevention, the correlation between the cultivation of ginseng and the parent rock of soil, and the psychological effect Korean ginseng can have on the capacity of mice to learn.[32]

Russian Research on Ginseng after World War II

Research on bioactive ingredients in ginseng began in earnest after the end of World War II. At the time, Russia was engaged in the mass cultivation of ginseng and various research projects using Korean ginseng seeds smuggled out of the country during the Korean War. A key figure involved in such research was Israel Brekhman (1921–1994), a pharmacologist working at the USSR Academy of Sciences' Far East Science Center in Vladivostok.

Brekhman clinically tested the efficacy of ginseng on hundreds of young soldiers. A few hours before being subjected to a three-kilometer run, soldiers were divided into two groups: one group was required to take ginseng extract while the other took a placebo that resembled the extract in color and taste. The group that took ginseng extract arrived at the destination one minute earlier on average compared to the placebo group. This test was the beginning of countless research papers Brekhman published on the pharmacological effects of ginseng, allowing him to be recognized as a pioneer in ginseng pharmacology even to this day.[33]

To prove his theory, Brekhman chose radio and telegraph operators as his next experimental group. The reason for choosing them was because their profession required detailed movement, concentration, and endurance. The treatment group and placebo group both exhibited a similar degree of improvement in terms of performance speed but the group that took ginseng made far fewer work-related errors. Brekhman actively engaged in animal testing as well. He dropped 120 mice into water to make them swim until exhaustion and allowed them a short break before repeating the routine. During the second round of swimming the mice injected with ginseng extract beforehand were able to swim twice as long when compared to those in the placebo group.[34]

Brekhman's experiments received considerable international attention. They inspired the Oxford-educated pharmacologist Stephen Fulder (b. 1946) to test the efficacy of ginseng on night shift nurses. The nurses who took ginseng showed lower degrees of fatigue and higher levels of achievement and concentration. Similar studies were also conducted in Germany.[35]

By the 1960s, great strides were made in researching the constituents of ginseng. A saponin called ginsenoside was isolated and purified to determine its chemical structure. At the forefront of such progress were researchers led by G.B. Elyakov at the Institute of Biologically-Active Substances under the USSR Academy of Sciences' Far Eastern Branch and researchers led by Shoji Shibata (紫田承二) of the University of Tokyo's Department of Pharmacy.[36] In Korea, Professor Han Byung-hoon and his colleagues at Seoul National University's Natural Products Research Institute attempted to isolate active ingredients from Korean ginseng to show they could stabilize serum albumin from heat denaturation. Isolating and observing the structure of Panax saponin A and C revealed that Panax saponin A was ginsenoside Rg1 and Panax saponin C was ginsenoside Re.

The scope of research on saponins in white and red ginseng widened thereafter and identified the chemical structure of thirty-seven different ginsenosides. Research is also being conducted on traces of ginsenoside in red ginseng. Scholars have so far made notable progress in terms of exploring the chemical constituents of Korean ginseng and that it would not be a stretch to say there is nothing left to discover, especially when it comes to saponin.[37]

Notes

1 Du Halde, *A Description of the Empire of China and Chinese-Tartary, Together with the Kingdoms of Korea, and Tibet* (London, 1741), 124.
2 Roberta Bivins, *Alternative Medicine?: A History* (Oxford: Oxford University Press, 2007), 38–39.
3 Barnes, *Needles, Herbs, Gods, and Ghosts*, 237.
4 Robley Dunglison, *A New Dictionary of Medical Science and Literature*, vol. 1 (Boston, MA: Charles Bowen, 1833), 184.
5 Bivins, *Alternative Medicine?*, 35.
6 Anna E. Winterbottom, "Of the China Root: A Case Study of the Early Modern Circulation of Materia Medica," *Social History of Medicine* 28, no. 1 (2015): 22.
7 Winterbottom, "Of the China Root," 41.
8 Cook and Walker, "Circulation of Medicine in the Early Modern Atlantic World," 341.
9 Cook and Walker, "Circulation of Medicine in the Early Modern Atlantic World," 340.
10 Bigelow, *American Medical Botany*, 94; Balfour, *Cyclopaedia of India and of Eastern and Southern Asia*, 1401.
11 Michael A. Flannery, "The Medicine and Medicinal Plants of C. S. Rafinesque," *Economic Botany* 52, no. 1 (1998): 28.
12 Rafinesque, *Medical Flora*, 56.
13 Rafinesque, *Medical Flora*, 55.
14 Samuel S. Garrigues, "Chemical Investigations on Radix Ginseng Americana, Oleum Chenopodii Anthelmintici and Oleum Menthae Viridis" (Doctoral dissertation, University of Göttingen, 1854).
15 Folliot de Saint-Vast, "Resp. Quaestio Medica, An Infirmis à Morbo Viribus Reparandis Gin Seng? Praes. F. Vandermonde."
16 Garrigues, "Chemical Investigations on Radix Ginseng Americana, Oleum Chenopodii Anthelmintici and Oleum Menthae Viridis," 7.
17 Garrigues, "Chemical Investigations on Radix Ginseng Americana, Oleum Chenopodii Anthelmintici and Oleum Menthae Viridis," 14.
18 Y. Asahina and B. Taguchi, "The Constituents of Ginseng," *Yakugaku zasshi* 26 (1906): 549.
19 Ko et al., *Uri insam ŭi ihae*, 24.
20 Shin Changgeon 신창건, "Kyŏngsŏngjeguktaehak e issŏsŏ hanyak yŏn'gu ŭi sŏngnip" 경성제국대학에 있어서 한약연구의 성립 [Institutionlization of Research on Traditional Medicine in Keijo Imperial University], *Sahoewa yŏksa* 사회와 역사 76 (2007): 105–106, 108, 115, 117.
21 Sugihara stated that "an investigation into the precise pharmacological effects of ginseng by Min (Pyŏng-ki), Kim (Ha-sik), and Yang at my laboratory revealed that the plant is essentially a stimulant of sorts." Sugihara Noriyuki 杉取徳行, "Chosen ninjin" 朝鮮人参 [Chosŏn Ginseng], *Chiryo yobi shoho* 治療及処方, 1932: 38–48.

Requoted from note 92 in Shin, "Kyŏngsŏngjeguktaehak e issŏsŏ hanyak yŏn'gu ŭi sŏngnip," 129.

22 Imamura, *Insamsa*, 2015, 1:173–174.

23 Chang, *Han'guk insam sanŏpsa*, 2018, 1:537–538.

24 Shin, "Kyŏngsŏngjeguktaehak e issŏsŏ hanyak yŏn'gu ŭi sŏngnip," 129–130.

25 Sun Insu, "Über die echte Ginsengwurzel (Panax Ginseng, Song-Sam)," *Naunyn Schmiedebergs Archiv für experimentelle Pathologie und Pharmakologie* 170 (1933): 443–457.

26 Sun Insu, "Über die echte Ginsengwurzel (Panax Ginseng, Song-Sam)," 444.

27 From April 1 to May 14, 1923, Son Pong-sang, Kong Sŏng-hak, Pak Pong-chin, Kim Wŏn-pae, and Amano Yunosuke embarked on a survey for forty-four days in China to pioneer a market for red ginseng, and Kong Sŏng-hak wrote an account of the survey under the title *Chungyu ilgi* (中遊日記). Five years later, Kong Sŏng-hak, Kong Sŏng-ku, Amano Yunosuke, and Ito Kikujiro headed to Hong Kong and Taiwan to conduct another survey for the same purpose. Major ginseng merchants from Kaesŏng joined this forty-two day trip with Mitsui bussan officials, and according to detailed records of the journey in the travelogue *Hyangdae giram* (香臺紀覽) by Kong Sŏng-ku. They were apparently well cared for by the Mitsui Shoji branches in China, Hong Kong, and Taiwan. Kong Sŏngku 공성구, *Hyangdaegiram: Kaesŏng sangin ŭi hongsam rodŭ kaech'ŏkki* 향대기람: 개성상인의 홍삼로드 개척기 [Hyangdaegiram: Kaesŏng Merchants' Journey to Establish an Export Route for Red Ginseng], trans. Pak Tonguk 박동욱 (Seoul: T'aehaksa 태학사, 2014).

28 Sun Insu, "Über die echte Ginsengwurzel (Panax Ginseng, Song-Sam)," 444. The remark was quoted from a handbook of pharmacognosy published in German: Alexander Tschirch, *Handbuch Der Pharmakognosie*, vol. 1 (Leipzig: Tauchnitz, 1909), 514ff.

29 Sun Insu, "Über die echte Ginsengwurzel (Panax Ginseng, Song-Sam)," 446–457.

30 Sun referred to ginseng-related studies from the 1930s published in the *Keijo Journal of Medicine*. See note 1 in Sun Insu, "Über die echte Ginsengwurzel (Panax Ginseng, Song-Sam)," 445.

31 In a chapter covering modern scientific research on ginseng, Imamura introduces fifty-three pharmacological studies published on ginseng prior to the mid-1930s. Imamura Tomo 今村鞆, *Insamsa* 人蔘史 [History of Ginseng], trans. Koh Seungtae 고승태, vol. 5: Insam ŭiyakp'yŏn 인삼의약편 [Ginseng Medication] (Yŏngju: Dongyang University 동양대학교, 2015), 613–743.

32 Summaries of such studies can be found in Imamura Tomo 今村鞆, *Insamsa* 人蔘史 [History of Ginseng], trans. Koh Seungtae 고승태, vol. 6: Insam chapkip'yŏn 인삼잡기편 [Miscellaneous Notes on Ginseng] (Yŏngju: Dongyang University 동양대학교, 2015), 402–407, 411, 415.

33 Schwemmer, *Wunderdroge Ginseng*, 83.

34 Schwemmer, *Wunderdroge Ginseng*, 87.

35 Schwemmer, *Wunderdroge Ginseng*, 85–86.

36 G.B. Elyakov et al., "Glycosides from Ginseng Roots," *Tetrahedron Letters* 5, no. 48 (1964): 3591–3597; Shibata Shoji et al., "Studies on the Constituents of Japanese and Chinese Crude Drugs. XI. Panaxadiol, A Sapogenin of Ginseng Roots," *Chemical and Pharmaceutical Bulletin* 11 (1963): 759–761. Requoted from Chang, *Han'guk insam sanŏpsa*, 2018, 1:540.

37 Ko et al., *Uri insam ŭi ihae*, 21.

13

THE DEPLETION OF WILD GINSENG AND THE BEGINNING OF CULTIVATED GINSENG

Ginseng used to grow in woodlands all over the Korean peninsula, except for coastal mountains in the Kyŏngsang or Chŏlla Provinces where the climate was warmer. The wild ginseng yield, however, experienced a continuous decline due to the indiscriminate collection of ginseng and deforestation. Korean wild ginseng began to show signs of impending extinction during the reign of King Sŏngjong in the mid-fifteenth century and vanished completely during the reign of King Yŏngjo in the mid-eighteenth century. In fact, *Sŭngjŏngwŏn ilgi*, or the Records of the Royal Secretariat, notes that "ginseng recently became extinct" in an entry for 1734, the tenth year of King Yŏngjo's reign.[1] Wild ginseng thereafter only, and barely, survived in the northern parts of the Korean peninsula, deep in the mountains. Imamura Tomo also pointed to deforestation as the reason wild ginseng, abundant in most parts of the Korean peninsula up until the middle of the Chosŏn Dynasty, grew scarce over the course of about 200 years.[2]

The cultivation of ginseng on the Korean peninsula appears to have begun long before wild ginseng faced the threat of extinction. Scholars like Steven Foster believe it has been about 1,000 years since ginseng started to be grown on the Korean peninsula.[3] Cultivation is commonly thought to have begun tacitly around the fifteenth century at the latest.[4] Documentation about such cultivation, however, emerged far later. The term *kasam* (家蔘), referring to locally grown ginseng, first appeared in the *Annals of King Chŏngjo*, among accounts of the year 1790. Judging from the frequent mention of ginseng seeds since the time of King Sukchong, scholars have come to believe that ginseng cultivation had grown common in certain areas around the early eighteenth century, such as the Yŏngnam area. By the second half of the eighteenth century, it became widespread enough for books to be compiled on cultivation methods. Agricultural books such as *Koundang p'ilgi* (古芸堂筆記) by Yu Tŭk-kong

DOI: 10.4324/9781003286691-16

(柳得恭, 1749–1807), *Samsŏ* (蔘書) by Yi Hak-kyu (李學逵, 1770–1835), and *Imwŏn kyŏngjeji* (林園經濟志) by Sŏ Yu-ku (徐有榘, 1764–1845) offer systematically organized chapters of information on how to grow *kasam*.[5]

The spread of ginseng cultivation changed the major areas of its production. When wild ginseng occupied most of Korea's ginseng output, the areas that mainly supplied ginseng were P'yŏngan Province, Hamgyŏng Province, Kangwŏn Province, and mountainous areas in the provinces of Ch'ungch'ŏng, Kyŏngsang, and Chŏlla. According to *Sejongshillok chiriji* (世宗實錄地理志), or the Geographical Appendix to the Annals of King Sejong, ginseng was collected as tax in kind from 112 counties and townships, which amounted to one-third of the total number of counties and townships in Korea.[6] As ginseng cultivation became prevalent beyond the nineteenth century, Kaesŏng surfaced as a major area of ginseng production. Beginning in the 1830s, Kaesŏng merchants started to cultivate ginseng at large scales and export red ginseng to China. From the 1850s, 24,000 kilograms were being produced and considering that about 12,000 kilograms were officially exported, Kaesŏng merchants must have smuggled the rest out to be sold in China. Red ginseng was almost entirely transported by land, which is why its export was less impacted by the opening of ports. Hence, the cultivation of ginseng as well as the production and export of red ginseng continued to revolve around Kaesŏng from the mid-nineteenth century until the Kabo Reform of 1894.[7]

As Korea went through the Kabo and Kwangmu Reforms and Japan installed its Residency-General in Korea and began plundering the country's economy, the policy on red ginseng changed and the Korean ginseng industry experienced dramatic change.[8] The Korean Empire was forced by Japan to launch a state monopoly system for red ginseng in 1908. The management and sale of red ginseng was thereafter up to the Japanese Government-General of Korea's Monopoly Bureau and Mitsui bussan, until Korea's liberation in 1945. Kaesŏng managed to maintain its reputation as a major ginseng producing area although it became part of North Korea after the Korean War. People who moved south from Kaesŏng during the war continued to grow ginseng in places like Kanghwa but failed to preserve their prestige while previously peripheral areas in the industry like Kŭmsan and P'unggi instead quickly emerged as major producers of ginseng in South Korea after the war.

Ginseng Cultivation in Japan

Although Panax japonicus, the ginseng native to Japan, was medicinally used by commoners, the upper class preferred the more effective Korean ginseng, so there was a constant demand for it in Japan.[9] It was therefore no coincidence that Japan fixed its eye on Korean ginseng during its invasion of Korea in the late sixteenth century. Japanese soldiers took ginseng from the Korean peninsula and had Korean captives grow it in Otokonomura (男子村), Japan.[10] In 1607, Tokugawa Ieyasu (徳川家康, 1542–1616) gave Korean ginseng seeds to Date Masamune (伊達政宗) and Take Yoshinobu (竹義宣) and ordered them to serve their country by planting and growing the seeds in the area they each governed, which had climates similar to Korea due to being located due east of the country.[11] Records indicate that another unsuccessful attempt to grow Korean ginseng in Japan was made at a mountain in a different area, where a ginseng farm of nearly 10,000 square meters was maintained until about 1860.[12]

As mentioned in Part 2, the demand for Korean ginseng surged under the rule of the Edo bakufu and caused a serious drain of silver, prompting the eighth shogun, Tokugawa Yoshimune, to devise a plan to cultivate Korean ginseng in Japan. Secretly charged with the mission of procuring live ginseng plants from Korea, the daimyo of Tsushima Domain smuggled three from Korea in 1721, six in 1722, eleven in 1727, and twenty-four in 1728, in addition to sixty ginseng seeds. In 1725, Yu Meiji (兪牧吉), a Manchurian merchant who regularly visited Nagasaki, is said to have brought three live plants and one hundred seeds of Korean ginseng.[13] Such Japanese efforts to cultivate ginseng were documented in detail, most likely because they were driven by the bakufu's aspiration to secure Korean ginseng.

The bakufu planted four roots on Sado (佐渡) Island in 1723 and succeeded in harvesting seeds for the first time in 1725. Another attempt to grow ginseng began in Nikko (日光) in 1719 and by 1733; seedlings harvested there were distributed all over Japan. This is why Japan named 1733 as the year imported ginseng started to be replaced. Books devoted to ginseng cultivation were published, including *Ninjinfu* (人蔘譜) in 1726, *Ninjinben* (人蔘辨) in 1728, *Wakan ninjinko* (和漢人蔘考) in 1746, and *Ninijin kosaku-ki* (人蔘耕作記) in 1747.[14] The bakufu continued to be directly involved in the cultivation and production of ginseng until 1787. Ginseng farms were created in the prefectures of Fukushima, Nagano (formerly Shinshu), and Shimane (formerly Unshu) and given licenses to harvest and sell ginseng.

Imamura Tomo believed the bakufu's efforts to cultivate ginseng were unsuccessful because they "required a considerable amount of investment without generating profits."[15] Once the bakufu liberalized the cultivation and sale of ginseng in 1790, output increased in Japan so that Korean ginseng grown in Japan became exported to Canton, China, for the first time. The bakufu entrusted the export of *otane ninjin* (御種人蔘: Japanese cognomen for Korean ginseng) to a Nagasaki merchant named Nakamura Seiemon (中村 盛右衛門). Nakamura thus became the exclusive exporter of Korean ginseng grown in Japan, a monopoly he passed down to his descendants for generations.[16]

After the Meiji Restoration, the bakufu handed all the ginseng factories and farms it managed over to ten civilians, thereby completely privatizing the Japanese ginseng industry.[17] However, the cultivation of Korean ginseng decreased rapidly in Japan when it could no longer be exported to China during World War II. Ginseng is now being grown in small batches in Nagano, Fukushima, and Shimane, some of which is being exported.[18]

Ginseng Cultivation in China

The first record indicating that ginseng was grown in China was *Tujing bencao* (圖經本草), compiled in 1061 during the Song dynasty. The book described ginseng's cycle of growth in detail, mentioning that "it germinates into a seedling in the spring. The plant is initially small ... bears five leaves after four to five years ... and gives birth to a root ten years later." Scholars consider this as proof that ginseng was already being cultivated in mountain regions by then.[19] Yet a more substantial description of ginseng cultivation can be found in Li Shizhen's *Bencao gangmu*, published during the Ming dynasty. The book states that "the seeds are sowed in October in the same way as any other vegetable."[20] While ginseng may have been grown in China at the time, the scale would have been very small, and since it was tricky to transplant ginseng elsewhere, farmed ginseng most likely did not impact the domestic distribution and use of wild ginseng.[21]

After the establishment of the Qing dynasty, ginseng was strictly controlled through the *fengjin* policy, which regarded Changbai (Paektu) Mountain as sacred and monopolized the area's natural resources. Moreover, farmed ginseng was discredited as fake and prohibited from being used for medicinal purposes. These circumstances made it troublesome to grow ginseng in China. However, when the amount of wild ginseng being collected gradually decreased under the Qianlong Emperor's rule (1736–1796), people in Jilin secretly began to grow ginseng. They would work in the mountains, marking seedlings they found and preserving them for years before collecting them, and even sowed seeds or transplanted seedlings.

Such operations, of course, had to be carried out furtively. From 1794, the Qing government launched several inspections to track down and punish ginseng growers for allowing farmed ginseng to be distributed alongside government-certified ginseng, thereby devaluing the latter.[22] By the 1820s, however, people grew increasingly open about growing ginseng, and in the face of a serious shortage in the supply of ginseng, the government had no choice but to gradually permit its cultivation.[23]

At first, people transplanted wild ginseng to an environment that would help it grow faster and therefore generate greater profits. The seeds collected from such wild ginseng were used to propagate it, which developed into a technique for cultivating *yuanshen* (園蔘), or "garden ginseng." *Yuanshen* was mainly grown around the Changbai Mountain and spread to areas nearby over time.[24] During the Tongzhi Emperor's reign (1862–1874), *yuanshen* was grown by approximately 400 households. The output, however, fluctuated heavily because techniques for cultivating such a tricky plant were yet to be refined. The number of households that grew *yuanshen* thus dropped to about 200 by 1901.[25]

Ginseng farming was able to get back on track by the time the Republic of China was established in 1912. Jilin settled down as a bona fide center of the Chinese ginseng industry. During the early years of the republic, Fusong (撫松) County in particular had around 470 households devoted to producing

35,000 kilograms of ginseng annually, which amounted to 70 percent of China's nationwide output. By 1918, the county established itself as the "hometown of ginseng" by generating an annual output of 200,000 kilograms.[26] The largest output of farmed ginseng from northeastern China occurred in 1929 when a total of approximately 900,000 kilograms was harvested: 300,000 kilograms from Fusong County, 60,000 kilograms from Ji'an (輯安), 180,000 kilograms from Antu (安圖), 120,000 kilograms from Linjiang (臨江), 120,000 kilograms from Tonghua (通化), and 120,000 kilograms from other areas.[27]

After causing the Mukden Incident in 1931, Japan brutally controlled Chinese ginseng farmers. To neutralize anti-Japanese resistance, the imperialist "*sanko*" policy (三光政策) that sought to "kill all, loot all, and burn all" was implemented in mountainous areas and thereby devastated the ginseng farms around Changbai Mountain.[28] Japan forced farmers to sell large amounts of ginseng at lower prices, leaving them with virtually no profits.[29] These measures led to a sharp drop in northeastern China's output of farmed ginseng. According to a 1938 report on a Japanese survey of Changbai Mountain, Fusong County produced a mere 6,000 kilograms of *yuanshen*.[30] By the time Japan surrendered in 1945, most of the ginseng farms in northeastern China were ruined, leaving farmers extremely impoverished. The region's output of wild ginseng was a mere 18.75 kilograms in 1948, along with approximately 16,800 kilograms of *yuanshen*.[31]

It was only beyond the 1980s when China began to develop its ginseng industry. The government devised a plan for the industry's development and launched projects to scientifically research methods to cultivate ginseng, prevent disease and insect damage, and develop processing techniques.[32] Around 2010, the Chinese government began to focus on promoting the ginseng industry in Jilin. Scholars seem to view this change in policy as a countermeasure against the Korean ginseng industry. In other words, China appears to be searching for a strategy to raise the market value of Jilin ginseng "to be on par with Korean ginseng, which is worth over ten times more despite occupying only twenty percent of the world's total output."[33]

Ginseng Cultivation in the United States

Concern that North American ginseng might go extinct surfaced soon after its discovery in Canada in the early eighteenth century. French and British merchants and the indigenous peoples they hired didn't hesitate to collect as much ginseng as possible. Obsessed with the profits to be reaped from exporting ginseng, people depleted wild ginseng in one area and simply moved on to the next as they gradually headed south. After the American Civil War (1861–1865), wild ginseng grew extremely scarce, especially because, during the war, virtually no efforts were made to bury the seeds after digging up the plant for its root.[34]

Due to these circumstances, the volume of exported ginseng in the 1890s dropped to one-third of its level a decade earlier. Unease that ginseng might soon become extinct mounted even at major ginseng habitats like the Appalachians,

TABLE 13.1 1929–1948 Output and Price of Northeastern Chinese Ginseng. [Fang, *Renshen jiqi shangpinxue*, 5]

Year	*Wild Ginseng*		*Farmed Ginseng*	
	Production (tael)	*Price (yuan)*	*Production (picul)*	*Price (yuan)*
1929	11,000	60	1,500,000	6
1930	8,000	60	600,000	6
1931	6,000	45	600,000	4
1932	3,000	45	150,000	3
1933	3,000	45	150,000	3
1934	2,000	45	150,000	3
1935	2,000	45	150,000	3
1936	2,000	45	Restricted	3
1937	2,000	45	Restricted	3
1938	2,000	45	Restricted	3
1939	2,000	45	Restricted	3
1940	1,000	80	Restricted	3
1941	1,000	120	Restricted	3
1942	1,000	120	Restricted	3
1943	1,000	120	Restricted	3
1944	1,000	120	Restricted	3
1945	700	200	30,000	120
1946	800	200	120,000	250
1947	700	200	70,000	600
1948	500	–	28,000	–

where ginseng had grown "as scarce as hen's teeth" according to one witness.[35] In the 1880s, ginseng was sold at fifty-one cents per pound, but the price jumped to three dollars and fifty cents by the 1890s.[36]

In 1887, the state of North Carolina promulgated a law that charged the collection of ginseng between the first of April and the first of September as a misdemeanor and fined each offender ten dollars per day of violation.[37] In 1891, the Canadian province of Ontario banned the collection of wild ginseng between January and September and decided to impose a penalty of between five and twenty dollars for violation. Save for the purpose of reclamation, the ban forbade plucking or damaging ginseng growing wild in the mountains.[38] In 1977, the United States and Canada designated American ginseng as an endangered species through the Convention on International Trade in Endangered Species of Wild Fauna and Flora.

The desire, and attempts, to grow ginseng were present far before the plant became recognized as an endangered species. Since the late seventeenth century, European botanists struggled and ultimately failed to grow ginseng at medicinal gardens. More serious efforts to cultivate ginseng started to be made in the United States beginning in the 1870s, although attempts around the time to transplant young plants ended in failure as well. Sporadic attempts to transplant the root of wild ginseng and sow ginseng seeds were made in the late 1880s, and Abraham Whisman in Virginia and George Stanton in New York succeeded in cultivating ginseng on flat land.

Stanton came to be called the "father of American ginseng" because he succeeded in growing marketable ginseng. The method Stanton developed was to plant ginseng in a plowed, open field and later install a canopy with wooden boards to sufficiently block sunlight. He had learned that the wild plant needed shade and stratification, wherein seeds are exposed to cold temperatures in order to break their dormancy.

The rising interest in growing ginseng led the United States Department of Agriculture to publish *American Ginseng: Its Commercial History, Protection, and Cultivation*.[39] As this manual gained popularity, the cultivation of ginseng gradually spread to the states of Wisconsin, Michigan, Ohio, and Minnesota between the 1900s and 1920s. By then ginseng was being grown on the homestead and Korean cultivation techniques were being implemented. This subsequently gave birth to enterprises that sold ginseng seeds or seedlings.[40]

With the spread of ginseng cultivation, universities began to actively research cultivation methods and various microorganisms that infect ginseng. In 1912, a highly detailed report on diseases in ginseng was published under the lead of Herbert Hice Whetzel (1877–1944), a plant pathologist at Cornell University.[41] Whetzel's report came to be regarded as a textbook on American ginseng cultivation and later largely contributed to the disease management section of manuals for ginseng growers. The introduction of such manuals commonly covered the history of ginseng cultivation, noting that it began two hundred years prior in Korea and Japan.[42]

All sorts of manuals for ginseng growers appeared by the early twentieth century. One manual was based on a compilation of answers to questions farmers sent by post on how to handle issues with growing ginseng. Another focused on eradicating the diseases ginseng could encounter. Reports were released on experiments testing the efficacy of ginseng at institutions like the University of Michigan and technical books were published on strategies for the commercialization and specialization of ginseng. Among the variety of guides worth consulting even today was the *Ginseng and Goldenseal Growers Handbook* (1912) by John Henry Koehler (1866–?), which was considered almost as a textbook at the time.

The book was packed with information ranging from the history of ginseng to cultivation and pest management techniques as well as marketing strategies. Having been involved in growing ginseng for thirty years, Koehler began to take an interest in commercializing the root after 1900 and became driven by a sense of duty to provide Americans with as much accurate information as possible. What is interesting about this comprehensive handbook is its high regard for Korean ginseng as opposed to Japanese ginseng. Koehler even went as far as to say that "Japanese ginseng is practically worthless; bringing such a low price in the Chinese [market that] it is barely enough to pay for transportation charges."

He also warned inexperienced buyers to beware of Japanese ginseng because it looked very similar to some kinds of American ginseng.[43]

A different handbook had a chapter titled "Don't Buy Japanese Stock," explaining that "ginseng is too expensive to take any chance in something that may prove worthless in the end."[44] Yet, these remarks indicate that Japanese ginseng seeds were already being widely distributed to and even grown by American ginseng farmers.

Books promoting ginseng not only to farmers but the general public also began to appear. The special feature on ginseng in an 1891 issue of *Scientific American* attracted enough attention for it to be translated and published by several Asian newspapers.[45] Such books would give detailed descriptions of Chinese ginseng, the root's efficacy, and the reputation it enjoyed or explained the fact that American ginseng was not the same as Chinese or Korean ginseng. However, they would also include rather dubious information, for instance, that while ginseng was sparsely consumed in the cold, dry northern parts of China, it was taken in copious amounts as tea, food, and medication in the hot, humid southern parts of the country.

Among introductory books on ginseng for general readers was *What Is Ginseng?* The book is intriguing in that its author Charles Marvin Root held Korean ginseng in very high regard. According to Root, Korean ginseng was considered the finest type even in China, hinted at in the following account of a Chinese dignitary unwrapping an elaborately packaged box of ginseng sent from Songdo.

> First comes a layer of scented wood dust mingled with fluffy cotton or the waste of silk cocoons. This layer is removed and now appears a layer of little packets of white and gold papers. Each packet contains a small quantity at unslaked lime, to avoid any moisture which might injure the root. These packets of lime lie both above and below the ginseng.
>
> The last act in unsealing the precious root for which all this preparation has been made is removing the last envelope of embroidered silk or of crimson and gold fish skin. When the real thing is reached it is found to be a small dried object 4 or 5 inches in length with a glistening surface something like dull amber, that rudely resembles in miniature the headless body of a man.[46]

The reason for including such an account was because Root hoped American ginseng growers could learn from "the extreme care in the preparation of ginseng for the market among the Coreans."[47] In Root's eyes, ginseng was "the most valuable crop in the world."[48] American ginseng may have been traded at dirt cheap prices, but to farmers with not much land to spare, it was a crop that could offer the greatest amount of profit with a small amount of labor. For women at a loss as to how to provide for their children after the sudden loss of their husband, Root's advice was to grow ginseng on a plot of land.

Root also amusingly suggested that ginseng farming could be a good way to determine which son a farmer should leave his farm to if he has more than one son. The farmer simply had to give ten dollars' worth of ginseng seeds to each son and see what happens. One son may sell the seeds to increase his savings, buy clothes, or pay for his tuition. Another may sell the seeds for money to travel. However, the one who plants the seeds to grow ginseng would be the son worthy of inheriting his father's farm and property because growing ginseng was a challenging business that required patience and management skills.[49]

About fifteen years after Americans had begun to farm ginseng, ginseng plantations started to emerge. At the center of this change was Marathon County, which was mainly settled by German and Polish immigrants. Beginning in 1904 the county began to grow ginseng and the Fromm Brothers Fur and Ginseng Farm there turned into a symbol of twentieth-century American ginseng farming. The Fromm brothers had been fascinated with silver fox fur and were looking for a way to raise enough seed money to create a fur farm when they happened to learn of ginseng's profitability from their neighbors. For the next few years, the brothers went into the mountains every August and collected thousands of ginseng roots, running into competitors who came for the same purpose.[50]

The Fromm brothers eventually figured that creating a ginseng farm would provide a far more stable source of income than collecting wild ginseng. They first succeeded in transplanting one hundred ginseng seedlings and created five feet long and wide, shaded beds. After struggling to protect their field by standing watch and installing a barbed-wire fence to drive thieves away in the fall, the brothers managed to turn it into a ginseng plantation.[51] In 1922, William Boehner & Co. from New York purchased more than 100,000 dollars' worth of American ginseng from the Fromm brothers. By 1929, the Fromm Brothers Farm earned a reputation as the greatest ginseng and fur producer in the West and came to supply its fur to the British royal family. The farm's ginseng was sold to Korea, Japan, Manchuria, Mongolia, and even to the Western Pacific Islands.

Ginseng Growers Association

As more people began to professionally cultivate ginseng, trade associations were formed in the United States to protect their interests, exchange information, and develop connections. Ginseng growers in the state of New York were the first to form an association, in 1902. By 1913, similar associations cropped up everywhere to reach the peak of their membership with the largest being in Wisconsin, Michigan, and Ohio. The time had come to organize a nationwide organization. In August 1916, Americans running large ginseng farms agreed to establish a nationwide ginseng association. The American Ginseng Growers Association started with 103 members who gathered for an intense three-day meeting in Lansing, Michigan, the following year to discuss the association's establishment. The minutes of this meeting are a valuable resource that clearly shows what the interests of American ginseng growers were in the early twentieth century.[52]

The meeting's attendees at first engaged in a heated discussion about whether it was necessary to have a nationwide association. State-level associations were already playing an active role in Michigan, Wisconsin, and Minnesota, where ginseng cultivation was popular. Such states were doubtful as to whether it was necessary to have an overarching nationwide organization. This was a stark example showing how central and regional control coexisted in a federation like the United States.

The need for a national ginseng association was raised for two main reasons. One was to build a network for the active exchange of information about diseases and pests to prevent and overcome them more efficiently. Quite a few farms at the time witnessed crops they had tended for years ruined overnight by infectious disease. Yet, the more important reason was because farmers wished to form a single channel for the export of American ginseng to China.

The second reason actually had to do with the desire to directly engage in trade deals.[53] In New York alone, there were 1,353 brokers involved in trade with China. Known as "Chinamen," such brokers determined the price of ginseng and practically monopolized export channels to China, which enabled them to collect high margins. Ginseng farmers were therefore left in the dark when it came to how much their products were being sold to the Chinese for. The fact that they were unaware of ginseng's exact market value was a source of constant unease. The following excerpt from the meeting's minutes reveals how isolated, frustrated, and helpless ginseng farmers felt.

> Mr. Vining: What is your idea of our ability to get right into the Chinese market?
> Mr. Kirk: I don't believe we will ever be able to get into China at all, and Mr. Koehler will agree with me.[54]

The minutes show that many at the meeting identified with Mr. Kirk's reply. The reality, however, was that Chinamen had to be involved at the beginning and end of each transaction. After a long discussion at the meeting, the attendees arrived at a compromise. They agreed to recruit a reliable Chinese middleman and have him reside in China as the association's delegate. The purpose of doing so was to stop the price of ginseng from collapsing, raise the efficiency of its export, and most of all, prevent Chinamen from acting arbitrarily because when smaller farms tried to individually export their products, brokers or Chinese merchants would often trick them into selling at unfair prices. Through its first meeting, the association elected its president who aspired to have all 4,000 ginseng growers across the country join as a member.

The 1880s to the 1920s was a time when the cultivation and trade of American ginseng flourished. The Great Depression of the 1930s, however, landed a heavy blow on the American ginseng industry. Furthermore, World War II and the subsequent break of relations with China obliterated the export market, driving ginseng farmers into grave difficulties. Most of the farmers in eastern Wisconsin and Ohio quit growing ginseng, leaving only the ginseng plantations around

Marathon County, Wisconsin, in business.[55] Those plantations that weathered the circumstances achieved considerable success when the United States resumed the export of its ginseng to China after the two countries normalized their relations in the 1970s. Marathon County, Wisconsin, where the Fromm Brothers Farm was located established itself as the center of farmed American ginseng. By then, ginseng had started to be grown in the American West and farms in Oregon and Washington began to commercially produce ginseng for export.

Most of the ginseng produced in the United States was exported to Hong Kong and Southeast Asia, the largest ginseng markets in the world. For quite some time, there was no market for ginseng in the United States, chiefly because ginseng had primarily been considered an item destined for export to China. Rather than trying to sample what they were growing, even farmers were too preoccupied with digging up and shipping as much ginseng as possible to China, which guaranteed a swift, sure, and high return. Once China opened its market in 1976, the production and export of American ginseng and related products increased until China started to mass produce American ginseng, prompting the United States to begin nurturing its domestic market or shift its gaze to Europe or South America.

Herbs, especially medicinal herbs, emerged as a new cultural trend in the United States from the 1980s. Ginseng and garlic happened to attract the most attention in the American herb market.[56] The Dietary Supplement Health and Education Act (DSHEA), passed in 1994, created a turning point for ginseng to "officially" enter the market of herbal dietary supplements. Rather than going through the tricky process of gaining approval as a medicine, ginseng was able to enter the category of food to be advertised and sold as a dietary supplement within legally permissible boundaries. Ginseng is described as an "energy enhancer" in the manual on dietary supplements the United States Department of Defense has been maintaining since the early 2000s to sustain and increase the combat power of American troops.[57]

The production per unit area of American ginseng surged in the 1980s and peaked by the 1990s.[58] American ginseng had been considered an export item from the moment it was discovered, but DSHEA set the stage for cultivated American ginseng's debut in the domestic market.

The Fading Nationality of Ginseng

The latest, greatest change involving ginseng is that it has started to be grown all over the world. Cultivation requires the import of seeds, and over the course of importing seeds, cultivating them, and selling grown roots, the nationality of ginseng has been blurred. As mentioned through previous chapters, Korea, Japan, and China began to actively cultivate ginseng as early as the late eighteenth century or as late as the late nineteenth century. The United States started to cultivate ginseng since the late nineteenth century as well. Russia was another country that showed a great interest in ginseng cultivation. After securing the

TABLE 13.2 United States' exports of domestic (cultivated and wild) ginseng, 1900–1983. [Carlson, "Ginseng," 241]

	1900–1909	*1910–1919*	*1920–1929*	*1930–39*	*1940–1949*	*1950–1959*	*1960–1969*	*1970–1979*	*1980–1983*	*Totals*	*(%)*
Lb	1,513,558	2,073,44	1,765,722	2,020,558	902,234	1,075,620	1,443,074	2,710,106	2,638,882	16,143,196	
Metric tons	686	940	801	916	409	488	654	1,229	1,197	7,320	
Value $	9,580,614	16,105,075	22,261,180	10,990,818	8,866,943	18,159,989	35,306,663	145,945,068	164,844,879	432,061,229	
Average value/lb	6.33	7.77	12.61	5.44	9.83	16.88	24.47	53.85	62.47	22.18	
Destinations (lb):											
Africa	–	–	–	–	786	–	44	6,863	20,573	28,266	(.18)
Asia:											
Far east	1,513,012	1,924,576	1,477,625	1,836,200	883,223	791,465	1,398,960	2,453,934	2,434,129	14,713,124	(91.14)
Southeast Asia	–	6,710	3,983	6,605	10,787	272,306	40,172	121,481	73,822	535,876	(3.32)
South Asia	71	13	35	29	199	–	–	–	–	347	(–)
Other	–	–	–	–	–	–	230	1,177	–	1,407	(.01)
Europe											
Northern	120	202	471	286	14	1,1754	384	31,140	19,030	53,401	(.33)
Southern	–	–	12	–	90	–	159	–	–	261	(–)
Latin America:											
Mexico & Cent. Amer	1	12	113	16	112	–	–	–	47,247	47,501	(.29)
South America	–	21	2,151	–	110	100	152	–	116	2,650	(.02)
West Indies	–	74	15	352	714	480	20	–	–	1,655	(.01)
Oceania:											
Australia	–	26	–	–	11	300	–	–	249	586	(–)
French Polynesia	–	2	–	28	419	177	20	–	–	646	(–)
Other Pacific	–	–	–	52	68	–	–	–	–	120	(–)
Canada:	3554	141,806	281,317	176,990	5,701	8,548	741	59,212	10,488	685,157	(4.25)
Other	–	–	–	–	–	490	2,192	36,299	33,218	72,199	(.45)

Source: U.S. Treasury Department, Statistics Bureau, Foreign Commerce and Navigation, Annual reports, 1900–1902; Department of Commerce and Labor, Bureau of Statistics, Foreign Commerce and Navigation, Annual reports, 1903–1912; Department of Commerce, Bureau of Foreign and Domestic Commerce, Annual reports, 1913–1940; and Department of Commerce, Bureau of the Census, United States Exports of Domestic and Foreign Merchandise, Commodity by Country, Annual reports, 1941–1983.[59]

*Pounds by country/area: Afghanistan (200), Argentina (2,132), Australia (586), Belgium (23), Bermuda (160), Brazil (21), British East Africa (22), British East Indies (4,855), British Malaya/Fed. Malaya (208,993), British Oceania (43), Burma (1,261), Canada (685,157), Canal Zone (19), Chile (37), China/Mainland (328,274), Colombia (32), Costa Rica (24,734), Cuba (1,355), Curacao (132), Dominican Republic (3), Dutch East Indies/Indonesia (5,839), Dutch Guiana (3), El Salvador (451), Formosa/Taiwan (219,699), France (78), French Polynesia (646), Gaza Strip (1,177), Germany (834), Guinea (20,573), Honduras (28), Hong Kong (14,005,209), India (276), Indochina (17,829), Italy (37), Jamaica (3), Japan (79,857), Korea Republic (80,085), Malaysia (15,888), Mauritius & Dependencies (717), Mexico (22,268), Mozambique (5), Netherlands (205), New Zealand (77), Nicaragua (1), Nigeria (6,863), Paraguay (114), Peru (80), Philippine Islands (14,531), Saudi Arabia (30), Siam/Thailand (66,168), Singapore (200,583), Spain (159), Sweden (12), Switzerland (65), Trinidad/Tobago (2), Union of South Africa (86), United Kingdom (12,209), Venezuela (230), West Germany (40,018), Other countries (72,199).

area north of the Amur River through the 1858 Treaty of Aigun and the area east of the Ussuri River through the 1860 Convention of Peking, Russia sought to create ginseng plantations in those areas with the intent of exporting the crop to China.[60]

The plan to mass produce ginseng, however, ultimately failed and Russia had to be satisfied with collecting wild ginseng in those areas. Yet, Russia was not ready to abandon its ambition to cultivate the plant. Apart from the purpose of exporting to China, ginseng was in constant demand in Russia because it was held in high esteem by Russian folk medicine. Upon the end of World War II, the Soviet Union jumped into the cultivation of ginseng. Even during the Korean War, it smuggled Korean ginseng seeds in for mass production and invested efforts into researching the active components of ginseng.[61] Like the aforementioned experiments by Israel Brekhman, clinical tests were done on animals as well as humans.

While the cultivation of American ginseng was on the rise in the early twentieth century, American farmers started to experiment with ginseng seeds from East Asia. In 1901, they included ginseng grown from imported Japanese seedlings in a batch of American ginseng exported to Qing China. However, when the ginseng's poor quality hurt their reputation, they decided to stop exporting it.[62] These circumstances led to the harsh criticism toward Japanese ginseng in John Henry Koehler's *Ginseng and Goldenseal Growers Handbook* (1912).

American ginseng farmers nevertheless refused to give up and continued to seek seeds from China. They didn't hesitate to place advertisements in newspapers. For instance, in 1937, an advertisement about a person in Los Angeles hoping to obtain ginseng seeds appeared in the *China Weekly Review*, an English-language newspaper published in China.[63] Hsu's Ginseng Enterprises Inc. in Wausau, Wisconsin, one of the largest ginseng farms in the United States today, is now growing ginseng with seeds brought from Korea. It is the only American company capable of handling the entire process of growing and curing American ginseng, in addition to manufacturing and selling finished products through wholesale and retail channels. The company even has its own booth in duty-free sections at airports including the Los Angeles International Airport. And now this company specializing in American ginseng has expanded its business to growing Korean ginseng.

In the summer of 2015, I visited the company's farm and factory and interviewed its vice president of operations, William Hsu. Hsu readily offered a tour of the fields where American ginseng was being grown but declined entry into the fields of Korean ginseng. When asked how the farm procured Korean ginseng seeds, Hsu replied that the information was confidential. When asked again, he said, "the seeds are now legally brought in from China, which means they are from Korean ginseng grown in China."[64] On how such seeds used to be procured in the past, Hsu said that was a question he'd have to ask his father.

Hsu in turn criticized that Korea has been too closed off to exporting its ginseng. He pointed out that despite being pretty much the only country in the world capable of satisfying the United States Food and Drug Administration's standards, Korea's government regulations and extreme pride have prevented it from exporting its ginseng, except in the form of finished products. Hsu believes Korea could achieve far more if it can allow its ginseng to be exported in all forms. According to Hsu, many American companies would be willing to buy Korean ginseng, even at high prices, but there were no channels that made it available in forms other than finished products, and the paperwork required for its import was far too complex.[65] Yet, from Korea's point of view, it seems debatable as to whether Korea would indeed benefit over the long term from completely opening its market.

For now, Canada is the greatest competitor and threat to American ginseng growers. Canada was relatively late in jumping into ginseng cultivation and it wasn't until the 1970s that plantations began to appear, mainly around British Columbia. Investment and support from the Chinese or Taiwanese made a significant difference early on. Ginseng farms gradually ventured out of the province so that ginseng is now being grown in the southwestern parts of Ontario adjoining Wisconsin. Unlike the United States, the Canadian government proactively supports and encourages the cultivation of ginseng. This approach was actually devised to aid tobacco farms on the verge of bankruptcy, as the consumption of tobacco decreased in both the United States and Canada. Ginseng requires soil conditions similar to that of tobacco and offers similar profits, which made it the best commercial substitute for tobacco.[66]

Meanwhile, it is also worth taking note of China's cultivation of American ginseng. The generally accepted explanation as to why China, after having favored Korean ginseng for so long, began to grow American ginseng has to do with a major change in the Chinese understanding of ginseng's medicinal properties. Since the 1970s, a belief began to spread that Korean ginseng raises the body temperature while Western ginseng lowers it. As briefly discussed in Part 1, the argument that ginseng should be administered in smaller doses to patients who are young or have high body temperatures had surfaced in Europe since the seventeenth century. However, it wasn't until the 1970s that Korean ginseng suddenly became firmly characterized worldwide as an ingredient responsible for raising the body temperature. Today, such a characterization is understood to have been formulated as a marketing strategy to compete with Korean ginseng.

This characterization has had a tremendous effect. Because of the belief that Korean ginseng raises the body temperature, people in the warm southern parts of China such as Hong Kong came to prefer Western ginseng instead. This not only weakened the reputation of Korean ginseng but gave rise to a major debate as to whether it really did cause the body temperature to rise. As the domestic demand for Western ginseng continued to increase under such circumstances, China began to bring American ginseng in for cultivation. In 1994, it first succeeded in mass producing American ginseng and since the 2000s American ginseng grown in China even started to be exported to the United States.[67]

Lately, companies that succeeded in artificially growing American and Korean ginseng have been appearing in Germany, Switzerland, Italy, Israel, France, Spain, Denmark, and Belgium. Ginseng has been successfully grown even in the southern hemisphere.[68] While small batches of it are being grown experimentally in Australia and Chile, New Zealand has been fiercely increasing its cultivation of ginseng. Both American and Korean ginseng are being grown in the dense pine tree forests of New Zealand.[69] Some ginseng growers choose to sow seeds on government-leased forests and harvest ginseng after about six years. In Turangi on the North Island, the labor necessary for growing ginseng has even been procured through a nearby prison's rehabilitation program.

Through the transplanting of ginseng all over the world, the nationality of ginseng has lost meaning. Korean ginseng grown in New Zealand is now labeled as New Zealand ginseng and American ginseng grown in Jilin, China, is labeled as Jilin ginseng. Tons of premium ginseng seeds are being smuggled out of Korea every year. Although approval from the Korean Ministry of Agriculture, Food, and Rural Affairs is required for the export of ginseng seeds, not once has an approval been officially granted.[70] Korean media reports on the illegal export of ginseng seeds or discussions on countermeasures merely point to the northeastern parts of China as the final destination of those seeds, when Korean ginseng has in fact been grown in the United States and the eastern end of Siberia for the past one hundred years and is now being grown even in the dense forests of New Zealand in the southern hemisphere.

Notes

1 Entry for January 1734, *Sŭngjŏngwŏn ilgi* [Daily Records of the Royal Secretariat], Book 43. Chang, *Han'guk insam sanŏpsa*, 2018, 1:245.

2 Imamura Tomo 今村鞆, "Yama ninjin saishuri no fushu" 山人蔘採取りの 風習 [Customs Involving the Collection of Wild Ginseng], *Ch'ŏnggu hakch'ong* 青丘學叢, no. 6 (1931): 111–113.

3 Steven Foster, "Towards an Understanding of Ginseng Adulteration: The Tangled Web of Names, History, Trade, and Perception," *HerbalGram*, no. 111 (2016): 46.

4 Ok Sun-chong 옥순종, *Kyoyang ŭro ingnŭn insam iyagi* 교양으로 읽는 인삼 이야기 [An Informed Account of Ginseng] (Seoul: Igasŏ 이가서, 2005), 32.

5 Jung Eun-joo 정은주, "Chosŏn hugi kasam chaebae wa samsŏ" 조선 후기 家蔘재배와 蔘書 [The Cultivated Ginseng in the Latter Part of the Joseon Dynasty and Samseo], *Han'guk shirhak yŏn'gu* 한국실학연구 24 (2012): 445–446.

6 Yang Chŏng-p'il 양정필, "Hanmal ilche ha Kŭmsan insam yŏn'gu 한말-일제하 錦山 人蔘 연구 [A Study on Geumsan Ginseng during Early Modern and Colonial Period of Korea]," *Han'guksa hakpo* 韓國史學報, no. 51 (2013): 200.

7 Yang, "Taehanjegukki Kaesŏng chiyŏk samŏp pyŏndong kwa samp'omin ŭi taeŭng," 138–155.

8 Yang Chŏng-p'il 양정필, "Taehanjegukki hwangshil ŭi hongsam chŏnmaeje shihaeng kwa t'onggambu ŭi samŏp chaep'yŏn" 대한제국기 황실의 홍삼전매제 시행과 통감부의 蔘業 재편 [The Korean Empire's Monopoly of Red Ginseng and the Japanese Residency-General's Reorganization of the Korean Ginseng Industry], in *Han'guk chŏnt'ongsahoe ŭi chaeinshik* 한국 전통사회의 재인식 [A New

Understanding of Traditional Korean Society] (Seoul: Kyŏngsewŏn 경세원, 2006), 583–610.

9 Miyake Hidetoshi 三宅英利, *Chosŏn t'ongshinsa wa Ilbon* 조선 통신사와 일본 [Chosŏn t'ongshinsa and Japan], trans. Kim Se-min 김세민 et al. (Seoul: Chisŏngŭi saem 지성의 샘, 1996), 168.

10 No Sung-hwan 노성환, "Imnanp'oro ka toeŏ Ilbon ŭro kŏnnŏgan Chosŏn ŭi tongshingmul" 임란포로가 되어 일본으로 건너간 조선의 동식물 [Chosŏn Wildlife Taken to Japan During the Japanese Invasions of Chosŏn], *Ilbonŏ kyoyuk yŏn'gu* 일본어교육연구 48 (2009): 245.

11 Imamura, *Insamsa*, 2015, 1:72.

12 No, "Imnanp'oro ka toeŏ Ilbon ŭro kŏnnŏgan Chosŏn ŭi tongshingmul," 245.

13 Imamura, *Insamsa*, 2015, 1:98-99; Chŏng Sŏngil 정성일, "Chosŏnsan insam chongja wa Ilbon ŭi insam suip taech'e" 조선산 인삼종자와 일본의 인삼수입 대체 [Chosŏn Ginseng Seedlings and the Replacement of Imported Ginseng in Japan], in *Ch'un'gye Pak Kwangsun kyosu hwagap kinyŏm kyŏngjehak nonch'ong* 춘계 박광순 교수 화갑기념 경제학 논총 [Collection of Economic Studies in Celebration of Professor Ch'un'gye Pak Kwangsun's Sixtieth Birthday] (Kwangju: Chonnam National University 전남대학교, 1993), 182; Chang, *Han'guk insam sanŏpsa*, 1:265–267.

14 Ok, *Kyoyang ŭro ingnŭn insam iyagi*, 54–55.

15 Imamura, *Insamsa*, 2012, 3:395–398, 404.

16 Imamura, *Insamsa*, 2015, 1:124.

17 Imamura, *Insamsa*, 2012, 3:424.

18 Chang, *Han'guk insam sanŏpsa*, 1:267, 271.

19 Ko Sung-kwon 고성권, "Sŏjihakchŏk kojŭng ŭl t'onghan Koryŏ insam ŭi chŏngch'esŏng" 서지학적 고증을 통한 고려인삼의 정체성: 기미(氣味), 효능을 중심으로 [Identity of Korean Ginseng through Bibliography: Focusing on Kimi (Property) and Efficacy], *Insam munhwa* 인삼문화 1 (2019): 3.

20 Li, *Shinjuhae ponch'o kangmok*, 4:47.

21 Imamura Tomo 今村鞆, *Insamsa* 人蔘史 [History of Ginseng], trans. Koh Seung-tae 고승태, vol. 4: Insam chaebaep'yŏn 인삼재배편 [Ginseng Cultivation] (Yŏngju: Dongyang University 동양대학교, 2010), 93.

22 Imamura, *Insamsa*, 2015, 1:130-131.

23 Imamura, *Insamsa*, 2010, 4:95, 97–98.

24 Wang, *Zhongguo renshen*, 6.

25 Wang, *Zhongguo renshen*, 34.

26 Wang, *Zhongguo renshen*, 24–25.

27 Fang Kun 方堃, ed., *Renshen jiqi shangpinxue* 人蔘及其商品學 [Ginseng and Merchandising] (Beijing: Renmin weisheng chubanshe 人民衛生出版社, 1958), 4.

28 Wang, *Zhongguo renshen*, 24–25.

29 Fang, *Renshen jiqi shangpinxue*, 4.

30 Wang, *Zhongguo renshen*, 25.

31 Fang, *Renshen jiqi shangpinxue*, 4.

32 Chen Jinghe 陳景河, "Renshen wenhua de kangdingzhizuo: Sun wencai jiaoshou zhongguo renshen wenhua xu 人蔘文化的扛鼎之作: 孙文采教授 中國人蔘文化序 [A Masterpiece on Ginseng Culture: The Preface of Professor Sun Wencai's Zhongguo Renshen Wenhua]," *Renshen Yanjiu* 人蔘研究, no. 3 (2013).

33 Park Ki-hwan 박기환, Hŏ Sŏng-yun 허성윤, and Li Jinghu 리징후, "Chungguk ŭi insam sanŏp hyŏnhwang kwa yuksŏng chŏngch'aek: Chungguk tongbuksamsŏng" 중국의 인삼산업 현황과 육성 정책: 중국 동북3성 지역 중심 [Current Status of the Ginseng Industry in China and Its Fostering Policy: Focusing on Three Northeastern Provinces of China] (Naju: Korea Rural Economic Institute 한국농촌경제연구원, 2014); Chung Chung-gil 정정길 and Li Jin, "Chungguk insam sanŏp palchŏn ŭi saeroun tonghyang" 중국 인삼산업 발전의 새로운 동향 [New Trends in the Development of China's Ginseng Industry], *Chungguk nongŏp tonghyang* 중국농업동향 5, no. 3 (2012): 29–39; Xu Shiwen 許十文 and Chen Xiaoping

陳曉平, "Renshen de Zhanzheng" 人蔘的戰爭 [A War of Ginseng], *21 shiji shangye pinglun* 21世紀商業評論, no. 21 (2013); Zhang He 張合, "Zhonghan renshen zhanzheng" 中韓人蔘戰爭 [A Sino-Korean Ginseng War], *Jiankang guanli* 健康管理, no. 2 (2012).

34 Luke Manget, "Nature's Emporium: The Botanical Drug Trade and the Commons Tradition in Southern Appalachia, 1847–1917," *Environmental History* 21, no. 4 (2016): 676.
35 "In Highland County," *The Richmond Dispatch*, October 16, 1901.
36 Manget, "Nature's Emporium," 676.
37 "Gleanings," *Birmingham Daily Post*, November 21, 1887.
38 "This Morning's News," *Daily News*, July 11, 1891.
39 Nash, *American Ginseng*.
40 Chang, *Han'guk insam sanŏpsa*, 1:277.
41 Herbert Hice Whetzel and Joseph Rosenbaum, *The Diseases of Ginseng and Their Control*, U.S. Department of Agriculture Bureau of Plant Industry Bulletin 250 (Washington D. C.: Government Printing Office, 1912).
42 James M. Van Hook, *Diseases of Ginseng*, Cornell University Agricultural Experiment Station Bulletin 219 (Ithaca, NY: Cornell University, 1904); Whetzel and Rosenbaum, *The Diseases of Ginseng and Their Control*, 7.
43 Koehler, *Ginseng and Goldenseal Growers' Handbook*, 21.
44 Root, *What Is Ginseng*, 36.
45 Nicolas Pike, "The Ginseng," *Scientific American* 64, no. 2 (1891): 19.
46 Root, *What Is Ginseng*, 25–26.
47 Root, *What Is Ginseng*, 26.
48 Root, *What Is Ginseng*, 24.
49 Root, *What Is Ginseng*, 24.
50 Katherene Pinkerton, *Bright with Silver* (New York: William Sloane Associates, Inc., 1947), 53.
51 Carlson, "Ginseng," 236.
52 John Henry Koehler, *Report of J. H. Koehler, Acting President of American Ginseng Growers' Association to the Ginseng Growers of America* (Wausau, WI, 1917).
53 Koehler, *Report of J. H. Koehler, Acting President of American Ginseng Growers' Association to the Ginseng Growers of America*, 9.
54 Koehler, *Report of J. H. Koehler, Acting President of American Ginseng Growers' Association to the Ginseng Growers of America*, 7.
55 Lee Dong-phil, "Hwagisam ŭi hyonŭng chujang kwa miguksam ŭi palchŏn kwajŏng e taehan koch'al" [A Study on the Cooling Effect Claim & Development Procedure of the American Ginseng], *Koryŏ insam hak'oeji* 30, no. 3 (2006): 162.
56 Mark Blumenthal, "Milestones in Pharmaceutical Botany Since 1960," *Pharmacy in History* 38, no. 1 (1996): 25.
57 Seok Yeong-dal, "Migun ŭi insam pokyong?: 20 segi mal insam ŭi Miguk shigiboch'ungje shijang p'yŏnip kwa migun maenyuŏl" ["The U.S. Military Uses Ginseng?": The Official Entrance of Ginseng to the U.S. Dietary Supplement Market and the U.S. Military's Dietary Supplement Manual in the Late 20th Century], *Insam munhwa* 1 (2019): 103–107.
58 W.A. Geyer et al., "Ginseng (Panax Quinquefolius L.) and Goldenseal (Hydrastis Canadensis L.) Trials in Eastern Kansas," *Transactions of the Kansas Academy of Science* 111, no. 1/2 (2008): 147.
59 Published data for 1978 and 1979 are incorrect. Correct figures were obtained from the Department of Commerce and Foreign Trade Division are included here.
60 "Russian Exploring Expedition," *The Morning Chronicle*, January 6, 1860; "Foreign intelligence," *The Times*, January 3, 1860.
61 Schwemmer, *Wunderdroge Ginseng*, 81.
62 Imamura, *Insamsa*, 2015, 1:156.
63 "Advertisement," *The China Weekly Review*, July 10, 1937.

64 William Hsu (vice president of operations, Hsu's Ginseng Enterprises Inc.), interview by Heasim Sul, June 30, 2015.
65 Hsu, interview.
66 Hsu, interview.
67 Chang, *Han'guk insam sanŏpsa*, 1:5.
68 W. Scott Persons, "Growing American Ginseng in Its Native Woodland Habitat" (North American Conference on Enterprise Development through Agroforestry, Minneapolis, MN, 1998).
69 Wei Chen, Prabhu Balan, and David G. Popovich, "Ginsenosides Analysis of New Zealand–Grown Forest Panax Ginseng by LC-QTOF-MS/MS," *Journal of Ginseng Research* 44, no. 4 (2020): 552–562.
70 *SBS News*, August 29, 2014.

PART 4
The Orientalism Surrounding Ginseng

Today, ginseng is not easy to come across in the Western history of medicine because it has been medically and culturally shunned in modern Europe and America. According to Roberta Bivins, "the persistence and success of a medical system is invariably contingent not only on its therapeutic efficacy, but on the historical and cultural climate within which it operates and to which it responds."[1] This seems to explain the way Western cultures repeatedly distanced themselves from ginseng by defining it as a thing of the East.

Ginseng was, however, brought up far more often in the everyday lives of Westerners in the nineteenth century than today. In 1859, the *Glasgow Herald* reported about a lecture on the main commodities traded between Shanghai and Japan, one of which was ginseng.[2] *The Morning Chronicle* in London published an article on a record discovered among the wreckage of an American ship, which indicated that a cargo of ginseng had been on board.[3] Newspaper reports on the Siamese embassy to Paris—an entertaining topic that surfaced in multiple papers for quite some time—mentioned that the embassy members enjoyed drinking ginseng julep.[4] Meanwhile, one commentary aimed at exposing errors in geography textbooks listed typical cases of erroneous spelling, one of which was to spell ginseng as "giuseg."[5]

Of course, many articles also included factual errors or misleading descriptions. In 1899, *The Times* of London published an article recommending crops for rotation to improve soil quality. Instead of the previously favored chicory, ginseng was recommended for its superior profitability. A successful American case had proved it possible to plant improved seeds from premium wild ginseng.[6] Such a recommendation is likely to have been made for readers all over Britain, but it was far from practical since farming ginseng was impossible in the British climate. Growing ginseng in a botanical garden was, however, a different story. One of the many articles satisfying the avid British interest in gardening

DOI: 10.4324/9781003286691-17

happened to feature gardening methods for subtropical plants including ginseng, which seems to have been misleading, not for identifying ginseng as a plant highly challenging to grow,[7] but for classifying it as a subtropical plant.

Upon the outbreak of the Cuban War of Independence (1895–1898), the world market for cigarettes was stirred by the possibility of a price surge. An editorial in *The Leeds Mercury* suggested developing a less harmful substitute for cigarettes, perhaps made of fragrant, nourishing ginseng.[8] For such random reasons, ginseng continued to be brought up in the news once in a while. In the meantime, mentions of ginseng in everyday life revealed a certain trend in the West. That trend involved both analogizing and ostracization, but the tendency to ostracize ginseng was far stronger than that to analogize and embrace it as part of their own culture.

Notes

1 Bivins, *Alternative Medicine?*, x.
2 "Lecture on Japan," *Glasgow Herald*, November 22, 1859.
3 "Imperial Parliament," *Freeman's Journal and Daily Commercial Advertiser*, August 5, 1840; "Untitled Article," *The Morning Chronicle*, August 12, 1840.
4 "France," *The Morning Chronicle*, June 27, 1861.
5 "Dr. Wm. Smith's School Manual of Modern Geography," *The Pall Mall Gazette*, April 27, 1876.
6 "Report of the American Minister of Agriculture," *The Times*, January 2, 1899.
7 "Subtropical Cultivation," *The Pall Mall Gazette*, October 18, 1886.
8 "Substitute for the Fragrant Weed," *The Leeds Mercury*, August 15, 1896.

14

ANALOGIZING AND OSTRACIZATION

Ginseng and Mandrake

When ginseng first arrived in Europe, people were rather confused about how to understand the exotic plant. In anthropology and history, reactions a group shows upon encountering a different culture have usually been classified as an analogy or opposition. An analogy involves denying or ignoring the cultural distance with someone or something else to assimilate the person or thing with oneself or one's neighbor. For instance, the crusaders regarded the Muslim warrior Saladin as the equivalent of a European knight, demonstrating that if an object is regarded as a subject's reflection, that object becomes reborn in the subject's imagination as something far from its original nature.

Analogy was the reaction Europeans initially showed toward ginseng. In seventeenth-century Europe, people sought to accept ginseng as a plant analogous to mandrake, a perennial sympetalous member of the Solanaceae family. According to Martino Martini, author of *Bellum Tartaricum*, ginseng and mandrake looked so alike that there was no reason to doubt whether their properties and efficacy were identical or not.[1] At an English Royal Society meeting in 1681, ginseng from Korea was observed to be "divided into two legs, as often the Mandrake [is]."[2]

Like ginseng, mandrake was characterized as resembling the human form in certain ways. The ancients believed mandrakes held mandragora, a demon that appears in the form of a beardless little man. Mandrake was also fabled to grow under the gallows and was therefore believed to be haunted by the spirits of the executed. In medieval Europe, mandrake was used as an aphrodisiac, love charm, or sometimes placed round the house to drive away bad luck. It was nevertheless stigmatized as being used in dark magic, such that in 1630, three women were executed in Hungary and Germany for keeping mandrakes in their house.[3]

DOI: 10.4324/9781003286691-18

FIGURE 14.1 Mandrake and ginseng.

Mandrake also made an appearance in Shakespeare's play *Romeo and Juliet*. Imagining waking up in her own tomb, Juliet says: "So early waking, what with loathsome smells, and shrieks like mandrakes torn out of the earth, that living mortals, hearing them, run mad."[4] At the time, mandrake was rumored to emit a shrill, humanlike cry when pulled from the ground. The mysterious root was effective in treating depression, anxiety, insomnia, and was also used as a surgical anesthetic. Its leaves were used to relieve pain when treating injuries, and while tea made from its leaves and root had a stimulating effect, administering it incorrectly could cause paralysis. Mandrake was also known to be effective in treating asthma and coughing.

Joseph François Lafitau, the French Jesuit missionary who discovered American ginseng in Canada, recalled that, "when I discovered ginseng, it occurred to me that it could be a species of mandrake. … it is almost similar to our mandrake, except that it is a little smaller."[5] Lafitau suspected that ginseng was a derivative of mandrake, which had been driven to extinction from being indiscriminately collected for its special effects. Proof to support his suspicion lay in the fact that ginseng physically resembled mandrake from root to fruit.[6]

Analogies between ginseng and mandrake continued to emerge until the late twentieth century. In his book *Life in Corea*, the British diplomat William Richard Carles remarks that, "All that most people know of the drug is that it is the root of the panax ginseng, and that, like the mandrake, in shape it frequently resembles the figure of a man."[7] A 1978 edition of *The American Biology Teacher* featured a comparison between ginseng and mandrake, noting that the two roots were both shaped like a man and "shrouded in mystery."[8]

What is interesting is that even in China, ginseng was thought to be similar to mandrake. The Chinese had been aware of mandrake since at least the Song dynasty (960–1279), which was far earlier than when the West became aware of ginseng. Through his works *Guixin zashi* (癸辛雜識) and *Zhiyatang zachao* (志雅堂雜鈔), the poet and painter Zhou Mi (周密, 1232–1298) introduced myths surrounding mandrake and how to use a dog to uproot the plant. Zhou described mandrake as "an extremely poisonous plant that grows hundreds of miles west of Huihuiguo [回回國, Arabia]," and added that, "it is similar to ginseng in terms of its great resemblance to the human form."[9] Hence, the belief that ginseng and mandrake are similar was formed over a long time in both the East and West. Comparing the two to determine their similarities was a cultural approach the East and West each took to draw ginseng or mandrake into a framework of understanding familiar to themselves.

Opposition and Ginseng Metaphors

While Lafitau attempted to understand ginseng as a reincarnation or variation of mandrake, ginseng increasingly became opposed rather than analogized in Europe. The fact that Europe was not ginseng's natural habitat was used to keep the plant at a distance. Such distancing began by projecting onto ginseng traits defined as unethical in European cultures. Even John Hill, a former quack who nevertheless enjoyed popularity, advised in the *History of the Materia Medica* that it would be necessary to "cut every root through" before buying ginseng because the Chinese who sold them were "such expert cheats, that they frequently find a way to introduce pieces of lead into it to increase the weight."[10]

Many European pharmacology books probed into the details of the tricks the Chinese used to cheat customers looking for ginseng. Ginseng roots lose marketability over time as their heads dry up, which is why Chinese ginseng diggers cut off the knob to prevent the root from appearing stale. Chinese merchants would also fill the holes worms made with yellow powder to make the root appear fit for sale. These tricks were described as "wonders ascribed by Chinese," showing that Europeans thought the Chinese had reached a level of mastery in cheating and were even a little jealous of their deft hands.[11] Such discussions indicate that while Europeans recognized ginseng as a product for sale, they regarded Chinese exporters as unreliable business partners in the ginseng trade. Ginseng thus came to be haunted by the image of cheats far away in China who had no respect for business ethics.

Western discussions about ginseng somehow seemed to assign *too much* meaning to it. On the meaning goods carry, Kenneth Pomeranz and Steven Topik have explained that "goods themselves have 'social lives' in which their meanings, their usefulness, and value are in flux." For instance, chocolate, which once helped warriors build up courage ahead of battles or experience religious ecstasy, turned into a sweet treat for children over time. The demand and supply of goods are therefore "culturally determined by people with loves, hatreds, and addictions, not by reified market forces," according to Pomeranz and Topik.[12] Ginseng was living a social life of its own in Western society, carrying cultural meaning and value far greater than the demand for ginseng or the frequency of its use. Almost without fail, writings mentioning ginseng would include the phrase "highly esteemed in China." This phrase appeared in narratives on ginseng's discovery soon after it was found on the American continent and Americans used it like a catchphrase to promote and export domestic ginseng. At a glance, the phrase seems to carry respect for ginseng's country of origin and rely on the authority China held from its lengthy tradition of studying and utilizing ginseng. However, the phrase could have also served as a means to tie ginseng to China, a world foreign to Westerners.

What is worth noting is that such an appraisal went beyond the realms of botany and medicine to be used as a metaphor in everyday life. The term "Chinese ginseng" sometimes stood for a good that was highly esteemed and valued in certain cultures,[13] or in other contexts it signified a means to quickly amass tremendous wealth.[14] On the other hand, the term was also used to explain the imaginary efficacy of a good from a different culture.[15] An example of this can be found in *A Letter to His Excellency, Marcus Morton, on Banking and the Currency* by the American historian and journalist Richard Hildreth (1807–1865).

> With respect to prices, there is an influence exercised over them, upon which political economists have not yet dwelt; but an influence which exerts a controling power—and that is, fancy, opinion. Ginseng is esteemed a worthless weed with us. In China it commands a high price. The Chinese believe it to possess medicinal qualities. The same diversity

> of value according to diversities of opinion, take place with respect to most other drugs, and in fact with respect to most, or rather all other things of every kind.[16]

Ginseng was also a symbol of Chinese pride and prejudice or used to describe people who gave themselves airs despite being nothing special.[17] This materialized into idiomatic expressions such as "like Chinese ginseng" or "like the faith the Chinese have in ginseng." Such expressions were tinged with disdain toward the Chinese as bluffers or people lacking objectivity from being self-absorbed in their own superiority.

Despite the fear that the Chinese would not approve of American ginseng, American botanists did not hesitate to belittle their potential trade partner by saying "they are so fanciful, it may not be as good as their own."[18] An editorial in *Philosophical Transactions* expressed sarcasm toward both China and ginseng by remarking that, "As for their Chemists, (of which they have also good store) they go beyond ours, promising not only to make Gold, but to give Immortality."[19] This editorial was published at a time when members of the Royal Society were enthusiastically studying ginseng and searching for ways to grow the plant in Britain. In *The History of John Juniper, Esq. Alias Juniper Jack*, the Irish novelist Charles Johnstone (c. 1719–1800) sarcastically remarked as follows: "On Ginseng, it is sufficient to say that it preserves life almost to immortality, as incontestibly appears by the empire of China's having flourished merely by the virtues of this plant above fifty thousand years more than the age of the world."[20]

The lagging level of medical sophistication in East Asia was the "rational" explanation that Europeans came up with as to why ginseng was admired as the best medicine there. In other words, Asians had to rely on herbs like ginseng because their medicine and medical supplies were not sophisticated enough.[21] This explanation, however, was suggested at a time when European medical professionals were mostly relying on medicinal herbs and the East was ahead of the West in the medical application of mineral waters. Despite having roamed all over Europe himself in search of medicinal (mineral) waters, the novelist and physician Tobias Smollett remarked that, "the Japanese have but very little skill in physic and surgery. In the cure of diseases they depend much on their medicinal waters, and on certain roots and plants, particularly the root ginseng, brought from China."[22]

Autocracy

From materia medica to newspaper articles, the scene most frequently cited in European descriptions of ginseng was one from a report the Jesuit missionary Pierre Jartoux sent to Europe.[23] As mentioned in Part 1, Jartoux personally came across ginseng along the Chinese border with Korea during a cartographic survey of Manchuria as per the Kangxi Emperor's orders.

> It is computed, that by this means the Emperor would get this year about twenty thousand Chinese pounds of it, which would not cost him above one fourth part of its value. We met by chance with some of these Tartars in the midst of those frightful Deserts. … This army of herbarists observed the following order. After they had divided a certain tract of land among their several companies, each company, to the number of an hundred, spreads itself out in a straight line to a certain fixt place, every ten of them keeping at a distance from the rest. … These poor people suffer a great deal in this expedition. They carry with them neither Tents nor beds, every one being sufficiently loaded with his provision, which is only millet parched in an oven, upon which he must subsist all the time of his journey. So that they are constrained to sleep under trees, having only their branches and barks, if they can find them, for their covering. Their Mandarins send them from time to time some pieces of beef, of such game as they happen to take, which they eat very greedily and almost raw. In this manner these ten thousand men passed six months of the year.[24]

The above scene was oft-relayed through all sorts of intermediaries in Europe until the late nineteenth century. The reason was perhaps because that particular image of collecting ginseng was the quintessence of the exoticism Europeans pictured in their minds when it came to the "other world" of the Far East. The vivid descriptions of the emperor's capacity to mobilize 10,000 people just for the purpose of collecting ginseng, the absolute obedience of the people, and the miserable conditions they had to endure out in the wild exhibited the commonly held concept of "Oriental autocracy." And since ginseng was obtained through the sacrifice of so many, it invoked a sense of class as something only the powerful could enjoy.

A Sense of Class

The reason ginseng was invaluable was not just because it was rare but because its high price made it available only to the few who could afford it. In China, ginseng was a gift exchanged among the upper class, presented to elders, or bestowed by the emperor. The emperor would often bestow ginseng to ailing bureaucrats or civilians and send it as a gift to vassal states. The Chinese culture of gifting ginseng reached the height of its popularity under the reigns of the Qianlong Emperor and the Jiaqing Emperor (嘉慶帝, r. 1796–1820). What was unique about this culture was that ginseng was a gift strictly passed down along a hierarchy. As a symbol of health, luck, and longevity, ginseng was the best possible gift a superior could give to a subordinate.[25]

The emperor's bestowal of ginseng to his subjects was therefore a highly political gesture, which is why the *Peking Gazette* gave it major coverage. Coverage involving ginseng in the *Peking Gazette* could be classified into three categories. The first category consisted of coverage of imperial orders for ginseng to be collected from northeastern regions like Jilin and sent to Beijing. Such coverage usually mentioned that the imperial family had urgently sent for wild ginseng whenever its stock ran low, reporting that three large-sized and ten smaller-sized sprigs have been discovered or that the cost of procuring the plants, amounting to 308 taels, was defrayed from the duties levied on cultivated ginseng. Articles would sometimes convey an apology for the insufficient amount of ginseng delivered to the imperial family. Such articles would also include excuses about how difficult it was to collect ginseng due to the lack of time or from being unable to access sealed-off areas as well as pledges to be more prompt in collecting and delivering ginseng to the imperial family.[26]

Coverage of the details of procurement also fell in the same category. One such article commended the loyalty of a Jilin official for faithfully carrying out the decree for wild ginseng to be sent as soon as it is discovered. The official is said to have sent six large, six small, and ten middle-sized wild ginseng roots to the imperial family.[27] Another article from February 1893 relayed the journey of ginseng collected as tax in kind as it was transported to the imperial family. Two officials took 10,000 *liang* [old Chinese unit of weight: 37.5 gram] of ginseng collected in Zhejiang and headed to Shanghai where they boarded a steamer to Tianjin and then traveled by land to Beijing.[28] Around the same time, a report from Jilin noted that the season's last shipment of wild ginseng was on its way to Beijing. Two officials had departed with two boxes that held more than eight pounds of premium-grade wild ginseng in total.[29]

The second category of ginseng-related coverage in the *Peking Gazette* involved illegal collection and smuggling. According to an imperial order issued in 1866, the offense of smuggling less than one hundred *liang* of ginseng was to be tried summarily on site and the exposer, often a customs officer, would be rewarded 20 percent of the smuggled ginseng.[30] Ginseng smuggling was frequently uncovered in the region of Shanhaiguan (山海關), one of the major passes on the Great Wall of China. Those arrested gave all kinds of excuses. Some implored that the ginseng for their old, ailing mother while others protested that they had been paid in kind with ginseng. When a laborer from Shandong was caught smuggling nineteen *liang* of ginseng out of Jilin in 1874, he claimed that he had bought it from a stranger for his sick, old mother. The ginseng was seized by the imperial family and the laborer was sent into exile for two years after receiving a penalty of eighty blows.[31]

The third category of ginseng-related coverage in the *Peking Gazette* aimed at announcing the emperor's bestowal of ginseng to high-ranking officials as part of his management of state affairs. The emperor would often bestow ginseng to retiring officials for them to restore their health. Once, when a loyal official suddenly passed, the emperor bestowed the official's seventy-year-old mother with some money and ginseng to console her.[32] In 1915, the *Gazette* reported that the warlord Yuan Shikai (袁世凱, 1859–1916) had gifted two ounces of Korean ginseng and 5,000 dollars to Duan Qirui (段祺瑞, 1865–1936) when Duan took sick leave for two months;[33] such a gesture was symbolic, suggesting that Yuan was exercising his prerogative as emperor, something many at the time accused him of having pretentions toward (in fact, later in the same year Yuan would declare himself the Hongxian Emperor of the short-lived "Empire of China").

In Korea, it was also customary for a king to bestow ginseng to an ailing subject. The king's orders to send ginseng can be found in historical documents such as *Sŭngjŏngwŏn ilgi* (承政院日記), or the Records of the Royal Secretariat, and *Chosŏnwangjo sillok* (朝鮮王朝實錄), or the Annals of the Chosŏn Dynasty. Such orders were sometimes given with detailed instructions. King Chŏngjo added the following advice when he bestowed ginseng to Ch'ae Che-kong (蔡濟恭, 1720–1799).

> Since ginseng should not be used lightly, it should be used only after recovering from exposure to outside air, fever, or cold sweat. Please carefully discuss its use with a physician and it would be best to inquire about and take into consideration the symptoms someone else suffered recently before taking ginseng. Depending on the patient's condition, ginseng can be prescribed to a person from the southeastern region but that in itself should not be done lightly. Although it is impossible to make any assessments from afar, food is the best cure, and while you may employ all means to make the patient sweat and lower the fever, be extremely careful with the use of any medication. How about sending over an account of how the patient has been treated so far?[34]

The press in the West, however, took note of how, in China, ginseng was a medicine the ultimate ruler used in emergencies. The plant was therefore described as a "wonder drug" the powerful used as a last resort. The article "A Physician in Ordinary at The Court Of Kwang-Hsu" in the March 31, 1899 edition of *The Times* in London read like a short story about how the Guangxu Emperor (光緒帝, r. 1874–1908) was cured. When the Chinese ruler fell ill, the best physician in the empire was summoned and a French physician was also consulted in the presence of the Empress Dowager Cixi. The emperor appeared to be suffering from a respiratory disease and a decoction was finally prescribed, which, according to the article, must have been "a decoction of ginseng." This careful, complex diagnosis and treatment for the Chinese emperor was an ultimate display of autocracy, one which stood in stark contrast to the simpler use of pharmacopoeias in Western medicine.[35]

Ginseng was also mentioned in the article "The Demise of Yuan Shih-Kai." Subtitled "His Last Hours," the article named ginseng as one of the last things the powerful Yuan Shikai ate shortly before his death.

> He said that in case he passed away, they [the officials] should each consider it their duty to maintain peace and order in the Metropolis. He then took a bowl of rice congee and a cup of ginseng syrup. He showed some signs

> of improvement; but this proved illusory and was but a prelude to the end. Soon after he again became unconscious from which he never recovered and at a little after ten o'clock he passed away.[36]

The following excerpt from an article on the death of Sun Yat-sen (孫中山, 1866–1925) is also worth examining for its placing of ginseng under the spotlight.

> Ginseng, the Chinese medicinal root, played a great part in prolonging Sun Yat-sen's life beyond the span allotted him by foreign doctors. Soon after their leader had been given up by his foreign advisers, his personal followers tried to persuade him to call in a Chinese physician, but without success until two weeks ago. Then the Doctor consented to see Lu Chung-an, a famous Chinese medical man, who had been advertising his ability in the cure of cancer for a month or so in the Chinese papers. Mr. Lu relied principally on ginseng, which served as a drink, is one of the most stimulating drinks in existence. After a copious draught of this concoction, Dr. Sun was able to sit up in bed, and confer with his friends for quite a long time; and during that time he displayed complete possession of his faculties. Gradually, however, the little life that ginseng invigorated sank into a state of torpor, which was proof against every effort at stimulation.[37]

The purpose of this article was not to report Sun Yat-sen's death but to negate the efficacy of ginseng and discredit it. This was evident from the article's title, which was "Ginseng's Effect on Dr. Sun: Remarkable Results Claimed for It as Tonic But No Lasting Cure." Furthermore, these discussions gave the impression that China rejected Western medicine and clung to its customs from the past. They also imparted the cynical conclusion that stubbornness deserved such a miserable ending. The East's efforts to preserve its traditions were interpreted as a rejection of the West and associated with obstinacy and self-righteousness. A newspaper article exposing the backwardness of Japanese medicine criticized the way Japanese physicians tended to hold only herbs like ginseng in high regard by remarking that, "still they are as proud and dogmatical as anywhere else in the world," and that, "many use spells and exorcisms, and most of them become rich."[38]

In 1916, the National Medical Association Conference was held in Shanghai. In his presentation "A Healthy Life," Wu Lien-teh (伍連德, 1879–1960) mentioned that while people took various things for their health, the wealthiest among them took "the best Korean ginseng." As a physician and public health specialist, Wu was the first student of Chinese descent to study at the University of Cambridge and the first Malayan to be nominated for the Nobel Prize in Physiology or Medicine in 1935. However, Wu's mention of Korean ginseng wasn't what the press sought to communicate through coverage of his presentation. What the press had intended to underline was that people were overlooking the fact that cleanliness and self-control were the true keys to a healthy life, which was a typical Western imperialist rhetoric that stressed hygiene.[39]

According to such rhetoric, the Chinese or Asians in general who relied on ginseng and neglected cleanliness and self-control could never be physically healthy. Linda L. Barnes has argued that "Chinese bodies suffered increased targeting as sites of a supposed convergence of vice and disease" by Western cultures over time.[40] Westerners projected onto the Chinese all the vices from the "ancient heathen world" and saw the Chinese as a reminder that a lack of piety and unchecked self-indulgence could end up "inundating the social system with the overflowings of ungodliness."[41] Social vices defined long ago in the West were fused with Chinese health practices to form an "anti-Chinese rhetoric."[42] In this sense, it was perhaps natural for ginseng the Chinese so admired to be accused as a symbol of extravagance and debauchery responsible for ruining civilizations.

Extravagance and Debauchery

While ginseng denoted high social status and wealth in the East, it became associated with extravagance and debauchery in Western discussions. Chinese eating practices, repeatedly described in newspapers, recounted various ingredients and grandiose meals as entertainment for the reader.[43] And ginseng never failed to be included in such descriptions. The purpose of mentioning Chinese dishes, however, was not to introduce their taste, cooking methods, or the dishes themselves, but to criticize the people who ate them. In other words, such mentions used food to delicately weave Orientalist discourses.

The Chinese were portrayed as people who did not hesitate to satisfy their epicurean desire through delicacies such as ginseng, whale oil, water snakes, toads, sea cucumber, and swallow's nest.[44] One article even remarked that, "in fact a Chinaman will eat everything but his own father."[45] In 1879, a rather lengthy passage about the Chinese dietary culture appeared in an article on British trade with China in *The Pall Mall Gazette*.

> Many other things go to China besides needles and matches. Rhinoceros horns, tigers' bones, and deer and buffalo sinews are imported for the benefit of timid and sickly Chinamen, who seek by swallowing decoctions made from these promising substances to acquire some of the strength and courage of their original owners. And there is no lack of enthusiasm among Chinese gourmets for the succulent bechedemer, which the shallow waters of the islands of the Pacific Ocean yield at their demand, or for the birds' nests which lend such a glutinous charm to their favourite soup.
>
> ...
>
> In return for these and other imports China sends into the outer world medicines of far greater value than those she accepts from it; though she has evidently some customers who are fond of rare remedies, and who look with a strange faith to lily flowers, ginseng, and lotus nuts for relief from some of the ills which flesh is heir to.[46]

At the center of such an inexplicable, unsatiable appetite was ginseng. Because it was worth 20 to 250 times or sometimes even 500 times more than the worth of silver,[47] obsession over ginseng became equated with the absence of temperance and economic sense. In 1933, an article in *The China Press* began with this sharp warning: "Watch yourself against over-eating!" The article featured Mr. Chu, a manager who worked in a downtown market in China. Physically and mentally overworked, Mr. Chu purchased and ate forty dollars' worth of ginseng before going to sleep, only to be found dead in bed by his servant the next morning.[48] The point was that faith in ginseng's efficacy had morphed into an act of greed and led to a tragic death.

In 1841, Western newspapers reported the dismissal of the Mongol nobleman and Qing official Qishan (琦善, 1786–1854) after the Qing dynasty lost the First Opium War (1840–1842). Appointed as an imperial commissioner (欽差大臣 *qinchai dachen*) in 1840, Qishan had been responsible for military diplomacy in Guangdong on behalf of Lin Zexu (林則徐). He argued for a compromise with the British during the First Opium War which caused him to be dismissed and condemned to exile after the war. The point of the news reports was not to criticize Qishan's role or the error he committed under China's political circumstances at the time but to expose the list of his possessions that were confiscated. This extensive list included 24 catties of ginseng, 25 catties of deer's horns, 94 large pearls, 270,000 taels of gold, 3,400,000 taels of silver, 4 pawn shops, 168 "female slaves," and an enormous amount of land.[49] The items on the list vividly revealed Qishan's extravagant taste. The same went for newspaper articles on the Empress Dowager Cixi. A lengthy article summarizing the Chinese imperial family's finances remarked that, "the Empress is very peremptory about ginseng and every now and then the court sends down a peremptory extra demand for more ginseng."[50] Ginseng had been inseparable from the empress dowager, who was portrayed as a symbol of extravagance, corruption, and tyranny.

In the eyes of the West, ginseng was coveted by all in China regardless of social rank. Foreigners who visited the country would remark that from the emperor down to slaves, all Chinese had faith in the efficacy of this strange root called ginseng.[51] In 1888, British and American newspapers revealed the prescription a Chinese physician in New York issued to an infirm Chinese laundress. The following comment was attached to the reported decoction made of two ounces of live deer horn and a half-ounce of "Corean ginseng" at a total price of eighteen pounds, five shillings, and two pence.

> Strange as it may seem, and even at these outrageous prices, there are hundreds of hard-working Chinese laundrymen all over the country who regularly take a dose or two of this remedy each year.[52]

These reactions toward ginseng had partly to do with the West's complete ignorance of the Chinese culture based on *wenbu* (溫補), which sought to replenish through warming. As epidemics grew rampant late in the Ming dynasty, people increasingly developed an interest in their health and appropriate treatments. Scholars suspect that this trend allowed ginseng to be widely understood by both physicians and patients as a lifesaving remedy. The plant thereafter became a popular ingredient in restoratives. The Chinese came to say that they feared death from infirmity rather than from disease or that only ginseng could cure because it guaranteed complete recovery. Hence, if a patient passed from taking something other than a restorative, the patient's family and friends were reproached for placing wealth ahead of health. Being viewed as unfilial was more disgraceful than spending the family's entire fortune to procure ginseng. By the first year of the Qianlong Emperor's reign, the upper class's fondness for restoratives had spread to the poor, who sought alternatives that had an effect similar to ginseng, since they couldn't afford the root. Among such alternatives were *dangshen* (黨蔘) and *shashen* (沙蔘).[53]

The Western discourse on ginseng, however, demonstrated more than a lack of understanding of other cultures or a lack of cultural relativism. It bore implications for not only the lower class in China but in Europe as well. In an ideal society in which people lived within their own means, ginseng was a luxury, one that was not to be made available to the laboring classes. Maintaining a clear hierarchy was a condition fundamental to sound social development and had to be fulfilled, at least in countries that shaped such a rhetoric.

In 1845, British newspapers quoted an article in *Punch* to cast criticism on a tariff reform carried out by then prime minister Robert Peel. The papers pointed out that tariffs had been removed mostly from luxury items and particularly called it foolish to treat ginseng as a common consumer good. They scoffed that, "the Premier will distribute ginseng to all who will pledge themselves to eat it," and that, "these are real proofs of what Sir Robert Peel has done for the poor man by the new tariff."[54] The premise behind such criticism was that while consumption corresponded to social status in Britain, that was not the case in China. Although China was the largest consumer of ginseng and had abundant human and material resources at its disposal, the British had concluded that China was trapped in a defective economic structure that forced it to rely on imports to procure miscellaneous manufactured goods such as needles or matches.[55]

Such a conclusion depicted China as lagging at a time when the West was in the process of modernization. This depiction was based on the diffusionist premise that despite being belittled, China would eventually follow in the West's footsteps. According to diffusionists, Western civilization has a historical superiority that has allowed Europe to retain a permanent superiority over non-Europe from past to present. Eurocentric diffusionism argues that those lagging outside Europe have had no choice but to imitate Europeans in order to achieve modernization.[56]

Meanwhile, discussions surrounding ginseng have defined the East as forever inexplicable and impossible to accommodate. In other words, even for a diffusionist framework, it was impossible to embrace the East. And ginseng was at the center of such efforts aimed at ensuring a distance between the East and West.

Notes

1 Lafitau, *Mémoire Presenté a Son Altesse Royale Monseigneur Le Duc d'Orléans, Regent Du Royaume de France*, 72.
2 Grew, *Musaeum Regalis Societatis*, 227.
3 Thomas L. Rost and Maureen L. Sandler, "The Common History and Popular Uses of Roots," *The American Biology Teacher* 40, no. 6 (1978): 338.
4 William Shakespeare, *Romeo and Juliet*, act 4, scene 3, lines 35–47.
5 Lafitau, *Mémoire Presenté a Son Altesse Royale Monseigneur Le Duc d'Orléans* 71.
6 Lafitau, *Mémoire Presenté a Son Altesse Royale Monseigneur Le Duc d'Orléans* 73–75.
7 Carles, *Life in Corea*, 4.
8 Rost and Sandler, "The Common History and Popular Uses of Roots," 338.
9 Imamura, *Insamsa*, 2015, 6:498.
10 Hill, *A History of the Materia Medica*, 589.
11 Rochon, *A Voyage to Madagascar and the East Indies*, 459–60; Hill, *A History of the Materia Medica*, 589; Hill, *The Vegetable System*, 5:25; Stearns, *The American Oracle*, 45.
12 Pomeranz and Topik, *The World that Trade Created*, xiii.
13 *Siris in the Shades: A Dialogue Concerning Tar Water* (London, 1744), 17.
14 Patrick Murray Elibank, *Thoughts on Money, Circulation, and Paper Currency* (Edinburgh, 1758), 28; Oliver Goldsmith, *The Citizen of the World; or Letters from a Chinese Philosopher, Residing in London, to His Friends in the East*, vol. 1 (London, 1762), 96–97.
15 James Anderson, *Recreations in Agriculture, Natural-History, Arts, and Miscellaneous Literature*, vol. 6 (London, 1802), 143.
16 Richard Hildreth, *Letter to His Excellency Marcus Morton on Banking and the Currency* (Boston, MA: Kidder and Wright, 1840), 9.
17 John Huxham, *Observations on the Air, and Epidemic Diseases*, vol. 2 (London, 1767), 241; Thomas Salmon, *Modern History: or, the Present State of All Nations*, vol. 1 (London, 1739), 20.
18 Darlington, "Collinson to Bartram, February 24, 1738-9, London, Pennsylvania Coffeehouse," 127.
19 "Of Some Books Lately Publish't : Relations of Divers Curious Voyages," *Philosophical Transactions* 1 (1665–1666): 249.
20 Charles Johnstone, *The History of John Juniper, Esq. Alias Juniper Jack*, vol. 2 (London, 1781), 167.
21 Luís de Camões, *The Lusiad: Or, the Discovery of India*, trans. William Julius Mickle (Oxford, 1776), 469.
22 Tobias Smollett, *The Present State of All Nations*, vol. 8 (London, 1769).
23 *Letters of the Missionary Jesuits* (Paris, 1713).
24 *Philosophical Transactions* 28 (1713), 241–242.
25 Sun Xiaoshu 孙曉舒, *Shanshen zhi "ye": Guanyu yiyi yu jiage zhi shengcheng de renleixue yanjiu* 山蔘之"野": 關于意義與價格之生成的人類學研究 ['Wild' Ginseng: An Anthropological Study of Its Significance and Price Formation] (Beijing: Zhishi chanquan chubanshe 知識産權出版社, 2012), 97–99.
26 "Abstract of Peking Gazettes," *The North-China Herald and Supreme Court & Consular Gazette*, December 20, 1881.
27 "Abstract of Peking Gazettes," *The North-China Herald and Supreme Court & Consular Gazette*, April 12, 1882.
28 "Abstract of Peking Gazettes," *The North-China Herald and Supreme Court & Consular Gazette*, February 3, 1893.
29 "Abstract of Peking Gazettes," *The North-China Herald and Supreme Court & Consular Gazette*, February 10, 1893.
30 "Abstract of Peking Gazettes," *The North-China Herald and Supreme Court & Consular Gazette*, December 5, 1878; "Abstract of Peking Gazettes," *The North-China Herald and Supreme Court & Consular Gazette*, April 12, 1877.

31 "Abstract of Peking Gazettes," *The North-China Herald and Supreme Court & Consular Gazette*, December 31, 1874.
32 "Abstract of Peking Gazettes," *The North-China Herald and Supreme Court & Consular Gazette*, September 11, 1875; "Abstract of Peking Gazettes," *The North-China Herald and Supreme Court & Consular Gazette*, June 17, 1876; "Abstract of Peking Gazettes," *The North-China Herald and Supreme Court & Consular Gazette*, March 21, 1878.
33 "General Tuan Chi-jui, 2 Ounces of Korean Ginseng and $5,000 as Gifts from H. E. Yuan," *The North China Herald and Supreme Court & Consular Gazette*, June 12, 1915.
34 Ch'ae Che-kong, "遺閣吏問病暘札," in *Pŏnamjip* 번암집 [A Collection of Pŏnam's Writings], vol. ha, n.d.; Kim Bo-sung김보성, "Han-Chung insamshi ŭi yangsang kwa t'ŭkching" 韓·中 人蔘詩의 양상과 특징 [Characteristics of Korean and Chinese Poems on Ginseng], *Hanmun'gojŏn yŏn'gu* 한문고전연구 36, no. 1 (2018): 313.
35 "A Physician in Ordinary at the Court of Kwang-Hsu," *The Times*, March 31, 1899.
36 "The Demise of Yuan Shih-Kai," *Peking Gazette*, June 8, 1916; "Final Scenes in the Late President's Life," *The North China Herald and Supreme Court & Consular Gazette*, June 30, 1916.
37 "Ginseng's Effect on Dr. Sun: Remarkable Results Claimed for It as Tonic but No Lasting Cure," *The North China Herald and Supreme Court & Consular Gazette*, March 28, 1925.
38 "The Voix de la Verité," *The Leeds Mercury*, July 30, 1859.
39 "A Healthy Life," *Peking Gazette*, February 14, 1916.
40 Barnes, *Needles, Herbs, Gods, and Ghosts*, 294.
41 Barnes, *Needles, Herbs, Gods, and Ghosts*, 294.
42 Barnes, *Needles, Herbs, Gods, and Ghosts*, 294.
43 "Miscellaneous: Chinese Delicacies," *The Manchester Guardian*, April 22, 1848; "Chinese Delicacies," *Freeman's Journal and Daily Commercial Advertiser*, September 12, 1848; "Chinese Delicacies," *The Manchester Times*, October 3, 1848; "Chinese Delicacies," *The Northern Star and National Trades' Journal*, December 1, 1849; "Curiosities of Trade in China," *The Pall Mall Gazette*, December 5, 1879; "A Chinese Banquet," *Aberdeen Weekly Journal*, January 16, 1880; "Miscellaneous Extracts," *Manchester Times*, January 17, 1880; "A Chinese Banquet," *The Hull Packet and East Riding Times*, January 23, 1880; "Literary Selections," *The Preston Guardian*, February 14, 1880.
44 "Curiosities of Trade in China," *The Pall Mall Gazette*, December 5, 1879.
45 "Miscellaneous: Chinese Delicacies," *The Manchester Guardian*, April 22, 1848.
46 "Curiosities of Trade in China," *The Pall Mall Gazette*, December 5, 1879.
47 "A Precious Drug," *Hampshire Telegraph and Sussex Chronicle*, September 9, 1893.
48 "$40 Worth of Ginseng Too Much for Eater," *The China Press*, December 16, 1933.
49 "Miscellaneous Extracts from the Indian Papers Received by the Overland Mail," *The Manchester Guardian*, November 10, 1841; "China," *Caledonian Mercury*, November 11, 1841; "Untitled Article," *The Derby Mercury*, November 17, 1841.
50 "Chinese Finance," *The North China Herald and Supreme Court & Consular Gazette*, March 23, 1883.
51 "Ginseng," *The Manchester Guardian*, April 25, 1867.
52 "Bleeding a Laundryman," *Hampshire Telegraph and Sussex Chronicle*, February 11, 1888.
53 Regarding the culture of *wenbu*, refer to Sun, *Shanshen zhi "ye,"* 95–99.
54 "The "Moral Lesson" of the Gallows," *Punch* 8 (1846), 159; "The Hangman's 'Moral Lessons'," *The Morning Chronicle*, April 3, 1845; "The 'Newspaper Man'," *The Manchester Times and Gazette*, April 5, 1845.
55 "Curiosities of Trade in China," *The Pall Mall Gazette*, December 5, 1879.
56 James Morris Blaut, *The Colonizer's Model of the World: Geographical Diffusionism and Eurocentric History* (New York: Guilford, 1993).

15

MYSTERIOUS ORIENTALITY

To Europeans, China or the East were places that operated according to different standards. Even accounts of having experienced the efficacy of ginseng noted in the end that the root nevertheless fell somewhat short of expectations that had been formed by Chinese testimonies.[1] Europeans would often conclude that the efficacy of ginseng failed to live up to its reputation as a cure-all and thus saw the root as more of a tonic helpful in restoring vigor.[2] What such conclusions meant, however, had less to do with whether ginseng was effective or not. This was because such conclusions exposed the European belief that their criteria for such a determination were entirely different from that of the Chinese, suggesting that they would never be able to accept the Chinese criteria. While *The American Farmer's Encyclopedia*, published in 1860, extolled the high commercial value of ginseng and proudly listed the annual volume of American ginseng exported to China, it firmly stated that "the extraordinary medical virtues formerly ascribed to ginseng, had no other existence than in the imaginations of the Chinese."[3]

Ginseng and the Diving Bell Accident

Ginseng was often considered a mystical object in the West. In 1783, it surfaced as a subject of rumor in Britain due to a major accident. In March, a merchant ship called the *Imperial East Indiaman* (also known as *Belgioioso*) sank near Dublin Bay in the Irish Sea on its way to China from Liverpool. The ship was carrying a considerable amount of silver and lead. To salvage the cargo, its owners hired an Edinburgh engineer and diver named Charles Spalding (1738–1783). On June 1, 1783, Spalding used the diving bell he'd modified to dive forty-two feet down to the wreck with his nephew. The two made three dives that day and managed to salvage some of the cargo, including lead. The next day, however, an entirely different scene unfolded. When seventy-five minutes went by without any signals

DOI: 10.4324/9781003286691-19

from Spalding and his nephew, the diving bell was lifted and the two were found dead inside.

The funeral for Spalding and his nephew was held on June 8, the seventh day after their death. Speculation ensued over why it took so long to hold the funeral. The problem was that the corpses had remained remarkably intact, without displaying any signs of discoloration. Prior to the accident, the divers had claimed that a terrible stench pervaded the wreck, possibly because of the rotten ginseng on board.

This matter attracted nationwide attention as it was covered by newspapers and magazines.[4] British scientists struggled to identify what had prevented the corpses' decomposition. The British Royal Society even held meetings twice to discuss the matter. One scientist argued that ginseng couldn't have been the cause of death because it was aromatic and wasn't likely to putrify so readily in salt water. Most people, on the other hand, believed that their death had been caused by "highly noxious effluvia, either arising from the putrid bodies in the Indiaman, or the great quantity of the medical plant called Ginseng."[5]

An inquest was held but the exact cause of death was never determined. While further speculations suggested that the accident could have been caused by the insufficient supply of fresh air or entangled signal ropes, people continued to be more convinced by the idea that the stench of rotten ginseng was to blame. Thanks to newspapers at the time that labeled ginseng plants as "strange," the root is still under suspicion to this day when it comes to discussions about the tragic death of Spalding.[6]

Superstitions and Tales

Western discussions of ginseng have been dotted with countless superstitions and inexplicable episodes. Tales involving ginseng are aplenty in China and Korea as well. One of the more well-known tales is that of how the infamous founding emperor of the Qin dynasty, Qin Shi Huang, sent people to Jeju Island and Japan in search of the mystical herb so as to fulfill his dream of immortality.[7] Ginseng is also known to have played a role in the early years of Nurhaci. After losing his mother, Nurhaci fled from his stepmother's abuse to the Changbai Mountains (Mount Paektu) where he collected and sold ginseng to accumulate wealth and power. He apparently sought a way to prevent ginseng from easily rotting and store it long term, so that it could be sold at a proper price. He is said to have eventually figured out a way to steam dry ginseng and managed to increase his profits. Of course, this tale is likely to have been adapted to highlight Nurhaci's brilliance.[8]

Imamura Tomo compiled ginseng-related myths, legends, stories, and tales for the sixth volume of the *History of Ginseng*, which covers miscellaneous details about ginseng. Imamura understood such legends and myths to have been influenced mainly by the Taoist belief in immortality, in addition to other beliefs in the spirits of mountains or plants, which were later infused with aspects of

Buddhism as well. He nevertheless concluded that ginseng was not so mystical after all, because its production was limited to certain areas and the history of its cultivation had been brief.[9] Ginseng-related legends and tales did tend to depict the root as a mysterious human-shaped object with supernatural powers, such as the ability to turn a person into a divine spirit, or as an object auspicious to a nation, but most of the time, ginseng served as a reward for demonstrating filial love to one's parents or doing virtuous deeds for the sake of others.[10]

Eastern tales involving ginseng therefore corresponded to the ideas and morals that formed the basis of society and came to be regarded as a natural part of Eastern history and culture. Such tales, however, were injected with a transtemporal mysticism in the West. In 1810, *The Observer* and *The Morning Chronicle* published articles about a plant discovered in China that turned into a dirty yellow worm in the winter and had a medicinal effect similar to ginseng.[11] Another article in *The Manchester Guardian* quoted a foreign official stationed in Niuzhuang (牛莊) who reported that ginseng took the form of man in secluded places and that the Chinese believed ginseng existed for the purpose of alleviating human pain.[12]

As a matter of fact, there happened to be an ancient Chinese tale in which wild ginseng rose out of the earth at the ripe old age of three hundred in the form of a man with white blood so powerful that a few drops of it could even resurrect the dead.[13] This very tale was introduced in the British weekly illustrated newspaper *The Graphic* in 1877. Yet, the article relayed it in a distant tone subtly underlining that it was only the Chinese who believed in the tale.

> After growing for three centuries, ginseng is inspired through the starlight by the spirits of the hills and rivers; then to burst into the shape and form of a man. In course of time the new creature can leave the earth and dwell among the stars; but the most wonderful part about him is his white blood, which is a sovereign cure for all diseases, and safeguard against mortality. It is very hard, however, to get this white blood, this divine ichor. To begin with, you must be extremely pious, and must pray and fast for some while before making the attempt. Then the plant-spirit may be deluded into believing that a red paper lamp with seven purple stars is the Great Bear and he comes near, being a star-worshipper. A net is kept handy, the spirit caught, and his arm cut with a knife of agate, and the drops of white blood caught in a vessel of the purest jade. As a few drops will bring a dead man to life, they are naturally valuable; and we commend them to the proprietor of the Amritaras, the Elixir of Immortality.[14]

Articles like this reeked of cynicism. Assigning supernatural attributes to ginseng and revering them or developing a futile desire for immortality through ginseng were ultimately interpreted as fundamental flaws of the Chinese. The West was thereby compelled to actively intervene and rectify such flawed premodern traits (Figure 15.1).

FIGURE 15.1 Walking Ginseng.

This sentiment happened to manifest through a meeting the China Emergency Committee held in Manchester in 1909. Those at the meeting called for the need to improve the sorely lagging Chinese medicine, which in the absence of surgeons prescribed tiger's teeth, snake skins, or ginseng as remedies. The meeting arrived at the consensus that active support for modernization should be given to the "peace-loving Chinese nation" as opposed to the hostile Japanese.[15]

Through discussions about ginseng, the mysterious Eastern panacea contended with its inexplicable efficacy that modern Western medicine found difficult to embrace. This contention encompassed the sense of inferiority Westerners had toward the sophisticated Chinese technique of curing ginseng, the rush to export that hindered the development of a domestic market for ginseng, and Western medicine's failure to identify a standard dosage of ginseng despite having been centered on standardization. These circumstances were mixed into an imperialist approach that was self-contradictory: claiming the superiority of ginseng produced in the West while stigmatizing ginseng produced in the East as a symbol of backwardness.

Like ginseng, countless objects originating from non-Western areas could also have become the victim of such self-contradiction, which often extended to the non-Westerners who produced and consumed those objects. As the abolitionist movement emerged in eighteenth-century Britain, abolitionists called for a boycott of goods produced by slave labor, such as sugar, indigo, and rice.[16] The consumption of sugar produced under conditions of brutal slave labor was likened to an act of cannibalism. The image of laborers slaving away to produce food was prevalent in the social imagination, reminding the British of the blood and tears slaves were forced to shed to produce the sugar they consumed.[17]

This gave rise to the sugar boycott in Britain, which became the origin of ethical consumerism. Sugar continues to be consumed, but ever since slavery was abolished, consumption has rarely triggered the image of the laborers producing it. Ginseng, however, has been treated differently by the West in that it has been portrayed negatively in association with the Chinese who have mainly consumed it. And such a negative portrayal extended to the producers of ginseng, causing ginseng diggers to become the subject of a similar social imagination. What is worth noting is the fact that social impressions about Chinese ginseng diggers have also been projected upon their American counterparts and continue to prevail to this day.

Notes

1 Woodville, *Medical Botany*, 2:272; Quincy, *Pharmacopoeia Officinalis, or a Complete English Dispensatory*, 61.
2 Brookes, *The General Dispensatory*, 42; Donald Munro, *A Treatise of the Materia Medica*, vol. 3 (Edinburgh, 1788), 119; Cullen, *A Treatise of the Materia Medica*, 2:161.
3 *The American Farmer's Encyclopedia*, 540.
4 *The Weekly Entertainer; or Agreeable and Instructive Repository*, September 15, 1783.
5 *The Terrific Register; or, Record of Crimes, Judgements, Providences, and Calamities*, vol. 2 (London: Sherwood, Jones, and Co. and Hunter, Edinburgh, 1825), 720.
6 John Bevan, "Charles Spalding's Diving Bells" (A Meeting of the Historical Diving Society at Norwegian Underwater Institute, Bergen, November 5, 2005).
7 Kim, "Insam kwa kangyŏk: Hugŭm-Ch'ŏng ŭi kangyŏk inshik kwa taeoegwan'gye ŭi pyŏnhwa," 233.
8 *Taizu Gao Huangdi shilu* (太祖高皇帝寶錄), vol. 3, 8b–9a (乙巳年 三月 乙亥朔). Kim, "Insam kwa kangyŏk," 234–235.
9 Imamura, *Insamsa*, 2015, 6:17.
10 Imamura, *Insamsa*, 2015, 6:17–220.
11 "Untitled Article," *The Observer*, June 3, 1810; "Ship News," *The Morning Chronicle*, June 4, 1810.
12 "Ginseng," *The Manchester Guardian*, April 25, 1867.
13 Kim, "Insam kwa kangyŏk," 234.

14 "A Marvellous Botanical Discovery," *The Graphic*, September 8, 1877. See also "Ginseng," *The North-China Herald and Supreme Court & Consular Gazette*, June 23, 1877.
15 Alicia Little, "Great Britain and the Development of China—to the Editor of the Manchester Guardian (Correspondence)," *The Manchester Guardian*, March 10, 1909.
16 Heasim Sul 설혜심, *Sobi ŭi yŏksa: Chigŭmkkot amudo chumok'aji anŭn "sobihanŭn in'gan" ŭi yŏksa* 소비의 역사: 지금껏 아무도 주목하지 않은 '소비하는 인간'의 역사 [A History of Consumption: On the Overlooked Aspect of Mankind as Consumers] (Seoul: Humanist 휴머니스트, 2017), 361–373.
17 Benjamin Moseley, *A Treatise on Sugar* (London, 1800), 166.

16

GINSENG DIGGERS IN THE EAST AND WEST

Chinese Ginseng Diggers

For a long time, the ginseng digger was a profession unique to East Asia.[1] In China, they were commonly referred to as *caishenren* (採蔘人), which meant ginseng gatherers. From the early days of the Later Jin, the privileges of collecting and selling ginseng were split among the nobility of the Eight Banners. Until the late seventeenth century, the authorities of Butha Ula (打牲烏拉) oversaw ginseng gathering in Manchuria and the people who hunted and gathered ginseng under their command were called Butha soldiers.

According to the government rules of 1713, Butha soldiers who gathered ginseng were each assigned with a quota of twenty *liang*. If they failed to fill the quota, they were whipped as punishment. By 1727, the rules of punishment were tightened so that a soldier would receive fifty whips for falling up to one *liang* short of his quota, one hundred whips for falling up to two *liang* short of his quota, and falling more than two *liang* short of his quota was punished with one hundred whips in addition to the wearing of a cangue for forty days. Not only were the soldiers punished for failing to fill their quotas, but the officials who supervised them were also whipped or demoted.[2]

Despite taking such harsh measures, the amount of ginseng presented to the Butha Ula superintendent continued to drop. By 1749, only 525 kilograms were secured, when the quota was 1,800 kilograms. In 1750, the imperial family admitted that it had become pointless to utilize Butha soldiers to gather ginseng and exempted the Butha Ula superintendent from paying ginseng as tax in kind.[3]

Apart from the soldiers under the Butha Ula superintendent's command, Eight Banner people in Shengjing were also dispatched to collect ginseng. Among the Eight Banners, the emperor classified three of them as "upper banners" and those in Shengjing who belonged to the three upper banners were in charge of

DOI: 10.4324/9781003286691-20

managing the imperial household's assets spread across Manchuria. In the early years of the Qing dynasty, the three upper banners in Shengjing sent 150 people, fifty from each banner, to collect ginseng every year.[4] When the ginseng gathered by the Eight Banners grew insufficient by the late seventeenth century, the Qing dynasty hired merchants to collect ginseng on consignment from the early eighteenth century.

Ginseng gathering was a costly task because it required staying in the mountains for four to five months at a time. The wealthy capitalists in Shengjing thus saw an opportunity. They used their financial means to acquire thousands of ginseng vouchers and then hired an agent to oversee their ginseng gathering operation. Unlike merchants who could afford to obtain ginseng vouchers, those who signed up to work as ginseng diggers were mostly from the lower class. These ginseng gathering operations financed by merchants led to the creation of new positions like contractors called *batou* (把頭) responsible for leading ginseng diggers in the mountains and guarantors who could vouch for the identity of each ginseng digger.

Anyone going into the mountains to gather ginseng was required to carry a government-issued permit called a *zhaopiao* (照票). All ginseng diggers as well as the soldiers who escorted them each carried a permit that had to be returned once they came down from the mountains. Although secretly collecting ginseng without a permit was punished if uncovered, thirty to forty thousand people took the risk each year.[5] A ginseng digger with a permit was supplied with shoes, knee pads, and fabric to make sacks. Such items, however, were supplied the year after delivering ginseng, forcing ginseng diggers to suffer financially in between.

Ginseng diggers were also provided with six months' worth of food which consisted of salt, 216 liters of rice, and 36 liters of flour per person. Every year they set out in early April and returned in early October. They traveled along a designated route that departed from Shengjing and passed through Hetu Ala, Huifa, and Jilin Ula before reaching Usuri Ula. However, more than half of the food would be consumed on the journey to Usuri Ula, and the ginseng diggers had to hunt animals or beg for food to make their way back to Shengjing.[6]

In 1792, an extreme drought displaced many in Zhili, causing the Chinese government to ease the ban on entry into northeastern areas. As a result, during the reigns of the Jiaqing Emperor and the Daoguang Emperor, many migrated to Manchuria and some flowed into previously sealed-off areas around the Amnok River basin.[7] Unlike people who used to be recruited to gather ginseng, those who relocated to northeastern areas turned ginseng gathering into a genuine profession.[8] The ginseng diggers that appear in Chinese sources after the nineteenth century mostly refer to those migrants and their descendants in northeastern China who hunted and collected wild ginseng for a living.

A rare description of such professional ginseng diggers appears in the travelogue *The Long White Mountain* by Henry Evan Murchison James.[9] While exploring Manchuria with two other Britons in 1886, James encountered young men in search of ginseng in the woods around Mount Paektu. According to

James, they traveled in groups of twelve to fifteen to find just one or two roots, which would be enough to compensate them all for an entire season's work. Below is a description of the ginseng diggers he ran into where the Ussuri River joined the Amur River.

> Those men, wretched in their entire being, have here no other means of sustaining life than that of giving themselves up, with incredible fatigue, to the search of the ginseng. Picture to yourself one of these miserable carriers, laden with more than twenty-four pounds weight, venturing without any road across immense forests, climbing up or descending the mountains; always left alone to his own thoughts, and exposed to every distemper; no knowing if to-day or to-morrow he may fall a victim to the wild beasts which abound around him, supported by the modicum of millet he brings with him, and a few wild herbs to season it. And all this during five months of the year, from the end of April to the end of September.[10]

James and his companions also ran into Koreans in the Changbai Mountains. The Koreans would hunt animals, dig for gold, or wander through the woods in search of wild ginseng, and some even cultivated ginseng at the foot of the mountains. "Colonists" was the word James used to refer to the people living in the woods, including Koreans. Such colonists had already formed guilds that operated under rules and regulations of their own. Jilin authorities tended to maintain good relations with these guilds and often asked them for help in capturing bandits.

Like such guilds, there were many occupational associations in northeastern China referred to as *xingbang* (行幇). Representative of such associations, according to a study by Ch'oe Chun, were *mubang* (木幇) for loggers, *shenbang* (蔘幇) for ginseng diggers, and *tufei* (土匪) for animal hunters and mounted bandits.[11] Ch'oe's research on *shenbang* offers a glimpse into the lifestyle ginseng diggers led in northeastern China and shows that they preserved their ginseng digging rituals and traditions to form a unique culture.

On an auspicious day, ginseng diggers would set out into the mountains with their tools and two weeks' worth of food. Upon entering a forest, they would first build a stick hut and perform a ritual for the mountain god. The ginseng diggers and loggers in northeastern China referred to the mountain god as *laobatou* (老把頭) but the myth surrounding the identity of *laobatou* varied depending on the area. According to the myth around the Changbai Mountains (Mount Paektu), a man named Sun Liang (孫良) went into the Changbai Mountains in search of ginseng but ran into the misfortune of starving to death. Upon death's door, Sun mustered everything he had left to write a poem about his hope to serve as a guide to ginseng diggers. That was how he came to guard the mountains as the mountain god.

While searching for wild ginseng, talking was taboo among ginseng diggers in Manchuria, and they strictly controlled their diet. They believed in dreams and drew distinctions between auspicious and inauspicious dreams. These Manchurian customs were highly similar to those of Korean ginseng diggers, suggesting a significant degree of mutual cultural exchange or influence over time.[12] After interviewing Korean ginseng diggers in the 1930s, Imamura Tomo discovered that Korean and Manchurian ginseng diggers shared strong similarities in terms of their practices, organizations, customs, and taboos. Imamura thus claimed that, "a traditional relationship exists between them, considering that the profession itself originated near the Korean border."[13]

The most interesting custom of ginseng diggers was how they interpreted the way birds sang to find ginseng. In northeastern China, ginseng diggers believed that the singing of a bird called *bangchuiniao* (棒棰鳥) at night offered hints as to where wild ginseng might be located. The bird now known as the varied tit was named after *bangchui* (棒棰), a word that refers to wild ginseng, because the bird apparently enjoyed eating wild ginseng seeds. If a *bangchuiniao* was hungry, it would clearly sing "wang gan gege" (王干哥哥), which sounded like it was calling out to "Brother Wang Gan." If a *bangchuiniao* was full, however, it would sing "wang gan geogeo" in a huskier tone. So, whenever ginseng diggers heard the bird sing in a huskier tone, they believed they'd be able to find wild ginseng by traveling in the opposite direction of the singing bird.[14]

Ginseng diggers also believed that a spirit, sometimes referred to as a "ginseng child," lived in wild ginseng and that the sound of ginseng diggers could easily startle the spirit and cause the wild ginseng to go into hiding. To prevent a wild ginseng from running away upon being discovered, ginseng diggers would immediately drive a wooden stick or hoe deep into the ground next to the plant and tie around its stems a red ribbon with an old coin hanging from it. A red cloth would be placed on the ground close to the plant to collect some of its precious seeds. Then the ginseng diggers would check the surrounding area to dig up all the wild ginseng in its vicinity. Finally, they would strip some of the bark off a pine tree nearby and carve on the bare spot the Chinese character *kou* (口) in different sizes to secretly mark the number of leaves the wild ginseng had and the number of ginseng diggers on site.[15]

Korean Ginseng Diggers

Ginseng diggers have been called by many names in Korea, including *shimmemani, shimkkun, samkkun, sammekkun, ch'aesamin* (採蔘人), *ch'aesamkkun* (採蔘軍 or 採蔘君), and *sanch'ŏk* (山尺).[16] In the case of *shimmemani*, the term is a compound of *shim*, an archaic word for wild ginseng, *me*, an archaic word for mountain, and *mani*, which means a great man. As previously explained in Part 2, ginseng gathering was a major government enterprise during the Chosŏn dynasty. It was therefore under strict state control, such that ginseng diggers would be punished for gathering without permission. For instance, in 1709, the twenty-ninth year of King Sukchong's reign, twenty ginseng diggers were sentenced to four years of imprisonment in Hamhŭng.[17] During the reign of King Chŏngjo, the Chosŏn court discussed when would be the best time to gather ginseng on the island of Ullŭngdo. An official in Samch'ŏk was originally in charge of the task, but because ginseng diggers were reluctant to cross the sea to reach the island, the districts of Kangnŭng, Yangyang, Samch'ŏk, P'yŏnghae, and Uljin each had to send three to ten ginseng diggers to carry out the task.[18]

During the Japanese occupation of Korea, the forest office of each region was responsible for managing ginseng diggers. The permit to enter mountains to gather ginseng was issued to teams of three diggers. Such permits expired in three months so that anyone who failed to come down from the mountains or return their permit by the end of that period would be considered missing. The number of ginseng diggers who received a permit from the forest office in Kanggye County of North P'yŏngan Province was 690 in 1928, 1,240 in 1929, and 1,038 in 1930. The fact that the authorities kept meticulous track of the number of permits issued each year suggests that ginseng was considered an invaluable resource and was therefore thoroughly managed by the Japanese.

To ginseng diggers, preparing to go into the mountains was more complicated than actually hunting for ginseng in the mountains. The reason was because they had to observe all sorts of taboos as they organized a team, prepared the necessary tools, and decided when to enter the mountains. To determine the date of departure, they would consult a fortuneteller or the team leader, referred to as the *ŏin* or *ŏinmani*, who was capable of performing divination on his own. The date would either be the day the god ginseng diggers worshiped descended from the heavens or the day after *Chungbok*, the middle dog day of the summer, because ginseng diggers believed that ginseng berries ripened overnight on that day. The *ŏin* was usually someone respected by the team and held absolute authority over his team members. According to Imamura Tomo, there were about three hundred *ŏins* in Kanggye alone and over one thousand *ŏins* nationwide near the end of the Chosŏn dynasty.[19]

Before heading into the mountains, a team of ginseng diggers had to decide whether they would have joint ownership over all the ginseng collected through their journey or recognize the individual ownership of the digger who first found each root. *Wŏnangme* or *tongme* referred to the equal division of profits from the joint collection and sale of ginseng. Even in that case, the *ŏin* would be allotted a portion slightly larger than his team members. *Tokme* or *kangme*, on the other hand, referred to the practice of recognizing individual ownership of the digger who first found a wild ginseng plant. This, however, left the matter of how ownership would be determined over the roots growing in the vicinity of the discovered root. Generally, the ginseng digger who first discovered a root would check its vicinity and then call out to his team members by yelling "*poshio!* (please look!)" or "*Somang poshio!* (please look forward to!)" so that they could come over and search for a root around the area for themselves.[20]

Once a team agreed on a method of division, it was customary to abide by it absolutely. This was apparently why ginseng diggers never experienced internal conflicts or disputes. Even if a digger ended up with nothing, he would never grow envious of a colleague who found many roots. Imamura Tomo found this custom "admirable" and described how impressed he had been with the personalities of the ginseng diggers he interviewed for his research. He went as far as to remark that

> although they are illiterate, they are kind, humble, and exude the goodness and beauty of nature, which must have been fostered unconsciously from roaming deep into the remote mountains and valleys for many years.[21]

Into the Mountains

With one week left until departure to the mountains, Korean ginseng diggers would begin to purify their bodies by bathing multiple times each day. They abstained from sexual intercourse and unhealthy foods. They used to strictly avoid red and white meat, but beginning in the early twentieth century, only dog and blowfish meat were prohibited. The items they prepared for the trip included clothes and a hat, gaiters, a wooden staff, and nine sheets of paper for rituals and other purposes.[22] Except for the sword they carried to clear paths, the tools they used to dig up ginseng were made of wood or animal bones, because they believed that ginseng disliked metal. For a two-week trip, each person usually packed about eighteen liters of rice in addition to soybean paste, soy sauce, and a bit of salted croaker. A live pig also used to be brought along to be offered during the sacrificial ritual held in the mountains, but this practice disappeared after Korea came under Japanese occupation.[23]

On the day of departure, ginseng diggers did not exchange words of farewell with their families.[24] And they strictly observed the rule against talking while traveling into the mountains. They also tried to avoid running into women while hiking and considered it most ominous for a woman to cross their path. If a woman appeared before them, she should have the courtesy to step aside. If the *ŏin* asked her for a piece of her skirt, she had to use her teeth to tear off two to three inches from the rear hem of her skirt for the ginseng diggers to carry throughout their journey. Imamura Tomo explained that this practice was a vestige of the ancient folk belief that female genitals had magical powers that could help defeat wild beasts and demons in the mountains.[25]

Ginseng diggers were greatly interested in dreams they had in the mountains. In fact, they were known to be conscious of their dreams all year round. Imamura claimed that, "the interpretations of dreams was a discipline in itself that could never be understood unless the person was someone who served as an *ŏin* for many years."[26] Still, some of the simpler principles of interpretation were considered common knowledge. Dreams of killing an animal or person or witnessing the death or funeral of a person were known to be auspicious. If the person dying was an adult, the dream augured the discovery of a large ginseng whereas a small ginseng was to be expected if the dream featured a child's death. A crane with a red forehead flying into one's arms was considered a sure sign that

TABLE 16.1 Auspicious or ominous scenes in dreams. [Wu, "Shimmani sŭpsok ŭi pyŏnhwa yangsang," 18]

Auspicious Scenes	*Ominous Scenes*
• Capturing a pig • Receiving a white radish from an old, white-haired man • Killing a person or animal • A wild ginseng transforming into a person • A crane flying into one's arms • Carrying a corpse or child down a mountain on one's back • Embracing a child • Witnessing a corpse or carrying it on one's back • Witnessing a funeral • Embracing a fairy coming down from the heavens • A wild dog or tiger seizing a person and running away	• A barking dog • Witnessing mountains or fields covered with snow or ice • Witnessing a child but being unable to carry the child on one's back • Giving away a white radish received from someone else • Being delighted at the sight of a woman • Fooling around with a woman • Losing a captured pig • A staff breaking in the middle of a journey • A wild dog or tiger escaping while one was riding it

the person would find a root of good quality because the red forehead and white feathers symbolized the colors of the berries and root of ginseng.[27] Below is a list Wu Sŭng-ha put together of scenes in dreams that ginseng diggers tended to consider auspicious or ominous.

Upon discovering wild ginseng, a digger was to repeatedly shout that he spotted ginseng or *pangch'o*. *Pangch'o* was a slang term for ginseng that sounded similar to the word *bangchui* used in Manchuria to refer to wild ginseng, which again points to the deep historical connection between Korean and Manchurian ginseng diggers. The ginseng digger then had to drive his staff into the ground near the wild ginseng or sit near it if he didn't have a staff and wait until his colleagues gathered around him. The *ŏin* would then let the man who discovered the ginseng check the vicinity by himself. The purpose of doing so was to give him the sole right to gather all the ginseng in the vicinity, because wild ginseng tended to grow in patches. Then he would clear an area of about three square meters around the wild ginseng before carefully digging it out of the ground so that even the root hairs remained intact. The unearthed ginseng would be wrapped in the moss lying around it, called *sŏgŭi*, then encased in pieces of bark, and bound together with string. The packaged root would finally be placed in the sack of the ginseng digger who found it.[28]

Since Korea's liberation, it has been difficult to gather statistics on ginseng diggers because the policy requiring permission to gather wild ginseng was discontinued.[29] Moreover, the profession of ginseng digging has nearly died out with the extinction of wild ginseng, so the unique customs and practices of ginseng diggers now only remain as intangible cultural heritage.

American Ginseng Diggers

On the North American continent, ginseng diggers began to appear from the early eighteenth century. Around the time Lafitau first discovered American ginseng in Canada, the plant was mainly gathered by local indigenous peoples such as the Iroquois. Yet, as larger amounts of wild ginseng were discovered in Wisconsin and Minnesota to the west and in the Appalachians to the south, gathering wild ginseng gradually turned into a profession for white Americans. In fact, the discovery and collection of American ginseng went in tandem with the westward expansion of white Americans. News of ginseng's discovery therefore signaled the arrival of white settlers in the area. And as the number of white settlers increased, the depletion of ginseng quickened.[30]

Ginseng proved to be a very useful source of cash for white Americans who had no other means of living. In some cases, it even anchored the swift recovery of an entire area that had fallen into economic difficulty. One such case was the Minnesota River Valley in the 1850s. When a large number of settlers suddenly poured into the area, a new town was formed but soon fell into an economic depression. In a state of devastation, farmers in the area shifted their gaze to the wild ginseng growing in the so-called "Big Woods." Before long, ginseng buyers caught wind of the news and the ginseng trade in the area prospered rapidly enough for a ginseng drying station to be built at Lake Washington.[31]

After their first major harvest of ginseng, people in the Minnesota River Valley went into celebration. Mankato even held a "ginseng ball" where people danced merrily to the "Ginseng Polka."[32] A bard went as far as to come up with the following poem, "Dig Ginseng," which was a parody of the famous poem "Excelsior" by Henry Wadsworth Longfellow (1807–1882).

> The shades of night were falling fast,
> As o'er the muddy highway passed
> A youth, who bore, across a stick,
> A tin-pail, knapsack, hoe and pick!
> Dig Ginseng!
> ...
> A peasant said, in tones of spite,
> "Beware of the mosquito's bite!
> The root is scarce, the soil is tough!"
> A voice replied, far up the bluff,
> Dig Ginseng![33]
> ...

This poem about ginseng seems to stand in stark contrast to the poems East Asians wrote about the same plant. In East Asia, ginseng was traditionally exchanged as a rare gift between heads of state or dignitaries. It therefore served as good subject matter for the literati, and poems lauding ginseng settled in as a literary tradition in China, Korea, and Japan. Most poems extoled the form and efficacy of ginseng, but some also warned about its evil effects. The following poem, "Gaoli renshenzan" (高麗人參贊), which can be roughly translated as "A Laud to Korean Ginseng," is one of the oldest Chinese poems about ginseng, although *Bencao gangmu* notes that it was in fact written by a Korean.[34]

三椏五葉 Three stems and five leaves
背陽向陰 Lean away from the sun, toward the shade
欲來求我 Should you come for me
椵樹相尋 Look under the tree of heaven

The poem below was written by the Qianlong Emperor of the Qing dynasty, probably as a cautionary message that the inappropriate use of ginseng could be costly.[35]

五葉三椏長白珍 The plant with five leaves and three stems is a treasure of the Changbai Mountains
年深形肖竟何因 How come it grows more like man over time
太原土貢今焉是 Compared to what was once offered as tribute at Taiyuan
上黨沙生寧有眞 How can the *shashen* (沙蔘) from Shangdang (上黨) be considered the same
具體幾曾五官具 Since when did it have the five sensory organs
陳筐徒訝四支陳 Baskets full of their limp legs is a strange sight
雖緣滋補稱延命 They say life can be extended by eating healthy
頗見輕投致喪身 But quite a few have died from medicating freely
大約佐饔圖利益 Hoping to benefit from taking it hastily with food
遂忘剜肉值艱屯 is to forget the suffering to come from the depletion of flesh
草莖誰悟文殊語 Who could possibly gain the wisdom of Manjushri through herbs
能活人還能殺人 that can save or kill a man.

The above poem shows that East Asian poems often aesthetically contemplated the botanical features and natural habitats of ginseng or raised caution about the harmful effects of abusing ginseng. The poem Minnesotans apparently chanted, on the other hand, focused on the profits to be reaped from digging ginseng and made no reflections about the plant itself. Their poem was a work song that had nothing to do with literary sensitivity or moral values.

Writing on the "ginseng rush" in Minnesota, Seth K. Humphrey (1864–1932) claimed that "outside of China, ginseng has never been credited with having any particular medicinal value," yet added that, "but for those desperate settlers in Minnesota, ginseng—no doubt about it—was 'good medicine.'"[36] What Humphrey meant by "good medicine" had nothing to with the health benefits ginseng could provide for Minnesotans. The phrase referred to the fact that ginseng was much esteemed in China, which was why Minnesotans were able to economically benefit from the herb. This leaves little doubt that while Americans were eager to gather ginseng, they had no intention of embracing the herb as part of their own culture.

Upon hearing that good money could be made from gathering ginseng, some farmers switched their profession and people from different states swarmed in to join the rush.[37] Full-time ginseng diggers were people who didn't have to commit to farming tasks in September and October and typically hired more than ten workers at a time to help dig ginseng in the mountains. Each trip into the mountains required days of camping out in the wilderness with each day spent searching for ginseng. The employer usually provided shelter and food for the trip and the ginseng diggers had to equip themselves with a rifle and a double-headed seng hoe to dig up ginseng.[38]

While spades made of wood or animal bones were used in East Asia due to the belief that metal scared wild ginseng,[39] seng hoes used in North America had a double-edged iron head fixed to a wooden handle. One end of the head would be shaped like a pickax to break up hard ground and the other end would be shaped like a hoe, or in many cases a forked hoe with two prongs. Because seng hoes had long handles, they often served as hiking sticks as well. In addition to such long-handled seng hoes, some ginseng diggers carried seng hoes with handles as short as spades. These tools were usually homemade and therefore one-of-a-kind heirlooms passed down from generation to generation.

LaDonna Yeadon is a professional ginseng digger who works in the woods of Wisconsin and Minnesota. Her fiancé initially led her to ginseng hunting, a rare profession for women, and she committed herself to it even after his death. She treasures the 1.5-inch wide, 8-inch long seng hoe her fiancé left her, an excellent tool for digging ginseng according to Yeadon. To dig the root up with all its hairs intact, she suggests using a seng hoe to clear the ground around the plant and then working carefully with only the index and middle finger.[40]

Considering how ginseng diggers in East Asia formed exclusive groups and established traditions over time, there was nothing particularly refined about the way Americans gathered and processed ginseng. Still, they had their own insights and methods. Americans were clearly aware of the environment ginseng grew in. Since colonialists arrived in the early eighteenth century, records already noted that ginseng "is fond of shade, and of a deep rich mould, and of land which is neither wet nor high" or grows "among the hills that lie far from the sea."[41] Similar statements were made by many ginseng diggers across North America.

Below is how the "natural home of the ginseng plant" was summarized in an extensive manual on growing ginseng from 1912, compiled by John Henry Koehler (1866–?), the president of the Ginseng Growers Association of America.

> On the hills and ridges of a forest where the butternet, the sugar-marple, rock-elm, slippery-elm, birch, white-oak and basswood (or linden)

> around. We find that the topographical conditions provide for surface drainage in very wet weather; the porous nature of the subsoil further provides for subdrainage, as well as allow moisture to come up from below in times of drought ...
>
> We further find on the surface of the ground in such forest an abundance of leaves and rotted wood, covering the ground like a blanket.[42]

Have these American practices and understandings changed over the past century? According to Kenny Salwey (1943), ginseng prefers the "north slope, plenty of shade, cool temp[erature]s in summer, plenty of drainage." He adds that ginseng particularly likes to grow near basswood trees around dead oak stumps because they pump nutrients into the soil.[43] Salwey is known as "the last river rat" in the United States. The term "river rats" refers to hermits living alongside nature in the Mississippi River valley. Salwey came to fame when his everyday life of hunting and gathering, surviving all four seasons, became the subject of televised documentaries and a book. He is well acquainted with the aforementioned female ginseng digger LaDonna Yeadon, but unlike Yeadon, who gathers ginseng full time, Salwey treats ginseng gathering as a side job he takes up in the fall to earn some extra cash.

Lonzo Mullins, a ginseng digger in Virginia, testifies that he would sometimes find large ginseng plants "especially round old walnut trees" where "the ground is awful rich."[44] People in southern West Virginia believe that the discovery of bloodroot guarantees the discovery of ginseng because places where bloodroot grow are ideal habitats for ginseng.[45] Yeadon, on the other hand, tends to often discover ginseng near a patch of Jack-in-the-pulpits.[46] While various plants may indicate the presence of ginseng, they all tend to grow in rich, shaded soil with good drainage.

Knowing the conditions of ginseng's natural habitat does not, however, make it any easier to discover ginseng in thick woods. The easiest way to identify ginseng has been to catch sight of the plant's red berries. This is why ginseng diggers often say that they feel a triumphant rush upon spotting red ginseng berries among lush forest vegetation. One even said he knew he'd hit the jackpot the moment he laid eyes on the red berries,[47] which wasn't entirely an exaggeration since ginseng tends to grow in patches, such that the discovery of one makes it likely for hundreds more to exist nearby. For instance, 1,000 pounds of ginseng was once found in a single spot. Such instances are the reason why ginseng gathering has sometimes been likened to treasure hunting.[48]

The leaves of ginseng have been an alternate means of identification besides its red berries. Mullins prefers to dig up ginseng late in the fall because "just before it goes to a dying it turns yellow," making it stand out against the forest's color palette.[49] Once ginseng is found in a particular spot, more tends to be discovered in the same spot, which thereby becomes a repository (or even a retirement plan) for the ginseng digger who makes the initial discovery.[50] Recently, full-time ginseng diggers have often begun to sow seeds around the spot where they just dug up a root in the hopes of harvesting a large amount of ginseng in five years' time.

Marking the spot where ginseng was discovered has therefore been an important part of the job. In East Asia, a piece of red cloth would be tied close to the spot,[51] while Americans would leave a mark on a nearby tree or stick a flag on the spot. Upon spotting red ginseng berries, some would leave other personal marks with the intent of returning to claim their reward later on. Ginseng berries come into fruit in the summer when ginseng gathering is prohibited, which is why ginseng diggers wait until the fall or until the plant is fully grown before they return to dig it up.

While ginseng is collected in September and October, Yeadon hints that she surveys for potential patches earlier in August, especially in areas with many squirrels and chipmunks because ginseng can be more difficult to discover once the animals devour its berries in the summer. Yeadon says she tries to leave less obvious marks by using small nails instead of flags or pieces of cloth.[52] More recently, ginseng diggers even use GPS receivers instead of leaving any marks, in order to hide their findings from other diggers.[53]

The season for collecting ginseng begins in the fall because the plant tends to mature as fall turns to winter. A seasonal restriction on collecting ginseng, however, was legally introduced in the late twentieth century.[54] Previously, people driven by profit began digging up ginseng from the spring or whenever they came across the plant, regardless of the season. Such indiscriminate collection caused several problems. One was the depletion and near extinction of ginseng and another was that premature ginseng collected before the fall failed to raise satisfactory profits. The excerpt below shows how François André Michaux bemoaned the North American practice of ginseng gathering as early as 1793.

> The ginseng exported from America was so badly prepared, that it fell very low in price, and the trade almost entirely ceased, ... In Chinese Tartary this gathering belongs exclusively to the emperor. ... It commences in autumn, and continues all the winter, the epoch when the root has acquired its full degree of maturity and perfection. ... In the United States, on the contrary, they begin gathering of ginseng in the spring, and end at the decline of autumn. Its root, then soft and watery, wrinkles in drying, terminates in being extremely hard, and loses thus a third of its bulk, and nearly half its weight.[55]

Like his father André Michaux (1746–1802), who served Louis XVI as a royal botanist, Michaux was also a botanist who had been dispatched to North America by the French government. As a bureaucrat in the age of mercantilism, Michaux's writings demonstrate that he was focused not on preserving ginseng as a species, but on managing its quality so as to reap more profits. Despite being a botanist, he doesn't seem to have been at all concerned about extinction. This tendency was maintained even after the United States gained independence and control over the export of American ginseng. Yet, no matter how much profit American ginseng yielded, it was still clearly dirt cheap compared to Chinese ginseng. To boost American ginseng's profitability, some involved in patriotic discussions argued that ginseng must be "collected [at] a proper season and cured [in] the Chinese manner."[56]

China had clearly been the final destination of American ginseng from the very beginning. Chinese methods were a frame of reference for collecting and processing ginseng that weighed on American ginseng diggers and merchants, giving rise to a sense of inferiority. Some of them complained that, "the Chinese do not esteem that which grows in America, valuing only their own,"[57] while others self-deprecatingly admitted that, "we cannot preserve any root as [the Chinese] do Ginseng."[58]

Moreover, the indigenous seemed more knowledgeable than white Americans when it came to ginseng. In the late eighteenth century, the American economist Matthew Carey witnessed the indigenous laughing out loud at the sight of white Americans washing ginseng at a stream. According to Carey, ginseng must never be washed because although washing may remove the dark speckles and make the root appear closer to the yellow tint the Chinese prefer, it simultaneously drains out the plant's components. He even added that one unwashed, properly processed root was worth more than fifty barrels of ginseng prepared in a different manner.[59] As a twentieth-century ginseng digger, Yeadon testifies that to receive a fair price for ginseng, it should never come into contact with water and any moist soil on it should immediately be brushed off carefully with one's fingers.[60] Most ginseng has nevertheless been washed at a stream or even in a washing machine in some cases, as we will see below.

Drying, however, was far more important than washing ginseng. Because raw ginseng rots easily, drying was crucial in order for the root to be shipped far away. Ginseng would shrink to less than 50 percent of its original volume when dried, but curing the root was a very tricky process. Sources related to the exporting of ginseng would frequently mention that the root was supposed to be cured into a "clear shining colour, like the Chinese tea."[61] Merchants were well aware of this, according to the following report von Linné's apostle Peter Kalm authored in 1748.

> After the Indians have sold the fresh roots to the merchants, the latter must take a great deal of pains with them. They are spread on the floor to dry, which commonly requires two months and upwards, according as the season is wet or dry. During that time they must be turned once or twice every day, lest they should putrify or moulder … no one ever had been entirely acquainted with the Chinese method of preparing it. However it is thought that amongst other preparations they dip the roots in a decoction of the leaves of ginseng. The roots prepared by the Chinese are almost transparent, and look like horn in the inside; and the roots which are fit for use, must be heavy and compact in the inside.[62]

Despite warnings not to dry the root under direct sunlight or with fire, people would still resort to whatever method they found convenient. An American botany book from the early nineteenth century advised its readers that "the roots may also be dried in the sun, or by the fire, and retain their qualities perfectly."[63] One chemistry journal even informed its readers that since air was detrimental to ginseng's components, the root had to be sealed up as soon as it had been dug up then placed in iron pans to be exposed to gentle heat in a baking oven.[64]

To this day, ginseng diggers working independently tend to stick to their own routines developed through trial and error instead of following a proper manual. Yeadon informed that some ginseng diggers around her even put wild ginseng in a washing machine to dry the root. She, on the other hand, chooses to dry ginseng slowly by laying it across cardboard beer boxes spread out in a refrigerator, which is the method highly regarded by "the Chinaman" who brokers her ginseng.[65]

The price of wild ginseng roots can vary even if they come from the same batch. Roots tend to be worth more if they are bigger and shaped like a human being, with two leg-like rootlets splitting out of the main body.[66] This criterion has been established purely according to the preferences of the Chinese. Like their East Asian counterparts, North American ginseng diggers estimate how old a root is based on the number of wrinkles formed on its head and regard older roots with more wrinkles as premium ginseng.

The horizontal wrinkles around the main body, which American ginseng diggers call "stress rings," are also a crucial indicator because they prove that the root is genuine wild ginseng.[67] Some in Manchuria went as far as to fabricate rings around the head and body to make wild ginseng appear more valuable. Those capable of such fabrication were called "wild ginseng mechanics" and were admired by ginseng diggers for their techniques. According to Salwey, the rings suggest that wild ginseng had "weathered storm and drought and pushed their way past rock and clay and tree roots to survive."[68] Compared to smooth-surfaced cultivated ginseng, Chinese buyers were willing to pay far more for wild ginseng with many wrinkles, which is why dried cultivated ginseng was sold at fifteen dollars per pound whereas wild ginseng was sold at an average price of five hundred dollars per pound in the 2000s.[69]

Notes

1 Piao, "Qingchao fengjin shiqi chaoxianren fanyue shili yanjiu," 6; Zhang, "Qing qianqi dui yalujiang fengjinqu de guanxia," 52–61; Zhang, "Liutiaobian, yinpiao yu qingchao dongbei fengjin xinlun," 78–85.

2 Jiang Zhushan 蔣竹山, *Renshen diguo: Qingdai renshen de shengchan xiaofei yu yiliao* 人蔘帝國: 清代人蔘的生産消費與醫療 [Ginseng Empire: Qing China's Production and Consumption of Ginseng and Medicine] (Hangzhou: Zhejiang daxue chubanshe 浙江大學出版社, 2015), 21.

3 Tong, *Zhongguo dongbeishi*, 1590–1594; Kim, "Manjujok kwa insam," 21.

4 Tong Yonggong 佟永功, "Qingdia shengjing shenwu huodong shulue" 清代盛京蔘務活動述略 [A Summary of Qing Chinese Activities Related to Shengjing Ginseng], *Qingshi Yanjiu* 清史研究, no. 1 (2000): 43; Wang Peihuan

王佩環, "Qingdai dongbei caishenye de xingshuai" 清代東北采蔘業的興衰 [The Ginseng Industry's Rise and Fall in the Northeastern Areas of Qing China], *Shehuikexue Zhanxian* 社會科學戰線, no. 4 (1982): 189; Kim, "Manjujok kwa insam," 21.

5 Kim, "17–18 segi ch'ŏngdae insam chŏngch'aek ŭi pyŏnhwa," 411.

6 *Shengjing shenwu dangan shiliao* 盛京蔘務檔案史料 [Archived Material on Affairs Related to Shengjing Ginseng], 37–38 (康熙25/閏4/22); Kim, "17–18 segi ch'ŏngdae insam chŏngch'aek ŭi pyŏnhwa," 412.

7 Piao, "Qingchao fengjin shiqi chaoxianren fanyue shili yanjiu," 8.

8 Imamura, *Insamsa*, 2015, 6:222–223.

9 Henry Evan Murchison James, *The Long White Mountain, or, A Journey in Manchuria: with Some Account of the History, People, Administration and Religion of That Country* (London: Longmans, 1888).

10 James, *The Long White Mountain, or, A Journey in Manchuria*, 433.

11 Ch'oe Chun 최준, "Chungguk tongbuk chiyŏk ŭi min'ganshinang" 중국 동북지역의 민간신앙 [Folk Religion in Northeast China], *Chungang minsok'ak* 중앙민속학 12 (2007).

12 Ch'oe, "Chungguk tongbuk chiyŏk ŭi min'ganshinang," 111, 115–117.

13 Imamura, *Insamsa*, 2015, 6:223, 261.

14 Ch'oe, "Chungguk tongbuk chiyŏk ŭi min'ganshinang," 116.

15 Ch'oe, "Chungguk tongbuk chiyŏk ŭi min'ganshinang," 116–117.

16 Wu Sŭng-ha, "Shimmani sŭpsok ŭi pyŏnhwa yangsang" [The Changing Patterns of Simmani's Folkways], *Minsok'ak yŏn'gu*, no. 35 (2014): 7–8.

17 Yŏn Ho-t'aek, "Shimmemani ŭnŏ ŭi yŏn'gu: Odaesan chiyŏk ŭl chungshimŭro" [A Study of Shimmemani Jargon: Focused on the Mount Odae Area], *Kwandongdae nonmunjip* 21 (1992): 80–81.

18 *Chosŏn wangjo sillok* [Annals of the Chosŏn Dynasty], vol. 42, entry for June 4, 1795; *Chosŏn wangjo sillok*, vol. 51, entry for March 18, 1799; Wu, "Shimmani sŭpsok ŭi pyŏnhwa yangsang," 9–10.

19 Imamura, "Yama ninjin saishuri no fushu," 114.

20 Wu, "Shimmani sŭpsok ŭi pyŏnhwa yangsang," 14.

21 Imamura, "Yama ninjin saishuri no fushu," 114, 120.

22 Imamura, "Yama ninjin saishuri no fushu," 114.

23 Imamura, "Yama ninjin saishuri no fushu," 114–116.

24 Ch'oe Sŭng-sun, "Kangwŏndo chibang ch'aesamin sŭpsok" [The Manners and Customs of Ginseng Diggers in Kangwŏndo], *Han'guk minsok'ak* 8 (1975): 50; Wu, "Shimmani sŭpsok ŭi pyŏnhwa yangsang," 16.

25 Imamura, "Yama ninjin saishuri no fushu," 116–117.

26 Imamura, "Yama ninjin saishuri no fushu," 118.

27 Imamura, "Yama ninjin saishuri no fushu," 118–119.

28 Imamura, "Yama ninjin saishuri no fushu," 119–120.

29 Wu, "Shimmani sŭpsok ŭi pyŏnhwa yangsang," 11.

30 Manget, "Ginseng, China, and the Transformation of the Ohio Valley, 1783–1840," 17.

31 Willam E. Lass, "Ginseng Rush in Minnesota," *Minnesota History* 41 (1969): 250–251.

32 Lass, "Ginseng Rush in Minnesota," 254.

33 A poem by Henry R. Hayden. Levi N. Countryman Diary, May 25, 1859, Countryman Papers (Minnesota Historical Society); *Mankato Weekly Independent*, June 4, 1859.

34 Li, *Shinjuhae ponch'o kangmok*, 4:44.

35 The Qianlong Emperor of the Qing dynasty清高宗 弘曆, *Yuzhishi sanji* 御製詩三集 [Three Collections of Imperial Poems], vol. 38, comp. Jing Pu 蔣溥等, Gujin ti yibai sishisan shou古今體一百四十三首 [143 poems in the ancient and modern style]·

Yong renxingshen liuyun 詠人形蔘六韻; Kim, "Han-Chung insamshi ŭi yangsang kwa t'ŭkching," 316–317.
36 Seth King Humphrey, *Following the Prairie Frontier* (Minneapolis, MN: University of Minnesota Press, 1931), 33.
37 Lass, "Ginseng Rush in Minnesota," 253.
38 Mary Hufford, "Knowing Ginseng: The Social Life of an Appalachian Root," *Cahiers de Littérature Orale* 53, no. 4 (2003): 275.
39 Jeff Talarigo, *The Ginseng Hunter* (New York: Anchor Books, 2009), 12.
40 LaDonna Yeadon (Wausau, Wisconsin), interview by Heasim Sul, June 29, 2015.
41 Kalm, *Travels into North America*, 3:115; Adair, *The History of the American Indians*, 361–362.
42 Koehler, *Ginseng and Goldenseal Growers' Handbook*, 25.
43 Salwey and Bestul, *The Last River Rat*, 127.
44 Steve Mooney, "Ginseng and Appalachian Culture: Settlement to Contemporary Times," *Appalachian Heritage* 18, no. 3 (1990): 41.
45 David A. Taylor, "Getting to the Root of Ginseng," *Smithsonian Magazine*, 2002, https://www.smithsonianmag.com/science-nature/getting-to-the-root-of-ginseng-65654374.
46 Yeadon, interview.
47 Manget, "Ginseng, China, and the Transformation of the Ohio Valley, 1783–1840," 3.
48 Manget, "Ginseng, China, and the Transformation of the Ohio Valley, 1783–1840," 4.
49 Mooney, "Ginseng and Appalachian Culture," 41.
50 Salwey and Bestul, *The Last River Rat*, 134.
51 Talarigo, *The Ginseng Hunter*, 6.
52 Yeadon, interview.
53 Taylor, "Getting to the Root of Ginseng."
54 Through the 1977 Convention on International Trade in Endangered Species of Wild Fauna and Flora, American ginseng was designated as an endangered species in the United States and Canada. The United States Fish and Wildlife Service regulates ginseng in the country, specifically the plant's roots rather than the leaves and seeds. The export of ginseng is permitted in nineteen states, although details involving the issue of permits, season of collection, and export destination slightly vary by state. In general, wild ginseng can only be collected with a permit during a designated season and ginseng seeds must be sowed immediately on the spot where a plant has been dug up. Digging up premature roots is legally banned. A permit is required to sell collected ginseng, not to mention a separate permit in order to sell ginseng out of state or to export overseas.
55 Michaux, *Travels to the West of the Alleghany Mountains*, 170–171.
56 *The Gentleman's Magazine* 23 (1753): 209; Carey, *The American Museum, or, Universal Magazine*, 2:126–127.
57 Dodsley, *The General Contents of the British Museum*, 155.
58 Hill, *The Valerian or, the Virtues of That Root in Nervous Disorders*, 17.
59 Carey, *The American Museum, or, Universal Magazine*, 2:126–127.
60 Yeadon, interview.
61 Adair, *The History of the American Indians*, 362.
62 Kalm, *Travels into North America*, 3:117–118.
63 Bigelow, *American Medical Botany*, 2:85.
64 M. Calau, "Pharmacology. On Rad. Ginseng from Chinese Sources," *The Chemical Gazette* 1 (1842): 238.
65 Yeadon, interview.
66 Taylor, "Getting to the Root of Ginseng."
67 Hufford, "Knowing Ginseng," 266.
68 Salwey and Bestul, *The Last River Rat*, 125.
69 Taylor, "Getting to the Root of Ginseng."

17

GINSENG DIGGERS' IMAGE AND INTERNAL COLONIALISM

In North America, ginseng was at first gathered by indigenous peoples. As the "ginseng rush" intensified, indigenous ginseng diggers who made a fair amount of money from selling ginseng would sometimes face a moral hazard. They often became an alcoholic or committed various misdemeanors.[1] As white Americans gradually joined the profession of ginseng gathering beginning in the mid-eighteenth century, the indigenous saw them as competition. In the 1770s, white American ginseng diggers were even attacked or killed by indigenous people on the Virginia frontier. Such tragedies occurred as a result of turf wars over resources like medicinal herbs, fish, and ginseng in the forest. By the 1790s, ginseng came to be gathered mostly by white Americans.[2]

From the mid-nineteenth century, however, ginseng diggers began to be associated with an image unique compared to that of other professions. That image, portraying them as poor, ignorant "white trash," was developed mainly by the press. In 1867, the *New York Herald* described ginseng diggers in western North Carolina as a "wretched class of poor white [that] abound in the mountains."

> They rove from place to place and never seem to have a settled habitation. ... With their matted hair, beetling brows and dull, rayless eyes, from which not a spark of intelligence or human feeling beams, they look like idiots.[3]

Other mediums adopted a similar rhetoric to illustrate ginseng diggers in a negative light. The American nature essayist John Burroughs (1837–1921) once remarked that, "in nearly every back-settlement in New York and New England may be found one or more ginseng hunters, half-wild men."[4] Ginseng hunters were essentially characterized as barbaric, filthy drifters.

DOI: 10.4324/9781003286691-21

What was graver from a social aspect, however, was that ginseng diggers were treated and characterized as a specific type of group: they were regarded as an untamed collective group with their own unique culture and customs that separated them from the rest of the world. This negative rhetoric was in some ways deliberately produced by the press of the north as they eagerly covered circumstances in the south after the American Civil War. Journalists eager to underline the backwardness and inferiority of the South targeted ginseng diggers as a group that had gone astray when compared to the progressive north. Newspaper articles also portrayed ginseng diggers as folks with a rebellious streak, such as emancipated slaves or soldiers who ran away from the Union or Confederate armies. Such articles even argued that ginseng gathering had originally been carried out by "negroes," thereby defining white ginseng diggers as people who had fallen to the status of black slaves.[5]

The culture and customs of ginseng diggers were indeed different from those in the civilized sphere. The press emphasized that ginseng diggers were an anti-civilized group that cared only about themselves and had no concept of law, property rights, or the institution of marriage.[6] The following is how ginseng diggers deep in the mountains of West Virginia were described in a political review magazine in 1850.

> The inhabitants of this secluded mountain country, cut off from all intercourse with the rest of the world, are as primitive in their dress and manners as the hills around them. Their clothes are chiefly fabricated from the dressed skins of the deer; as well the women as the men. This article is well adapted to their occupation of digging "sang roots," and traversing the woods in quest of game; which affords much of their animal food. Mounted astride, on the back of a little pony, on top of a huge bag of roots, the women were hardly to be distinguished from the men. Huts, covered with bark, were erected in the most productive localities for ginseng; and the months of August and September, when the plant is in perfection, were spent in its collection. … Their code of morals was as rude and aboriginal as their diet. The men often exchanged their wives with each other, giving or taking some article as the difference in value; and sometimes sold them outright for a desirable horse or a fine rifle gun.[7]

The reason ginseng hunters had such barbaric customs, it was understood, was because their livelihoods depended entirely on ginseng. The press went as far as to define them as "a race separate and apart, whom progress has left full a century behind."[8]

From a civilized, urban point of view, ginseng diggers may have seemed like people living on the boundary between man and nature. The search for ginseng in fact involved struggles with nature. Roaming around the woods alone for days on end is a lonesome, dangerous affair that entails defending oneself from wild animals such as bears, snakes, and bees.[9] In an interview, Chang Seok-hoon, who has been a ginseng digger in the woods of Kentucky, Virginia, and West Virginia, mentioned the threats one can potentially face in the mountains. Since wild ginseng tends to be deep in the woods, it's very common for ginseng diggers to run into large animals like bears, although, according to Chang, bears can become less terrifying if a ginseng digger comes across the same bear often enough for them to recognize each other.

Rather, snakes happen to be the most threatening creature. In Chang's experience, snakes in American forests tend to be very large, yet nimble, and because many of them live in trees they are likely to attack from behind or bite the neck. This is why Chang suggests it is necessary to carry a backpack tall enough to reach above one's head.[10] Yeadon also named snakes like the timber rattlesnake as the most dangerous creature a ginseng digger can run into in the woods of Wisconsin and Minnesota. A smell tart like dill pickles indicates that a rattlesnake is lurking nearby, and she added that it's necessary to be cautious with snakes in the process of shedding their skin because they can be particularly aggressive when the skin compromises their vision.[11]

In the post-Civil War years, some writers in the north nevertheless romanticized the lives of ginseng diggers, calling them "happy-go-lucky figures totally free from the shackles of civilization." This was most likely a contrived definition that marked the growing number of laborers and the poor in the country as their antithesis.[12] Ginseng diggers who chose freedom appeared to enjoy a better quality of life than the many immigrant laborers who were surfacing as a threat to employment in the north or the poor tied to their land in the south. The following passage from 1882 by Guy La Tourette reflects this romanticization of ginseng diggers.

> But I confess that wandering the mazes of the wild hills and mountains, by the side of rocky, foaming trout streams, and through the cool wind-swept forests in pursuit of one's livelihood is far more agreeable to one's senses and feelings than hoeing corn on a blistering hillside during the dog days, and even for those who do not have to dig ginseng for a living there is a strange fascination in the search for the plant that cannot be fully understood except by those who have experienced it.[13]

In some ways, however, that "strange fascination" bordered on supernatural or shamanistic properties impossible for the rationality of the civilized to grasp. Based on dialectical versions of the word ginseng such as *seng* or *sang*, ginseng diggers were sometimes called *seng digger*, *senger*, *sang digger*, *sanger*, or *shang diggers*. They were also commonly referred to as ginseng hunters because unlike other plants that could simply be picked, ginseng was understood as a plant that had to be hunted. To its hunters, ginseng seemed like an animal on the move rather than a plant rooted to the ground. They often believed ginseng had the remarkable ability to hide or run away from its original location.[14] A 1908 manual on ginseng gathering remarked that ginseng "hides away from man with seeming intelligence."[15]

It is therefore no surprise that mysterious, evasive, and elusive are the adjectives ginseng diggers most frequently use to describe ginseng. Experienced ginseng diggers know that ginseng grows "where the brambles are thickest, the hills steepest, and loggers have left enough oak tops to stop a Humvee."[16] Ginseng is known to go dormant at times when conditions grew detrimental or too dry. One ginseng digger confessed that, "you never know where you're going to find ginseng," and ginseng "seems to reveal itself on its own terms, making contact with the digger before the digger notices it."[17] Salwey remarked that *shang* hunters "talk about how a plant 'lays' on a slope" and try not to "lose their souls to the plant."[18]

Oddly enough, the mysterious aura surrounding ginseng became associated with Orientalism toward China. The following was brought up in an editorial from 1846 about the export of American ginseng published in the bulletin of the National Institution for the Promotion of Science.

> As the Chinese are very superstitious and whimsical in their opinions and actions, and governed or influenced more or less by them, it is owing to this that they put up so much more value on that brought from Tartary, as I was informed by several Chinese, that their ginseng comes from the "cold country (Tartary)," and is found but on one island, which is inhabited by tigers, making it very dangerous to visit it, and that the ginseng is without leaves, and therefore cannot be seen in the day-time, but at night a flame issues from it, at which time the island is visited by those who wish to procure it, and shoot arrows at the place, leaving them to mark the spot, until the next day, when the roots are dug up.[19]

The editorial originally sought to argue that the quality of clarification through steaming and drying has to be improved to export ginseng at higher prices. What stands out more than this argument is, however, the way the customers of ginseng are described as "peculiar people, who are so exceedingly tenacious of their prejudices and predilections."[20] Despite being customers of an American commodity, the author draws a line drawn between his compatriots and the Chinese and mocks the latter by referring to them as peculiar people.

This derisive view was not only directed toward the outside. American ginseng diggers who breathed animation into ginseng were considered akin to the Chinese, characterized as peculiar people for their supernatural tales about ginseng and attachment toward the plant. The rhetoric that otherized ginseng as an exclusive property of China pushed American ginseng diggers out of the realm of ordinary citizens. The testimony by ginseng diggers that gathering ginseng is a very lonesome, covert affair can therefore be understood in more than one sense.[21] Loneliness may be a natural consequence of roaming the vast wilderness alone, but cultural prejudice against ginseng diggers may have been caused them to grow lonelier and secretive.

Although ginseng played a crucial role in eighteenth- to nineteenth-century North American economy, American mainstream culture strictly identified ginseng as a Chinese item and thereby marginalized people whose lives depended on the plant. The merchants and investors who exported ginseng, on the other hand, made their mark on the history of American capitalism's development. However, their connection to ginseng was thoroughly concealed. Mentions of ginseng are very difficult to find in American history textbooks and many Americans today are still unaware of the fact that ginseng is being grown in their own country.

The people who hunt ginseng and the communities they form have thus become characterized as economically primitive and culturally disparate. Their places of living have come to exhibit characteristics of an internal colony.[22] Lenin and Antonio Gramsci took note of the potential for colonialism to exist not only between different countries but within a country as well. Their conceptualization of internal colonialism suggested that severe economic inequalities between regions within a state can allow the core to exploit and marginalize the periphery.

The central Appalachians, spread across West Virginia, Virginia, Kentucky, and Tennessee, can be referred to as an internal colony in the United States. The region is the most economically lagging in the country. Yet, it produces more than half of the wild ginseng the country exports, not necessarily because wild ginseng grows profusely in the region but because many professional ginseng diggers are based there.[23] The region's underdevelopment is not, however, limited to its economic circumstances. It is a place where a mysterious world of incantations reminiscent of China and a past Americans have overcome coexist. People who dig up ginseng there are ordinary American citizens, but they tend to be perceived as a completely different race.

In 2014, the History Channel broadcast *Appalachian Outlaws*. The documentary/reality show followed five ginseng diggers in West Virginia during the ginseng gathering season from September 1 to November 30 to show what happens while they are in the woods. It vividly captured the dynamic scenes that unfolded between professional ginseng diggers, their family members, landowners, brokers, and occasional drifters who came into the mountains looking for ginseng.

When the "ginseng fever" surfaces every fall, ginseng diggers take turns standing watch at night and lay traps to drive thieves away. They do not hesitate to get into fistfights with folks from a neighborhood nearby or aim rifles at them for trespassing into their own ginseng hunting area. Brokers travel through multiple areas and fiercely engage in schemes, conciliations, and conflicts to reap more profits. In the Appalachians, where ginseng is the ticket to power and status, some are lucky enough to hit the jackpot while others suffer misfortune as they each take part in a cut-throat competition for profit. When *Appalachian Outlaws* premiered between January and March in 2014, more than three million watched the show.

Appalachian Outlaws reflected, reinforced, and spread the American society's distorted view of ginseng and ginseng diggers. Through it, the negative image of ginseng diggers formed in the late nineteenth century was being reproduced and widely distributed in the twenty-first century. Through a medium with an impact incomparable to newspapers, ginseng diggers were turned into a spectacle, a human zoo. They were portrayed as emotional characters without an ounce of rationality. The rampant swearing and violence made the documentary seem more like a reality show presenting a summation of crudeness, which made it hard to believe that it was actually produced by the History Channel.

American folklorist Mary Hufford accused the show of using ginseng diggers to reenact the Wild West frontier.[24] The main characters seemed to be more familiar with force than law and acknowledged nothing but their internal rules, and a major theme of the show featured their aversion toward and exclusion of people from the outside. Hufford criticized that the show for depicted ginseng diggers as isolated, violent figures who looked like the successors of the outlaws of the Wild West. Equally problematic was the way the camera glamorized the ginseng diggers' trespassing into other people's property and poaching the ginseng in the vicinity; an image reminiscent of the acquisition of land through homesteading in the Wild West.

What Hufford overlooked is the role that ginseng itself plays at the center of this chaotic social and economic environment. Ginseng has overthrown the legend of the American frontier. Unlike the days when the indigenous Americans were slaughtered and Chinese laborers were exploited for gold mining, Chinese Americans now call the shots as white Americans dig up ginseng. Chinese Americans travel through areas producing ginseng to buy the root or run wholesale businesses in major cities such as New York and San Francisco that monopolize export channels to China. They are the ones who order ginseng and determine its grade and price, which means they have the power to affect the livelihoods of white American ginseng diggers.

These circumstances can be witnessed in *Appalachian Outlaws* when the main characters face their Chinese American wholesaler in New York. They panic because their harvest falls short of the ordered amount and travel all the way to New York to bribe and appeal to the wholesaler. Following their journey to New York, the show accentuates the foreignness of Chinatown by featuring a neighborhood flooded with Chinese characters.

The Chinese American wholesaler is blurred or filmed from the back but never from the front. His presence nevertheless seems as omniscient as Big Brother in George Orwell's novel *Nineteen Eighty-Four.* The show thereby portrays such formidable wholesalers as Americans who built a China of their own in New York and treat ginseng diggers like colonists.

The final destination of the ginseng amassed by such wholesalers is China, which means the root can never become wholly American. While ginseng diggers are people linked to the root's mysterious appeal, they can never create the appeal on their own and are therefore stuck in between Chinese and American cultural frames. Americans have not been able to embrace the mysterious export item as part of their own culture. Even in the twenty-first century, American ginseng diggers seem to have little choice but to continue bearing the image of anti-civilized, estranged barbarians trapped in the past.

Notes

1 Schorger, "Ginseng: A Pioneer Resource," 67.
2 Manget, "Ginseng, China, and the Transformation of the Ohio Valley, 1783–1840," 15.
3 "North Carolina," *New York Herald*, April 29, 1867.
4 John Burroughs, "Ginseng-Hunting," *St. Nicholas: An Illustrated Magazine for Young Folks* 15, no. 7 (1888): 518.
5 Manget, "Sangin'io the Mountains," 39.
6 "Roots and Herbs," *The Farmer's Cabinet*, September 20, 1871; "The Shy Sang Diggers," *New York Sun*, December 20, 1894; "Kentucky Mountaineers," *Morning Oregonian*, January 18,1895; "Saugers," *Springfield Republican*, November 8, 1878.
7 "A History of the Divining Rod; with the Adventures of an Old Rodsman," *United States Magazine and Democratic Review* 26 (1850): 323–324.
8 "The Ginseng Digger," *Cincinnati Commercial Tribune*, March 8, 1889.
9 "Seng Talk and Ginseng Tales" in the Coal River Folklife Collection (AFC 1999/008), American Folklife Center, Library of Congress.
10 Chang Seok-hoon (Los Angeles), interview by Heasim Sul, July 7, 2015.
11 Yeadon, interview.
12 Manget, "Sangin'io the Mountains," 45.
13 Guy la Tourette, "Ginseng and Its Diggers," *The Pharmaceutical Journal and Transactions* 7 (1882): 379.
14 Hufford, "Knowing Ginseng," 283–284.
15 Arthur Robert Harding, "Ginseng Habits," in *Ginseng and Other Medicinal Plants* (Columbus, OH: A. R. Harding Publishing Co., 1908).
16 Salwey and Bestul, *The Last River Rat*, 125.
17 Interview with Ernie Scarbrough, a ginseng digger in Rock Creek, quoted from Hufford, "Knowing Ginseng," 273.
18 Salwey and Bestul, *The Last River Rat*, 130–131.
19 The National Institute for the Promotion of Science, *Fourth Bulletin of the National Institute for the Promotion of Science, February 1845 to November 1846*, 554.
20 The National Institute for the Promotion of Science, *Fourth Bulletin of the National Institute for the Promotion of Science, February 1845 to November 1846*, 555.
21 Salwey and Bestul, *The Last River Rat*, 126; Taylor, "Getting to the Root of Ginseng"; Adam Federman, "Digging the Root," *Adirondack Life*, no. September/October (2012): 36.
22 Michael Hechter, *Internal Colonialism* (Berkeley, CA: University of California Press, 1975).
23 Hufford, "Knowing Ginseng," 267.
24 Mary Hufford, "Review of Appalachian Outlaws," *Journal of Appalachian Studies* 20, no. 2 (2014): 234–239.

EPILOGUE

In 1974, Immanuel Wallerstein published *The Modern World-System I*, proposing that the modern world be analyzed as an interrelated system.[1] He argued that based on modes of production, a world can be divided into a core, periphery, and semi-periphery, which altogether emerged as a world economic system around 1550 and developed into the capitalist world economy. The core dominates highly profitable activities of production under a transnational division of labor and gains surplus production from the non-core, demonstrating a process that runs through an intricate nexus between capital and state apparatuses. Unlike the core, where wage labor is predominant, the periphery depends on coercive modes of production—such as slavery on plantations—and surrenders surplus production to the economically dominant core. Meanwhile, the semi-periphery is dominated by the core but dominates the periphery, thereby serving as an intermediary for the smooth operation of the world economy.

Wallerstein's world-systems theory greatly stirred academic circles in its breaking from previous historical narratives that revolved around an individual country to suggest a globally interconnected perception of the world. Surely enough, the theory has continued to receive much criticism ever since. Critiques varied: some were resistant to its perceived excessive schematization, some mentioned a lack of empirical evidence to support the theory, and some pointed out that the theory's characterization of the state's relationship with capitalism is overly consolidated or independent. Arguing against Wallerstein's regarding of world capitalism as an invention of modern Europe, Janet L. Abu-Lughod even claimed that a premodern world-system already existed across Eurasia by the thirteenth century.[2]

Meanwhile, Kenneth Pomeranz argues that from the ancient to medieval times, China and India were far more developed than Europe, so that upon entering the modern times, there was almost no difference between them and

Europe in terms of economic capability. The change Pomeranz refers to as the "Great Divergence" was triggered by coincidence and violence around 1820, which means Europe only managed to gain hegemony a mere two centuries ago.[3] Andre Gunder Frank goes further to insist that Europe has never held a central position within the world-system. According to Frank, the origin of a single world-system already manifested 5,000 years ago, and China has always been at its center.[4] What Pomeranz and Frank's argument have in common is that they basically reject Wallerstein's Eurocentrism. Unlike its original intent to overcome Eurocentrism, Wallerstein's theory is typically and erroneously Eurocentric insofar as it illustrates the process through which a system born in Western Europe expands and absorbs the world.

In terms of focusing on a particular commodity to examine the world-systems theory, ginseng can serve as an example to establish that Wallerstein's Eurocentric approach is flawed. As a result of the Age of Discovery, ginseng turned into a global commodity soon after its introduction to Europe in the early seventeenth century, but Western Europe was never able to take a central position when it came to ginseng. To begin with, the ginseng trade operated under a dual structure, with a global trade network surrounding East Asia at the core. Over a long period of time, Korea, China, and Japan weaved a complex distribution network through which ginseng was offered as a tributary item or diplomatic gift, or traded via authorized and unauthorized channels. A network outside East Asia, on the other hand, only emerged in the seventeenth century and consisted of two different routes for trading ginseng.

Through one route, Korean ginseng was shipped west, passing through several trade ports in Southeast Asia before arriving in Europe. Through the other route, ginseng discovered in North America in the early eighteenth century set out on a long journey around the globe to reach Guangzhou. The leading force in this external trade network then became replaced. America began to nearly monopolize the ginseng trade between East and West, replacing the hegemony Britain had held since the late eighteenth century. At a time when absolute hegemony was supposed to lie in the hands of Western Europe according to Wallerstein's theory, the axis of this outer circuit for trading ginseng had soon shifted to America.

Moreover, although the West traded ginseng, it could never become a Western commodity. During the 300 years between the voyages of Christopher Columbus and the Industrial Revolution, three types of trade were responsible for establishing a capitalist world-system: slaves traded from Africa to the New World, tremendous amounts of gold and silver mined in the Americas and exported to Europe and Asia, and lastly, "drugs" such as sugar, coffee, tea, chocolate, and tobacco.[5] Like other addictive luxuries, ginseng attracted great interest among Europeans and surfaced as an object of detailed botanical studies for prominent scientific groups at the time.

Nevertheless, while other addictive foods ran into the fate of being produced through slave labor at colonial plantations, mercantile Europe, despite its many efforts, failed at transplanting and cultivating ginseng. Instead, the discovery of ginseng in North America sparked a ginseng rush, allowing the United States, a newborn state struggling to find an exportable commodity, to succeed in initiating trade with China by sending a ship full of ginseng. Other crops grown at plantations were sent to Europe to be transformed into a "European commodity" before being distributed for sale around the world, but North America was in a haste to ship ginseng to China as soon as it went through a minimal drying process. As such, American ginseng never managed to escape its status as a second-rate commodity.

Although it exported vast amounts of ginseng, the United States failed at securing dominance over the commodity. The demand for, grading of, and pricing of ginseng were all determined by the importing country, China. Being no match for East Asia in terms of techniques for processing ginseng, the United States suffered from a sense of inferiority but had to settle for the fact that it was able to export ginseng. And because the country had been preoccupied with exporting ginseng, it could never become a domestic product and thus deprived Americans of opportunities to thoroughly experience and use it.

Paradoxically, the West's inability to seize hegemony in the ginseng trade caused the consumption of ginseng to be limited to East Asia. China seemed to suck in all of the world's supply, like a massive grave of ginseng. Yet, this notion did not only describe the manner in which ginseng flowed to China. It also spawned the perception that ginseng was an exclusive property of China.

Wallerstein considered "geoculture" as a cultural framework that allows modern world-systems to function efficiently.[6] According to the concept of geoculture, based on liberalism and scientism, ginseng was an object a West-centric geoculture could never subsume. Nineteenth-century Western scientists laid the foundations for modern medicine and pharmacy as they extracted active components from beneficial foreign plants. However, they failed to do so with ginseng. Without a precise understanding of ginseng's medicinal properties, the West remained unable to challenge the knowledge system of East Asia that had a far longer history of utilizing ginseng. Eventually, instead of incorporating ginseng into their own knowledge system, Western medicine and pharmacy chose to depreciate and ostracize the root's efficacy. This was contradictory to the West's dependence on Eastern medical traditions when exporting American ginseng, arguing that the efficacy of American ginseng was on par with that of Korean ginseng.

As a result, Western discourse marginalized ginseng from its mainstream culture by defining ginseng as a mysterious exclusive property of China that embodied autocracy, extravagance, debauchery, and irrationality. This discriminating gaze also extended to the people and places where ginseng was used, perpetuating a distinction between themselves and others across all terrains of knowledge. As the main consumers of ginseng, Asians became agents of actions projecting all the negative attributes associated with ginseng. Even American ginseng hunters have been perceived as people of the periphery, and who have

"Oriental" traits. Ginseng is still trapped in an inferior, irrational Orientality even as ginsenoside has been clearly identified an active component in ginseng and many countries in the West now grow and export ginseng. This speaks to a history of clashes between a global ginseng economy revolving around East Asia and a West-centrism wishing to deny this reality. Such clashes and discord are the reason why Western historical studies have neglected to examine ginseng.

A global history of ginseng validates the proposition that the success or failure of medical therapy depends not only on its efficacy but also on the historical, cultural conditions under which it is administered. Cultural lines are drawn across all spheres of science and such a disposition possesses a persistence that cannot be easily corrected through the objective results of an experiment. In today's turbulent currents of globalization, the social life of commodities like ginseng needs to be studied from the perspective of the humanities and social sciences, especially from a historical perspective, so as to look beyond their pharmacological action or present, commercial effects to form a truly balanced worldview.

Notes

1 Immanuel Wallerstein, *The Modern World-System I: Capitalist Agriculture and the Origins of the European World-Economy in the Sixteenth Century* (New York: Academic Press, 1974).
2 Janet L. Abu-Lughod, *Before European Hegemony: The World System A.D. 1250–1350* (New York: Oxford University Press, 1989).
3 Kenneth Pomeranz, *The Great Divergence: China, Europe, and the Making of the Modern World Economy* (Princeton, NJ: Princeton University Press, 2000).
4 Andre Gunder Frank and Barry Gills, eds., *The World System: Five Hundred Years or Five Thousand?* (Lanham, MD: Routledge, 1996); Andre Gunder Frank, *Reorient: Global Economy in the Asian Age* (Berkeley, CA: University of California Press, 1998).
5 Pomeranz and Topik, *The World That Trade Created*, Part 3 The Economic Culture of Drugs.
6 Conceived in analogy to geopolitics, geoculture refers to norms and forms of discourse broadly recognized for their legitimacy within a world-system. Wallerstein argued that a geoculture is created instead of being automatically guaranteed to exist with the establishment of a world-system. Immanuel Wallerstein, *World-Systems Analysis: An Introduction* (Durham, NC and London: Duke University Press, 2004), Ch. 4 The Creation of a Geoculture.

BIBLIOGRAPHY

1. Archival Sources and Interviews

BM. Dept. of MSS., Sloane MS 1847, f. 68. 2 April [1679].

L. C. John Holker Papers (JHP), reel 15, folio 5888.

Levi N. Countryman Diary, May 25, 1859, Countryman Papers [the Minnesota Historical Society].

Nat. Hist. Museum (BM), Botany Library, Sir Hans Sloane-Vegetables and vegetable substances, nos. 887, 12140 and 12141.

The Coal River Folklife Collection (AFC 1999/008) [Library of Congress collection].

Interview with LaDonna Yeadon [June 29, 2015, Wausau, Wisconsin].

Interview with Will Hsu [June 30, 2015, Wausau, Wisconsin].

Interview with Chang Seok-hoon [July 7, 2015, Los Angeles].

2. Newspapers

Aberdeen Weekly Journal

Birmingham Daily Post

Caledonian Mercury

Cincinnati Commercial Tribune

Daily News

Freeman's Jounal and Daily Commercial Advertiser

Glasgow Herald

Hampshire Telegraph and Sussex Chronicle

Joongang Ilbo

Liverpool Mercury

London Gazette

Manchester Times
Mankato Weekly Independent
Morning Oregonian.
New York Herald
New York Sun
North China Daily News
Oil and Drug News
Peking Gazette
Reynold's Newspaper
Springfield Republican
The Belfast News-Letter
The China Press
The China Weekly Review
The Derby Mercury
The Dong-A Ilbo
The Era
The Examiner
The Farmer's Cabinet
The Graphic
The Hull Packet and East Riding Times
The Hull Packet and Humber Mercury
The Leeds Mercury
The Manchester Guardian
The Manchester Times
The Manchester Times and Gazette
The Morning Chronicle
The Newcastle Weekly Courant
The North China Herald and Supreme Court & Consular Gazette.
The Northern Star and National Trades' Journal
The Observer
The Pall Mall Gazette
The Preston Guardian
The Richmond Dispatch
The Times
Western Mail
Wilmington Daily Herald

3. Printed Materials

A Companion to Every Place of Curiosity and Enjoyment in and about London and Westminster. London, 1767.

"A Great Market for Ginseng, Annual Report of Consul Johnson, Dated Amoy, China, July 29, 1897." In *Consular Reports: Commerce, Manufactures, Etc.*, Vol. 60. Washington, DC: Government Printing Office, 1897.

"A History of the Divining Rod; With the Adventures of an Old Rodsman." *United States Magazine and Democratic Review*, Vol. 26 (1850): 218–25.
Abercrombie, John. *The Propagation and Botanical Arrangements of Plants and Trees*, Vol. 2. London, 1784.
Abu-Lughod, Janet L. *Before European Hegemony: The World System A.D. 1250–1350*. New York: Oxford University Press, 1989.
Adair, James. *The History of the American Indians*. London, 1775.
Adams, John. *Modern Voyages: Containing a Variety of Useful and Entertaining Facts*, Vol. 2. London, 1790.
Aikin, John. *A Manual of Materia Medica*. Yarmouth, 1785.
Ainslie, Whitelaw. *Materia Indica*, Vol. 1. London, 1826.
Akin, James. *Encyclopaedia: Or, a Dictionary of Arts, Sciences, and Miscellaneous Literature*, Vol. 8. Philadelphia, PA, 1798.
Alleyne, James. *A New English Dispensatory*. London, 1733.
American Philosophical Society. *Transactions of the American Philosophical Society*, Vol. 1. Philadelphia, PA, 1771.
Anderson, James. *Recreations in Agriculture, Natural-History, Arts, and Miscellaneous Literature*, Vol. 6. London, 1802.
Anderson, Stuart. "Pharmacy and Empire: The 'British Pharmacopoeia' as an Instrument of Imperialism 1864 to 1932." *Pharmacy in History*, Vol. 52, no. 3 (2010): 112–21.
Anderson, William. *The London Commercial Dictionary and Sea-Port Gazetteer*. London: Printed for Effingham Wilson, 1819.
Appleby, John H. "Ginseng and the Royal Society." *Notes and Records of the Royal Society of London*, Vol. 37, no. 2 (1983): 121–45.
Asahina, Y., and B. Taguchi. "The Constituents of Ginseng." *Yakugaku Zasshi*, Vol. 26 (1906): 549–73.
Balfour, Edward, ed. *Cyclopaedia of India and of Eastern and Southern Asia*. Madras: The Scottish Press, 1857.
Bankes, Thomas, Edward Warren Blake, and Alexander Cook. *A New Royal Authentic and Complete System of Universal Geography Antient and Modern*. London, 1790.
Barnes, Linda L. *Needles, Herbs, Gods, and Ghosts: China, Healing, and the West to 1848*. Cambridge, MA: Harvard University Press, 2005.
Barton, William P. C. *Compendium Florae Philadelphicae*, Vol. 2. Philadelphia, PA: M. Carey and Son, 1818.
Batsaki, Yota, Sarah Burke Cahalan, and Anatole Tchikine, eds. *The Botany of Empire in the Long Eighteenth Century*. Washington, DC: Dumbarton Oaks, 2017.
Bayle, Antoine Laurent Jessé. *Encyclopédie Des Sciences Médicales*. Paris, 1841.
Belchingen, Count, and J. A. Cope. *An Essay on the Virtues and Properties of the Ginseng Tea*. London, 1786.
Belden, Louise Conway. "Humphry Marshall's Trade in Plants of the New World for Gardens and Forests of the Old World." *Winterthur Portfolio*, Vol. 2 (1965): 106–26.
Berg, Maxine. "In Pursuit of Luxury, Global History and British Consumer Goods in the Eighteenth Century." *Past and Present*, no. 182 (2004): 85–142.
Bevan, John. "Charles Spalding's Diving Bells." Presented to a meeting of the Historical Diving Society at Norwegian Underwater Institute, Bergen, 5 November 2005.
Bigelow, Jacob. *American Medical Botany*, Vol. 2. Boston: Cummings and Hilliard, 1818.
Birch, Thomas. *The History of the Royal Society of London*. London, 1737.
Bivins, Roberta. *Alternative Medicine?: A History*. Oxford: Oxford University Press, 2007.
Blaut, James Morris. *The Colonizer's Model of the World: Geographical Diffusionism and Eurocentric History*. New York: Guilford, 1993.

Blumenthal, Mark. "Milestones in Pharmaceutical Botany Since 1960." *Pharmacy in History*, Vol. 38, no. 1 (1996): 24–28.

Board of Trade. *Tables of the Revenue, Population, Commerce of the United Kingdom, Part III*. London: William Clowes, 1834.

Boerhaave, Herman. *Boerhaave's Treatise of the Materia Medica*. London, 1739.

Boivin, Bernard. "La Flore Du Canada En 1708: Étude d'un Manuscrit de Michel Sarrazin et Sébastien Vaillant." *Études Littéraires*, Vol. 10, no. 1–2 (1977): 223–97.

Bossu, Jean-Bernard. *Travels through That Part of North America Formerly Called Louisiana by Mr. Bossu, Captain in the French Marines*. Translated by John Reinhold Forster, Vol. 1. London, 1771.

Breen, Timothy H. "An Empire of Goods: The Anglicization of Colonial America, 1690–1776." *Journal of British Studies*, Vol. 25, no. 4 (1986): 467–99.

Brookes, Richard. *The General Dispensatory*. London, 1773.

Buchan, William, and Joseph Granville Norwood. *Domestic Medicine: A Treatise on the Prevention and Cure of Diseases*. Cincinnati, OH: U. P. James, 1838.

Burroughs, John. "Ginseng-Hunting." *St. Nicholas: An Illustrated Magazine for Young Folks*, Vol. 15, no. 7 (1888): 518–20.

Byrd, William. *The Prose Works of William Byrd of Westover*. Edited by Louis B. Wright. Cambridge, MA: Harvard University Press, 1966.

———. *The Writings of Colonel William Byrd of Westover in Virginia Esqr*. Edited by John Spencer Bassett. New York: Doubleday, Page & Co., 1901.

Calau, M. "Pharmacology. On Rad. Ginseng from Chinese Sources." *The Chemical Gazette*, Vol. 1 (1842): 236–38.

Camões, Luís de. *The Lusiad: Or, the Discovery of India*. Translated by William Julius Mickle. Oxford, 1776.

Carey, Mathew, ed. *The American Museum, or Repository of Ancient and Modern Fugitive Pieces, & c*, Vol. 2. Philadelphia, PA, 1787.

———, ed. *The American Museum, or, Universal Magazine*, Vol. 7. Philadelphia, PA, 1790.

Carles, William Richard. *Life in Corea*. London: Macmillan, 1888.

Carlson, Alvar W. "Ginseng: America's Botanical Drug Connection to the Orient." *Economic Botany*, Vol. 40, no. 2 (1986): 233–49.

Carver, Jonathan. *The New Universal Traveller*. London, 1779.

Cauwenberghe, Eddy van, ed. *Precious Metals, Coinage and the Changes of Monetary Structures in Latin-America, Europe and Asia*. Leuven: Leuven University Press, 1989.

Chakrabarti, Pratik. *Materials and Medicine: Trade, Conquest and Therapeutics in the Eighteenth Century*. Manchester: Manchester University Press, 2010.

———. "Medical Marketplaces beyond the West: Bazaar Medicine, Trade and the English Establishment in Eighteenth-Century India." In S. R. Mark Jenner and Patrick Wallis, eds. *Medicine and the Market in England and Its Colonies, c. 1450 –c. 1850*. Basingstoke: Palgrave Macmillan, 2007: 196–215.

Chang, Il-moo 장일무. *Han'guk insam sanŏpsa* 한국인삼산업사 [*A History of the Korean Ginseng Industry*], Vol. 2. Seoul: Korean Ginseng Corporation 한국인삼공사, 2018.

Charlevoix, Pierre-François-Xavier de. *Journal d'un Voyage Fait Par Ordre Du Roi Dans l'Amérique Septentrionale*. Edited by Pierre Berthiaume, Vol. 2. Montréal, QC: Les presses de l'Université de Montréal, 1994.

Chen, Jinghe 陳景河. "Renshen wenhua de kangdingzhizuo: Sun wencai jiaoshou zhongguo renshen wenhua xu" 人蔘文化的扛鼎之作: 孙文采教授 中國人蔘文化序 [A Masterpiece on Ginseng Culture: The Preface of Professor Sun Wencai's Zhongguo Renshen Wenhua]. *Renshen yanjiu* 人蔘研究, Vol. 25, no. 3 (2013): 62–64.

Chen, Wei, Prabhu Balan, and David G. Popovich. "Ginsenosides Analysis of New Zealand–Grown Forest Panax Ginseng by LC-QTOF-MS/MS." *Journal of Ginseng Research*, Vol. 44, no. 4 (2020): 552–62.

Ch'oe, Chun 최준. "Chungguk tongbuk chiyŏk ŭi min'ganshinang" 중국 동북지역의 민간신앙 [Folk Religion in Northeast China]. *Chungang minsok'ak* 중앙민속학, Vol. 12 (2007): 96–121.

Ch'oe, Sŭng-sun 최승순. "Kangwŏndo chibang ch'aesamin sŭpsok" 강원도지방 채삼인습속 [The Manners and Customs of Ginseng Diggers in Kangwŏndo]. *Han'guk minsok'ak* 한국민속학, Vol. 8 (1975), 46–59.

Chŏng, Sŏngil 정성일. "Chosŏnsan insam chongja wa Ilbon ŭi insam suip taech'e" 조선산 인삼종자와 일본의 인삼수입 대체 [Chosŏn Ginseng Seedlings and the Replacement of Imported Ginseng in Japan]. In *Ch'un'gye Pak Kwangsun kyosu hwagap kinyŏm kyŏngjehak nonch'ong* 춘계 박광순 교수 화갑기념 경제학 논총 [*Collection of Economic Studies in Celebration of Professor Ch'un'gye Pak Kwangsun's Sixtieth Birthday*]. Kwangju: Chonnam National University 전남대학교, 1993, 173–88.

Chung, Chung-gil 정정길, and Li Jin 리금. "Chungguk insam sanŏp palchŏn ŭi saeroun tonghyang" 중국 인삼산업 발전의 새로운 동향 [New Trends in the Development of China's Ginseng Industry]. *Chungguk nongŏp tonghyang* 중국농업동향, Vol. 5, no. 3 (2012): 29–39.

Chung, Ha-mie 정하미. "Pŏmnyŏngjip Ohure Gaki Shūsei e nat'anan edo makpu ŭi insam chŏngch'aek" 법령집 어촉서집성(御燭書集成)에 나타난 에도막부의 인삼정책 [The Edo Shogunate Policy about Ginseng Showed in Statute Ohure-Gaki Syusei]. *Pigyo ilbonhak* 비교일본학, Vol. 39 (2017): 179–96.

Clarke, John James. *Oriental Enlightenment: The Encounter between Asian and Western Thought*. London: Routledge, 2002.

Cocks, Richard. *Diary of Richard Cocks*. London: Hakluyt Society, 1883.

Collins, Jackie. *Hollywood Wives*. New York: Pocket Books, 1994.

Comte, Louis Daniel le. *Nouveau Mémoire Sur l'état Présent de La Chine*, Vol. 1. Paris, 1696.

Cook, Alexandra. "Linnaeus and Chinese Plants: A Test of the Linguistic Imperialism Thesis." *Notes and Records of the Royal Society of London*, Vol. 64, no. 2 (2010): 121–38.

Cook, Harold J. "Testing the Effects of Jesuit's Bark in the Chinese Emperor's Court." *Journal of the Royal Society of Medicine*, Vol. 107, no. 8 (2014): 326–27.

Cook, Harold J., and Timothy D. Walker. "Circulation of Medicine in the Early Modern Atlantic World." *Social History of Medicine*, Vol. 26, no. 3 (2013): 337–51.

Coxe, John Redman. *The American Dispensatory*. Philadelphia, PA: Thomas Dobson, 1818.

———. *The Philadelphia Medical Dictionary*. Philadelphia, PA: Thomas Dobson, 1808.

Croker, Temple Henry, Thomas Williams, and Samuel Clark. *The Complete Dictionary of Arts and Sciences*, Vol. 2. London, 1765.

Cullen, William. *A Treatise of the Materia Medica*, Vol. 2. Edinburgh, 1789.

———. *Lectures on the Materia Medica*. London, 1772.

Curtis, Thomas, ed. *A London Encyclopaedia, or Universal Dictionary of Science, Art, Literature, and Practical Mechanics*, Vol. 16. London: Thomas Tegg, 1829.

Curtis, William. *A Catalogue of the British, Medicinal, Culinary, and Agricultural Plants, Cultivated in the London Botanic Garden*. London, 1783.

Damrosch, Leo. *Jean-Jacques Rousseau: Restless Genius*. Boston, MA: Houghton Mifflin Company, 2007.

Darlington, William, ed. *Memorials of John Bartram and Humphry Marshall*. Philadelphia, PA: Lindsay & Blakiston, 1849.

Davis, Jeanine, and W. Scott Persons. *Growing and Marketing Ginseng, Goldenseal and Other Woodland Medicinals*. Gabriola Island: New Society Publisher, 2014.

Demos, John. *The Unredeemed Captive: A Family Story from Early America*. New York: Alfred A. Knopf, 1994.

Devlin, Michael. *Pillula Salutaris; Or, the Justly Celebrated Dr. Anthony's Irish Pills*. London, 1790.

Dewhurst, Kenneth. *John Locke (1632–1704), Physician and Philosopher: A Medical Bibliography with an Edition of the Medical Notes in His Journals*. London: The Wellcome Historical Medical Library, 1963.

Diderot, Denis, and Jean le Rond d'Alembert, eds. *Encyclopédie, Ou Dictionnaire Raisonné Des Sciences, Des Arts et Des Métiers*. Chicago, IL: University of Chicago Press, 2008.

Dillwyn, Lewis Weston. *Hortus Collinsonianus: An Account of the Plants Cultivated by the Late Peter Collinson*. Swansea: W. C. Murray and D. Rees, 1843.

Dodsley, Robert. *The General Contents of the British Museum: With Remarks Serving as a Directory in Viewing That Noble Cabinet*. London, 1762.

Du Halde, Jean-Baptiste. *A Description of the Empire of China and Chinese-Tartary, Together with the Kingdoms of Korea, and Tibet*. London, 1741.

———. *Description Géographique, Historique, Chronologique, Politique, et Physique de l'empire de La Chine et de La Tartarie Chinoise*, Vol. 4. Paris, 1735.

———. *The General History of China: Containing A Geographical, Historical, Chronological, Political and Physical Description of the Empire of China, Chinese-Tartary, Corea and Thibet, Including an Extract and Particular Account of Their Customs, Manners, Ceremonies, Religion, Arts and Sciences*, Vol. 4. London, 1736.

Du Hamel, Jean-Baptiste. *Regiae Scientiarum Academiae Historia*. Revised. Paris, 1701.

Dunglison, Robley. *A New Dictionary of Medical Science and Literature*, Vol. 1. Boston, MA: Charles Bowen, 1833.

East India Company. *First, Second, and Third Reports of the Select Committee, Appointed by the Court of Directors of the East India Company*. London, 1793.

Edmonds, Richard. "The Willow Palisade." *Annals of the Association of American Geographers*, Vol. 69, no. 4 (1979): 599–621.

Elibank, Patrick Murray. *Thoughts on Money, Circulation, and Paper Currency*. Edinburgh, 1758.

Elliot, John. *The Medical Pocket-Book*. London, 1791.

Elyakov, G. B., L. I. Strigina, N. I. Uvarova, V. E. Vaskovsky, A. K. Dzizenko, and N. K. Kochetkov. "Glycosides from Ginseng Roots." *Tetrahedron Letters*, Vol. 5, no. 48 (1964): 3591–97.

Evans, Brian L. "Ginseng: Root of Chinese-Canadian Relations." *The Canadian Historical Review*, Vol. 66, no. 1 (1985): 1–26.

Ewell, James. *The Medical Companion, or Family Physician*. Washington, DC, 1827.

Fang, Kun 方堃, ed. *Renshen jiqi shangpinxue* 人參及其商品學 [*Ginseng and Merchandising*]. Beijing: Renmin weisheng chubanshe 人民衛生出版社, 1958.

Federman, Adam. "Digging the Root." *Adirondack Life*, no. September/October (2012), 35–39.

Fei, Chi 費馳. "17 shijimo 18 shijichu de dongya shanglu jiqi yingxiang" 17世紀末18世紀初的東亞商路及其影響 [East Asian Trade Routes and Their Impact Between the Late Seventeenth to Early Eighteenth Century]. *Zhongguo bianjiang shidi yanjiu* 中國邊疆史地研究, Vol. 21, no. 4 (2011), 95–101.

Fenton, William N. "Contacts between Iroquois Herbalism and Colonial Medicine." In *Annual Report of the Smithsonian Institute*. Washington, DC: Smithsonian Institute, 1941. 503–526.

Flannery, Michael A. "The Medicine and Medicinal Plants of C. S. Rafinesque." *Economic Botany*, Vol. 52, no. 1 (1998): 27–43.

Flaumenhaft, Eugene, and Carol Flaumenhaft. "Asian Medicinal Plants in Seventeenth Century French Literature." *Economic Botany*, Vol. 36 (1982): 147–62.

Fleets Pocket Almanack for the Year of Our Lord 1790. Boston, MA, 1789.

Floris, Peter. *Peter Floris, His Voyage to the East Indies in the Globe, 1611–1615: The Contemporary Translation of His Journal*. Edited by William Harrison Moreland. London: Hakluyt Society, 1934.

Folliot deSaint-Vast, Lucas Augustin. "Resp. Quaestio Medica, An Infirmis à Morbo Viribus Reparandis Gin Seng? Praes. F. Vandermonde." University of Paris, 1736.

Fontenoy, Paul E. "Ginseng, Otter Skins, and Sandalwood: The Conundrum of the China Trade." *The Northern Mariner*, Vol. 7, no. 1 (1997): 1–16.

Foster, Steven. "Towards an Understanding of Ginseng Adulteration: The Tangled Web of Names, History, Trade, and Perception." *HerbalGram*, no. 111 (2016): 36–57.

Fox, Richard Hingston. *Dr. John Fothergill and His Friends: Chapters in Eighteenth-Century Life*. London: Macmillan and Co. Ltd., 1919.

Foyster, William, ed. *Letters Received by the East India Company*, Vol. 5. London: Sampson Low, Marston & Co., 1901.

Frank, Andre Gunder. *Reorient: Global Economy in the Asian Age*. Berkeley, CA: University of California Press, 1998.

Frank, Andre Gunder, and Barry Gills, eds. *The World System: Five Hundred Years or Five Thousand?* Lanham, MD: Routledge, 1996.

Franquet, Louis. *Voyages et Mémoires Sur Le Canada En 1752–1753*. Montréal, QC: Editions Elysée, 1974.

Games, Alison. *The Web of Empire: English Cosmopolitans in an Age of Expansion, 1560–1660*. New York: Oxford University Press, 2008.

Garrigues, Samuel S. "Chemical Investigations on Radix Ginseng Americana, Oleum Chenopodii Anthelmintici and Oleum Menthae Viridis." Doctoral dissertation, University of Göttingen, 1854.

Geyer, W. A., R. Janke, C. K. Barden, and E. Carey. "Ginseng (Panax Quinquefolius L.) and Goldenseal (Hydrastis Canadensis L.) Trials in Eastern Kansas." *Transactions of the Kansas Academy of Science*, Vol. 111, no. 1/2 (2008): 147–52.

Goldsmith, Oliver. *The Citizen of the World; or Letters from a Chinese Philosopher, Residing in London, to His Friends in the East*, Vol. 1. London, 1762.

Goldsmith, Oliver, and G. F. Shaw. *A History of the Earth and Animated Nature, Together with the Elements of Botany*. London: R. Edwards, 1819.

Gordon, J., T. Dermer, and A. Thomson. *A Catalogue of Trees, Shrubs, Plants, Flower Roots, Seeds, &c. Sold by Gorden, Dermer, and Thomson, Seed and Nurserymen, at Mile End, Near London*. London, 1783.

Grau, Shirley Ann. *The Keepers of the House*. Baton Rouge, LA: Louisiana State University Press, 1995.

Grew, Nehemiah. *Musaeum Regalis Societatis*. London, 1681.

Guo, Weidong 郭衛東. "Xiyangshen: Zhongmei zaoqi maoyi zhong de zhongyao huopin" 西洋蔘: 中美早期貿易中的重要貨品 [Western Ginseng: A Major Commodity in the Early Trade Between China and America]. *Guangdong shehuikexue* 廣東社會科學, no. 2 (2013) 122–32.

Hale, Nathan. *The American System, or the Effects of High Duties on Imports Designed for the Encouragement of Domestic Industry*. Boston, MA: Nathan Hale's Press, 1826.

Hamauzu, Tetsuo 浜渦哲雄. *Taeyŏngjeguk ŭn Indo rŭl ŏttŏk'e t'ongch'i hayŏnnŭn'ga: Yŏngguk tongindo hoesa 1600–1858* 대영제국은 인도를 어떻게 통치하였는가: 영국 동인도 회사 1600–1858 [*How the British Empire Ruled India: The British East India Company 1600–1858*]. Translated by Kim Sŏng-tong 김성동. Seoul: Shimsan 심산, 2004.

Hanbury, William. *A Complete Body of Planting and Gardening*, Vol. 1. London, 1770.

Haneda, Masashi 羽田正. *Tongindo hoesa wa Asia ŭi pada* 동인도회사와 아시아의 바다 [*The East India Company and the Waters of Asia*]. Translated by Yi Su-yŏl 이수열 and Ku Chi-yŏng 구지영. Seoul: Sŏnin 선인, 2012.

Han'guk insamsa p'yŏnch'an wiwŏnhoe 한국인삼사 편찬위원회. *Han'guk insamsa* 한국인삼사 [*History of Korean Ginseng*], Vol. 1. Seoul: Han'guk insamsa p'yŏnch'an wiwŏnhoe 한국인삼사 편찬위원회, 2002.

Hansen, Carlo, and Anne Fox Maule. "Pehr Osbeck's Collections and Linnaeus's Species Plantarum (1753)." *Botanical Journal of the Linnaean Society*, Vol. 67, no. 3 (1973): 189–212.

Hanson, Marta, and Gianna Pomata. "Medicinal Formulas and Experiential Knowledge in the Seventeenth-Century Epistemic Exchange between China and Europe." *Isis*, Vol. 108, no. 1 (2017): 1–25.

Harding, Arthur Robert. *Ginseng and Other Medicinal Plants*. Columbus, OH: A. R. Harding Publishing Co., 1908.

Harris, Steven J. "Jesuit Scientific Activity in the Overseas Missions, 1540–1773." *Isis*, Vol. 96, no. 1 (2005): 71–79.

Hechter, Michael. *Internal Colonialism*. Berkeley, CA: University of California Press, 1975.

Hildreth, Richard. *Letter to His Excellency Marcus Morton on Banking and the Currency*. Boston, MA: Kidder and Wright, 1840.

Hill, John. *A History of the Materia Medica*. London, 1751.

———. *The Valerian or, the Virtues of that Root in Nervous Disorders; and the Characters Which Distinguish the True from the False*. London, 1758.

———. *The Vegetable System*, Vol. 5. London, 1759.

Histoire de l'Académie Royale Des Sciences. Paris, 1718.

Hobbs, Christopher. "The Medical Botany of John Bartram." *Pharmacy in History*, Vol. 33, no. 4 (1991): 181–89.

Hocking, G. M. "A Chronology of Ginseng." *Quarterly Journal of Crude Drug Research*, Vol. 14 (1976): 168.

Hou, Fuzhong 侯馥中. "Mingdai Zhongguo Yu Chaoxian Maoyi Yanjiu" 明代中國與朝鮮貿易研究 [A Study of the Sino-Korea Trade in the Ming Dynasty]. Doctoral dissertation, Shandong University 山東大學, 2010.

Hu, Shiu Ying. "The Genus Panax (Ginseng) in Chinese Medicine." *Economic Botany*, Vol. 30 (1976): 11–28.

Huc, Évariste-Régis. *Le Christianisme En Chine, En Tartarie et Au Tibet*, Vol. 3. Paris, 1857.

Hufford, Mary. "Knowing Ginseng: The Social Life of an Appalachian Root." *Cahiers de Littérature Orale*, Vol. 53, no. 4 (2003): 265–91.

———. "Review of Appalachian Outlaws." *Journal of Appalachian Studies*, Vol. 20, no. 2 (2014): 234–39.

Humphrey, Seth King. *Following the Prairie Frontier*. Minneapolis, MN: University of Minnesota Press, 1931.

Huxham, John. *Observations on the Air, and Epidemic Diseases*, Vol. 2. London, 1767.

Iannini, Christopher P. *Fatal Revolutions: Natural History, West Indian Slavery, and the Routes of American Literature*. Chapel Hill, NC: University of North Carolina Press, 2013.

Imamura, Tomo 今村鞆. *Insam Shinch'o, Insamsa* 인삼신초, 인삼사 [*The Mystical Herb Ginseng and Its History*]. Translated by Yang Chŏng-p'il 양정필, Vol. 1. Han'guk kŭndae minsok illyuhak charyo taegye 한국근대 민속·인류학자료대계 21. Seoul: Minsogwŏn 민속원, 2009.

———. *Insamsa* 인삼사 [*History of Ginseng*]. Translated by Koh Seung-tae 고승태, Vol. 1: Insam sasangp'yŏn 인삼사상편 [Thoughts on Ginseng]. Yŏngju: Dongyang University 동양대학교, 2015.

———. *Insamsa* 인삼사 [*History of Ginseng*]. Translated by Koh Seung-tae 고승태, Vol. 2: Insam chŏngch'ip'yŏn 인삼정치편 [Ginseng Politics]. Yŏngju: Dongyang University 동양대학교, 2015.

———. *Insamsa* 인삼사 [*History of Ginseng*]. Translated by Koh Seung-tae 고승태, Vol. 3: Insam kyŏngjep'yŏn 인삼경제편 [Ginseng Economy]. Yŏngju: Dongyang University 동양대학교, 2012.

———. *Insamsa* 인삼사 [*History of Ginseng*]. Translated by Koh Seung-tae 고승태, Vol. 4: Insam chaebaep'yŏn 인삼재배편 [Ginseng Cultivation]. Yŏngju: Dongyang University 동양대학교, 2010.

———. *Insamsa* 인삼사 [*History of Ginseng*]. Translated by Koh Seung-tae 고승태, Vol. 5: Insam ŭiyakp'yŏn 인삼의약편 [Ginseng Medication]. Yŏngju: Dongyang University 동양대학교, 2015.

———. *Insamsa* 인삼사 [*History of Ginseng*]. Translated by Koh Seung-tae 고승태, Vol. 6: Insam chapkip'yŏn 인삼잡기편 [Miscellaneous Notes on Ginseng]. Yŏngju: Dongyang University 동양대학교, 2015.

———. *Insamsa* 인삼사 [*History of Ginseng*]. Translated by Koh Seung-tae 고승태, Vol. 7: Sammyŏng hwigop'yŏn 삼명고휘편 [Reflections on Ginseng Names]. Yŏngju: Dongyang University 동양대학교, 2012.

———. *Ninjinshi* 人蔘史 [*History of Ginseng*], Vol. 7. Keijō: Chōsen sōtokufu senbaikyoku 朝鮮總督府專賣局, 1934.

———. "Yama ninjin saishuri no fushu" 山人蔘採取りの 風習 [Customs Involving the Collection of Wild Ginseng]. *Ch'ŏnggu hakch'ong* 靑丘學叢, no. 6 (1931). 110–23

Jackson, Donald, and Dorothy Twohig, eds. *The Papers of George Washington, Diaries*, Vol. 4. Charlottesville, VA: University of Virginia Press, 1976.

James, Henry Evan Murchison. *The Long White Mountain, or, a Journey in Manchuria: With Some Account of the History, People, Administration and Religion of That Country*. London: Longmans, Green, and Company, 1888.

Jartoux, Pierre. "The Description of a Tartarian Plant, Call'd Gin-Seng; with an Account of Its Virtues. In a Letter from Father Jartoux, to the Procurator General of the Missions of India and China." *Philosophical Transactions* 28 (1713): 237–47.

Jiang, Zhushan 蔣竹山. *Renshen diguo: Qingdai renshen de shengchan xiaofei yu yiliao* 人蔘帝國: 清代人蔘的生産消費與醫療 [*Ginseng Empire: Qing China's Production and Consumption of Ginseng and Medicine*]. Hangzhou: Zhejiang daxue chubanshe 浙江大學出版社, 2015.

Johnstone, Charles. *The History of John Juniper, Esq. Alias Juniper Jack*, Vol. 2. London, 1781.

Jordan's Parliamentary Journal, for the Year MDCCXCIII, Vol. 2. London, 1793.

Jou, Kyung-chul 주경철. *Taehanghae shidae: Haesang p'aengch'ang kwa kŭndae segye ŭi hyŏngsŏng* 대항해 시대: 해상팽창과 근대세계의 형성 [*The Age of Discovery: Maritime Expansion and the Formation of the Modern World*]. Seoul: Seoul National University Press 서울대학교 출판부, 2008.

Jung, Eun-joo 정은주. "Chosŏn hugi kasam chaebae wa samsŏ" 조선 후기 家蔘재배와 蔘書 [The Cultivated Ginseng in the Latter Part of the Joseon Dynasty and Samseo]. *Han'guk shirhak yŏn'gu* 한국실학연구 24 (2012): 443–77.

Kains, Maurice Grenville. *Ginseng: Its Cultivation, Harvesting, Marketing and Market Value, With a Short Account of Its History and Botany*. New York: Orange Judd Company, 1901.

Kalm, Peter. *Travels into North America*. Translated by John Reinhold Forster, Vol. 3. London, 1770.

Kempfer, Engelbert. *Amoenitatum Exoticarum Politico-Physico-Medicarum Fasciculi V.* Lemgo, 1712.

Kim, Bo-sung 김보성. "Han-Chung insamshi ŭi yangsang kwa t'ŭkching" 韓·中人蔘詩의 양상과 특징 [Characteristics of Korean and Chinese Poems on Ginseng]. *Hanmun'gojŏn yŏn'gu* 한문고전연구, Vol. 36, no. 1 (2018): 299–329.

Kim, Kwang-jae 김광재. "Ilcheshigi sanghae Koryŏ insam sangindŭl ŭi hwaltong" 일제시기 상해 고려인삼 상인들의 활동 [The Activities of Korean Ginseng Dealers in Shanghai During the Japanese Colonial Period]. *Han'guk tongnibundongsa yŏn'gu* 한국독립운동사연구, Vol. 40 (2011): 221–64.

Kim, Seon-min 김선민. "17-18 segi ch'ŏngdae insam chŏngch'aek ŭi pyŏnhwa" 17-18세기 청대 인삼정책의 변화 [Qing Ginseng Monopoly During the 17th to 18th Century]. *Chungguk'akpo* 중국학보, Vol. 74 (2015): 405–24.

———. *Ginseng and Borderland: Territorial Boundaries and Political Relations Between Qing China and Choson Korea, 1636–1912.* Oakland, CA: University of California Press, 2017.

———. "Insam kwa kangyŏk: Hugŭm-Ch'ŏng ŭi kangyŏk inshik kwa taeoegwan'gye ŭi pyŏnhwa" 人蔘과 疆域: 후금-청의 강역인식과 대외관계의 변화 [The State Development from the Later Jin to the Qing and the Boundary Making in the Early Seventeenth Century]. *Myŏngch'ŏngsa yŏn'gu* 명청사연구, Vol. 30 (2008): 227–57.

———. "Manjujok kwa insam" 만주족과 인삼 [The Manchus and Ginseng in the Qing Period]. *Insam munhwa* 인삼문화, Vol. 1 (2019): 11–27.

Ko, Sung-kwon 고성권. "Sŏjihakchŏk kojŭng ŭl t'onghan Koryŏ insam ŭi chŏngch'esŏng" 서지학적 고증을 통한 고려인삼의 정체성: 기미(氣味), 효능을 중심으로 [Identity of Korean Ginseng through Bibliography: Focusing on Kimi (Property) and Efficacy]. *Insam munhwa* 인삼문화, Vol. 1 (2019): 1–10.

Ko, Sung-kwon 고성권, Kim Yun-su 김윤수, Kim Yun-yŏng 김윤영, Kim Chong-ki 김종기, Mok Sŏng-kyun 목성균, Pak Chong-tae 박종대, Sin Ch'a-kyun 신차균, Im Pyŏng-ok 임병옥, Chŏng Chae-hun 정재훈, and Chŏng Hŏn-pae 정헌배. *Uri insam ŭi ihae* 우리 인삼의 이해 [*An Understanding of Korean Ginseng*]. Seoul: Chung-Ang University Press 중앙대학교 출판부, 2005.

Koehler, John Henry. *Ginseng and Goldenseal Growers' Handbook.* Wausau, WI: P. F. Stolze, 1912.

———. *Report of J. H. Koehler, Acting President of American Ginseng Growers' Association to the Ginseng Growers of America.* Wausau, WI: J. H. Koehler, 1917.

Kong, Sŏng-ku 공성구. *Hyangdaegiram: Kaesŏng sangin ŭi hongsam rodŭ kaech'ŏkki* 향대기람: 개성상인의 홍삼로드 개척기 [*Hyangdaegiram: Kaesŏng Merchants' Journey to Estalish an Export Route for Red Ginseng*]. Translated by Pak Tong-uk 박동욱. Seoul: T'aehaksa 태학사, 2014.

Kwak, Yi-seong 곽이성. "Koryŏ insam ŭi yurae mit hyonŭng ŭi sŏjihakchŏk koch'al" 고려인삼의 유래 및 효능의 서지학적 고찰 [Bibliographic Consideration on the Efficacy and the Origin of Korean Ginseng]. *Insam munhwa* 인삼문화, Vol. 1 (2019): 43–56.

Lach, Donald F. "China and the Era of the Enlightenment." *The Journal of Modern History*, Vol. 14, no. 2 (1942): 209–23.

Lach, Donald Frederick. *The Preface to Leibniz' Novissima Sinica: Commentary, Translation, Text.* Honolulu: University of Hawai'i Press, 1957.

Lafitau, Joseph-François. "Le Genseng, Plante Si Précieuse à La Chine, Découverte Dans Le Canada." *Mémoires Pour l'histoire Des Sciences et Des Beaux-Arts*, no. January (1717): 121–24.

———. *Mémoire Presenté a Son Altesse Royale Monseigneur Le Duc d'Orléans, Regent Du Royaume de France: Concernant La Précieuse Plante Du Gin-Seng de Tartarie, Découverte En Canada Par Le P. Joseph François Lafitau, de La Compagnie de Jesus, Missionnaire Des Iroquois Du Sault Saint Louis*. Paris, 1718.

Lan, Weiji 藍偉吉. "18 shijimo Zhongguo xiyangshenre yuanyin qianxi" 18世紀末中國西洋蔘热原因淺析 [An Analysis of the Craze for Western Ginseng in Late Eighteenth Century China]. *Heilongjiang shizhi* 黑龍江史志, no. 23 (2013): 21–24

Lass, Willam E. "Ginseng Rush in Minnesota." *Minnesota History* 41 (1969): 249–66.

Lee, Chul-sung 이철성. "Kaesŏng insam i wae yumyŏnghage toeŏssŭlkka?" 개성 인삼이 왜 유명하게 되었을까? [How Did Kaesŏng Ginseng Earn Its Fame?]. *Naeirŭl yŏnŭn yŏksa* 내일을 여는 역사, no. 13 (2003): 85–97.

Lee, Dong-phil 이동필. "Hwagisam ŭi hyonŭng chujang kwa miguksam ŭi palchŏn kwajŏng e taehan koch'al" 화기삼의 효능 주장과 미국삼의 발전과정에 대한 고찰 [A Study on the Cooling Effect Claim & Development Procedure of the American Ginseng]. *Koryŏ insam hak'oeji* 고려인삼학회지 30, no. 3 (2006): 158–64.

Lee, Hye-min 이혜민. "Rui 14se ŭi insam: 17segi Mal - 18segi ch'o p'ŭrangsŭ ŭi ponch'ohak chishik hyŏngsŏng" 루이 14세의 인삼: 17세기 말-18세기 초 프랑스의 본초학 지식 형성 [Louis XIV's Ginseng: Shaping of Knowledge on an Herbal Medicine in the Late 17th and the Early 18th Century France]. *Ŭisahak* 의사학, Vol. 25, no. 1 (2016): 111–45.

Lee, Sharon Wai-Seung. "Evolution of the 'Shang' (American Ginseng) Industry in Marathon County." Master's Thesis, University of Wisconsin, Madison, 1998.

Leibniz, Gottfried Wilhelm. *Der Briefwechsel Mit Den Jesuiten in China (1689–1714)*. Edited by Rita Widmaier and Malte L. Babin. Hamburg: Felix Meiner Verlag, 2006.

———. *Sämtliche Schriften Und Briefe: Politische Schriften, 1667–1676*. IV. Darmstad: Otto Reichl Verlag, 1931.

Letters of the Missionary Jesuits. Paris, 1713.

Lettres Édifiantes et Curieuses, Écrites Des Missions Étrangères, Par Quelques Missionnaires de La Compagnie de Jésus, Vol. 10. Paris, 1713.

Leupp, Gary P. *Interracial Intimacy in Japan: Western Men and Japanese Women, 1543–1900*. London: Continuum, 2003.

Lewis, William. *An Experimental History of the Materia Medica*, Vol. 1. Dublin, 1769.

———. *The Edinburgh New Dispensatory*. 5th ed. Edinburgh, 1797.

———. *The New Dispensatory*. Dublin, 1782.

Li, Shizhen 李時珍. *Shinjuhae Ponch'o kangmok* 신주해 본초강목 [*Newly Annotated Bencao Gangmu*]. Translated by Kim Chong-ha 김종하, Vol. 1. Seoul: Yŏil ch'ulp'ansa 여일출판사, 2007.

———. *Shinjuhae Ponch'o Kangmok* 신주해 본초강목 [*Newly Annotated Bencao Gangmu*]. Translated by Kim Chong-ha 김종하, Vol. 4. Seoul: Yŏil ch'ulp'ansa 여일출판사, 2007.

Lin Zexu quanji bianji weiyuanhui 林則徐全集編輯委員會. *Lin Zexu quanji* 林則徐全集 [*The Complete Works of Lin Zexu*], Vol. 3. Fuzhou: Haixia wenyi chubanshe 海峡文藝出版社, 2002.

Lin, Zhongfan 林仲凡. "Ming Qing shidai woguo dongbei gedi renshen de kaicai yu jingying" 明清時代我國東北各地人蔘的開採與經營 [The Collection and Management of Ginseng in Different Areas of Northeastern China During the Ming-Qing Dynasties]. *Zhongguo nongshi* 中國農史, no. 4 (1988): 33–40.

Linnæi, Caroli. *Species Plantarum, Exhibentes Plantas Rite Cognitas Ad Genera Relatas, Cum Differentiis Specificis, Nominibus Trivialibus, Synonymis Selectis, Locis Natalibus, Secundum Systema Sexuale Digestas*, Vol. 2. Holmiæ [Stockholm], 1753.

Linnaeus, Carolus. *Hortus Cliffortianus*. Amsterdam, 1737.

———. *Materia Medica, Liber I. de Plantis*. Holmiæ [Stockholm], 1749.

Linné, Carl von. *Miscellaneous Tracts Relating to Natural History, Husbandry, and Physick*. Translated by Benjamin Stillingfleet. London, 1759.

Long, Wu 龍武. "Mingmo Liaodong mashi maoyizhan he nuzhen" 明末遼東馬市貿易戰和女真諸部興衰 [Trade War at Horse Markets in Late Ming China and the Rise and Fall of Jurchen Ministries]. Master's Thesis, Graduate School of Chinese Academy of Social Sciences 中國社會科學研究生院, 2014.

Loskiel, George Henry. *History of the Mission of the United Brethren among the Indians in North America*. Translated by Christian Ignatius La Trobe. London, 1794.

MacLeitch, Gail D. *Imperial Entanglements: Iroquois Change and Persistence on the Frontiers of Empire*. Philadelphia, PA: University of Pennsylvania Press, 2011.

———. "'Red' Labour: Iroquois Participation in the Atlantic Economy." *Labor: Studies in Working-Class History of the Americas*, Vol. 1, no. 4 (2004): 69–90.

Manget, Luke. "Ginseng, China, and the Transformation of the Ohio Valley, 1783–1840." *Ohio Valley History*, Vol. 17, no. 3 (2017): 3–23.

———. "Nature's Emporium: The Botanical Drug Trade and the Commons Tradition in Southern Appalachia, 1847–1917." *Environmental History*, Vol. 21, no. 4 (2016): 660–87.

———. "Sangin'io the Mountains: The Ginseng Economy of the Southern Appalachians, 1865–1900." *Appalachian Journal*, Vol. 40, no. 1/2 (2012): 28–56.

Martini, Martino. *Bellum Tartaricum, or The Conquest of the Great and Most Renowned Empire of China, by the Invasion of the Tartars*. London, 1654.

Maurice, Thomas. *Indian Antiquities*, Vol. 7. London, 1800.

Meares, John. *Voyages Made in the Years 1788 and 1789, from China to the North West Coast of America*. London, 1790.

"Medical and Physical Society of Calcutta." *The Asiatic Journal and Monthly Miscellany*, Vol. 25 (1828): 493–494 .

Michaux, François André. *Travels to the West of the Alleghany Mountains*. London, 1805.

Millar, James. *A New Course of Chemistry*. London, 1754.

Miller, Philip. *The Gardener's Kalendar*. 11th ed. London, 1757.

Millspaugh, Charles F. *American Medicinal Plants*. Philadelphia, PA: Boericke & Tafle, 1887.

"Miscellaneous Notices." *The Quarterly Journal of Agriculture*, Vol. 11 (1841 [1840]). 120–21

Miyake, Hidetoshi 三宅英利. *Chosŏn t'ongshinsa wa Ilbon* 조선 통신사와 일본 [*Chosŏn t'ongshinsa and Japan*]. Translated by Kim Se-min 김세민, Kang Tae-tŏk 강대덕, Yu Chae-ch'un 유재춘, and Ŏm Ch'an-ho 엄찬호. Seoul: Chisŏngŭi saem 지성의샘, 1996.

Moon, Kwang-kyun 문광균. "18 segi Kanggye chiyŏk kongsamje ŭi unyŏng kwa pyŏnhwa" 18세기 강계지역 공삼제의 운영과 변화 [18th Century Practice of the Taxation System in Ginseng and Its Change in Kanggye]. *Chosŏn shidaesa hakpo* 조선시대사학보, Vol. 57 (2011): 161–206.

Mooney, Steve. "Ginseng and Appalachian Culture: Settlement to Contemporary Times." *Appalachian Heritage*, Vol. 18, no. 3 (1990): 36–43.

Morse, Hosea Ballou. *The Chronicles of the East India Company Trading to China 1635–1834*, Vol. 2. Cambridge, MA: Harvard University Press, 1926.

Morse, Jedidah. *Geography Made Easy: Being an Abridgement of the American Universal Geography*. Boston, MA, 1790.

Morton, Oren Frederic. *A History of Monroe County, West Virginia.* Dayton, VA: Ruebush-Elkins, 1916.

Moseley, Benjamin. *A Treatise on Sugar.* London, 1800.

Munro, Donald. *A Treatise of the Materia Medica*, Vol. 3. Edinburgh, 1788.

Murray, Lady Charlotte. *The British Garden: A Descriptive Catalogue of Hardy Plants, Indigenous, or Cultivated in the Climate of Great Britain.* Bath, 1799.

Nash, George Valentine. *American Ginseng: Its Commercial History, Protection and Cultivation.* Revised. U. S. Department of Agriculture Division of Botany Bulletin 16. Washington, DC: Government Printing Office, 1898.

Nees von Esenbeck, Theodor Friedrich Ludwig. *Plantae Medicinales.* Düsseldorf: Arnz & Co., 1833.

Nieuhof, Johannes. *L'ambassade de La Compagnie Orientale Des Provinces Unies Vers l'Empereur de La Chine, Ou Grand Cam de Tartarie, Faite Par Les Srs. Pierre de Goyer, & Jacob de Keyser.* Leiden: Pour Jacob De Meurs, Marchand Libraire & Graveur de la Ville d'Amsterdam, 1665.

No, Sung-hwan 노성환. "Imnanp'oro ka toeŏ Ilbon ŭro kŏnnŏgan Chosŏn ŭi tongshingmul" 임란포로가 되어 일본으로 건너간 조선의 동식물 [Chosŏn Wildlife Taken to Japan During the Japanese Invasions of Chosŏn]. *Ilbonŏ kyoyuk yŏn'gu* 일본어교육연구, Vol. 48 (2009): 233–49.

Nott, John. *A Posologic Companion to the London Pharmacopoeia.* London, 1794.

Ok, Sun-chong 옥순종. *Kyoyang ŭro ingnŭn insam iyagi* 교양으로 읽는 인삼 이야기 [*An Informed Account of Ginseng*]. Seoul: Igasŏ 이가서, 2005.

Osbeck, Pehr. *A Voyage to China and the East Indies.* Translated by John Reinhold Forster, Vol. 2. London, 1771.

Park, Ki-hwan 박기환, Hŏ Sŏng-yun 허성윤, and Li Jinghu 리징후. *Chunggguk ŭi insam sanŏp hyŏnhwang kwa yuksŏng chŏngch'aek: Chunggguk tongbuksamsŏng* 중국의 인삼산업 현황과 육성 정책: 중국 동북3성 지역 중심 *[Current Status of the Ginseng Industry in China and Its Fostering Policy: Focusing on Three Northeastern Provinces of China*]. Naju: Korea Rural Economic Institute 한국농촌경제연구원, 2014.

Park, Pyeong-sik 박평식. "Chosŏn chŏn'gi ŭi insam chŏngch'aek kwa insam yut'ong" 조선전기의 인삼정책과 인삼유통 [Ginseng Policy and Its Distribution in the Early Choson Dynasty]. *Han'guksa yŏn'gu* 한국사연구, Vol. 143 (2008): 201–41.

———. "Sŏnjojo ŭi taemyŏng insam muyŏk kwa insam sangin" 宣祖朝의 對明 인삼무역과 인삼상인 [Ginseng Trade with Ming and Ginseng Merchants during the Years of King Sônjo]. *Yŏksa gyoyuk* 역사교육, Vol. 108 (2008): 127–58.

Parsons, Christopher M. "The Natural History of Colonial Science: Joseph-François Lafitau's Discovery of Ginseng and Its Afterlives." *The William and Mary Quarterly*, Vol. 73, no. 1 (2016): 37–72.

Payne, John. *Geographical Extracts, Forming a General View of Earth and Nature.* London, 1796.

Pearson, Richard. *A Practical Synopsis of the Materia Medica*, Vol. 2. London: C. and R. Baldwin, n.d.

Persons, W. Scott. *Growing American Ginseng in Its Native Woodland Habitat.* Minneapolis, MN, 1998.

Piao, Fulan 朴福蘭. "Qingchao fengjin shiqi chaoxianren fanyue shili yanjiu" 「清朝封禁时期朝鲜人犯越事例研究 [A Study of Border Violations by Chosŏn People During Qing China's Practice of the Fengjin Policy]. Master's Thesis, Yanbian University 延邊大學, 2013.

Pike, Nicolas. "The Ginseng." *Scientific American*, Vol. 64, no. 2 (1891): 19.

Pinkerton, Katherene. *Bright with Silver.* New York: William Sloane Associates, Inc., 1947.

Polczinski, Len C. "Ginseng (Panax Quinquefolius L.) Culture in Marathon County, Wisconsin: Historical Growth, Distribution, and Soils Inventory." Master's Thesis, University of Wisconsin, 1982.

Pomeranz, Kenneth. *The Great Divergence: China, Europe, and the Making of the Modern World Economy*. Princeton, NJ: Princeton University Press, 2000.

Pomeranz, Kenneth, and Steven Topik. *The World That Trade Created: Society, Culture, and the World Economy, 1400 to the Present*. Armonk, NY: M.E. Sharpe, 2006.

Pomet, Pierre. *A Complete History of Drugs*. London, 1748.

Preston, David L. *The Texture of Contact: European and Indian Settler Communities on the Frontiers of Iroquoia, 1667–1783*. Lincoln: University of Nebraska Press, 2009.

Qi, Lian-Wen, Chong-Zhi Wang, and Chun-Su Yuan. "Ginsenosides from American Ginseng: Chemical and Pharmacological Diversity." *Phytochemistry*, Vol. 72, no. 8 (2011): 689–99.

Quincy, John. *Pharmacopoeia Officinalis, or a Complete English Dispensatory*. London, 1782.

Rafinesque, Constantine Samuel. *Medical Flora; or Manual of the Medical Botany of the United States of North America*, Vol. 2. Philadelphia, PA: S. C. Atkinson, 1830.

Ray, John. *Historia Plantarum*, Vol. 2. London, 1688.

Rhind, William. *A History of the Vegetable Kingdom*. Glasgow: Blackie & Son, 1841.

Rochon, Alexis. *A Voyage to Madagascar and the East Indies*. Translated by Joseph Trapp. London, 1792.

Roos, Anna Marie. "Naturalia: The History of Natural History and Medicine in the Seventeenth Century." *Notes and Records of the Royal Society of London*, Vol. 66, no. 4 (2012): 313–21.

Root, Charles Marvin. *What is Ginseng: An Account of the History and Cultivation of Ginseng*. Omaha, NE: J. M. Roucek, 1905.

Rost, Thomas L., and Maureen L. Sandler. "The Common History and Popular Uses of Roots." *The American Biology Teacher*, Vol. 40, no. 6 (1978): 338–41.

Rowbotham, Arnold H. "The Jesuit Figurists and Eighteenth-Century Religious Thought." *Journal of the History of Ideas*, Vol. 17, no. 4 (1956): 471–85.

Rutty, John. *Observations on the London and Edinburgh Dispensatories*. London, 1776.

Salmon, Thomas. *Modern History: Or, the Present State of All Nations*, Vol. 27. London: Printed for T. Longman and et al., 1735.

———. *Modern History: Or, the Present State of All Nations*, Vol. 1. London, 1739.

Salwey, Kenny, and J. Scott Bestul. *The Last River Rat: Kenny Salwey's Life in the Wild*. Stillwater, MN: Voyageur Press, 2001.

Schlesinger, Jonathan. "The Qing Invention of Nature: Environment and Identity in Northeast China and Mongolia, 1750–1850." Doctoral dissertation, Harvard University, 2012.

Schorger, A. W. "Ginseng: A Pioneer Resource." *Transactions of the Wisconsin Academy of Science, Art and Letters* 57 (1969): 65–74.

Schwediauer, Franz. *Practical Observations on the More Obstinate and Inveterate Venereal Complaints*. London, 1784.

Schwemmer, Ulrike. *Wunderdroge Ginseng: Vom Einzug Einer Mythischen Heilpflanze in Die Moderne Medizin*. Wien-München: Franz Deuticke Verlag, 1998.

Semedo, Alvaro. *Relatione Della Grande Monarchia Della Cina*. Rome, 1643.

Seok, Yeong-dal 석영달. "Migun ŭi insam pokyong?: 20 segi mal insam ŭi Miguk shigiboch'ungje shijang p'yŏnip kwa migun maenyuŏl" 미군의 인삼복용?: 20세기 말 인삼의 미국 식이보충제 시장편입과 미군 매뉴얼 ["The U.S. Military Uses Ginseng?": The Official Entrance of Ginseng to the U.S. Dietary Supplement Market and the U. S. Military's Dietary Supplement Manual in the Late 20th Century]. *Insam munhwa* 인삼문화, Vol. 1 (2019): 93–109.

Shannon, Timothy J. "Dressing for Success on the Mohawk Frontier: Hendrick, William Johnson, and the Indian Fashion." *The William and Mary Quarterly*, Vol. 53, no. 1 (1996): 13–42.

Shaw, Samuel. *The Journals of Major Samuel Shaw*. Taipei: Ch'eng-Wen Publishing Co., 1968.

Shibata, Shoji, Fujita Mtiiti, Itokawa Hideji, Tanaka Osamu, and Ishii Tastuo. "Studies on the Constituents of Japanese and Chinese Crude Drugs. XI. Panaxadiol, A Sapogenin of Ginseng Roots." *Chemical and Pharmaceutical Bulletin*, Vol. 11 (1963): 759–61.

Shin, Chang-geon 신창건. "Kyŏngsŏngjeguktaehak e issŏsŏ hanyak yŏn'gu ŭi sŏngnip" 경성제국대학에 있어서 한약연구의 성립 [Institutionlization of Research on Traditional Medicine in Keijo Imperial University]. *Sahoewa yŏksa* 사회와 역사, Vol. 76 (2007): 105–39.

Shteir, Ann B. "Gender and 'Modern' Botany in Victorian England." *Osiris*, Vol. 12 (1997): 29–38.

Siris in the Shades: A Dialogue Concerning Tar Water. London, 1744.

Sloane, Hans. *A Voyage to the Islands Madera, Barbadoes, Nieves, St Christophers, and Jamaica*, Vol. 2. London, 1707.

Smedley, Edward, Hugh James Rose, and Henry John Rose, eds. *Encyclopaedia Metropolitana*, Vol. 19. London, 1845.

Smith, Philip Chadwick Foster. *The Empress of China*. Philadelphia, PA: Philadelphia Maritime Museum, 1984.

Smithies, Michael. *The Discourses at Versailles of the First Siamese Ambassadors to France, 1686–1687*. Bangkok: Siam Society, 1986.

Smollett, Tobias. *Humphry Clinker*. London: G. Routledge & Co., 1857.

———. *The Present State of All Nations*, Vol. 8. London, 1769.

Smyth, J. F. D. *A Tour in the United States of America*, Vol. 1. Dublin, 1784.

Song, Chengji 宋承吉. "Gu shangdang renshen shi jin zhi yaoyong renshen" 古上黨人蔘是今之藥用人蔘 [Yesterday's Shangdang Ginseng Is Today's Medicinal Ginseng]. *Mingbao yuekan* 明報月刊, Vol. 9 (1984): 83–84.

———. "Shilun Zhongguo Gudai Renshen de Zhuchanqu" 試論中國古代人蔘的主產區 [A Study of Major Ginseng Producing Areas in Ancient China]. *Zhongguo nongshi* 中國農史, Vol. 3 (1986): 56–59.

Song, Chengji 宋承吉, and Zhan Xiujuan 張秀娟. "Zhongguo yaoyong renshen shigang" 中國藥用人参史綱 [A Historical Outline of Chinese Medicinal Ginseng]. *Renshen yanjiu* 人蔘研究, Vol. 1 (1993): 41–44.

Song, Junling 宋軍令. "Ming Qing shiqi meizhou nongzuowu zai zhongguo de chuanzhong jiqi yingxiang yanjiu" 明清時期美洲农作物在中國的傳種及其影響研究 [A Study of American Crops Bred in Ming and Qing China and Their Impact]. Doctoral dissertation, Henan University 河南大學, 2007.

Sonnedecker, Glenn. "The Founding Period of the U. S. Pharmacopeia: I. European Antecedents." *Pharmacy in History*, Vol. 35, no. 4 (1993): 151–62.

Stearn, William T. "The Influence of Leyden on Botany in the Seventeenth and Eighteenth Centuries." *The British Journal for the History of Science*, Vol. 1, no. 2 (1962): 137–58.

Stearns, Samuel. *The American Oracle: Comprehending an Account of Recent Discoveries in the Arts and Sciences*. London, 1791.

Sul, Heasim 설혜심. "19 segi Yŏngguk shinmun e nat'anan insam" 19세기 영국신문에 나타난 인삼 [Ginseng as It Appeared in 19th-Century British Newspapers]. *Yŏngguk yŏn'gu* 영국연구, Vol. 34 (2015): 1–42.

———. *Grand Tour: Elite kyoyuk ŭi ch'oejong tan'gye* 그랜드 투어: 엘리트 교육의 최종단계 [*Grand Tour: The Final Stage of Elite Education*]. Seoul: Humanist 휴머니스트, 2020.

———. *Sobi ŭi yŏksa: Chigŭmkkŏt amudo chumok'aji anŭn "sobihanŭn in'gan" ŭi yŏksa* 소비의 역사: 지금껏 아무도 주목하지 않은 '소비하는 인간'의 역사 [*A History of Consumption: On the Overlooked Aspect of Mankind as Consumers*]. Seoul: Humanist 휴머니스트, 2017.

Sun, Insu. "Über Die Echte Ginsengwurzel (Panax Ginseng, Song-Sam)." *Naunyn Schmiedebergs Archiv Für Experimentelle Pathologie Und Pharmakologie*, Vol. 170 (1933): 443–57.

Sun, Xiaoshu 孙晓舒. *Shanshen zhi "ye": Guanyu yiyi yu jiage zhi shengcheng de renleixue yanjiu* 山蔘之"野": 關于意義與價格之生成的人類學研究 [*'Wild' Ginseng: An Anthropological Study of Its Significance and Price Formation*]. Beijing: Zhishi chanquan chubanshe 知識産權出版社, 2012.

Swann, John P. "The Evolution of the American Pharmaceutical Industry." *Pharmacy in History*, Vol. 37, no. 2 (1995): 76–86.

Talarigo, Jeff. *The Ginseng Hunter*. New York: Anchor Books, 2009.

Tashiro, Kazui. "Exports of Japan's Silver to China via Korea and Changes in the Tokugawa Monetary System during the Seventeenth and Eighteenth Centuries." In *Precious Metals, Coinage and the Changes of Monetary Structures in Latin-America, Europe and Asia*. Edited by Eddy van Cauwenberghe. Leuven: Leuven University Press, 1989: 99–116.

Taylor, David A. "Getting to the Root of Ginseng." *Smithsonian Magazine*, 2002. https://www.smithsonianmag.com/science-nature/getting-to-the-root-of-ginseng-65654374.

The American Farmer's Encyclopedia. New York: A. O. Moore, Agricultural Book Publisher, 1860.

"The 'British Pharmacopœia.'" *The British Medical Journal*, Vol. 2 (1885): 1025–1026.

The Casket, Flowers of Literature, Wit and Sentiment, Vol. 5. Philadelphia, PA: Samuel C. Atkinson, 1830.

The London Practice of Physic. London, 1769.

The National Institute for the Promotion of Science. *Fourth Bulletin of the National Institute for the Promotion of Science, February 1845 to November 1846*. Washington, DC: W. Q. Force, 1846.

The New Annual Register, or General Repository of History, Politics and Literature for the Year 1792. London, 1793.

The Pharmacopœia of the United States of America. Sixth Decennial Revision. New York: William Wood & Company, 1882.

The Royal College of Physicians of London. *Medical Transactions*, Vol. 3. London, 1785.

———. *The New Pharmacopoeia of the Royal College of Physicians of London*. Translated by Thomas Healdes. 3rd ed. London, 1788.

The Terrific Register; Or, Record of Crimes, Judgements, Providences, and Calamities, Vol. 2. London: Sherwood, Jones, and Co. and Hunter, Edinburgh, 1825.

The Weekly Entertainer; or Agreeable and Instructive Repository, Vol. 1. Sherborne, 1783.

Thévenot, Melchisédech. "Of Some Books Lately Published : Relations of Divers Curious Voyages." *Philosophical Transactions*, Vol. 1, no. (1665–1666): 248–54.

Thunberg, Charles Peter. "Travels in Japan and Other Countries." In *Historical Account of the Most Celebrated Voyages, Travels, and Discoveries*, Vol. 15. London, 1797.

Tinling, Marion, ed. *The Correspondence of the Three William Byrds of Westover, Virginia, 1684–1776*, Vol. 2. Charlottesville, VA: Virginia Historical Society Documents, 1977.

Titford, W. J. *Hortus Botanicus Americanus*. London: C. Stower, 1811.

Tong, Dong 佟冬, ed. *Zhongguo dongbeishi* 中國東北史 [*A History of Northeastern China*], Vol. 4. Changchun: Jilin wenshi chubanshe 吉林文史出版社, 1998.

Tong, Yonggong 佟永功. "Qingdai shengjing shenwu huodong shulue" 清代盛京蔘務活動述略 [A Summary of Qing Chinese Activities Related to Shengjing Ginseng]. *Qingshi yanjiu* 清史研究, no. 1 (2000): 42–49.

Tourette, Guy la. "Ginseng and Its Diggers." *The Pharmaceutical Journal and Transactions*, Vol. 7 (1882): 379–80.

Touwaide, Alain. "Nature's Medicine Cabinet: Notes on Botanical Therapeutics at the Birth of the New World." *Journal of the Washington Academy of Sciences*, Vol. 89, no. 3/4 (2003): 141–50.

Tschirch, Alexander. *Handbuch Der Pharmakognosie*, Vol. 1. Leipzig: Tauchnitz, 1909.

Vaillant, Sébastien. "A New Genus of Plants, Call'd Aralistrum, of Which the Famous Nin-Zin or Ginseng of the Chinese, is a Species." *Philosophical Transactions*, Vol. 30 (1717–1719): 705–707.

Vallée, Arthur. *Un Biologiste Canadien, Michel Sarrazin, 1659–1735: Sa Vie, Ses Travaux et Son Temps*. Québec: Le Quotidien, 1927.

Van Hook, James M. *Diseases of Ginseng*. Cornell University Agricultural Experiment Station Bulletin 219. Ithaca, NY: Cornell University, 1904.

Voltaire. *The Works of M. de Voltaire: Translated from the French with Notes, Historical and Critical*. Translated by T. Smollet and T. Francklin, Vol. 12. London, 1761.

Wallerstein, Immanuel. *The Modern World-System I: Capitalist Agriculture and the Origins of the European World-Economy in the Sixteenth Century*. New York: Academic Press, 1974.

———. *World-Systems Analysis: An Introduction*. Durham and London: Duke University Press, 2004.

Wallis, George. *Annual Oration, Delivered March 8th, 1790 before the Medical Society*. London, 1790.

———, ed. *The Works of Thomas Sydenham, M. D., on Acute and Chronic Diseases*, Vol. 2. London, 1778.

Wallis, Patrick. "Exotic Drugs and English Medicine: England's Drug Trade, c. 1550–c. 1800." *Social History of Medicine*, Vol. 25, no. 1 (2012): 20–46.

Wang, Dave. "Chinese Civilization and the United States: Tea, Ginseng, Porcelain Ware and Silk in Colonial America." *Virginia Review of Asian Studies*, Vol. 13 (2011): 113–31.

Wang, Jingze 王景澤. "Dui Qingdai fengjin dongbei zhengce de zairenshi" 對清代封禁東北政策的再認識 [A Reexamination of Qing China's Fengjin Policy Toward Its Northeastern Areas]. *Dongbei shida xuebao* 東北師大學報, Vol. 166 (1997): 45–55.

Wang, Peihuan 王佩環. "Qingdai dongbei caishenye de xingshuai" 清代東北采蔘業的興衰 [The Ginseng Industry's Rise and Fall in the Northeastern Areas of Qing China]. *Shehuikexue zhanxian* 社會科學戰線, Vol. 4 (1982): 189–92.

Wang, Tiesheng 王鐵生, ed. *Zhongguo renshen* 中國人蔘 [*Chinese Ginseng*]. Shenyang: Liaoning kexuejishu chubanshe 遼寧科學技術出版社, 2001.

Whetzel, Herbert Hice, and Joseph Rosenbaum. *The Diseases of Ginseng and Their Control*. U.S. Department of Agriculture Bureau of Plant Industry Bulletin 250. Washington, DC: Government Printing Office, 1912.

Whitney, Peter. *The History of the County of Worcester in the Commonwealth of Massachusetts*. Worcester, MA, 1793.

Willich, Anthony Florian Madinger, and James Mease. *The Domestic Encyclopaedia; or, a Dictionary of Facts, and Useful Knowledge*, Vol. 3. Philadelphia, PA: William Young Birch, 1804.

Wilson, Fairbank, & Co. *Interesting History of the Panax (Quinquefolium) of Linnaeus: The Ginseng of the Chinese from the Archives of History and Medical Science*. Boston, MA: White & Potter, 1851.

Wilson, Renate. "The Traffic in Eighteenth-Century Medicines and Medical Ideas and the 'Medicina Pennsylvania' of George de Benneville." *Pharmacy in History*, Vol. 44, no. 4 (2002): 142–51.

———. "Trading in Drugs through Philadelphia in the Eighteenth Century: A Transatlantic Enterprise." *Social History of Medicine*, Vol. 26, no. 3 (2013): 352–63.

Winterbottom, Anna E. "Of the China Root: A Case Study of the Early Modern Circulation of Materia Medica." *Social History of Medicine*, Vol. 28, no. 1 (2015): 22–44.

Wittie, Robert, and William Simpson. *Some Observations Made Upon the Root Called Nean, or Ninsing, Imported from the East-Indies*. London, 1680.

Woodville, William. *Medical Botany*, Vol. 1. London: William Phillips, 1810.

Wu, Sŭng-ha 우승하. "Shimmani sŭpsok ŭi pyŏnhwa yangsang" 심마니 습속의 변화 양상 [The Changing Patterns of Simmani's Folkways]. *Minsok'ak yŏn'gu* 민속학 연구, Vol. 35 (2014): 5–28.

Xu, Shiwen 許十文, and Chen Xiaoping 陳曉平. "Renshen de zhanzheng" 人蔘的戰爭 [A War of Ginseng]. *21 shiji shangye pinglun* 21世紀商業評論, Vol. 21 (2013): 41–47.

Yang, Chŏng-p'il 양정필. "17-18 segi chŏnban insam muyŏk ŭi pyŏndong kwa kaesŏng sangin ŭi hwaltong" 17-18세기 전반 인삼무역의 변동과 개성상인의 활동 [Changes in the Ginseng Trade and Operations of Gaesung Merchants in the 17th to Early 18th Century]. *T'amna munhwa* 탐라문화, Vol. 55 (2017): 107–44.

———. "1910 nyŏndae ilche ŭi samŏp chŏngch'aek kwa Kaesŏng samp'oju ŭi hwaltong" 1910년대 일제의 삼업정책과 개성 삼포주의 활동 [Japanese Imperial Authorities' Policy Regarding Jinseng Production during the 1910s, and the Activities of the Jinseng Farm Owners in the Gaeseong Region]. *Yŏksamunje yŏn'gu* 역사문제연구, Vol. 24, no. 2 (2010): 265–97.

———. "1910–20 nyŏndae Kaesŏng sangin ŭi paeksam sangp'umhwa wa p'anmae hwaktae hwaltong" 1910–20년대 개성상인의 백삼 상품화와 판매 활동 [White Ginseng Commercialization and Sales Expansion Activities of Gaesung Merchants in the 1910s and 1920s]. *Ŭisahak* 의사학, Vol. 20, no. 1 (2011): 83–118.

———. "Hanmal ilche ha kŭmsan insam yŏn'gu" 한말 일제하 錦山 人蔘 연구 [A Study on Geumsan Ginseng during Early Modern and Colonial Period of Korea]. *Han'guksa hakpo* 韓國史學報, Vol. 51 (2013): 199–226.

———. "Taehanjegukki hwangshil ŭi hongsam chŏnmaeje shihaeng kwa t'onggambu ŭi samŏp chaep'yŏn" 대한제국기 황실의 홍삼전매제 시행과 통감부의 蔘業 재편 [The Korean Empire's Monopoly of Red Ginseng and the Japanese Residency-General's Reorganization of the Korean Ginseng Industry]. In Lee Sang-tae ed., *Han'guk chŏnt'ongsahoe ŭi chaeinshik* 한국 전통사회의 재인식 [*A New Understanding of Traditional Korean Society*], 583–610. Seoul: Kyŏngsewŏn 경세원, 2006.

———. "Taehanjegukki Kaesŏng chiyŏk samŏp pyŏndong kwa samp'omin ŭi taeŭng" 대한제국기 개성지역 삼업 변동과 삼포민의 대응 [A Crisis of Ginseng Capital and the Countermeasures of the Ginseng-Cultivating People during Daehan Empire]. *Ŭisahak* 의사학, Vol. 18, no. 2 (2009): 133–55.

Yang, Chŏng-p'il 양정필, and Yŏ In-sŏk 여인석. "'Chosŏn insam' ŭi kiwŏn e taehayŏ" '조선인삼'의 기원에 대하여 [A Study on the Origins of 'Korean Ginseng']. *Ŭisahak*, Vol. 13, no. 1 (2004): 1–19.

———. "'Chungguk insam' ŭi shilch'e e taehan pip'anjŏk koch'al" [A Study on the True Nature of 'Chinese Jinseng']. *Ŭisahak* 의사학, Vol. 12, no. 2 (2003): 144–66.

———. "Samguk-Shilla t'ongilgi insam saengsan kwa taeoegyoyŏk" 삼국-신라통일기 인삼 생산과 대외교역 [The Ginseng Growing District, Taxation and Trade in Ancient Korea]. *Ŭisahak* 의사학, Vol. 13, no. 2 (2004): 177–97.

Yŏn, Ho-t'aek 연호택. "Shimmemani ŭnŏ ŭi yŏn'gu 2: Odaesan chiyŏk kwa sŏraksan chiyŏk ŭnŏ charyo ŭi pigyo rŭl chungshimŭro" 심메마니 은어의 연구 2: 오대산 지역과 설악산 지역 은어자료의 비교를 중심으로 [A Study of Shimmemani Jargon 2: Focused on Comparing Material Related to Jargon from the Mount Odae and Mount Sŏrak Areas]. *Kwandongdae nonmunjip* 관동대논문집, Vol. 21 (1993): 79–93.

———. "Shimmemani ŭnŏ ŭi yŏn'gu: Odaesan chiyŏk ŭl chungshimŭro" 심메마니 은어의 연구: 오대산 지역을 중심으로 [A Study of Shimmemani Jargon: Focused on the Mount Odae Area]. *Kwandongdae nonmunjip* 관동대논문집, Vol. 21 (1992): 79–93.

Youngman, Anna. "The Fortune of John Jacob Astor." *Journal of Political Economy*, Vol. 16, no. 6 (1908): 345–68.

Yu, Lei 于磊. "Lun Qingdai qianqi dongbei shenwe guanlitizhi de yanbian ji yingxiang" 論清代前期東北蔘務管理體制的演變及影響 [Changes and Effects of the Northeastern Ginseng Management System in Early Qing China]. Bachelor's Thesis, Liaoning University 遼寧大學, 2009.

Yun, Sŏn-cha 윤선자. "Ilche ŭi kyŏngje sut'al kwa Kaesŏng ŭi samŏp" 일제의 경제수탈과 개성의 삼업 [The Economic Plundering of Japanese Colonial Rule and the Ginseng Industry of Gaesung]. *Han'guk kŭnhyŏndaesa yŏn'gu* 한국 근현대사 연구, no. 35 (2005): 92–123.

Zhang, He 張合. "Zhonghan renshen zhanzheng" 中韓人蔘戰爭 [A Sino-Korean Ginseng War]. *Jiankang guanli* 健康管理, no. 2 (2012): 32–33.

Zhang, Jie 張傑. "Liutiaobian, yinpiao yu qingchao dongbei fengjin xinlun" 柳條邊, 印票與清朝東北封禁新論 [A Reexamination of the Willow Palisades, the Yinpiao System, and Qing China's Fengjin Policy Toward Its Northeastern Areas]. *Zhongguo bianjiang shidi yanjiu* 中國邊疆史地研究, no. 1 (1999): 78–85.

———. "Qing qianqi dui yalujiang fengjinqu de guanxia" 清前期對鴨綠江封禁區的管轄 [A Study of Closed Off Areas Near the Yalu River in Early Qing China]. *Zhongguo bianjiang shidi yanjiu* 中國邊疆史地研究, no. 4 (2004): 52–61.

Zhao, Yunan 趙郁楠. "Qingdai dongbei shenwu guanli kaoshu" 清代東北蔘務管理考述 [A Study of the Qing Dynasty's Management of Ginseng-Related Affairs in Northeastern China]. Master's Thesis, Minzu University of China 中央民族大學, 2007.

Zhu, Qianzhi 朱謙之. *Chungguk i mandŭn yurŏp ŭi kŭndae: Kŭndae yurŏp ŭi chungguk munhwa yŏlp'ung* 중국이 만든 유럽의 근대: 근대 유럽의 중국문화 열풍 [*China's Influence on the Formation of Modern Europe: The Chinoiserie Craze*]. Translated by Chŏn Hongsŏk 전홍석. P'aju: Ch'ŏnggye 청계, 2003.

INDEX

Note: Page numbers in *italics* indicate figures, **bold** indicate tables in the text, and references following "n" refer endnotes.